Companies, International Trad

The book focuses on the role of corporations within the trading system, and the complex relationships between corporations, nation states and international organisations. The actions and motives that drive corporations are considered as well as the structure of the international trading system. Remedial devices such as codes of conduct and human rights instruments are assessed for effectiveness.

The book seeks reasons for what is a growing understanding that international trading regimes are not meeting objectives found in many international agreements, including both the international trade agreements themselves (WTO, GATT, TRIPS etc.) and human rights instruments. In particular it is clear that the prevalence and severity of poverty is not being adequately addressed. This work sets out to investigate the role played by companies in this failure in the globalisation of trade to realise its aims, in particular the failure to achieve the minimum of basic rights, the right to food.

JANET DINE was, while writing this book, Professor of Law at the University of Essex. She is now Professor of International Economic Law at the Centre for Commercial Law Studies, Queen Mary College, University of London, a Senior Visiting Fellow at the Institute of Advanced Legal Studies, London, and Visiting Professor at Queen's University, Belfast.

Cambridge Studies in Corporate Law

Series Editor
Professor Barry Rider,
University of London

Corporate or Company Law encompasses the law relating to the creation, operation and management of corporations and their relationships with other legal persons. **Cambridge Studies in Corporate Law** offers an academic platform for discussion of these issues. The series is international in its choice of both authors and subjects, and aims to publish the best original scholarship on topics ranging from labour law to capital regulation.

Janet Dine
The Governance of Corporate Groups
0 521 66070 X

A. J. Boyle
Minority Shareholders' Remedies
0 521 79106 5

Gerard McCormack
Secured Credit under English and American Law
0 521 82670 5

Janet Dine
Companies, International Trade and Human Rights
0 521 82861 9

Companies, International Trade and Human Rights

Janet Dine

CAMBRIDGE
UNIVERSITY PRESS

CAMBRIDGE UNIVERSITY PRESS
Cambridge, New York, Melbourne, Madrid, Cape Town, Singapore,
São Paulo, Delhi, Dubai, Tokyo

Cambridge University Press
The Edinburgh Building, Cambridge CB2 8RU, UK

Published in the United States of America by Cambridge University Press, New York

www.cambridge.org
Information on this title: www.cambridge.org/9780521141826

First published 2005
Third printing 2007
This digitally printed version 2010

A catalogue record for this publication is available from the British Library

Library of Congress Cataloguing in Publication data
Dine, Janet.
Companies, international trade and human rights / Janet Dine.
    p. cm. – (Cambridge studies in corporate law)
Includes bibliographical references and index.
ISBN 0 521 82861 9
1. International trade – Social aspects.   2. Human rights – Economic aspects.
3. Foreign trade regulation.   4. Social responsibility of business.   5. Corporate
governance.   I. Title.   II. Series.
HF1379.D56   2004   382 – dc22   2004051109

ISBN 978-0-521-82861-1 Hardback
ISBN 978-0-521-14182-6 Paperback

Contents

Preface

This book is written from a perspective shared with Thomas Pogge:

We, the affluent countries and their citizens, continue to impose a global economic order under which millions avoidably die each year from poverty-related causes. We would regard it as a grave injustice if such an economic order were imposed within a national society. We must regard our imposition of the present global order as a grave injustice unless we have a plausible rationale for a suitable double standard. We do not have such a plausible rationale. (T. Pogge, *World Poverty and Human Rights* (Polity Press, Oxford, 2002))

This book is the result of an investigation into a phenomenon that I found extremely puzzling: the fact that kind-hearted, intelligent, well-informed people could be found taking diametrically opposed views on the issues of international trade and the global economy and the operation of companies within that system. Take just one example: a firm believer in the 'trickle-down effect', Moore (in *World Without Walls* (Cambridge University Press, 2002), p. 146) encourages the 'race to the bottom' as an instrument for improvement. If jobs are shifted from Korea and Indonesia to China because wages are lower, so much the better – 'I hope I live long enough to see wages in China rise so high that those jobs go to Ethiopia'. But an opponent of 'trickle down' notes that in China 'at least 30 million city dwellers are jobless, up to 200 million peasants have no real work and up to 200 million more subsist as day labourers . . . Enormous wealth is being created, but too much is being pocketed by too few' (R. Righter, *The Times*, 30 September 2003). In such a climate, why should wages rise?

In the course of the investigation I have been shocked and angry at the ability of those of us from the rich and powerful nations to 'turn a blind eye' to desperate suffering and to construct our thinking and language and develop philosophies which are self-serving. But I have also come to understand how complex the issues are and am now quite sure that any 'simple answer' is almost certain to be a wrong answer. It is difficult to carry a protest banner reading 'It might be a good idea to sequence trade and capital account liberalisation for small economies so that domestic industries and the financial sector are protected from the worst of the "herd" behaviour of the international financial sector' – but simplistic 'wrecking' answers such as 'Ban WTO' or 'Kill Coke' are unlikely to achieve justice in the trading system. The book is therefore an attempt to indicate how difficult the issues are. This is done by looking at the debate at a general level and following with a detailed study of a single issue. It is a wide canvas and the detailed studies are intended as a counterbalance to the allegations which are hurled to and fro at the generalised level. On one question, however, I am utterly convinced. We have an international trading and financial system which creates destitution and injustice as well as extreme wealth. It is unjust. And it needs experts of considerable sophistication to try and unpick the injustice. Most of all, it needs the compassion and goodwill of people of the wealthy world to demand the reconstruction of the trading system and the companies operating within it, which provide so much of that wealth.

The book starts by asking whether there is a global crisis. Chapter 2 puts forward some reasons for the present situation, considering especially the various ways in which global injustice is rationalised in philosophy, economics and language in order to comfort us. Chapter 3 deals with the international institutions, the IMF, World Bank and WTO, together with detailed studies of issues which expose the complexity of what these institutions seek to achieve: banking and financial liberalisation; the construction of a Poverty Reduction Strategy Plan; the EU sugar regime and its proposed reform in line with WTO rules. Chapter 4 considers the moves to control companies and international institutions by imposing human rights norms on them and, in the context of the right not to self-incriminate, discusses the complex arguments about whether companies can or should be able to claim rights. Direct and indirect imposition of human rights responsibilities on the international organisations is also discussed, together with the possibility of a 'right to trade' becoming part of WTO jurisprudence. Chapter 5 considers the growing corporate social responsibility debate, calling for careful formulation of the underlying justifications for its imposition on companies, particularly in the light of the corruption of one of its mainstays, the concept of sustainable development. Chapter 6 contains some suggestions for change, including a new conceptualisation of the operation of companies, directors' duties, the central place of risk analysis and reform of company law remedies. It also calls for a reassessment of our conception of property rights and the consequences this might have for international relations if the concept of international co-operation in the UN Covenant on Economic, Social and Cultural Rights were to be taken seriously. There are suggestions for further research on a number of reform agendas: state bankruptcy, international free movement of people, changes in understanding sovereignty and banking reform, as well as reform of voting procedures at the WTO, IMF and World Bank. The issues covered mean that a positive deluge of literature is available and it has not been possible to read it all. I hope I have considered a representative sample and I am grateful to everyone who has supplied information. I am especially grateful to the British Academy for funding a trip to Barbados to research the sugar industry, although my colleagues were less than impressed with the absolute *necessity* of travelling to Barbados in January! Many thanks also to Sally Painter who helped with that application and provided valuable information and support throughout the writing of this book. As always, thanks to my family for their support and concern about the injustice of the trading system. Thanks also to the 'starship' colleagues Steve Anderman, Jim Gobert, Sheldon Leader, David Ong and Bob Watt for discussions on corporate governance, to Michael Blecher who provided invaluable help on systems theory (and red wine), Alastair Macauley for assistance with economics, Marios Koutsias for help with research, Stephen Bottomley and members of the Corporate Law Teachers Association of Australia and New Zealand for helpful suggestions, Chris Richards for keeping me fit enough to complete the project and Barry Rider, Finola O'Sullivan and Kim Hughes for agreeing to publish the result.

Table of statutes, agreements, convenants and treaties

Table of cases

Abbreviations

ACP	African, Caribbean and Pacific States
BIS	Bank for International Settlements
CEDAW	Convention on the Elimination of All Forms of Discrimination Against Women
CEO	chief executive officer
CESCR	UN Committee on Economic, Social and Cultural Rights
CSR	corporate social responsibility
EBA	Everything But Arms Initiative
ECHR	European Convention on Human Rights
ECtHR	European Court of Human Rights
ECLA	Economic Commission for Latin America
EPZ	Export Processing Zone
FDI	foreign direct investment
FSA	Financial Services Authority
GATT	General Agreement on Tariffs and Trades
GCC	Global Climate Coalition
GDP	gross domestic product
HIPC	Heavily Indebted Poor Countries
ICCPR	International Covenant on Civil and Political Rights
ICESCR	International Covenant on Economic, Social and Cultural Rights
ICFTU	International Confederation of Free Trade Unions
ICSID	International Centre for the Settlement of Investment Disputes
IDA	International Development Association
IFC	International Finance Corporation
IFI	international financial institution
ILO	International Labour Organization
IMF	International Monetary Fund
IPO	initial public offer
ISO	International Sugar Organisation
LDC	Least Developed Country

MAI	Multilateral Agreement of Investment
MFN	Most Favoured Nation
MIGA	Multilateral Investment Agency
MNE	multinational enterprise
MSN	maximum supposed needs
PFI	private finance initiative
PIG	public interest group
PRGF	Poverty Reduction and Growth Facility
PRSP	Poverty Reduction Strategy Plan
SAP	Structural Adjustment Plan
SDR	Special Drawing Right
SPS	Special Preferential Sugar Scheme
TNC	transnational corporation
TRIMS	Trade-Related Investment Measures
TRIPS	Agreement on Trade-Related Aspects of Intellectual Property
UDHR	Universal Declaration of Human Rights
UNCTAD	United Nations Conference on Trade and Development
UNEP	United Nations Environment Programme
WHO	World Health Organization
WTO	World Trade Organization

1   A global crisis?

Is there 'a rapidly accelerating and potentially fatal human crisis of global proportions?'[1] And if there is, are 'the systemic forces nurturing the growth and dominance of global corporations . . . at the heart of the current human dilemma?'[2]

On these questions, there is something amounting to a war of statistics seeking to prove that the world is richer than it ever has been,[3] that many people have been lifted out of poverty,[4] and that the economic systems in place are benefiting the world.[5] On the other hand, statistics also show that the gap between rich and poor is widening both within and between nations and that in many countries, poverty is both increasing by numbers and by depth.[6] Using almost any statistics 'we certainly know that the problem of world poverty is catastrophic'.[7] Of 6,133 million human beings in 2001, some:

- 799 million people are undernourished;[8]
- 50,000 people daily die of poverty-related causes.[9]

---

[1] D. Korten *When Corporations Rule the World* (Kumarian Press, 1995), p. 3.

[2] Korten, *When Corporations Rule*, p. 9.

[3] 'Between 1965 and 1998 average incomes more than doubled in developing countries': *World Bank Development Report 2000–2001, Attacking Poverty* (Oxford: Oxford University Press, 2001), p. vi.

[4] 'In 1990–1998 alone the number of people in extreme poverty fell by 78 million': *World Bank Development Report 2000–2001*, p. vi.

[5] See, e.g., T. Larsson, *The Race to the Top: The Real Story of Globalisation* (Cato Institute, Washington, 1999); D. Irwin, *Free Trade Under Fire* (Princeton University Press, New Jersey 2002), a slightly more balanced approach in M. Moore, *World Without Walls* (Cambridge University Press, 2002).

[6] UNCTAD Report, *The Least Developed Countries Report 2002* (UN, 2002). See ILO, *A Fair Globalisation: The Final Report of the World Commission on the Social Dimension of Globalisation* (ILO, Geneva, 2004).

[7] T. Pogge, 'The First Millennium Development Goal' (www.etikk.ne/globaljustice/).

[8] United Nations Development Programme, *Report 2003*, p. 87.

[9] Such as starvation, pneumonia, tuberculosis, measles, malaria, pregnancy-related causes: World Health Organisation, *The World Health Report 2001* (WHO Publications, Geneva, 2001), Annex, Table 2.

This means that 'the global poverty death toll over the 15 years since the end of the Cold War was around 270 million, roughly the population of the US'.[10] And the figures go on and on:

- 34,000 children under five die daily from hunger and preventable diseases;[11]
- 1,000 million lack access to safe drinking water.[12]

What are we to make of this barrage of statistics with their apparently contradictory messages? As with all statistics, it depends on how they are compiled and precisely what is counted. There are definitional problems, for example the definition of poverty is hotly disputed,[13] as are the ways of arriving at the statistics.[14] Take just one example, the definition of poverty and the trends in poverty reduction. Reddy and Pogge show that both are highly questionable.[15] Trends are falsified by comparing different poverty 'lines' arrived at in different ways and targets are moderated by switching from an estimate of the *numbers* of persons in poverty to the *proportion* of the world's population in poverty. The numbers themselves are greatly affected by using flawed methodology for comparing the purchasing power of the poor across countries.

There is also the great danger posed by aggregation and averaging. Gaps in wealth disappear when some persons or nations are hugely wealthy and their wealth is increasing. In aggregate statistics the poor become invisible.[16] Aggregate counting disguises growing inequality and makes it possible to assert, as Moore does:

---

[10] Pogge, *Millennium Goal*, p. 11.

[11] US Department of Agriculture, *US Plan on Food Security, 1999*, p. iii (www.fas.usda.gov/summit/pressdoc.hmtl).

[12] UNDP, *2003 Report*, p. 9; Wateraid, 'The Education Drain' (www.wateraid.org.uk).

[13] Most thoughtful studies now rely not *just* on income data but on a multifactorial definition which takes account of insecurity, vulnerability and powerlessness: A. Sen, *Development as Freedom* (Oxford University Press, 1999); D. Narayan, P. Petesch, M. Shah and R. Chambers, *World Bank Development Report 2000–2001: Voices of the Poor – Can Anyone Hear Us?* (Oxford University Press, New York, 2000).

[14] See the detailed discussion of methodology in *World Bank Development Report 2000–2001*, ch. 1. UNCTAD, *Least Developed Countries Report 2002*, notes that its statistics differ from those of the World Bank because they are collected on a national-accounts-consistent basis which adds to the household survey basis used by the World Bank the further dimension of average annual private consumption per capita as reported in national accounts data.

[15] S. Reddy and T. Pogge, 'How Not to Count the Poor' (www.socialanalysis.org) and Pogge, *Millennium Goal*.

[16] 'Dealing with Aggregation' in *World Bank Development Report 2000–2001*, p. 22. See also *ibid.*, p. 25.

One fact is that developing countries are not losing out in world trade, despite what the WTO's critics say. The opposite is the case. Over the past decade, developing countries have consistently outperformed industrialised countries in terms of export growth – an average increase of almost 10 per cent a year, compared to 5 per cent for the industrialised countries.[17]

This statement uses averaging to disguise differences in performance; the average is skewed by the dazzling performance of China and good performance of India. Sub-Saharan Africa is getting poorer.[18] It also disguises poverty by using percentages: 5 per cent of the GDP of developed nations in real terms is many times 10 per cent of the GDP of the least developed nations. The inequality in wealth is staggering: 'The average income in the richest 20 countries is 37 times the average in the poorest 20 – a gap that has doubled in the past 40 years'.[19] It is not the task of this book to attempt a critique of the detail of the statistics. Even at an optimistic reading of reliable estimates, in our rich world,[20] the situation is dire:

of 6 billion people, 2.8 billion – almost half – live on less than $2 a day, and 1.2 billion – a fifth – live on less than $1 a day[21] . . . In rich countries fewer than 1 child in 100 does not reach its fifth birthday, while in the poorest countries as many as a fifth of children do not. And while in rich countries fewer than 5% of all children under five are malnourished, in poor countries as many as 50% are.'[22]

There is therefore certainly a deep human crisis which is worsening in certain parts of the world, particularly the poorest or Least Developed Countries (LDCs).[23] Why? Are 'the systemic forces nurturing the growth and dominance of global corporations . . . at the heart of the current human dilemma?'[24] Note that Korten does not point at corporations as the cause but at the underlying systemic forces. This is important because the blaming of corporations provides the wealthy world with a convenient scapegoat to point at. It needs to be recognised that all of us living in comfort in the rich nations of the world are benefiting from the deeds of corporations regularly vilified in the anti-globalisation press.

---

[17] Moore, *World Without Walls*, p. 169.

[18] UNCTAD, *Least Developed Countries Report 2002*, p. 7.   [19] *Ibid.*, n. 9, p. 3.

[20] 'Human conditions have improved more in the past century than in the rest of history – global wealth, global connections, and technological capabilities have never been greater': *World Bank Development Report 2000–2001*, p. 3.

[21] Oxfam puts the latter figure at 1.1 billion: *Rigged Rules and Double Standards* (Oxfam, 2002).

[22] *World Bank Development Report 2000–2001*, p. 3.

[23] UNCTAD, *Least Developed Countries Report 2002*, p. iii.   [24] *Ibid.*, p. 9.

Most of us will be shareholders, if not in a direct sense, then in the sense that our pensions and savings depend on the profit maximisation of large corporations. Indeed, corporations have 'no soul to damn and no body to kick' which leaves them as faceless and convenient repositories for the guilt of the societies which invented them, profit from them and tolerate their operations.[25] The creation of the legal fiction of separate corporate personality cannot absolve from responsibility the societies for whose benefit they operate, any more than the fiction of dehumanising the negro could absolve the society that tolerated slave-trading from its responsibilities.

In his seminal work charting how dependent on the slave trade was the rise of capitalism, Eric Williams describes the massive profits made as a result of the 'triangular trade': manufactured goods shipped from England to Africa, exchanged at a profit for slaves which were taken to the West Indies and exchanged at a profit for sugar and rum which were imported at a profit into England. He shows how the West Indian slave trade and slavery in the West Indies was abolished only when the sugar colonies which used slaves became uneconomical and humanitarian voices were joined by those who would benefit economically from its abolition. Not only were great profits made from this trade but Williams shows that these profits provided the capital for the Industrial Revolution, with many of the traders becoming bankers and financing the great industrial projects. Colonisation further enriched Western countries. One small but telling example was recently revealed by Roy Moxham. In *The Great Hedge of India* he chronicles how he set out to find 'an English folly', a 2,300 mile long hedge built across India and found that instead of an amusing folly he was on the trail of a vicious instrument of oppression, a customs barrier that had been built to enforce a salt tax which was pitched at a level which the poor could not afford, was ruthlessly enforced even in times of famine and which may well have been responsible for millions of deaths. It was also the source of great wealth for a number of Englishmen, including Clive, operating through the East India Company:

Clive's wealth had come indirectly from the Indian peasants who earned a fraction of what was earned by their English counterparts. An agricultural labourer in England earned perhaps the equivalent of 15 rupees (£1.50) a month, whereas the Indian labourer received only one rupee. What was more, the money was taken out of the country. That was to become the norm. Richard Burwell, one of Clive's colleagues, who made 400,000 rupees a year from illicit salt contracts, brought 6,000,000 rupees back to England. British individuals, and most of all

---

[25] For a more detailed examination of this aspect of the debate, see chapter 2.

the East India Company itself, took vast sums out of India and spent it in Britain
. . . India, which when the British arrived had been relatively well off, became
much poorer.[26]

Much of the riches now enjoyed in the West were built on slavery and colonialism, is the same system being perpetuated by economic imperialism?

In view of the voices raised in protest at the way in which the global
economy creates extreme poverty, it is necessary to ask whether our
system today is replicating the inhumanity of the past:

Seen in historical perspective, it [slavery] forms part of that general picture
of the harsh treatment of the underprivileged classes, the unsympathetic poor
laws and severe feudal laws and the indifference with which the rising capitalist class was beginning to reckon prosperity in terms of pounds sterling, and
. . . becoming used to the idea of sacrificing human life to the deity of increased
production.[27]

To what extent is the extreme impoverishment of millions of persons a
result of legal and economic forces similar to those underlying the slave
trade, with tragically similar results – the systematic deprivation of the
poor of all human dignity?

Although many of the poorest states are 'independent' in political
terms, in contrast to their vassal status under colonial rule, they are nevertheless economic prisoners of the rich West and of the transnational corporations (TNCs) which are the economic and political tools of Western
societies.

What, then, are the 'systemic forces'? Many would point to 'globalisation'. Globalisation is a slippery concept which means different things
to different people in different contexts. Here I adopt the following
definition: 'it is the closer integration of the countries and peoples
of the world which has been brought about by the enormous reduction
of costs of transportation and communication, and the breaking down of
artificial barriers to the flows of goods, services, capital, knowledge and
(to a lesser extent) people across borders'.[28]

Put thus, it sounds benign. Why has it become the focus of both passionate support and equally passionate denigration?

As we were corralled behind barbed wire barricades [at Seattle], I found myself
wondering how such fine, noble, principled expressions of universal values and
rights as internationalism and solidarity had become so denigrated. Globalisation

[26] R. Moxham, *The Great Hedge of India* (Constable and Robinson, London, 2001), p. 41.
[27] E. Williams, *Capitalism and Slavery* (1944, new edn, University of North Carolina Press,
1994), p. 5, citing M. James, *Social Problems and Policy During the Puritan Revolution,
1640–1660* (London, 1930), p. 111.
[28] J. Stiglitz, *Globalisation and its Discontents* (Penguin, London, 2002), p. 9.

as a word, a slogan, an explanation of history, all too frequently now conjures up a vision of elitism, dominance and power by the few; suppression of human rights, unbridled, unregulated capitalism and privilege. By contrast, universal values, internationalism and solidarity were perceived as words of comfort, unity and tolerance. And yet what is globalisation, or should it be, but the implementation of just this drive to spread universal values and solidarity? Is this just a marketing problem? What truth is there to the accusations of the aggressive protesters and NGOs – not all of whom are mad or bad – who claim everything is getting worse and that globalisation is a threat to freedom, development, indigenous peoples and local cultures.[29]

As Stiglitz remarks 'The differences in views are so great that one wonders, are the protesters and the policy makers talking about the same phenomena?'[30]

As always in human affairs, much depends on the institutions which have been involved in the process and the underlying philosophies which they have adopted. Many commentators will immediately identify as the agents of change the International Monetary Fund (IMF), the World Trade Organisation (WTO) and the World Bank, prime movers in the globalisation process.[31] While this is undoubtedly correct, it may have tended to obscure the multiplicity of other players. Drahos and Braithwaite identify the various trading blocks of the rich world as significant players, in particular the USA and EU.[32] There has also been considerable discussion of the role of nation states. This is often concerned with the diminishing powers of the state in the face of a number of apparent threats: increased power at regional and/or international level and the disparity of power between some nation states and international corporations. While the disparity in power can be demonstrated by a raft of economic indicators,[33] the economics do not tell the whole story. Recent commentators have understood that it is not only the naked power balance that has wrought a change in the role of the state, but the underlying expectations of the role that the state *ought* to play that has changed. Rowan Williams argues that the state is increasingly seen as enabling citizens to fulfil their individual expectations, but has ceased to provide what could be termed a 'moral collectivity'. The new 'market state' may be seen as a response to globalisation[34] but may also be seen as a result of

[29] Moore, *World Without Walls*, p. 8.   [30] Stiglitz, *Globalisation*, p. 9.

[31] Stiglitz, *Globalisation*, S. Skogky, *The Human Rights Obligations of the IMF and World Bank* (Cavendish, London, 2001); D. Kennedy and J. Southwick (eds.), *The Political Economy of International Trade Law* (Cambridge University Press, 2002) (esp. WTO). Their roles are discussed in chapter 3.

[32] P. Drahos and J. Braithwaite, *Global Business Regulation* (Cambridge University Press, 2000).

[33] J. Dine, *The Governance of Corporate Groups* (Cambridge University Press, 2000).

[34] Rowan Williams, *Guardian*, 27 February 2003.

different expectations of citizens. And many of these different expectations have been fuelled by a 'triumph of ideology over science',[35] most particularly by the neo-classicist doctrine that rational actors will, if left undirected, make maximally efficient economic decisions which will maximise their welfare, leading to an efficient economy where all will eventually benefit:

For more than 20 years economists were enthralled by so-called 'rational expectations' models which assumed that all participants have the same (if not perfect) information and act perfectly rationally, that markets are perfectly efficient, that unemployment never exists (except when caused by greedy unions or government minimum wages) and where there is never any credit rationing.[36]

That this model is becoming increasingly discredited does not alter the fact that believers in this model now act as policy-makers in many countries and are trying to implement programmes based on the ideas that have come to be called 'market fundamentalism'.

In particular, such views lead to the undermining of the state as a responsible entity the purpose of which is to represent a collective morality and achieve a fair distribution of goods. It also inevitably points to the individual as providing the salvation for all, most importantly through the use of property transactions. The consumer as saviour is a direct descendant of these ideas. Globalisation is thus both driven by philosophies of open markets and fuelled by the consumerist, individual culture which operates at citizen level. Thus, the citizen becomes a consumer with considerable impact on our understanding of democracy. If the state exists merely to mend 'market failure' so that the invisible hand of the market can create paradise for all, what use is a vote at nation state level? Further, if the 'market' can manipulate politicians in the shape of threats and bribes from powerful companies, where is the citizen to exercise any influence? In *The Silent Takeover*, Hertz chronicles instances of companies providing benefits for society in the provision of infrastructure, education and environmental benefits and wonders:

who, in this latest stage of the takeover, is taking over whom? Politicians are spending some of their time acting like salesmen, and corporations some of their time acting like politicians. Consumers are voting with their pockets while the electorate is increasingly staying away from the polling station . . . Can this fusion of consumer politics and corporate power provide satisfactory solutions to the problems created and encouraged by untrammelled capitalism, or even be a satisfactory replacement for traditional politics? Or is it a chimera? And if it is a monster, will it devour us?[37]

[35] J. Stiglitz, Guardian, 20 December 2002.   [36] *Ibid.*
[37] N. Hertz, *The Silent Takeover* (Heinemann, 2001), p. 184.

The forces of globalisation and the institutions that are prominent in its creation are not the only forces which require examination if reform is to be attempted. The roots of the present 'World We're In'[38] run very deep indeed:

The world today behaves like a madhouse. The worst of it is that the values we had more or less defined, taught, learned, are thought of as archaic as well as ridiculous. Respect for the world: who is that important to? The human being should be the absolute priority. And it isn't. It's becoming less and less so. It seems that it's more important to reach Mars than prevent 13 million Africans dying of hunger. Why would I want to know if there's water on Mars if we're polluting the water here on Earth, doing nothing to avoid it? Priorities need to be redefined, but there's no chance of redefining those priorities if we don't confront the need to know what democracy is. We live in a very peculiar world. Democracy isn't discussed, as if democracy had taken God's place, who is also not discussed.[39]

Perhaps the discussion should begin with the understanding that markets are not all-powerful: 'Adam Smith's invisible hand – the idea that free markets lead to efficiency as if guided by unseen forces – is invisible, at least in part, because it is not there'.[40] The redefinition of the role of governments, and, in this particular arena, trade negotiators must follow if they are no longer seeking to obey the invisible hand.

Growing inequality

We have seen that the average income in the world's richest twenty countries is thirty-seven times the average in the poorest countries, a gap that has doubled in the past forty years.[41] There is a simultaneous and linked environmental crisis.[42] Few studies doubt that the giant transnational corporate enterprises have played their part in creating both strands of this 'globalisation of poverty',[43] in particular because of their embrace of the free market classical economic theories, which underpins so much of corporate activity. The World Bank *World Development Report* is uncompromising. Setting out the numbers trying to live on less than US $2 or US $1 dollar a day (see above) it notes that:

[38] W. Hutton, *The World We're In* (Little Brown, London, 2002).
[39] Jose Saramago, *Guardian*, 28 December 2002.   [40] Stiglitz, n. 35 above.
[41] *World Bank Development Report 2000–2001*, p. 3.
[42] M. Hertsgaard, *Earth Odyssey* (Abacus, London, 1999); H. Heerings and I. Zeldenrust, *Elusive Saviours* (International Books, Utrecht, 1995); J. Karliner, *The Corporate Planet* (Sierra Club, 1997).
[43] In 1990, there were at least 212 million people without income or assets to guarantee the necessities for a basic existence. See United Nations Development Programme, *Human Development Report 1992* (Oxford University Press, 1992); United Population Fund, *The State of World Population 1992* (New York, 1992).

This destitution persists even though human conditions have improved more in the past century than in the rest of history – global wealth, global connections and technological connections have never been greater. But the distribution of these gains is extraordinarily unequal . . . And the experience in different parts of the world has been very diverse. In East Asia the number of people living on less than $1 a day fell from around 420 million to around 280 million between 1987 and 1998 – even after the setbacks of the financial crisis. Yet in Latin America, South Asia, and sub-Saharan Africa the numbers of poor people have been rising. And in the countries of Europe and Central Asia in transition to market economies, the number of people living on less than $1 rose more than twentyfold.[44]

And, as we have already seen, some scholars argue that these figures underestimate the problem.[45] Similar conclusions about growing inequality were reached by the International Labour Organisation (ILO) in its 2004 report, *A Fair Globalisation*;[46] while recognising that globalisation has great potential for good:

we also see how far short we still are from reaching this potential. The current process of globalisation is generating unbalanced outcomes, both between and within countries. Wealth is being created but too many countries and people are not sharing in its benefits . . . Many of them live in the limbo of the informal economy without formal rights and in a swathe of poor countries that subsist precariously on the margins of the global economy. Even in economically successful countries some workers and communities have been adversely affected by globalisation. Meanwhile the revolution in global communications, heightens awareness of these disparities.[47]

The 'systemic forces' driving globalisation and companies' part in globalisation are thus widely seen as the economics underlying capitalism and in particular the so-called 'Washington consensus' of neo-liberalism arguing for free and open world markets. Although there is a possibility that true free trade might benefit all, what seems clear is that trade rules which impose open borders on small and vulnerable nations, while keeping closed borders and subsidies for the benefit of rich nations, has a vicious effect.[48] However, while arguing that the claim that rich country markets are more closed and protected than those of developing countries is 'a distortion', Moore agrees that the tariffs imposed by the USA, EU and Japan on foods that are in competition with those grown in those countries and clothing and shoes are 'indefensible' and creating a burden on the poor. Citing Edward Gresser, Moore agrees that 'The

---

[44] *World Bank Development Report 2000–2001*, p. 3. See also Hertz, *Silent Takeover*, pp. 40–1.
[45] Reddy and Pogge, 'How Not to Count the Poor'.
[46] ILO, Geneva, 2004.   [47] ILO, *Fair Globalisation*, p. x.
[48] Oxfam, *Rigged Rules*; J. Dunning (ed.), *Making Globalisation Work* (Oxford University Press, 2003).

US tariff system . . . could have been maliciously designed as a burden for the poor . . . Any tax that focuses, as tariffs do, on the necessities of life, will hit poor families harder than rich families'.[49] The ILO reports that unemployment worldwide has reached 185 million whereas the richest 1 per cent of the American population 'raked in 17% of the country's income, the highest level of income inequality since the 1920s'.[50]

Companies

The same economic dogma also forms the basis for the growth of the largest corporations and its consequences for their structure and operations will be revisited in chapter 2. Here, we will put aside the discussion of the 'systemic forces' and look at the catalogue of complaints which are lodged against the companies without (I hope) losing sight of the fact that a 'company' is a legal fiction created to benefit (some of) mankind. However, most studies accept the central role played by companies in globalisation and international trade:

Transnational companies (TNCs) are the driving force behind globalisation. Through their production, trade and investment activities, they are integrating countries into a global market. Through their control over resources, access to markets, and development of new technologies, TNCs have the potential to generate enormous benefits for poverty reduction. However, that potential is being lost. The weakness of international rules, bad policies and weak governance in developing countries, and corporate practices which prioritise short-term profit over long-term human development are undermining the capacity of poor countries – and poor people – to benefit from international trade.[51]

The immense power of corporations is indicated by a comparison between the economic wealth generated by corporations, measured by sales, compared with a country's gross domestic product (GDP). On this basis 'the combined revenues of just General Motors and Ford . . . exceed the combined GDP for all of sub-Saharan Africa[52] and fifty-one of the largest one hundred economies are corporations.[53] Further, the number of transnational corporations jumped from 7,000 in 1970 to 40,000 in 1998, and they account for most of the world's trade. They also stand

[49] Moore, *World Without Walls*, p. 170, quoting E. Gresser, *Hidden Tax on the Poor: The Case for Reforming US Tariff Policy* (Progressive Policy Institute Report, 25 March 2002).
[50] *Guardian*, 25 February 2004.   [51] Oxfam, *Rigged Rules*, p. 175.
[52] Karliner, *Corporate Planet*, p. 5; 'Global 500: The World's Largest Corporations', *Fortune*, August 1995, *World Bank Development Report 2000–2001*.
[53] S. Anderson and J. Cavanaugh, *The Rise of Global Corporate Power* (Institute for Policy Studies, Washington DC, 1996).

accused of creating the current trade rules by their influence on government. Drahos and Braithwaite note that American trade representatives ask the large corporations what they want from a trade negotiation and then negotiate accordingly.[54]

These corporations and their 250,000 foreign affiliates account for most of the world's industrial capacity, technological knowledge and international financial transactions. They mine, refine and distribute most of the world's oil, gasoline, diesel and jet fuel. They build most of the world's oil, coal, gas, hydroelectric and nuclear power plants. They extract most of the world's minerals from the ground. They manufacture and sell most of the world's automobiles, airplanes, communications satellites, computers, home electronics, chemicals, medicines and biotechnology products. They harvest much of the world's wood and make most of its paper. They grow many of the world's agricultural crops, while processing and distributing much of its food. All told, the transnationals hold 90% of all technology and product patents worldwide and are involved in 70% of world trade.[55]

The deluge of literature cataloguing complaints against the operation of companies[56] makes sensible categorisation difficult. For the sake of clear discussion it may be useful to consider five categories[57] and look at the immediate driving forces, leaving for later consideration more fundamental causes. Of course, the substance discussed under any one heading influences and overlaps with issues discussed under others. However, the following division may be useful:

- environmental issues;
- labour concerns;
- relationship with the IMF/ World Bank/WTO;
- distortion of governments;
- marketing and public relations.

[54] P. Drahos and J. Braithwaite, *Global Business Regulation* (Cambridge University Press, 2000).

[55] Karliner, *Corporate Planet*, p. 5; UNCTAD, *World Investment Report 1995: Transnational Corporations and Competitiveness* (UNCTAD, Division on Transnational Corporations and Investment, New York, 1995), pp. xix–xx.

[56] Just some of them are George Monbiot, *Captive State: The Corporate Takeover of Britain* (Macmillan, 2000); Korten, *When Corporations Rule*; N. Klein, *No Logo* (Picador, 1999); N. Klein, *Fences and Windows* (Picador, 2002); Hertz, *Silent Takeover*; N. Chomsky, *Profit over People* (Seven Stories Press, New York, 1999); G. Palast, *The Best Democracy Money Can Buy* (Pluto, 2002); B. Ehrenreich, *Nickel and Dimed* (Granta, London, 2002); E. Schlosser, *Fast Food Nation* (Penguin, London, 2002); M. P. Toynbee, *Hard Work* (Bloomsbury, London, 2003); W. Hutton, *The World We're In* (Little Brown, London, 2002); M. Chossudovsky, *The Globalisation of Poverty* (Pluto, Halifax, Nova Scotia, 1998); P. Harrison, *Inside the Third World* (3rd edn, Penguin, Harmondsworth, 1993); Hertsgaard, *Earth Odyssey*; Karliner, *Corporate Planet*.

[57] The list is not dissimilar from the six categories briefly discussed in Dine, *Governance of Corporate Groups*, ch. 5.

Environmental concerns

The literature on environmental issues and complaints against transnational corporations is huge and growing.[58] There is no doubt that there has been a significant export of 'dirty' industries and significant pollution from the activities of mining and manufacturing operations masterminded by TNCs across the world. It is sufficient here to update what I wrote in 2000; there is no evidence of a lessening of the problem, although individual companies may have improved.

One of the keys to understanding the global problem of waste and pollution, is that much of its incidence in the developing world is due to developed nations' illegal shipment of their own waste to these regions . . . trucks entering Eastern Europe [from Germany] export hundreds of thousands of tons of waste that Westerners find too expensive or too inconvenient to dispose of themselves. The pressure is mostly financial. Under US and European environmental laws today, the cost of disposing of hazardous industrial and mining waste can be as high as several thousand dollars per ton . . . Shipping such materials abroad is often much cheaper.[59]

The exporting nations can pose as environmentally aware:

Japan has reduced its aluminium smelting capacity from 1.2 million tons to 149,000 tons and now imports 90% of its aluminium. What this involves in human terms is suggested by a case study of the Philippine Associated Smelting and Refining Corporation (PASAR). PASAR operates a Japanese-financed and constructed copper smelting plant in the Philippine province of Leyte to produce high grade copper cathodes for shipment to Japan. The plant occupies 400 acres of land expropriated by the Philippine Government from local residents at give-away prices. Gas and waste water emissions from the plant contain high concentrations of boron, arsenic, heavy metals, and sulfur compounds that have contaminated local water supplies, reduced fishing and rice yields, damaged the forests, and increased the occurrence of upper respiratory diseases among local residents. Local people whose homes, livelihoods and health have been sacrificed to PASAR are now largely dependent on the occasional part-time or contractual employment they are offered to do the plant's most dangerous and dirtiest jobs.[60]

Karliner[61] chronicles the migration of the chlorine industry from developed nations to Brazil, Mexico, Saudi Arabia, Egypt, Thailand, India,

---

[58] M. Chossudovsky, *The Globalisation of Poverty* (Pluto, Halifax, Nova Scotia, 1998); P. Harrison, *Inside the Third World* (3rd edn, Penguin, Harmondsworth, 1993); Hertsgaard, *Earth Odyssey*; Karliner, *Corporate Planet*. See Oxfam, *Global Finance Hurts the Poor* (Oxfam America, 2002), p. 46 and Oxfam, *America Oil, Gaz and Mining: Poor Communities Pay the Price* (Oxfam, Boston, 2001).

[59] M. Czinkota, I. Ronksinen and M. Moffett, *International Business* (4th edn, Dryden, 1996).

[60] Korten, *When Corporations Rule.*   [61] Karliner, *Corporate Planet*, pp. 81–2.

Taiwan and China, and similar strategies being followed by the nuclear power industry, the automobile industry and tobacco marketing.

Mark Hertsgaard[62] gives graphic accounts of industrial conditions in developing nations which would not be tolerated in developed nations, including the chlorine discharged from the Chongquing paper factory:

a vast roaring torrent of white, easily thirty yards wide, splashing down the hillside from the rear of the factory like a waterfall of boiling milk . . . Decades of unhindered discharge had left the rocks coated with a creamlike residue, creating a perversely beautiful white-on-white effect. Above us, the waterfall had bent trees sideways; below, it split into five channels before pouring into the unfortunate Jialing.

The Bush programme of deregulation may have halted the export of degradation to the detriment of his own citizens: 'America's largest power generator has found a unique way to avoid legal challenges from a town it has polluted – buy it lock, stock and barrel for $20million'.[63] Yet another product of deregulatory neo-classical policies. However, damage done by past operations continues. Chevron Texaco is currently being sued by 30,000 citizens of Ecuador who allege that their livelihoods and health has been damaged by oily waste disposed of in open, unlined pits, many of which have leaked and affected water supplies.[64] Coca Cola is alleged to be extracting water from an aquifer at a wholly unsustainable rate, lowering the water table in Karalla, India.[65] There are hundreds of horror stories.[66]

Labour

During the era of the slave trade, local African chiefs were paid to sell their fellow citizens into a life of bondage. Now, governments are paid to sell their citizens into a life of bondage. National Geographic estimates that there are 27 million slaves in the world.[67] The citizens in question are not exclusively those of the poorer nations of the world. Under the heading 'Modern Slavery', Korten gives details of cruel conditions across the world, including in contract clothing shops: 'Many of them are dark, cramped and windowless . . . Twelve hour days with no days off and a break only for lunch are not uncommon . . . "The workers

---

[62] Hertzgaard, *Earth Odyssey*.
[63] B. Hale, 'Power Giant Buys Town to Avoid Pollution Lawsuits', *The Times*, 14 May 2002.
[64] *Guardian*, 25 October 2003 (www.amazonwatch.org/amazon/EC).
[65] 'You and Yours' programme, BBC website.
[66] See Oxfam, *Global Finance*, esp. p. 46 and Oxfam, *Oil, Gaz and Mining*.
[67] Andrew Cockburn, '21st Century Slaves', *National Geographic*, September 2003 and L. Warren, 'Inhuman Profit', *National Geographic*, September 2003.

were not allowed to talk to each other and they didn't allow us to go to the bathroom" says one Asian garment worker'.[68] And the location – San Francisco.

Evidence of the dreadful conditions in factories is readily available.[69] The structure and operation of TNCs are vital ingredients in understanding the treatment of workers. Note that the key word here is 'workers' rather than 'employees'. This is because the essence of the modern TNC is that it has the minimum number of employees as they are a threat to its flexibility in responding to market conditions. They might combine in a union, they might demand reciprocal loyalty for long service or build up employment rights such as maternity leave or a right not to be unfairly dismissed. For this reason, the largest companies have the fewest employees. Korten explains the theory of 'downsizing':

Drastic cuts in personnel are the most visible aspect of downsizing, but they are in most instances only one part of a larger organisational strategy. The larger scheme is to trim the firm's in-house operations down to its 'core competencies' – generally the finance, marketing and proprietary technology functions that represent the firm's primary source of economic power. The staffing of these functions is reduced to the bare minimum and consolidated within the corporate headquarters. Peripheral functions, including much of the manufacturing activity, is farmed out to networks of relatively small outside contractors – often in low wage countries . . . This restructuring creates a two-tiered or dualistic employment system. Those employees engaged in the core corporate headquarters functions are well compensated, with full benefits and attractive working conditions. The peripheral functions – farmed out either to subordinate units within the corporation or to outside suppliers dependent on the firm's business – are performed by low-paid, often temporary or part-time 'contingent' employees who receive few or no benefits and to whom the corporation has no commitment.[70]

The President of Levi Strauss, Americas division, explained his company's decision to shut down twenty-two plants and lay off 13,000 workers during 1997–1999:

Our strategic plan in North America is to focus intensely on brand management, marketing and product design as a means to meet the casual clothing wants and needs of consumers. Shifting a significant portion of our manufacturing from the US and Canadian markets to contractors throughout the world will give the company greater flexibility to allocate resources and capital to its brands. These steps are crucial if we are to remain competitive.[71]

[68] Korten, *When Corporations Rule*, p. 230.
[69] See sources already cited ILO website, International Confederation of Free Trade Unions (ICFTU) website, extensive research findings in Oxfam, *Rigged Rules*, ch. 7. See J. Pilger, *The New Rulers of the World* (Verso, London, 2002), especially 'The Model Pupil' for an account of conditions in EPZs in Indonesia; Klein, *No Logo*, pp. 204–29.
[70] Korten, *When Corporations Rule the World*, pp. 216–217.   [71] Klein, *No Logo*.

Naomi Klein attributes some of this shift to the growth of brands. The corporate headquarters concentrates on inventing and promoting the brand while shedding its production of the actual objects that are sold: 'marketing departments charged with the management of brand identities have begun to see their work as something that occurs not in conjunction with factory production but in direct competition with it'. 'Products are made in the factory', says Walter Landor, president of the Landor branding agency, 'but brands are made in the mind'.[72] The low status thus afforded to the actual manufacturing means that 'it stands to reason that the people doing the work of production are likely to be treated like detritus – the stuff left behind'.[73] 'There is no value in making things any more. The value is added by careful research, by innovation and by marketing'.[74]

This arrangement has several 'comfort factors' for the central management team, including minimum outlay on wages and benefits and extreme flexibility of numbers – contingent, outsourced or part-time labour can usually be shed at will, particularly if employed via an agency. Invisibility is an added benefit. The company can disclaim responsibility for the workers employed by agencies or suppliers, they are not physically apparent at the comfortable headquarters and 'out of sight' is conveniently 'out of mind'. 'From El Paso to Beijing, San Francisco to Jakarta, Munich to Tijuana, the global brands are sloughing the responsibility of production on to their contractors; they just tell them to make the damn thing, and make it cheap, so there's lots of money left over for branding. Make it *really* cheap.'[75]

This two-tier structure goes a long way to explain the disparities between 'executive pay' and survival wage levels noted in so many studies not only of the poorer countries of the world but also of its richest nations. Outsourcing labour has spread beyond manufacturing to the service sector. In *Nickel and Dimed*, Barbara Ehrenreich describes the lifestyle to which the lower half of the restructured equation are condemned in the richest country of the world. Her evaluation of a research project during which she took jobs as a waitress, a cleaner, a care home assistant and a Wall Mart employee, concludes that, even working seven days a week or taking two jobs at the same time, it was almost impossible to live on the wages offered. To a large extent this was because of the way in

[72] *Ibid.*, p. 195, quote from Landor website.   [73] Klein, *No Logo*, p. 197.
[74] Phil Knight, CEO Nike, taken from D. Katz, *Just Do It: The Nike Spirit in the Corporate World* (Adams Media Corporation, Holbrook, 1994), p. 204, cited in Klein, *No Logo*, p. 197.
[75] Klein, *No Logo*, p. 198, emphasis in the original.

which housing costs had clearly responded to market forces while wages have not:

When the rich and poor compete for housing on the open market, the poor don't stand a chance. The rich can always outbid them, buy up their tenements and trailer parks, and replace them with condos, Mc Mansions, golf courses, or whatever they like. Since the rich have become more numerous, thanks largely to rising stock prices and executive salaries, the poor have necessarily been forced into housing that is more expensive, more dilapidated, or more distant from their places of work.[76]

Why had wages not responded by rising even when '[e]very city where I worked in the course of this project was experiencing what local business-people defined as a "labor shortage" – commented on in the local press and revealed by ubiquitous signs saying "Now Hiring" or, more imperiously "We are Now Accepting Applications"'.[77] Why haven't wages moved upwards? 'According to the American Policy Institute the poorest 10% of US workers saw wages rise from $5.49 per hour in 1996 to $6.05 per hour in 1999. The next poorest saw a rise from $6.80 an hour in 1996 to $7.35 an hour in 1999.'[78] This tiny rise means that '[i]n the first quarter of 2000, the poorest workers were earning only 91% of what they earned in [1973]'.[79] Alan Greenspan 'went so far as to suggest that the economic laws linking low employment to wage increases may no longer be operative'.[80] If this has any substance, significant factors must be at work. As Ehrenreich suggests, the most obvious factor is the resistance of employers to pay rises, often offering benefits such as free meals rather than raising wages, as the 'benefits' can be withdrawn at will. Flexibility appears again to be a factor. However, this does not explain why workers do not move into higher paid jobs. Ehrenreich indicates that the constrained mobility of the poor is one factor, as is their lack of information which operates both at the level of information about alternative work and also and particularly about the wages being paid to fellow workers.[81] It seems altogether likely that this tendency to non-mobility is exacerbated by the two-tier workforce identified by Korten. With the 'jobs' outsourced and the 'employment' isolated within the company headquarters, there is no progression from the poorest work to the better jobs. A great chasm separates the two workforces. The upheaval of a move is therefore only for a marginal wage increase and if this involves geographical complications, such as difficulty with childcare, there is no incentive to undertake the change. In a similar experiment undertaken

[76] B. Ehrenreich, *Nickel and Dimed* (Granta, London, 2002), p. 199.
[77] *Ibid.*, p. 201.   [78] *Ibid.*, p. 202.   [79] *Ibid.*, p. 203 (because of inflation).
[80] 'An Epitaph for a Rule that Just Won't Die', *New York Times*, 30 July 2000, cited in Ehrenreich, *Nickel and Dimed*, p. 202.
[81] Ehrenreich, pp. 205–7.

in the United Kingdom, Polly Toynbee worked as a hospital porter, a dinner lady, a nursery assistant and a care home worker with the elderly.[82] She came to startlingly similar conclusions to those of the American study, although her researches were concentrated in what used to be the public sector. Just as TNCs are downsizing, for the erstwhile public sector in the United Kingdom 'the words are "outsourcing", "subcontracting", "market testing", "best value", "externalisation" – for people working on the bottom rung of the public sector, all these words have meant just one thing: lower pay, worse conditions, less security. It has reduced the idea of public service to a cheap and expendable commodity'.[83] In public administration there was a 66.6 per cent increase in the use of temporary workers between 1980–1985 as a result of compulsory competitive tendering.[84] The downward pressure on Wages was exacerbated by the abolition of the Fair Wages Resolution in 1983. This had obliged any company contracting with a public authority to give the same national pay and conditions.[85] The trend was continued by the abolition of Wages Councils that had set a minimum threshold in each occupation. In 1993, the Department of the Environment reported that in 51 per cent of councils, manual workers had suffered cuts in basic wages, bonuses, hours, holidays and sick pay due to contracting out.[86] The transfer of employees from the public sector to the private sector is covered by the Transfer of Undertakings Regulations[87] but the large turnover of workers in low paid jobs mean that new entrants are not protected. UNISON found[88] that '62% of new starters were paid less; 44% had more unsocial working hours; 58% had worse sick pay; 73% had less holiday; 51% had worse pensions; 44% had worse job security. Of the 1.5 million workers affected 71% are women'.[89] With the expansion of Public Finance Initiatives and Public Private Partnership Plans, the trend seems set to continue.[90]

So far as the mobility of labour is concerned, Toynbee found that it was impossible to move from one job to another without a break in employment. This was partly to do with the way in which to gain a new job meant extensive travelling and attendance at interviews during working hours. Since a break in employment at survival levels of pay almost

---

[82] Toynbee, *Hard Work Nickel and Dimed.*   [83] *Ibid.,* p. 75.
[84] T. Colling, *Employee Relations in the Public Services* (Routledge, 1999).
[85] *Hard Work*, p. 77.
[86] Walsh, Kiernon and Davis, *Competition and Service: The Impact of the Local Government Act 1988* (HMSO, 1993), cited in *Hard Work*, p. 78.
[87] Directive 77/187/EEC, [1977] OJ L61/26, Transfer of Undertakings (Protection of Employment) Regulations 1981, S1 1981/1794; S. Sachdev, *Contracting Culture: From CCT to PPPs* (UNISON, 2001).
[88] *Ibid.* and see *Hard Work*, p. 79.
[89] *Hard Work*, p. 79, quoting UNISON survey, n. 83.
[90] *Hard Work*, p. 79, UNISON survey, n. 83.

inevitably meant getting into debt, it could rarely be contemplated. In the United Kingdom there are no benefits available to tide jobseekers over time between unemployment and the arrival of the first pay cheque or the equivalent period which may elapse between jobs. Add to this the fear of failure of finding a new job and the fear of failure in attending at a new workplace and the failure to desert low paid jobs becomes easily explicable. Both Toynbee and Ehrenreich reported the anxiety that failure to secure jobs afforded them. Since neither of them needed the jobs either for their long-term image of themselves nor for their financial security, it can be imagined that where persons on survival wages are between jobs, the equivalent risk will be assessed in much higher terms and it will be a risk that few will be prepared to take. Both researchers also reported the use made of employers of the impossibility of finding childcare at an affordable rate so that they could offer 'mother's hours' jobs at rock bottom wages.

Management tactics are also instrumental in suppressing mobility, whether by the carrot such as 'the profit-sharing plan, with Wal-Mart's stock price posted daily in a prominent spot near the break room. There was the company's much heralded patriotism . . . There were "associate" meetings that served as pep rallies, complete with the Wal-Mart cheer "Gimme a 'W', etc."'.[91] More disturbingly are the 'sticks' of searches, drug testing, rules against talking and other minor indignities which are enforced by fear of dismissal and which combine to create a lack of self-worth: 'If you're made to feel unworthy enough, you may come to think that what you're paid is what you are actually worth'.[92]

Both researchers also recognise the 'invisibility' factor as part of the equation. Fallows notes the lack of shared spaces and services in the USA:

As public schools and other public services deteriorate, those who can afford to do so send their children to private schools and spend their off-hours in private spaces – health clubs, for example, instead of the local park. They don't ride on public buses and subways. They withdraw from mixed neighbourhoods into distant suburbs, gated communities or guarded apartment towers; they shop in stores that, in line with prevailing 'market segmentation' are designed to appeal to the affluent alone.[93]

Toynbee writes that 'London was a sadder, duller, more impoverished place . . . Wherever I walked, everything I passed was out of bounds, things belonging to other people but not to me . . . This is what

---

[91] Ehrenreich, *Nickel and Dimed*, p. 208.   [92] *Ibid.*, p. 211.
[93] Ehrenreich, *Nickel and Dimed*, p. 216, citing J. Fallows, 'The Invisible Poor', *New York Times*, 19 March 2000.

"exclusion" means, if you have ever wondered at this modern wider definition of poverty. It is a large No Entry sign on every ordinary pleasure'.[94] This polarisation of society is neatly summed up in Klein's metaphor of 'fences and windows' to describe the separation of the haves and have-nots (fences) and the opportunities for hope (windows).

Traditional justifications for low wages are: that these are 'entry-level' jobs and people will move on, that they are unskilled jobs which can be abandoned if workers acquired more skills and training, and that they are a necessary consequence of the need for 'flexibility' of response to market forces. The first and second are no longer the case. The huge divide between the outsourced workforce and the central planners, whether in the public or the private sector, means that ladders of opportunity have been withdrawn. Many remain in this type of work. Further, as Toynbee points out, both caring and cleaning are essential jobs. Even if the present workforce moved out, this does not excuse payment at sub-survival rate and the acquisition of new skills is irrelevant for the carrying out of those particular tasks. A relentlessly optimistic view is espoused by Moore:

Nowhere has globalisation had more impact than on what we eat. There are many more Chinese, Thai and Indian restaurants in major cities, than there are KFCs and Macdonalds. Most of the developed world can take for granted the fresh fish from Chile, tomatoes from Israel, dates from Tunisia, chilled lamb from New Zealand and beef from Uruguay arrayed on supermarket shelves . . . In lonely desert outposts in the midst of political chaos a working refrigerator selling Coca Cola can stand as a temple to consumerism, choice, global integration and corporate organisation.[95]

However, this comes at a huge cost to the labour market.

As for the argument concerning flexibility, it is clear that employers have the ultimate right to dispose of workers at will under this system but it is equally plain that they suffer a very high turnover of poorly motivated staff whose qualifications, honesty and reliability are unknown to them (both Ehrenreich and Toynbee report that references were rarely taken up). More disturbingly still, the rigidity of the division of responsibilities among the various contracted out private companies was the enemy of flexibility when it came to actually getting the job done. Thus, a hospital porter may not assist a nurse in lifting a patient as the firm employing the porter has not contracted for that service. Similarly, a cleaner may only clean 'office space', and not 'kitchen space' or 'medical space', which may be contracted out to two other firms.[96]

---

[94] *Hard Work*, p. 239.   [95] Moore, *World Without Walls*, p. 43.
[96] *Hard Work*, pp. 165–6.

In the United Kingdom, some progress may be made following an agreement between unions and government to reverse some of the effects of privatisation on jobs by preventing the creation of poorer packages for those entering the erstwhile public sector.[97] However, the ambit of this initiative is most unclear. Agency workers will not be included in the package and they will remain unprotected at EU level. The United Kingdom was instrumental in blocking a proposed directive to protect agency workers[98] while Hank Paulson, chief executive of Goldman Sachs, received (impossible to write earned) US $21.4 million in cash and shares.[99]

Export Processing Zones

The worst employment conditions for which TNCs are blamed may be found in Export Processing Zones (EPZs). The role and operation of these areas is discussed along with the concept of foreign direct investment below. However, one issue is often mentioned in respect of EPZs and applies also to poorly paid employment in rich countries: the employees may be happy to have jobs where none were available before: 'along the northern border of Mexico, where the Maquilla export zone has been set up following the establishment of NAFTA in 1994, multinational production created over half a million new jobs where virtually none existed before, often providing better benefits and paying high (sic) wages than local companies'.[100] Does this 'benefit' justify the behaviour of the TNCs? This question will be discussed in some detail below.

Relationship with international governance

As we will see in chapter 3, the IMF and World Bank 'agree' that, in return for the provision of finance to poor countries, the economies of these countries will be restructured. The packages always include privatisation measures, opening of the economy to foreign companies and capital account liberalisation.[101] Palast lists 167 'conditionalities for Ecuador' including 'raise the price of cooking gas by 80% by November 1st 2000 . . . eliminate 26,000 jobs and cut real wages for the remaining

[97] *The Times*, 14 February 2003.

[98] P. Toynbee, 'A Cringing Appeasement of the Rich and Powerful', *Guardian*, 24 March 2004.

[99] *Financial Times*, 22 March 2004.   [100] Hertz, *Silent Takeover*, p. 36.

[101] G. Palast, 'Sell the Lexus, Burn the Olive Tree: Globalisation and its Discontents' in *Best Democracy*.

workers by 50% in four steps in a timetable specified by the IMF. By July 2000, Ecuador had to transfer ownership of its biggest water system to foreign operators, then Ecuador would grant British Petroleum's ARCO unit rights to build and own an oil pipeline over the Andes'.[102] The questions surrounding the utility of foreign direct investment are discussed below, the dangers of capital account liberalisation are also discussed in chapter 3. Moore's claim is in line with standard 'Washington consensus' dogma. He claims that 'countries which are open to trade grow faster than those that aren't'.[103] As we shall see in chapter 3, this is not clearly borne out by careful research, nor does it apparently rely on more than a crude 'GDP' growth factor, thus ignoring the inequality debate. The economy of Barbados grew exponentially during the slave trade years but this clearly did not benefit all who lived there.

All three of the Washington consensus measures benefit large multi-national companies. The opening up of a country's economy means that TNCs have the opportunity to acquire local companies. Moore admits that whole industries have been wiped out by the effects of trade liberalisation, giving as an example the clothing industry in Zambia: 'the challenge for developing countries like Zambia is to establish the infrastructure that will allow it to attract investment, redirect resources from uncompetitive industries and put more into education and healthcare, giving current and future generations a better chance of competing in a globalised world'.[104] Difficult to achieve if whole industries disappear. Of course, the cutting of wages and jobs means a ready cheap compliant workforce for incoming TNCs. Once the economy has 'opened' it is also very much more likely that TNCs will win contracts for large infrastructure projects, including those financed by the World Bank. It is very difficult for small local companies to tender at a competitive rate against TNCs with all their economies of scale. Because of the insistence by the IMF and World Bank on privatisation, the tendering will often include bids to take over essential public services such as water, fuel and communications. Again, TNCs with their expertise and economies of scale are ideally suited to bid for these contracts but will then control the price of the commodity and whether or not there should be universal provision. The advantages to large banks of capital account liberalisation are similar, with the added benefit that the IMF has hitherto provided a form of guarantee of repayment. All eyes are on Argentina to see if that will change.

[102] Palast, *Best Democracy*, p. 46.   [103] Moore, *World Without Walls*, p. 25.
[104] Moore, *World Without Walls*, p. 25.

Distortion of government priorities: the role of FDI

The growing polarisation of world resources,[105] with wealth increasingly concentrated in the hands of the few both in terms of disparities among nations and within nations,[106] is exacerbated by one of the foundation stones of development policy over the latter part of the twentieth century, namely Foreign Direct Investment (FDI). This is a mechanism with great potential benefits, including the provision of stable capital, the importation of skills and technology and access to the largest markets of them all: 'Exchanges *within* TNCs now account for around two-thirds of world trade flows, reflecting the growth of intra-product trade'.[107] FDI has also been associated with investment in research and development leading to the development of local technological capacity: 'Companies such as Cisco systems, Texas Instruments, and Hewlett Packard have set up software R&D facilities in India. Similarly, the Sony Corporation has established nine R&D units in Asia, including a number of design units'.[108] Despite these beneficial examples, the general picture remains grim with Oxfam identifying two linked problems which may be called selectivity and quality.

The first difficulty is the selectivity of the distribution of FDI:

> very little private capital goes to the poorest countries. The 15 recipients of the largest amounts, such as China, Thailand, Indonesia, Malaysia, Brazil and Mexico, account for more than four-fifths of the total . . . Almost entirely neglected is sub-Saharan Africa, which receives just over one percent of FDI. Thus the countries that are most desperately in need of increased financial resources to integrate more successfully into the world trading system are being left behind.

The ability to benefit from FDI seems to depend on the pre-existing conditions and is greater if there is a significant 'absorptive' capacity

---

[105] Even according to (probably conservative) estimates, more than 1.2 billion people live in absolute poverty, i.e. on less than US $1 dollar a day. See UN Development Programme, *Human Development Report 1999–2000* (Oxford University Press, New York, 2000); *World Bank Development Report 2000–2001*; Third World Network, 'A World in Social Crisis: Basic Facts on Poverty, Unemployment and Social Disintegration' *Third World Resurgence* (No. 52, 1994).

[106] United Nations, *Human Development Report 1992* (Oxford University Press, New York, 1992) found that the 20 per cent of the people who live in the world's wealthiest countries receive 82.7 per cent of the world's income, only 1.4 per cent of the world's income goes to the 20 per cent who live in the world's poorest countries. See Korten, *When Corporations Rule*; Chossudovsky, *Globalisation of Poverty*; P. Harrison, *Inside the Third World* (3rd edn, Penguin, 1993); R. Chambers, *Whose Reality Counts* (Intermediate Technology, 1997).

[107] Oxfam, *Rigged Rules*, p. 43, citing G. Bird and R. Rajan, 'Economic Globalisation: How Far and How much Further?' (Adelaide University Centre for International Studies, Discussion Paper 117, 2001), p. 3.

[108] Oxfam, *Rigged Rules*, p. 177.

which would include a well-educated workforce.[109] This difficulty is exacerbated by falling aid budgets which, in any event 'amount to less than one-quarter of the $208 billion provided in FDI'.[110]

Counting FDI

As we saw at the beginning of this chapter, methods of collecting statistics are of vital importance in understanding the detailed picture. Nowhere is this clearer than in the estimation of the benefits of FDI. It is often assumed that the inward investment is a net figure which is wholly for the benefit of the host country. This ignores a range of negative factors such as profit repatriation, imports of goods and services, and benefit packages. The World Bank calculates that for sub-Saharan Africa, profit repatriation represents three-quarters of FDI inflows.[111] The average for all developing countries is approximately 32 per cent.[112]

Imports of goods and services may also impose high costs. Woodward calculates that between 1993 and 1995, imports by foreign investors into Mexico increased the annual current account deficit by an amount equivalent to 2 per cent of GDP.[113] In 1995, Mexico experienced a severe financial crisis. UNCTAD estimates that in Thailand between 1990 and 1997, FDI had a negative effect on balance of payments.[114] Hanson cites a number of studies which show that foreign companies are more efficient than domestic ones; they benefit from global economies of scale and it may be that their multinational status is itself evidence of efficiency.[115] Hanson identifies three potentially significant benefits from FDI:

- training of employees who may then transfer skills to domestic firms;
- competition and emulation by domestic companies within industries where foreign firms are present;
- 'forward and backward' linkages with other industries, i.e. sale of foreign firm's products to domestic firms or vice versa.[116]

On the other hand, foreign firms may push domestic firms out of business or buy them up to create their own monopoly which may then be

---

[109] Oxfam, *Rigged Rules*, p. 177.   [110] *Ibid.*

[111] World Bank, *Curbing the Epidemic-Governments and the Economics of Tobacco Control* (World Bank, Washington, 1999).

[112] Oxfam, *Rigged Rules*, p. 178.

[113] D. Woodward, *The Next Crisis? Direct and Equity Investment in Developing Countries* (Zed, London, 2001).

[114] UNCTAD, *Trade and Investment Report 1997* (UNCTAD, Geneva, 1997), cited in Oxfam, *Rigged Rules*, p. 178.

[115] G. Hanson Should Countries Promote Foreign Direct Investment? (UNCTAD, G-24 Discussion Paper Series 9, Geneva, 2001).

[116] Hanson, 'Should Countries Promote FDI?', p. 5 and see Oxfam, *Global Finance*, p. 45.

exploited (the replacement of local industry might be beneficial where domestic industries were very inefficient).[117] Borenszstein, De Gregorio and Lee show that FDI only benefits countries which have average male schooling above one year of secondary education. Below that, FDI has a negative effect.[118] The World Bank's research supports this finding.[119] Oxfam concludes 'A lot of research remains to be done to determine under which conditions the positive effects outweigh the negative ones . . . FDI should not be assumed as being always beneficial or at least benign, particularly for low income countries'.[120] In particular, the dangers of FDI for employment of low-skilled workers is highlighted:

In many low-income countries, FDI is sought not so much for transfers of technology and management skills but for employment of low-skilled workers (mostly in low-technology manufacturing activities) and for foreign exchange (in either natural resource sectors or manufacturing industries). For cash-strapped countries both reasons make perfect economic sense. Nonetheless, tax reliefs and subsidies aimed at attracting FDI have real economic costs too and should be used only after careful economic analysis.[121]

This, quite apart from the social and environmental costs: 'Millions of workers employed in low-technology manufacturing industries in export-processing zones, most of whom are women coming from rural areas, are trapped in appalling working environments.'[122] For a discussion of environmental effects, see below.

The packages which governments put together to attract foreign investment are notorious and have a significant impact on the debate concerning labour relations (with the creation of Export Processing Zones) and environmental issues. Korten quotes an advert in *Fortune* magazine placed by the Philippine government: 'To attract companies like yours . . . we have felled mountains, razed jungles, filled swamps, moved rivers, relocated towns . . . all to make it easier for you and your business to do business here.'[123] This is the 'race to the bottom'. Environmental impacts aside, the packages almost always include tax concessions or holidays. Hanson[124] reports that 'the governments of Rio Grande do Sul and Bahia in Brazil gave General Motors and Ford respectively financial

[117] Oxfam, *Global Finance*, p. 45.
[118] E. Borensztein, J. De Gregorio and J. Lee, 'How Does Foreign Direct Investment Affect Economic Growth?' (2000) *Journal of International Economics* 45.
[119] World Bank, *Global Development Finance 2001* (World Bank, Washington, 2001).
[120] Oxfam, *Global Finance*, pp. 45–6.   [121] *Ibid.*, p. 46.
[122] ILO, *Fair Globalisation*, p. x; Oxfam, *Global Finance*, p. 46.
[123] Korten, *When Corporations Rule*, p. 159.
[124] G. Hanson, 'Should Countries Promote Foreign Direct Investment?' (G-24 Discussion Paper, Geneva, 2001), cited Oxfam, *Rigged Rules*, p. 179.

packages worth $3billion in total to locate factories in their states'. A further problem is the possibilities raised by the growth of intra-company trade. It makes it very easy to adjust prices between different departments of a company to minimise profit levels and thus taxation. The US government charges tax on global profits but the administrative capacity and leverage to follow suit is beyond the capacity of developing nations.

Export Processing Zones: poor quality FDI[125]

The International Labour Organisation figures for 1998 estimated that there were at least 850 EPZs in 70 countries, employing at least 27 million workers[126] with between US $200 and US $250billion worth of trade flowing through them.[127] The employment figures for 2002–2003 show an increase to 41,934,133.[128] The most startling example of the *genre* are the *maquiladoras*[129] of Mexico, a country which 'has come to symbolise the "quantity not quality" approach to FDI'.[130] The adoption of FDI as part of a national development strategy was given a huge boost by the adoption of the North American Free Trade Area[131] and:

at one level, the results have been spectacular. Flows of FDI averaged more than $10bn a year in the second half of the 1990s. More than half of these inflows have gone into manufacturing, predominantly into high-technology sectors such as automobiles, electronics and computers. Exports have boomed, with their share in GDP rising to almost one-third by the end of the 1990s. The *maquiladora* zone accounts for more than half of these exports . . . Foreign companies now account for two-thirds of Mexico's exports.[132]

However, what appears to be a success story fails to be a path to development. Not only is the success achieved at the expense of the labour employed in these areas by the systematic lowering of regulations, but the EPZs remain simply assembly zones with the materials being imported by the firms, assembled and then exported: 'Ford's state-of-the-art engine-assembly plant in Chihuahua exports more than 90% of its production, and uses almost no local inputs other than labour.'[133] Similarly with the computer industry, 'despite exports of computer products growing from $1.5million in 1994 to $6.5million in 1998 . . . linkages between exporters

---

[125] See Pilger, *New Rulers*, esp. 'The Model Pupil' for an account of conditions in EPZs in Indonesia; Klein, *No Logo*, pp. 204–29.
[126] ILO website (www.ilo.org), figures for March 1998, cited in Klein, *No Logo*, p. 205.
[127] Klein, *No Logo*, p. 205, figures supplied by WTO official.
[128] ILO database on EPZs.   [129] Derived from *maquillar*, to make up or assemble.
[130] Oxfam, *Rigged Rules*, p. 180.   [131] North American Free Trade Agreement.
[132] Oxfam, *Rigged Rules*, p. 180, citing Economic Commission for Latin America (ECLA), *Foreign Investment in Latin America and the Caribbean 1999* (ECLA, Santiago, 1999).
[133] Oxfam, *Rigged Rules*, p. 180.

and local firms are negligible'.[134] If this is coupled with the tax concessions given to the companies to locate their plants in the country it can be seen that the development benefits from this strategy are negligible. All that transpires are poorly paid work in bad conditions, with little in government revenue to improve the infrastructure of the country and no possibility of local firms breaking into the supply chain. Once again we see the development of a two-tier structure with the workers fenced off from prosperity, with no ladders to escape by. Similarly, the profits from the added-value of assembly go to the benefit of the TNCs and their executives and shareholders. Thus, apparent success means that it is all the more important to develop an accurate method of 'counting FDI', including an assessment of its quality. The conditions for the workforce can be desperate.[135] Lee Kil-soo was found guilty of human trafficking. He owned the Daewoosa Samoa factory near Pago Pago, Samoa. Workers made clothes sold principally under Sears and JC Penney labels. The factory employed 251 immigrant workers from Vietnam and China in conditions described by John Ashcroft, US Attorney General, as 'nothing less than modern-day slavery'. The workers paid US $200 a month for room and board, for which they received a bunk in a thirty-six bed dormitory and little food. Their pay was routinely withheld and after a strike to recover lost earnings managers switched off the electricity making the heat unbearable. In 2000 one of the seamstresses was dragged from her sewing machine and her eye was gouged out with a plastic pipe.[136]

There are success stories. Hertz cites India as a particular example: 'In India, which in recent years has relaxed its hostility to foreign investment and liberalisation, the economy is booming; car sales in cities jumped by 57% during the first nine months of 2000 and Indian software developers are making a global impact with software sales grossing approximately $4billion in 2000'.[137] Oxfam cites the case of Intel's US $300million investment in Costa Rica where the company has moved beyond assembly to provide 'a new centre for software development and the design of semi-conductors. It has also invested heavily in staff training, and in developing teaching and research facilities in universities and the Technology Institute'. However, as we have seen, the ability to benefit from FDI is dependent on 'absorptive capacity' so that the poorest, least educated nations are least likely to benefit. More assistance is required before they can benefit from quality FDI.[138]

---

[134] *Ibid.*   [135] *Ibid.*
[136] D. Flickling, 'Misery of Rag-Trade Slaves in America's Pacific Outpost', *Guardian*, 1 March 2003.
[137] Hertz, *Silent Takeover*, p. 36. Other examples are Mexico and China.
[138] ILO, *Fair Globalisation*.

Distortion of government priorities: the 'willing capture'
of governments

In the United Kingdom, a number of authors have identified disturb-
ing evidence that corporations are influencing government behaviour
at the expense of the normal democratic processes. George Monbiot[139]
writes that 'Corporations, the contraptions we invented to serve us, are
overthrowing us. They are seizing powers previously invested in government, and using them to distort public life to suit their own ends.'
The role of privatisation in this process is generally perceived as significant. The Thatcher/Regan consensus of small government fuelled by
the neo-liberal economic Chicago school argued for a 'vision of a good
society [which] rested on the strength and productive potential of free
men in free markets'.[140] The IMF and World Bank have disseminated
this doctrine worldwide as part of the 'Washington consensus'.

Clearly, it is in the interests of concerns which seek to maximise profits
to ensure that the standards of health and safety laws, of labour rights
and of environmental restrictions, are as low as possible. 'It is not hard to
see why corporations might wish to infiltrate government. By bypassing
the electoral process, communicating directly with ministers and officials, they can pre-empt legislation which might be popular, but could
restrict their ability to make money.'[141] Why would a government be
open to this sort of behaviour? 'The first and most obvious [reason] is
that the simplest means of obtaining power is to appease those who possess it already.'[142] And governments are vulnerable. It is simple for a
company to threaten to leave the jurisdiction with multiple job losses
and loss of tax revenue if the government does not acquiesce in policies which it desires. This threat operates on a European level as well as
in the United Kingdom.[143] Indeed, '[t]he creed of free market capitalism, Anglo-American style, was soon disseminated across the world'.[144]
Governments may also see themselves as representing powerful interests
for the general good, a sort of willing 'capture'. Clinton is alleged to

---

[139] *Captive State: The Corporate Takeover of Britain* (Macmillan, London, 2000).
[140] David Stockman, *The Triumph of Politics* (London, 1986), p. 6, cited in Hertz, *Silent Takeover*, p. 23. David Stockman was President Reagan's Budget Director.
[141] *Ibid.*, p. 8.   [142] *Ibid.*, p. 9.
[143] Monbiot chronicles the influence of the European Round Table of industrialists, 'an association of the chief executives of forty-six of the biggest companies in Europe', on the negotiations which preceded the Single European Act: 'Dekker and other Round Table executives began threatening national governments that if they did not lend their support to the integration scheme, big business would move its operations elsewhere, making much of the European workforce redundant.' 8 Monbiot, *Captive State*, p. 321.
[144] Hertz, *Silent Takeover*, p. 23.

have reasoned that 'What is good for Boeing is good for America'[145] and decreed that industrial espionage should be one of the main tasks of the CIA. This approach can be clearly seen in international negotiations and is reported by Drahos and Braithwaite, quoting an American trade representative: 'One USTR [Office of the US Trade Representative] was remarkably frank in saying that the US has no intellectual plan about the long-term national interest, no consistent commitment to any principle. Rather the "client state" is the model of the USTR: "It's too socialist to plan . . . the businessman is the man who knows. So you respond to him".'[146] The theory is that the government should do its best for its citizens; it is a trustee for their interests.[147] The citizens include the powerful money-making corporations.[148] The best for citizens is explained by neo-classical economists as more money, the best way to get more money into the economy is by unstinting support for corporations. Thus, the job of government is to act as trustee for the corporations and act as an adversary when other interests get in the way:

> Because of their dependence on the success of the private sector and exports for wealth, stability, rising aggregate standards of living, jobs – factors that can today be equated with political power – governments do not just sit back and let the market take its course. Instead they actively pursue policies that benefit business, giving up in the process their ability to set an independent agenda and favouring corporate Goliaths over individual Davids.[149]

Monbiot relates a number of power struggles concerning the 'public private finance initiative'[150] (PFI) which tend to show that once private funding on a significant scale is involved, threats to withdraw can bring significant lapses in regulatory enforcement, the companies gaining bargaining power which can overwhelm democratic processes. Similar concerns surround the behaviour of supermarket chains and the role of corporations in universities[151] and schools.

Ethics disappear: the 'ethical foreign policy' of the newly elected Labour government in 1997 included the approval of a contract reportedly worth £438 million for arms sales to Indonesia, a country involved

---

[145] *Ibid.*, p. 65.
[146] P. Drahos and J. Braithwaite, *Global Business Regulation* (Cambridge University Press, 2000).
[147] This is further discussed in chapter 6.
[148] This issue is further discussed in chapter 3.   [149] Hertz, *Silent Takeover*, p. 66.
[150] Monbiot, Captive State, 'The Skye Bridge Mystery', 'Hospital Cases', 'The Smashing of Southampton'.
[151] Nottingham University recently obtained over £3 million for a Centre for Corporate Social Responsibility from BAT plc, formerly British American Tobacco. The web of networking between highly placed corporate managers and government departments is ingeniously laid out in Monbiot's 'Fat Cats Directory', *Captive State*, ch. 6.

in significant human rights abuses at that time,[152] and the USA stands accused of military interventions in Iran in 1953, Guatemala in 1954, Brazil in 1964, all in pursuit of American corporate interests.[153]

Environmentalists are also worried:

The intensity of the corporate counter-attack against a burgeoning environmental and consumer rights opposition has been so powerful that in countries like America, it has, at best, derailed, at worst, destroyed democracy itself. If democracy is meant to signify a representative government for all the people, in which everyone has an equal chance of being heard, of being able to influence their local politician, then democracy is dead, killed by the monoliths of the modern age – transnational corporations.

Overtly and covertly, by stealth and by design, big business has perverted the democratic process by buying politicians, by bribing them, by funding "independent" think-tanks, by forming "corporate front groups", by bullying citizens, by lobbying and by lying – all in the name of profit. At the same time, they have told us how much they care.[154]

Rowell cites Liberal Democrat MP, David Alton:[155] 'the most insidious form of corruption is that which breaches no law but is part and parcel of the system'. Alton found that:

Past Ministers soon find solace in directorships and consultancies outside government. On the backbenches the same holds true. One hundred and thirty-five Conservative MPs hold 287 directorships and 146 consultancies between them, and the other parties are not immune. Twenty-nine Labour members share sixty directorships and forty-three consultancies; while Liberal Democrats hold a total of fifteen.[156]

It is easy to see how conflicts of interest will arise when any restriction on the freedom of operation of a company where such a stake is held by an MP is debated in Parliament. 'But', asks Rowell 'does actual corporate manipulation actually influence the way a politician will vote.'[157] And the answer is 'yes' according to a 1991 report by the American Center for Public Integrity[158] in whose poetic language: 'We found that on critical matters which affect our daily lives, for the Congress of the United

---

[152] Hertz, *Silent Takeover*, p. 69.

[153] W. LaFeber, 'The Tension Between Democracy and Capitalism during the American Century' in *Diplomatic History*, vol. 23, no. 2 (Malden, 1999), cited in Hertz, *Silent Takeover*, p. 78.

[154] A. Rowell, *Green Backlash: Global Subversion of the Environment Movement* (Routledge, 1996).

[155] D. Alton, 'Standards in Public Life', *Independent on Sunday*, 30 October 1994, cited in Rowell, *Green Backlash*, p. 78.

[156] *Ibid.*   [157] *Ibid.*, p. 81.

[158] *Corporate Crime Reporter*, vol. 5, no. 27, 8 July 1991, p. 9: 'Two reports indicate public corruption may be endemic to the current political system', cited in Rowell, *Green Backlash*, p. 81.

States, money talks and the public interest walks. In some instances, we have documented how some members of the House and Senate actually switched their votes to support special interests whose money they had received in thousands of dollars.'[159] Although direct campaign contributions cannot be made to finance American electioneering, 'soft money' contributions, often used for television advertising, are estimated to have reached US $393 million in the 2000 elections;[160] '[i]n the run up to the 2000 presidential elections the candidates seeking nomination raised and spent over $1billion'[161] and when 'Charles Keating, the boss of an American thrift company, Lincoln Savings and Loan that later defaulted and cost the US government and people hundreds of billions of dollars, was asked whether the $1.3million he had donated to five senators' campaigns had influenced their behaviour, he replied "I certainly hope so".'[162] The list of links between campaign donations and votes in Congress is almost endless. Jennifer Shecter of the Center for Responsive Politics collates campaign contributions and the resultant votes by legislators who receive them. She notes that '[t]he ten House and ten Senate members who received the largest contributions from the American Sugar Industry all voted to preserve a sugar quota that keeps prices high for consumers. Similar matchups are made for the timber industry, the B-2 bomber, the gambling industry, and even drunk-driving'.[163] These votes may, of course, reflect a genuine political belief in the protection of local industry and jobs or in the righteousness of a particular course of action, but its scale and pervasiveness is at the very least throwing doubt on the independence of the political decision-makers.

One tactic used by corporations is formation of apparently 'white hat' organisations ostensibly devoted to independent research but in reality a 'front' for particular industries. The Global Climate Coalition (GCC), for example, is, according to its own lights, involved in co-ordinating 'business participation in the scientific and policy debate on the global climate change issue'[164] but includes in its membership an alliance of major energy users and producers.[165] However, this appeasement of companies may be counterproductive, particularly where revenue is to be raised for government purposes which might include redistribution and/or

---

[159] Including a change of votes in favour of the automobile industry on legislation which would have forced them to increase fuel efficiency standards for vehicles.
[160] Hertz, *Silent Takeover*, p. 91.   [161] *Ibid.*, p. 94.
[162] *Ibid.*, p. 96, taken from 'You Pays Your Money', *Economist*, 31 July 1999. For a list of similar examples see Hertz, *Silent Takeover*, pp. 96–100.
[163] Hertz, *Silent Takeover*, p. 97.   [164] Rowell, *Green Backlash*, p. 85.   [165] *Ibid.*, p. 86.

provision of public services. Rupert Murdoch's News Corporation pays only 6 per cent tax worldwide; and in the United Kingdom, up to the end of 1998, it paid no net British corporation tax at all, despite having made £1.4 billion profit there since June 1987.[166]

There are other concerns, too. Many of them may be picked up from daily press reports. 'Railtrack's chief executive has been awarded a £50,000 pay rise, the company disclosed to-day.'[167] 'In an announcement that attracted immediate condemnation from passenger groups and politicians, Railtrack confirmed that Steve Marshall's pay had been increased by 12.5 per cent to £450,000. The move follows widespread outrage last month about a £1.3 million "golden goodbye" to Gerald Corbett, the former chief executive who resigned after the Hatfield disaster.' Railtrack was at that time responsible for the track and infrastructure of the railway network in the United Kingdom. The company explained[168] that the remuneration committee, which consisted of non-executive directors, had examined the pay of chief executives in 'comparable companies' and had decided that the pay of their chief executive should be in line with them in order to ensure that the company was seen as a major competitor at a national level. During the period of office of the two men named in *The Times* report, Railtrack had been severely criticised for its safety record and blamed as at least partially responsible for a number of passenger deaths, including those at a crash at Hatfield. A victim who was injured in that crash described the pay rise for Steve Marshall as 'obscene'.[169] This tale of executive pay raises many issues. Cheffins cites a 1994 study by Bacon and Woodrow which found that the average remuneration of chief executives was 'over 20 times the annual salary of the typical rank and file worker'.[170] The disparity in pay is matched by a huge disparity in treatment. The redundancy payments for workers whose jobs are lost in efficiency drives will amount to no more than a few thousands. Both this and the methods of announcing redundancies without prior consultation have been the subject of intense debate. 'Marconi sheds over 4,000 jobs' was front page news on 5 July 2001.[171] At the time of the announcement '[i]t was unclear how many of the jobs would be lost at Marconi's sites in the UK'.[172] The relevant union 'called for urgent talks with Marconi's management'.[173]

---

[166] Hertz, *Silent Takeover*, p. 7, figures taken from 'Business: Rupert Laid Bare', *Economist*, 20 March 1999.
[167] *The Times*, 9 July 2001.
[168] Radio 4 'Today' programme, 9 July 2001.   [169] *The Times*, 9 July 2001.
[170] B. Cheffins, *Company Law* (Oxford University Press, 1997), p. 112.
[171] *The Times*, 5 July 2001.   [172] *Ibid.*   [173] *Ibid.*

Marketing and PR

'We are drip-fed images that reinforce [the] . . . capitalist dream. Studios and networks beautify the very essence of capitalism . . . Procter and Gamble explicitly prohibits programming around its commercials "which could in any way further the concept of business as cold or ruthless"'.[174] Two difficulties lie in the way of finding out about company behaviour; the first is that the prime source of information is the company itself and there is a clear incentive to put the best face possible on its activities; the second is the power of the media, especially television and, in particular, the reliance on revenue from advertising. Any expose story runs the risk of a loss of advertising revenue from the targeted company. On 18 August 2000, a Florida state court jury found that Robert Murdoch's 'Fox 13' television station in Florida 'acted intentionally and deliberately to falsify or distort the plaintiff's news reporting', that the plaintiff's threat to reveal this misconduct was the sole reason for the termination of their contracts of employment and awarded damages of US $425,000.[175] The dispute had arisen because two reporters (Steve Wilson and Jane Akre) had uncovered a practice of the supply of milk contaminated with a bovine growth hormone BGH made by Monsanto. The hormone was feared to be linked with some forms of cancer. The major Florida milk wholesaler had announced that it would not buy milk from cows treated with the hormone but the reporters discovered that it was in fact doing so. After threats from Monsanto they lost their jobs and the television station broadcast a distorted version of their research. It is not only advertisements that give a rosy view of companies and their products, commercial television, radio, newspapers and magazines may also do so.[176]

Is the international economic system just?

Is the economic order unjust? We have seen from the discussion above that the defining characteristic of the international economic order is its inequality. Perhaps that is just?

The unequal society

To what extent can an unequal society remain a 'just' society? And to what extent does the international legal order differ from national or local legal order?

---

[174] Hertz, *Silent Taqkeover*, p. 6.   [175] *Ibid.*, p. 136.
[176] For other examples see *ibid.*, ch. 6; Rowell, *Green Backlash*; Palast, *Best Democracy*.

Rawls and the 'just difference principle'

Rawls may be seen as an apologist for inequalities existing within a society which nevertheless may be regarded as 'just'. Rawls believes that 'deep inequalities [in] . . . initial chances in life . . . are inevitable in the basic structure of *any* society'.[177] Rawls sets out his 'Main Idea'[178] – 'justice as fairness'. The principles to govern this 'just society' are to be arrived at from 'behind a veil of ignorance', that is, 'no-one knows his place in society, his class position or social status, nor does anyone know his fortune in the distribution of natural assets and abilities, his intelligence, strength, and the like'.[179] From this 'original position' Rawls postulates that the choice would be in favour of two principles: 'the first requires equality in the assignment of basic rights and duties, while the second holds that social and economic inequalities, for example inequalities of wealth and authority, are just only if they result in compensating benefits for everyone, and in particular for the least advantaged members of society'.[180] Rawls accurately distances himself from the neo-classicists by remarking that 'These principles rule out justifying institutions on the grounds that hardships of some are offset by a greater good in the aggregate.'[181] This rejects the measure of 'efficiency' commonly used to justify free market transactions (see below).

It is notable, however, that elsewhere Rawls defends a market system (but not necessarily a free market) in terms that seem both quaint and old-fashioned. Thus, 'a system of markets decentralises the exercise of economic power'[182] an unlikely conclusion now in a world of transglobal corporations. Rawls is perhaps making the old-fashioned assumption that the state is more powerful than other economic actors.

However, to return to the inequalities debate, Rawls holds that the inequalities in distribution may not only remain but be regarded as just on the basis of the difference principle, i.e. inequality is justified because it benefits the worst off in society: 'the social order is not to establish and secure the more attractive prospects of those better off unless doing so is to the advantage of those less fortunate'.[183] As explained by Cohen:[184] 'the difference principle licences an argument for inequality which centres on the device of material incentives. The idea is that talented people will produce more than they otherwise would if, and only if, they are paid more than an ordinary wage, and some of the extra which they will then

---

[177] J. Rawls, *A Theory of Justice* (revised edn, Oxford University Press, 1999), p. 7.
[178] *Ibid.*, p. 10.   [179] *Ibid.*, p. 11.   [180] *Ibid.*, p. 13.
[181] *Ibid.*   [182] *Ibid.*, p. 241.   [183] *Ibid.*, p. 65.
[184] G. Cohen, *If You're an Egalitarian How Come You're so Rich?* (Harvard University Press, Cambridge, 2000), p. 124.

produce can be recruited on behalf of the worse off'. Now, quite apart from ecological and philosophical arguments concerning the wisdom of promoting to the status of a value ever-increasing production, Cohen argues persuasively that Rawls' contentions contain a number of flaws as a *justification* for inequality rather than as a factual explanation of it. The Rawlsian principle rests on the self-interested market motivation of the actors in the free market. It is they who will only produce more if rewarded with incentives greater than the norm. Cohen points out that this contrasts with the notion that '[c]itizens in everyday life affirm and act from the first principles of justice' in order that 'their nature as moral persons is most fully realised',[185] since the 'talented' appear to be refusing to perform their task to the best of their ability without extra reward. A just society, according to Rawls, is one where all its members affirm the correct principles of justice. However, the 'talented':

could not claim, *in self-justification* at the bar of the difference principle, that their high rewards are necessary to enhance the rewards of the worst off since . . . it is they themselves who *make* those rewards necessary, through their own unwillingness to work for ordinary rewards as productively as they do for exceptionally high ones . . . High rewards are therefore, necessary only because the choices of talented people are not appropriately informed by the difference principle.[186]

Cohen defends this criticism of Rawls against the possible objection that, according to Rawls, the difference principle applies only to 'the basic structure of society' and not to decisions made by individuals within that just basic structure by arguing that this objection shows clearly the imperfections of the Rawlsian scheme. Cohen distinguishes between a just *society* and a just *distribution*, the latter consisting in a certain egalitarian profile of rewards.[187] Cohen argues that the Rawlsian conception of just basic structures leaving individuals free to act as selfish free marketeers cannot deliver the benefits of a truly just society in the way in which Rawls himself understands them. That can only be achieved by individuals acting in accordance with an egalitarian ethic which will deliver distributive justice. Thus, Rawls believes that institutions structured so as to accept the difference principle will foster feelings of fraternity: 'Those better circumstanced are willing to have their greater advantages only under a scheme in which this works out for the benefit of the less fortunate'[188] but Cohen points out that this motivation is 'incompatible

---

[185] J. Rawls, *Kantian Constructivism in Moral Theory* (Harvard University Press, Cambridge, Mass, 1999), p. 521 and *Theory of Justice*, p. 528.
[186] Cohen, *If You're an Egalitarian*, p. 127.   [187] *Ibid.*, pp. 132–3.
[188] Rawls, *Theory of Justice*, p. 90.

with the self-interested motivation of market maximisers, which the difference principle does not condemn'.[189] Similarly frail is Rawls' argument that the establishment of 'just' institutions as a 'desire to act justly' will coincide with 'the desire to express our nature as free moral persons',[190] leading to just choices in individual transactions. Cohen enquires 'how can they, without a redolence of hypocrisy, celebrate the full realisation of their natures as moral persons, when they know that they are out for the most that they can get in the market?'.[191] A further problem is the frailty of Rawls' reasons for focusing on 'basic structures'. Rawls says: 'The basic structure of society is the primary subject of justice because its effects are so profound and present from the start.'[192] Cohen, however, argues: 'Why should we *care* so disproportionately about the coercive basic structure, when the major reason for caring about it, its impact on people's lives, is *also* a reason for caring about informal structure and patterns of personal choice?'.[193] To Cohen, therefore, *the personal is political.*[194] The establishment of 'just' institutions is not enough, an egalitarian ethic is also necessary. Pogge believes that Rawls has important reasons for limiting the range of his principles of justice to the basic structure – the fact of pluralism, as well as a desire not to be overdemanding and thus risk instability.[195] Rawls thus accepts that a just society may be composed of those who are not motivated by the desire to achieve justice. There is a division between the description of a just society and the judgment that should be made about personal motivation. The complex link between motivation, causation and justice is further explored by Pogge in a sophisticated criticism of the Rawlsian concept of justice. Pogge believes that the Rawlsian understanding of justice is simplistic in that it postulates parties that 'are conceived as interested solely in the quality of life of prospective citizens, irrespective of the institutional mechanisms that may condition such quality of life'.[196] Institutions and the mechanisms they use to deliver a good lifestyle are important because of the complex relationship between institutions and human flourishing. In essence, this is a causation or *mens rea* relationship: injustice arises not only through deprivation of certain goods or rights but because of the reason that deprivation occurs. Pogge illustrates this by arranging the same deprivation in order of injustice inflicted:

[189] Cohen, *If You're an Egalitarian*, p. 135.   [190] Rawls, *Theory of Justice*, p. 501.
[191] Cohen, *If You're an Egalitarian*, p. 135.   [192] Rawls, *Theory of Justice*, p. 7.
[193] Cohen, *If You're an Egalitarian*, p. 140, emphasis in the original.
[194] *Ibid.*, p. 122, emphasis in the original.
[195] T. Pogge, *World Poverty and Human Rights* (Polity Press, Oxford, 2002), p. 105.
[196] Pogge, *World Poverty*, p. 44.

a certain group of innocent persons is avoidably deprived of some vital nutrients V – the vitamins contained in fresh fruit, say, which are essential to good health. The six scenarios are arranged in order of their injustice, according to my preliminary intuitive judgment. In scenario 1, the shortfall is *officially mandated*, paradigmatically by the law: legal restrictions bar certain persons from buying foodstuffs containing V. In scenario 2, the shortfall results from *legally authorized* conduct of private subjects: sellers of foodstuffs containing V lawfully refuse to sell to certain persons. In scenario 3, social institutions *forseeably and avoidably engender* (but do not specifically require or authorise) the shortfall through the conduct they stimulate: certain persons, suffering severe poverty within an ill-conceived economic order cannot afford to buy foodstuffs containing V. In scenario 4, the shortfall arises from private conduct that is *legally prohibited but barely deterred*: sellers of foodstuffs containing V illegally refuse to sell to certain persons, but enforcement is lax and penalties are mild. In scenario 5, the shortfall arises from social institutions *avoidably leaving unmitigated the effects of a natural defect*: certain persons are unable to metabolise V owing to a genetic defect, but they avoidably lack access to the treatment that would correct their handicap. In scenario 6, finally, the shortfall arises from social institutions *avoidably leaving unmitigated the effects of a self-caused defect*: certain persons are unable to metabolise V owing to a treatable self-caused disease – brought on perhaps, by their maintaining a long-term smoking habit in full knowledge of the medical dangers associated therewith – and avoidably lack access to the treatment that would correct their ailment.[197]

Emphasis is also on the avoidability of the shortfall. As Pogge points out, correcting injustice has its own costs and the degree of injustice is proportional not only to its causation but with the costs that would be imposed in trying to correct it. The Rawlsian concept of justice ignores the role of institutions in its delivery. This more complex understanding of justice has far-reaching effects in judgments that need to be made both about the world trading system institutions and the company institutions that operate within it. This understanding leads also to a different perspective on human rights, pointing out that none are absolute: the right to life is not violated by a death 'that could have been prevented by expensive medical treatment that the patient was unable and the state unwilling to pay for'.[198] This means that it makes more sense to talk about 'non-fulfilment' or 'underfulfilment' of human rights rather than a violation of them, which suggests a more absolute definition of a right. The centrality of institutions in Pogge's conception of human rights means that it escapes the criticism of being individualistic legally-based rights. Instead, the focus is on institution-building: 'human rights are not supposed to regulate what government officials must do or refrain from doing, but

---

[197] *Ibid.*, pp. 41–2.   [198] *Ibid.*, p. 47.

are to govern how all of us together ought to design the basic rules of our common life'.[199] 'The pre-eminent requirement on all coercive institutional schemes is that they afford each human being secure access to minimally adequate shares of basic freedoms and participation of food, drink, clothing, shelter, education, and health care. Achieving the formulation, global acceptance and realisation of this requirement is the pre-eminent moral task of our age.'[200] Pogge argues that this conception of rights is supported by Article 28 of the Universal Declaration on Human Rights: 'Everyone is entitled to a social and international order in which the rights and freedoms set forth in this Declaration can be fully realised.' So, far from the more traditional understanding which reads the rights agenda as imposing duties not to violate rights, Pogge sees a 'responsibility [on governments and individuals] to work for an institutional order and public culture that ensure that all members of society have secure access to the objects of their human rights'.[201]

The primary focus on institution-building means that, as with markets, the only time when legally individually enforceable rights would have significance is in case of institutional failure. This creates an intriguing relationship between the concepts of institutional failure and market failure. If the market is an institution, the traditional concept of market failure[202] may need to be revised in this context since, in the case of institutional failure, it would be necessary to define and enforce individual rights.

It is hard to see how one can, on the one hand, be committed to the claim that societies, for the sake of the persons living in them, ought to be organised so that these persons need not endure inhuman and degrading treatment and yet, on the other hand, not consider it morally wrong for persons to treat others in inhuman or degrading ways. A commitment to human rights goes along with interactional moral commitments; but this is no reason to identify the former with the latter.[203]

Duties become more complex, not merely a matter of enforcement mechanisms but a moral duty to advocate social programmes that would be likely to alleviate the problem. If a coercive order avoidably restricts access to basic necessities 'all human agents have a negative duty . . . not to cooperate in upholding it unless they compensate for their cooperation by protecting its victims or by working for its reform. Those violating this duty share responsibility for the harms (insecure access to basic necessities) produced by the unjust institutional order in question.'[204]

[199] *Ibid.*, p. 47.   [200] *Ibid.*, p. 50.   [201] *Ibid.*, p. 65.   [202] See chapter 5.
[203] Pogge, *World Poverty*, p. 65.   [204] *Ibid.*, p. 67.

National orders and international orders: another just difference?

In the context of the international community, Rawls departs radically from his national concepts of justice.[205] Although Rawls seeks to internationalise his original position theory, a number of scholars have criticised its inadequacy. Rawls seeks to extend the concept of the original position to 'representatives of different nations'[206] who are to choose the fundamental principles of justice to adjudicate conflicting claims among states. The parties know nothing about the particular circumstances of their own society, in particular its power in comparison with other countries. This creates equity and 'is fair between nations; it nullifies the contingencies and biases of historical fate'.[207] It throws up three principles: the status of states as free and equal; self-determination ('the right of a people to settle its own affairs without the intervention of foreign powers')[208] and adherence to treaty obligations. Pogge argues that there are two possible readings of this account: the parties to the international original position may represent persons from the different societies or they may represent states.[209] Hayden argues that, although these two competing accounts can be advanced as a way of determining an international original position, only the latter reading is intended by Rawls: 'the parties are to be understood in Rawls's own account as representatives of nation-states, and not of persons'.[210] This is the logical consequence of settling the principles of justice applicable within states as a priority over the establishment of an international regime of justice.

In the international context, Rawls rejects the difference principle because it is unacceptable for one group of people to bear costs of decisions chosen by others – decisions on industrialisation or the birth rate are examples. This appeal to 'choice' must be met with two objections: first that the 'choice' argument has many historical inaccuracies. Especially where countries still suffer the result of economic systems imposed by colonisation, the degree of 'choice' is very limited as is the geographical accidents which can determine wealth. Secondly, Rawls 'fails to explain why this ground should not analogously disqualify the difference principle for national societies as well. Why is it not likewise unacceptable for one province, township or family to bear such costs of decisions made by another?'.[211] Rawls concedes that the difference principle could be

---

[205] J. Rawls, *The Law of Peoples* (Harvard University Press, Cambridge, 1999).
[206] Rawls, *Theory of Justice*, p. 378.   [207] *Ibid.*, p. 378.   [208] *Ibid.*, p. 378.
[209] T. Pogge, *Realising Rawls* (Cornell University Press, Ithaca, NY, 1989), p. 242.
[210] P. Hayden, *John Rawls: Towards a Just World Order* (University of Wales Press, Cardiff, 2002), p. 89.
[211] Pogge, *World Poverty*, p. 105.

replaced by some other liberal criterion of economic justice,[212] but again fails to transfer this requirement to the global economic order. This omission is explained on the basis of the need to accommodate certain 'decent' non-liberal societies. Pogge points out that this logic would only make a difference if the failure to reform the international order was at the request of the non-liberal societies which liberal societies are bound to accommodate. On the contrary '[t]he much more affluent liberal societies are the ones blocking such reforms . . . when there exists no "decent" society actually opposing the reforms, then the concern to accommodate decent societies cannot be a reason for liberal societies to block them contrary to the minimal criterion, and hence to every more specific criterion, of liberal economic justice'.[213]

Further, Rawls imposes double standards of justice on national and international economic orders. A decent, non-liberal society must have a system of law that follows 'a common good idea of justice that takes into account what it sees as the fundamental interests of everyone in society'[214] – the global international order is just if no peoples have to live 'under unfavourable conditions that prevent their having a just or decent political and social regime'.[215] Pogge notes that this demand constrains only 'peoples' and not global economic institutions so that '[w]e may impose a global economic order that generates centrifugal tendencies and ever increasing international inequality, provided we "assist" the societies impoverished by this order just enough to keep them above some basic threshold'.[216] Since both formulations are vague and abstract it is perhaps not crystal clear that the two could not equate – if so, why use different formulations? Rawls seems *prima facie* to be guilty of double standards once again. Thus

it seems clear, then, that Rawls endorses double standards on three different levels: in regard to national economic regimes, the difference principle is part of Rawls's highest aspiration for justice; in regard to the global economic order, however, Rawls disavows this aspiration and even rejects the difference principle as unacceptable. Rawls suggests a weaker minimal criterion of liberal justice on the national level; but he holds that the global order can fully accord with liberal conceptions of justice without satisfying this criterion. And Rawls suggests an even weaker criterion of economic decency on the national level; but he holds that the global order can be not merely decent, but even just, without satisfying this criterion. Insofar as he offers no plausible rationales for these three double standards, Rawls runs afoul of moral universalism. He fails to meet the burden of

---

[212] J. Rawls, *Political Liberalism* (Columbia University Press, New York, 1993), p. 227.
[213] Pogge, *World Poverty*, p. 107.   [214] Rawls, *Law of Peoples*, pp. 67–8.
[215] *Ibid.*, pp. 67–8.
[216] T. Pogge, 'Rawls on International Justice' (2001) 51 *Philosophical Quarterly* 246.

showing that the application of different moral principles to national and global institutional schemes does not amount to arbitrary discrimination in favour of affluent societies and against the global poor.[217]

The discrimination is arbitrary according to Pogge because an essential element of moral universalism is 'the assignment of the burden of proof to those who *favor* a double standard'.[218] It is worth repeating the opening paragraph of this book: this book is written from a perspective shared with Thomas Pogge:

We, the affluent countries and their citizens, continue to impose a global economic order under which millions avoidably die each year from poverty-related causes. We would regard it as a grave injustice if such an economic order were imposed within a national society. We must regard our imposition of the present global order as a grave injustice unless we have a plausible rationale for a suitable double standard. We do not have such a plausible rationale.[219]

---

[217] Pogge, *World Poverty*, pp. 107–8.   [218] *Ibid.*, p. 109.   [219] *Ibid.*, p. 109.

2   Why we are here[1]

'Imagine some visionary statesman, in 1830 say, posing the question of how the advanced states of Europe and North America can preserve and, if possible, expand their economic dominance over the rest of the world even while bringing themselves into compliance with the core norms of Enlightenment morality. Find the best solution to this task you can think of and then compare it to the world today. Could the West have done any better?'.[2] This question is posed by Thomas Pogge explaining the ability of rational humans to shape their thinking to suit their interests. Pogge does not believe that any such grand plan existed or exists but nevertheless believes that the prevalence of extreme poverty and the reasons given for not tackling the issue are a prime example of avoidance techniques by the rich: 'moral norms, designed to protect the livelihood and dignity of the vulnerable, place burdens on the strong. If such norms are compelling enough, the strong make an effort to comply. But they also, consciously or unconsciously, try to get around the norms by arranging their social world so as to minimise their burdens of compliance'.[3] In this chapter I examine some of the most important devices for achieving this effect. One of the most important is the limited liability company and the demands made on its managers to maximise the profits of shareholders. A common method of minimising the burden of compliance is to interpose an agent to carry out reprehensible acts: Pogge gives the example of appointing a lawyer to manage an apartment block. The most efficient use of the block would be to convert the flats into luxury accommodation and double the rent. Some of the flats are occupied by poor elderly tenants who would be forced to leave and would have difficulty finding accommodation elsewhere. The lawyer is appointed to manage the block 'efficiently'

---

[1] Where essential to the arguments advanced here I have repeated material which appears in *The Governance of Corporate Groups* (Cambridge University Press, 2000) and I am grateful to Cambridge University Press for permission to do this.

[2] T. Pogge, *World Poverty and Human Rights* (Polity Press in association with Blackwell, Oxford, 2002), p. 5.

[3] Pogge, *World Poverty*, p. 5.

thus saving the owner from himself evicting the elderly residents. Pogge argues that this solution cannot absolve the owner of his moral responsibility.[4] Companies are used by rich societies in an exactly equivalent way, to be the agents carrying out reprehensible moral acts from which rich societies benefit. Companies are doubly useful in this respect as they can also be blamed for the reprehensible acts while those who invented them and profit from them can express moral outrage, thus feeling good about taking the moral high ground. Other devices are nation states, which are used in a variety of ways – one is to attribute the cause of poverty to the state within the border of which the poverty occurs. As with companies, this allows proponents of the theory to take the moral high ground by vilifying such states. This role is supported by the structure of international law and international human rights law which focus almost exclusively on nation states. This leaves the role of the international financial institutions (IFIs) and the negotiating power of rich trading states very much in the background. Other devices examined are the misuse of philosophy and the 'capture' of language by the neo-classical economists who drive the IFIs. Other moral deflection devices include the misuse of statistics which was examined in the last chapter. A further instance of the misuse of language relating to property rights is examined in chapter 6.

Helplessness?

Is it possible that avoidance techniques are adopted because individuals feel unable to alter the situation and so take refuge in comforting euphemisms and other deflecting devices? 'Why do we citizens of the affluent western states not find it morally troubling, at least, that a world heavily dominated by us and our values gives such very deficient and inferior starting positions and opportunities to so many people?'[5]

Pogge believes that part of the answer lies in history: 'Fifty years ago, the eradication of severe poverty worldwide would have required a major shift in the global income distribution',[6] now the cost would be less than 1 per cent of global income[7] but attitudes lag behind reality. Further, moral universalism was not generally accepted, i.e. the equal moral status of all human beings was not established. Even in the context of established moral universalism, however, '[w]e know that billions abroad are exposed to life threatening poverty. We think that we should perhaps help these people with sporadic donations ... But few of us believe that this extensive

---

[4] *Ibid.*, p. 77.   [5] *Ibid.*, *World Poverty*, p. 9.
[6] *Ibid.*, p. 92.   [7] World Bank Report 2002.

and severe poverty, even if avoidable, shows our global economic order to be unjust.'[8]

Moral deflection devices

In examining the current economic consensus we will find many examples of devices which, consciously or unconsciously, disguise the moral choices which, if clearly presented, might change the course of decision-making. The tricks we use are closely interrelated and it is therefore extremely difficult to disentangle the threads. With this caveat let me suggest that moral deflection devices can be categorised into:

- institutions, companies and nation states;
- taking philosophies out of context;
- statistical representation (dealt with in chapter 1);
- language devices.

The role of institutions and perceptions of institutions

Companies

Companies are used to provide ethical 'loopholes':

Consider the ethical view that as a member of a social arrangement one may sometimes – when acting in behalf of other members or of the entire group – deliberately harm outsiders in some specific way, even though one may not do so when acting on one's own. Such views are, I believe, widely held. In the business world, those who implement a corporate policy that is harmful to consumers, employees, or to the general public often stress their status as managers and their obligations towards the firm's owners, whose financial interests they were hired to promote. How is this supposed to be ethically relevant? . . . Ethical views of this sort guide their adherents to form or join social arrangements in order to effect, through the special ties these involve, a unilateral reduction of responsibility toward those left out of these arrangements.[9]

This points up both the concept of exclusion – the company is an exclusive club – and hints at the mechanism by which the connection between 'ownership' of the company as property and the polarisation of income and power can come about because of the sloppy ethical understanding that creation of a corporation can, in some way, reduce ethical and human rights responsibilities. Pogge argues that where an ethic has fixed 'those basics that persons owe all others in the absence of any special ties and

---

[8] Pogge, *World Poverty*, p. 96.   [9] *Ibid.*, p. 76.

relations . . . [imposing an agent] should not enable persons unilaterally to reduce or dilute them. Specifically, it should not allow them, by forming or joining a social arrangement, to subject themselves to new, countervailing obligations to its members that may outweigh, trump, or cancel their minimal obligations to everyone else.'[10]

Companies are created by laws adopted by societies. Creating a company to obtain or manufacture goods cheaply and to provide investment opportunities means that rich societies are benefiting from the cheap prices obtained for resources from poorer societies – resources here include labour. Thus, appointing a company to achieve objectives which would be ethically deplored in an individual means that we can conveniently blame others while reaping the reward of their behaviour. Ireland uses the image of a man lying on a sofa together with the assertion that he is 'working highly profitably' making money from his investments to reveal 'the irresponsibility that is built into the prevailing structure of corporate rights and the regulatory institutions that support them, for it is precisely the no-obligation, no-responsibility nature of corporate income rights which enables their owners to relax on sofas, blissfully ignorant of and uninterested in precisely how the dividends and interest accruing to them is generated'.[11] He also points out the wide complicity in corporate behaviour through the growth in private pensions. Using companies to generate our wealth and provide cheap food and commodities is the first moral deflection device.

A second moral deflection device comes into play when we vilify companies for their behaviour. This gives us the moral high ground while still living comfortably because of the benefits they provide. Moral indignation at the terrible behaviour of some corporations as discussed in chapter 1 must not be allowed to obscure the fact that companies are designed by societies and their profits underpin much of our wealth. So when they strike bargains with evil regimes, repatriate their profits and sell us goods produced at low prices because of sweated or slave labour, this is not because of the inherent evil of the people that work in corporations but as a direct result of the legal design of corporations and the operation of the international legal system which provides them with many opportunities yet fails to regulate.

A variant of the second device is provided by the immense energy put into codes of conduct and corporate social responsibility.[12] Since these are voluntary and very liable to capture by the public relations departments

[10] *Ibid.*, pp. 78–9.
[11] P. Ireland, 'Property and Contract in Contemporary Corporate Theory' (2004) *Legal Studies* 453 at 506.
[12] See chapter 5.

of companies, it is likely that a great deal of energy will be spent to little effect. The participants have a 'feel good' factor which deflects them from the more important structural issues causing the problems.

In truth it is necessary (to use a New Labour slogan) to be tough on companies and *on the causes of companies.* The avoidance of moral blame is assisted by the distortion of our understanding of companies by deconstructing their power and by a false understanding of their structure. The American/UK contractual model has shareholders as the primary focus; the company must serve the interests of shareholders and directors are appointed and dismissed by shareholders. Nevertheless, directors are to act in the interests of the company and usually owe no direct duties to shareholders. This structure does not *necessarily* equate shareholders with the company nor does it equate shareholder interests with 'profit maximisation' and impose a duty on directors to achieve such a goal. Nevertheless, recent discourse has imposed the concept of profit maximisation on the assumption that this is what shareholders require and the second assumption that shareholders and the company are one and the same thing. Such an understanding of corporate aims has wide implications for their behaviour since all considerations other than profit are seen as 'negative externalities' to be adhered to minimally or to be bargained away if possible. It has also been one of the underlying causes of spectacular bankruptcies such as Enron and WorldCom (see further discussion of this below). In terms of moral responsibility, such a construct of corporations means that they become another method of moral deflection: because the purpose of corporations is to make as much money as possible, the societies that tolerate and profit from their existence have no responsibility for the methods they pursue. This ignores the fact not only that companies are structured by national laws but also that those who profit from an activity have a responsibility to prevent that activity harming others. The corporate social responsibility movement rarely addresses the fundamental issue of the design of companies as we shall see in chapter 5 – because of this, it is much less effective than it otherwise could be.

Moral deflection devices are turned into laws. So far as companies are concerned, they benefit both from national laws which permit groups of companies to operate as a power block while treating them in law as separate companies and operations, and international laws which impose difficult jurisdictional barriers between the different component companies in groups so that it becomes exceptionally difficult to call companies to account for any wrongs that may be committed.

Effectively, law performs a conjuring trick in order to disguise the power concentrations and opportunity for manipulation in corporate groups.

Scott[13] traces this distorted perception back to classic economic analysis: 'Economic analysis was predicated on the role played by the individual entrepreneur in organising production. Classical economists assumed that "entrepreneurs" headed firms which they personally owned; and they could see no obvious reason to modify this view when analysing the behaviour of the modern, large scale business corporation.'[14] Blumberg[15] identifies two other reasons in the context of American law: the fact that not until 1888–93[16] was it possible for one corporation to become a shareholder in another corporation,[17] and that when the issue of the liability of parent corporations first came before the courts not only had the limited liability of shareholders been accepted for decades but that at the time 'American law was experiencing the high tide of formalism, or conceptualism, as the only legitimate form of legal analysis. Shareholders were not liable for the obligations of the corporations of which they were shareholders. A parent company was a shareholder. Ergo, a parent corporation was not liable for the obligations of its subsidiary corporations of which it was a shareholder.'[18]

Despite the 'dramatic change in the underlying relationship'[19] which occurs when companies form themselves into groups, this analysis prevailed and is still evident today in both American and UK[20] jurisprudence. Just as the nexus of contracts approach to single corporations deconstructs the institution, denying its public role and the status of its constitution, so groups of companies are deconstructed so that they are seen as related to each other only as majority or minority shareholders. The effects of the aggregation of power have been missed and are only taken account of in extreme cases[21] or where the state has intervened following financial scandals.[22] Prentice[23] regards the fragmentation of laws relating to group issues consequent on the contractual approach as beneficial on the ground that once rules relating to particular issues such as

[13] J. Scott, 'Corporate Groups and Network Structure' in J. McCaherty, S. Picciotto and C. Scott (eds), *Corporate Control and Accountability* (Clarendon, Oxford, 1993).
[14] *Ibid.*, p. 292.
[15] P. Blumberg, 'The American Law of Corporate Groups' in McCaherty, Picciotto and Scott, *Corporate Control*.
[16] First in New Jersey: New Jersey Act, 4 April 1888, ch. 269 s.1 (1888 N. J. Laws 385).
[17] See also T. Hadden, 'An International Perspective on Groups' in McCahery, Picciotto and Scott, *Corporate Control*, p. 345.
[18] Blumberg, 'American Law', p. 308.   [19] *Ibid.*
[20] Despite the fact that there never was a ban on companies holding shares in other companies.
[21] *Adams v. Cape Industries plc* [1990] Ch. 433.
[22] See discussion of protection of creditors, below.
[23] D. Prentice, 'Some Comments on the Law of Groups' in McCaherty, Picciotto and Scott, *Corporate Control*.

'consolidation of accounts, disclosure, taxation, directors' dealings within the context of groups, minority shareholder oppression, and insolvency' have been formulated, 'there will be little left to be mopped up by a law which specifically addresses the problem of groups'. However, in a non-legalistic (real life) context, the consequences of this fragmentation are severe.

The reality of corporate power is rather different from the fragmented vision of the economists. Very few inhabitants of the planet are untouched by the activities of companies and some argue that they are taking over the world at the expense of the nation state[24] and to the detriment of developing nations and the environment. 'At the heart of the . . . capitalist system, the free market economy, lies company law.'[25] It is through the medium of companies that wealth is created. More than this, the way in which companies are regulated says a great deal about the values that each society and the global community gives preference to.

The concept of a company carrying on business in several countries is far from new. However, this activity has increased enormously in recent years and current statistics contain a rather frightening message. According to the UN's *World Investment Report 2001*, the world has about 45,000 transnational firms controlling 280,000 foreign affiliates. Worldwide sales of the latter amounted to about US $7 trillion. The largest 100 companies own about US $1.7 trillion of foreign assets – one-fifth of the estimated global total. Multinational companies account for fifty-one of the world's largest economic entities (the other forty-nine are nation states).[26] The important characteristic of the multinational phenomenon is that management are increasingly responsible for activities on an *international basis*. Their horizons are no longer limited by national or local considerations. A useful definition is that put forward by the Commission of Transnational Corporations in its draft Code of Conduct for Transnational Corporations. The emphasis is on 'a system of decision making, permitting coherent policies and a common strategy through one or more decision-making centres'.[27] The whole decision-making structure has the world as its focus. This, coupled with the reason for the existence of companies, which is often seen to be to make the maximum profit

[24] N. Hertz, *The Silent Takeover* (Heinemann, 2001); George Monbiot, *Captive State: The Corporate Takeover of Britain* (Macmillan, London, 2000); D. Korten, *When Corporations Rule the World* (Kumarian Press, 1997); N. Klein, *No Logo* (Flamingo, 2001).

[25] B. Pettet, *Company Law* (Pearson Education, Edinburgh, 2001), p. 3.

[26] S. Anderson and J. Cavanaugh, *The Rise of Global Corporate Power* (Institute for Policy Studies, Washington DC, 1996).

[27] United Nations Economic and Social Council, *Work on the Formulation of the United Nations Code of Conduct on Transnational Corporations – Outstanding Issues in the Draft Code of Conduct on Transnational Corporations* (E/C10/1985/5/2, 22 May, 1985).

for shareholders, creates a system which lays poorer countries open to exploitation.

Multinational and transnational companies do not exist as an entity defined or recognised by law. They are made up of complex structures of individual companies with an enormous variety of interrelationships. In order to understand the legal complexity which this brings with it, it is necessary to start with an understanding of single companies. Companies are regarded as separate legal entities, owning their own property and with their own liability for contracts, crimes and other wrongs they may commit. The liability of their shareholders is limited to the amount paid for the ownership of their share. Companies played a vital role in first the industrial and subsequently the technological revolutions by limiting the risk faced by investors, enabling the raising of large sums of money from many sources in order to fund large projects (such as railways and canals) and undertake expensive research and development (for example into new medical treatments and drugs). The fact that shareholders knew with certainty the maximum amount they could lose enabled them to calculate what they could afford to invest.

The number of investors also meant that it was impossible for each of them to have a say in the day-to-day decision-making of the business, and it became necessary to appoint dedicated managers. The growth of the so-called multinational or transnational corporations is possible because the legal systems of most countries regard one company holding shares in another in exactly the same way as if it were a human individual shareholder. Thus, the legal systems take no account of the reality of the accumulation of power represented by a large number of companies related by interlocking shareholdings. Many companies are organised in this 'group' structure where control is exercised over a number of subsidiaries by a parent company which holds a significant number of the shares in one or more subsidiary companies. The simplest arrangement is a hierarchy with 100 per cent shareholding by a parent company, but there are numerous other ways of creating effective control of one company over others by different share structures.

Where all the component companies of a group are situated in one legal jurisdiction, it is open to the laws of that country to treat the group as a single entity where the formal legal structure is being used for fraudulent purposes. This is often termed 'lifting the corporate veil' and many jurisdictions (including the countries of the European Union) collect tax from groups of companies on this basis.

However, where companies use group structures but spread themselves across different legal jurisdictions many problems arise. Because many developing states are desperate for foreign direct investment they will

offer tax holidays and lax regulatory regimes in order to entice the powerful multinationals to invest (see chapter 1). Take an example where a
parent company is situated in a rich OECD country (as most of them
are). It has control over a subsidiary in a developing country because of
its shareholding in that subsidiary. The parent and its associated group
have a turnover which is greater than that of the state where its subsidiary
is located and has therefore been able to bargain for a very loose regulatory regime in the subsidiary's host state. The subsidiary is causing
environmental degradation and imposing terrible working conditions on
its labour force.

What legal results follow from this scenario?

(1) The subsidiary's host state is in breach of its duty to protect its citizens
    who are forced to work in poor conditions and endure the environ-
    mental damage. It will be reluctant to try and enforce higher stan-
    dards if the parent company is likely to withdraw the subsidiary from
    the country. This is the 'race to the bottom' in regulatory standards.
(2) In the host state of the subsidiary the parent company will probably
    be viewed as a separate entity from the subsidiary and, because it
    owes its existence to the laws of a foreign country (the rich state) it
    has no legal presence in the host state and can incur no liability.
(3) In the unlikely event that the host state 'lifts the veil' and finds the
    parent liable it will be difficult for those damaged to enforce judgment
    against a parent situated in a foreign country and funds may also be
    diverted elsewhere in the group and/or the company may liquidate.

To turn attention to the legal results of this scenario in the home state of
the parent:

(a) the separate legal status will *prima facie* allow the parent corporation
    to escape from any liability for the actions of its subsidiary;
(b) in the unlikely event of the laws of the home state of the parent 'lifting
    the veil' and imposing liability on the parent corporation, they may
    be criticised for imposing extra-territorial liability.

It is argued that for home states to 'lift the veil' in these circumstances
may cause a conflict between the laws and standards of the home state and
those of the host (subsidiary's) state. Some argue that this would require
an 'extraterritorial application of law'.[28] Muchlinski postulates three
circumstances: prescribing laws that apply to the whole of the multinational enterprise group regardless of its presence in another jurisdiction;
imposing disclosure requirements on the parent over documents held by a

---

[28] P. Muchlinski, *Multinational Enterprises and the Law* (Blackwell, Oxford, 1995).

subsidiary abroad; and insolvency of a subsidiary requiring action against the parent to recover funds.[29] All of these situations would require laws with an extra-territorial reach with the possible 'serious political effects' of imposing the policies of the regulating state on the foreign jurisdiction and breaching the target state's exclusive territorial jurisdiction.[30] However, these are not the only situations. The focus should be exclusively on the state where the parent of the TNC is situated, the 'home' state. Muchlinski argues that:

the regulating state seeks to make the overseas unit of the MNE act in accordance with the law that governs the activities of the unit present within the regulating state. In the home state, that will involve the regulation of an overseas subsidiary through the imposition of legal duties on the parent to direct the acts of the subsidiary in the required manner . . . This may have the effect that obedience to one legal system will result in a violation of the law of the other, or, at least, in the imposition of legal standards not accepted under the law of that other.[31]

This would indeed be the case if the regulations simply insisted that particular standards be observed by the foreign subsidiary and insisted that the parent use its control to abide by those standards. However, the situation is more complex. The home state is regulating the ability of the parent to control. This control is conferred on the parent by its ownership of the shares in the subsidiary. The locus of the place of control is a matter of discussion. In English law there is no clearly settled doctrine.[32] It can thus be argued that the home state has a duty to regulate the way in which the parent exercises its control over the subsidiary. There are many cases which have located the residence of a corporation at the place where central management and control is situated. Where a parent exercises control over its subsidiary and that subsidiary is involved in a state's breach of human rights or other standards, the relevant activity of the *parent* has occurred within the jurisdiction of the home state.

There thus arises a duty resting on home states to ensure the protection of human rights and other standards by regulation of the parent company's exercise of control within its legal jurisdiction. Any objection on the grounds of imposition of different standards by the two jurisdictions could be met by a requirement that the parent should be under an obligation to require adherence *at least* to local standards and to report why it is necessary to depart from the standards of the home state. This issue is discussed further in chapter 4.

In terms of the globalisation debate, the problems associated with multinational companies are compounded because they may not even be shareholders of the companies which they use to supply their component

[29] *Ibid.*, pp. 108–9.   [30] *Ibid.*, p. 109.   [31] *Ibid.*
[32] Dine, *Governance of Corporate Groups*, ch. 3.

parts. Many companies are linked only by contracts of supply so that although they are effectively entirely dependent on retaining the goodwill of the central management of the multinational, they are legally not connected to them by structural ties. This problem is made worse when the suppliers contract out work to home-workers whose conditions are impossible to monitor or inspect. There are a multitude (well over 400) of codes of conduct which seek to impose control over the operation of TNCs but none of these have any legal remedies for breach. Monitoring the compliance of corporations with these codes is extremely difficult, not least because much of the relevant information is under the control of the company itself.

The details of the English company law which supports this scenario can be gleaned from looking at the details of just two cases: *Salomon* v. *Salomon*[33] and *Adams* v. *Cape Industries*.[34] Mr Salomon was a boot and shoe manufacturer who had been trading for over thirty years. He had a thriving business. He also had a large family to provide for. To enable the business to expand, he turned it into a limited liability company. As part of the purchase price he took shares in the company and lent the company money in return for 'debentures', which are paid off preferentially in the event of a liquidation. The company did not last very long. Almost immediately there was a depression in the boot and shoe trade and a number of strikes. Mr Salomon tried to keep the company afloat by lending it money and by transferring his debentures to a Mr Broderip for £5,000, which he handed over to the company on loan. However, liquidation was not long in coming. The sale of the company's assets did not realise enough to pay the creditors. The liquidator claimed that the debentures had been fraudulently issued and were therefore invalid. He also denied that the business had been validly transferred from Mr Salomon to the company. The grounds for both these claims were that the business had been overvalued at £39,000 instead of its true worth of around £10,000 and that the whole transfer to a limited company amounted to a scheme to defeat creditors. The judge who heard the case first admitted that the transfer had been legally carried out and could not be upset. However, he suggested (*Broderip* v. *Salomon*)[35] that Mr Salomon had employed the company as an agent and that he was therefore bound to indemnify the agent. He said that the creditors of the company could have sued Mr Salomon despite the existence of the company to whom the business had been legally transferred. At first instance and in the Court of Appeal the view was taken that the transaction was contrary to the intent of the Companies Act and was either a 'fraudulent' transaction in the sense of a misuse of the statute (rather than a dishonest act) or

[33] [1897] AC 442.   [34] [1990] BCLC 479.   [35] [1895] 2 Ch. 323.

that the company stood in such a relationship to Mr Salomon (agency, trust or nominee) that he should contribute to the fund available for the creditors. In the Court of Appeal, Mr Salomon's appeal was dismissed. However, the House of Lords took a different view. Lord MacNaughten said:

> The company is at law a different person altogether from [those forming the company]: and, though it may be that after incorporation the business is precisely the same as it was before, and the same persons are managers, and the same hands receive the profits, the company is not in law the agent of the subscribers or trustee for them. Nor are the subscribers as members liable, in any shape or form, except to the extent and in the manner provided by the Act . . . If the view of the learned judge were sound, it would follow that no common law partnership could register as a company limited by shares without remaining subject to unlimited liability.[36]

The case established the complete separation between a company and those involved in its operation. Here we can see the law in operation, shifting the risk from shareholders to creditors by the creative use of separate corporate personality and the corporate veil. Gower comments:[37]

> This decision opened up new vistas to company lawyers and the world of commerce. Not only did it finally establish the legality of the 'one man' company and showed that incorporation was as readily available to the small private partnership and sole trader as to the large public company, but it also revealed that it was possible for a trader not merely to limit his liability to the money which he put into the enterprise but even to avoid any serious risk to the major part of that by subscribing for debentures rather than shares. This result seems shocking and has been much criticised.[38]

The risk is likely to weigh particularly heavily on 'the little man, whom the law should particularly protect'[39] since it is unlikely that a small business or individual will study the accounts of a company before dealing, even if that were satisfactory in determining the state of finances (which it is not, since they will inevitably be out of date). Similarly, employees are in a poor position.

This shifting of the risk is, of course, an instance of state interference reflecting use of the concession doctrine. Concession theorists would argue that such a fundamental shift justifies a network of regulation aimed at the protection of creditors and others who have dealings with the company in order to rebalance the risk. Economic contractualists who play

[36] At p. 51.
[37] Gower, *Principles of Modern Company Law* (6th edn, P. Davies (ed.), Sweet and Maxwell, London, 1997), p. 79.
[38] Citing O. Kahn-Freund, 'Some Reflections on Company Law Reform' (1944) *7 MLR* 54.
[39] *Ibid.*

down the importance of limited liability so as to de-emphasise the role of the state would not give credence to the concession theorists demand that if the state has been involved in tipping the risk substantially in favour of shareholders it must have a right and duty to regulate in order to protect other participants against whom the balance has been tilted.[40] They believe that 'the market' would somehow have created limited liability without state interference.

What is clear at present is that the fictitious separate personality of a company is taken very seriously by the courts. As we have seen, this has especial difficulties when groups of companies seek to evade regulation by creating structures of linked companies operating in different jurisdictions. For the shareholder, however, this strict upholding of the legal fiction is wholly beneficial, creating a shelter and refuge which enables her to minimise risk.

Separate corporate personality: handle with care

The beneficial consequences for shareholders of the separate personality of the company include:

(a) ease of change of membership because the property of the business is owned by the company; members simply transfer shares without the need to divide the property of the business;
(b) perpetual succession, which means that the death or illness of shareholders has no effect on the continued existence of the company;
(c) a company may be sued and sue in its own name thus preventing the necessity for identifying all the participants.[41]

Although generally beneficial for shareholders, the separate personality of the company can, if strictly construed by the courts, have some unexpected and sometimes unwelcome effects. In *Neptune (Vehicle Washing Equipment) Ltd* v. *Fitzgerald*,[42] the defendant was a sole director of a company. Despite this he was obliged to make disclosure of a personal interest in a resolution which he passed purporting to terminate his contract of employment although the court held that 'it may be that the declaration does not have to be out loud'. Although this sounds strange it emphasises that the contract was one between the director and the company so that in his capacity as an official acting in the interests of the company

---

[40] R. Posner, *Economic Analysis of the Law* (4th edn, Little Brown, Boston, 1992), p. 392.
[41] For a more detailed coverage of these issues see J. Dine, *Company Law* (4th edn, Palgrave, 2001), chs 1 and 2; B. Pettet, *Company Law* (Pearson Education, Edinburgh, 2001), ch. 2.
[42] [1995] 1 BCLC 352.

the director must remind himself of his personal interest before determining a course of action. In *Macaura* v. *Northern Assurance Co.*[43] the court refused to ignore the separateness of the company and 'lift the veil' despite the fact that the consequence of so doing was to deny a remedy to someone whose personal fortune had gone up in smoke. Macaura had sold the whole of the timber on his estate to a company. He owned almost all of the shares in the company and the company owed him a great deal of money. Macaura took out an insurance policy on the timber in his own name. When almost all the timber was later destroyed by fire he claimed under the insurance policy. The House of Lords held that he could not do so. He no longer had any legal interest in the timber and so fell foul of the rule that an insurance policy cannot normally be taken out by someone who has no interest in what is insured.

In the past the courts have been willing to disregard the corporate veil 'in the interests of justice'. However, it is unlikely that this approach has survived the Court of Appeal decision in *Adams* v. *Cape Industries*[44] (see below). The courts have moved from a concession-based imposition of notions of justice to a more contractually based approach.

Two cases provide an illustration of the older approach where the courts were prepared to disregard the separate personality of the company if that would achieve a just result, but equally would keep the veil of personality firmly in place where that would benefit someone for whom the court feels sympathy. In *Malyon* v. *Plummer*,[45] a husband and wife had full control of a company. The husband was killed by the defendant in a car accident and the widow was unable to continue the business of the company. An insurance policy had been taken out on the man's life and £2,000 was paid to the company on his death. The shares of the company were therefore more valuable than they had been prior to his death. The plaintiff (widow) had received an inflated salary from the company prior to her husband's death. The court had to assess the future financial situation of the widow in order to set the amount of damages payable to her. It was decided that the excess of the plaintiff's salary over the market value of her services was a benefit derived from the plaintiff's relationship as husband and wife. It was therefore a benefit lost by his death and only the market value of her services should be taken into account in assessing her future position. This ignores the fact that she was employed by a company which should in accordance with *Salomon's* case have been regarded as a completely separate entity from both husband and wife. It did mean, however, that the widow got more. Similarly, the court held that the insurance money was money which should be regarded as having been paid to the wife as a

[43] [1925] AC 619.   [44] [1990] Ch. 433.   [45] [1963] 2 All ER 344.

result of the death of the husband. The shares owned by the wife should therefore be valued at the lower value before the £2,000 was paid.

It is very difficult to see a distinction in principle between *Malyon* v. *Plummer* where the veil was not just pierced but torn to shreds and *Lee* v. *Lee's Air Farming*[46] where the emphasis was laid heavily on the separate legal personality of the company. In this case the widow would have lost everything if the *Malyon* v. *Plummer* approach had been adopted. In *Lee*, the appellant's husband was the sole governing director and controlling shareholder of a company. He held all but one of the shares in the company. He flew an aeroplane for the company which had taken out an insurance policy which would entitle his widow to damages if when he died he was a 'worker' for the company. He was killed in a flying accident. It was held that the widow was entitled to compensation. Lee's position as sole governing director did not make it impossible for him to be a servant of the company in the capacity of chief pilot because he and the company were separate and distinct legal entities which could enter and had entered into a valid contractual relationship.

Fraud

The Court of Appeal in *Adams* v. *Cape Industries*[47] accepted that 'fraud' should be a ground for lifting the veil. The ability to hide behind the corporate veil could be a powerful weapon in the hands of those with fraudulent tendencies. The courts have therefore always reserved the right to ignore a company which is formed or used merely to perpetrate a dishonest scheme. Here we see the tension between the private law contractual approach which would tend to read the legislation and the constitutional documents literally and a broader, public law imposition of 'justice' norms.

In the *Salomon* cases, both the Court of Appeal and the judge in the first instance thought that they had before them a case of fraudulent use of the corporate veil. Since there was no evidence of dishonest intent in that case it seems that these courts were using 'fraud' in a very wide sense. Indeed, they seem to have regarded the formation of the company so that the business could henceforth be carried on with limited liability as sufficient evidence of 'fraud'. To take such a wide view would defeat the whole notion of the separate existence of the company and the attachment of limited liability to the company and make it impossible for small private companies to function in any way differently from partnerships. The importance of the decision in *Salomon* in the House of Lords is clear. A mere wish to avail oneself of the benefits of limited liability is not of itself

---

[46] [1916] AC 12.   [47] [1990] Ch. 433.

to be regarded as fraudulent. This view was emphatically endorsed by
the court in *Adams*, where rejigging the structure of a group to avoid liability to employees was held not to be 'fraudulent'. This leaves in doubt
how much of the previous law remains valid. In a 1960s case, *Jones v.
Lipman*,[48] the first defendant agreed to sell land to the plaintiffs. When
he later wished to avoid the sale he formed a company and transferred
the land to it. The court held that the company was a 'cloak' for the first
defendant, that he had the power to make the company do as he wished
and the court would order the transfer of land to the plaintiff. The right
of the buyer to have the house transferred to him had 'vested' as he was
entitled to an order for specific performance. Similarly, in another case
decided before *Adams*, *Gilford Motor Co. v. Horne*,[49] the court refused to
allow the defendant to avoid an agreement that he would not compete
with former employers. He had attempted to do so by competing with
them in the guise of a limited company.[50] One of the issues arising from
the *Adams* case is the extent to which these cases can be distinguished.
The Court of Appeal in *Adams* accepted the validity of *Jones v. Lipman*
but in fact the two cases are difficult to distinguish and reached opposite
results. It could be argued that the right of the purchaser in Jones had
'vested', that is become actionable but, as we shall see, the employees
in *Adams* had already been injured at the time of the reorganisation of
the group, so their cases were also actionable at that time. Is there a real
difference?

Groups

There are two definitions of a group in UK law, one definition for accounting purposes and another, which applies in all other circumstances. The
general definition (Companies Act 1985, s.736) reads as follows:

(1) A company is a 'subsidiary' of another company, its 'holding company', if
that other company –

(a) holds a majority of the voting rights in it, or
(b) is a member of it and has the right to appoint or remove a majority of its
   board of directors, or
(c) is a member of it and controls alone, pursuant to an agreement with other
   shareholders or members, a majority of the voting rights in it,

or if it is a subsidiary of a company which is itself a subsidiary of that other
company.

(2) A company is a 'wholly owned subsidiary' of another company if it has no
members except that other and that other's wholly owned subsidiaries or persons
acting on behalf of that other or its wholly owned subsidiaries.

[48] [1962] 1 All ER 442.   [49] [1933] Ch. 935.
[50] See also *Re Darby* [1911] 1 KB 95, *Re H* [1996] 2 BCLC 500.

The emphasis is on control of voting rights which are further defined by the Companies Act 1985. The definition for accounting purposes is even wider. Where companies are operating together, a fairer picture of the financial health of the enterprise as a whole will be given by 'consolidated' or 'group' accounts. Accordingly, Companies Act 1985, s.227 provides that if at the end of a financial year a company is a parent company, the directors, as well as preparing accounts for individual companies, have an additional duty to prepare group accounts, which must give a true and fair view of the state of affairs of the parent and its subsidiaries at the end of the year and also a true and fair view of the profit and loss of the undertakings included in the consolidation during that year. These accounts must comply with the Companies Act 1985, Sch. 4A.

Companies Act 1985, s.258, contains the following definition of the relationship which applies for accounting purposes:

(2) An undertaking is a parent undertaking in relation to another undertaking, a subsidiary undertaking, if –

(a) it holds a majority of the voting rights in the undertaking, or
(b) it is a member of the undertaking and has the right to appoint or remove a majority of the board of directors, or
(c) it has the right to exercise a dominant influence over the undertaking –
   (i) by virtue of provisions contained in the undertaking's memorandum or articles, or
   (ii) by virtue of a control contract, or
(d) it is a member of the undertaking and controls alone, pursuant to an agreement with other shareholders or members, a majority of the voting rights in the undertaking . . .

(4) An undertaking is also a parent undertaking in relation to another undertaking, a subsidiary undertaking, if it has a participating interest in the undertaking and –

(a) it actually exercises a dominant influence over it, or
(b) it and the subsidiary are managed on a unified basis.

A 'participating interest' is defined by s.260. It means an interest held on a long-term basis for the purposes of exercising influence or control, that is, other than for investment purposes. A holding of 20 per cent or more is presumed to be a participating influence unless the contrary is shown.

This definition, particularly the references to 'dominant influence', are wider than the definition of the same relationship which is used for all other purposes. The definitions do not give clear guidance to the courts as to the circumstances in which a group of companies is to be regarded as one entity. Different jurisdictions have reached different answers.[51] The

[51] See Dine, *Company Law* and Dine, *Governance of Corporate Groups*.

importance of this debate, particularly in the context of the problems caused by multinationals, cannot be underestimated. Control over the operations of a large company can be exercised by those holding as little as 20 per cent of the shares. Many companies are organised in a 'group' structure where control is exercised over a number of subsidiaries and a significant number of the shares are held by another 'parent' company. The simplest arrangement is a hierarchy with 100 per cent shareholding but there are numerous other ways of creating effective control of one company over others by different share structures.[52]

Lifting the veil in group situations

The approach of the UK courts is epitomised by Templeman LJ in *Re Southard & Co Ltd*:[53]

English company law possesses some curious features, which may generate curious results. A parent company may spawn a number of subsidiary companies, all controlled directly or indirectly by the shareholders of the parent company. If one of the subsidiary companies, to change the metaphor, turns out to be the runt of the litter and declines into insolvency to the dismay of its creditors, the parent company and the other subsidiary companies may prosper to the joy of the shareholders without any liability for the debts of the insolvent subsidiary.

The approach is confirmed by the cavalier treatment by the courts of 'letters of comfort'. Thus, in *Re Augustus Barnett & Son Ltd*,[54] the company was a wholly owned subsidiary of a Spanish company. The subsidiary traded at a loss for some time but the parent company repeatedly issued statements that it would continue to support the subsidiary. Some of the statements were made in letters written to the subsidiary's auditors and published in the subsidiary's annual accounts for three successive years. Later, the parent company allowed the subsidiary to go into liquidation and failed to provide any financial support to pay off the debts of the subsidiary. In deciding that this did not constitute fraudulent trading on the part of the parent company, Hoffman J accepted that the assurances of the parent were without legal effect.[55] Prentice notes 'there was no serious argument in the case that the [parent company] might have misled its subsidiary's creditors and that this would constitute a basis for piercing the corporate veil'.

---

[52] Dine, *Governance of Corporate Groups*, ch. 2.   [53] [1979] 3 All ER 556.

[54] [1986] BCLC 170, and see *Kleinwort Benson Ltd* v. *Malaysia Mining Corp. Bhd* [1988] 1 WLR 799. For a discussion of Augustus Barnett and an assessment that the result would have been the same under Insolvency Act 1986, s.214, see D. Prentice, 'Corporate Personality, Limited Liability, and the Protection of Creditors' in R. Grantham and C. Rickett (eds), *Corporate Personality in the 20th Century* (Hart Publishing, 1998).

[55] They were not fraudulent because Hoffman J accepted that they were true when made. The subsequent change of mind did not make them retrospectively fraudulent.

In general, the courts have been hostile to developing a notion of 'enterprise law'. Thus, in *Kodak Ltd* v. *Clark*,[56] it was held that a 98 per cent controlling interest in a company does not *of itself* give rise to an agency relationship so as to treat the parent and subsidiary as one enterprise. In *Smith, Stone & Knight Ltd* v. *Birmingham Corporation*,[57] Atkinson J tried to extract the relevant principles. The issue in the case was that land owned by a subsidiary was compulsorily purchased. The land had been used to carry on the business of the parent company. The subsidiary was not itself able to claim compensation.[58] The court held that the parent could recover. According to Atkinson J, the overall question was whether the subsidiary was carrying on the parent's business or its own. This was a matter of fact to be answered by assessing six factors:

> I find six points which were deemed relevant for the determination of the question: Who was really carrying on the business? In all the cases, the question was whether the company, an English company here, could be taxed in respect of all the profits made by some other company, being carried on elsewhere. The first point was: Were the profits treated as the profits of the company? – when I say 'the company' I mean the parent company – secondly, were the persons conducting the business appointed by the parent company? Thirdly, was the company the head and brain of the trading venture? Fourthly, did the company govern the adventure, decide what should be done and what capital should be embarked on the venture? Fifthly, did the company make the profits by its skill and direction? Sixthly, was the company in effectual and constant control?

Farrah notes that questions 4, 5 and 6 cover much the same ground and criticises the approach as 'incoherent',[59] although it was subsequently followed in *Hotel Terrigal Pty Ltd* v. *Latec Investments Ltd (No. 2)*[60] by the New South Wales Supreme Court.

Even where these questions can be answered in the affirmative it is unlikely that the group will be treated as a single entity, because recent cases, particularly *Adams* v. *Cape Industries*,[61] seem to indicate that 'enterprise doctrine' has lost rather than gained ground recently. Further, the answers to the questions posed in *Smith, Stone & Knight* can only provide guidelines and the court will determine each case according to its own facts and the context in which the case arises. The background to such cases can be very varied. *Unit Construction Co.* v. *Bullock*[62] involved the determination of the residence of a company registered in Kenya but managed by a parent in the United Kingdom. The company was held to

---

[56] [1903] 1 KB 505; see also *Delis Wilcox Pty* v. *FCT* (1988) 14 ACLR 156.
[57] [1939] 4 All ER 116.
[58] Because the subsidiary had a short tenancy and the corporation could have given notice under the Lands Clauses Consolidation Act 1845, s.121.
[59] J. Farrah and B. Hannigan, *Farrar's Company Law* (Butterworths, London, 1998).
[60] [1969] 1 NSWLR 676.   [61] [1990] Ch. 433.   [62] [1960] AC 35.

be resident in the United Kingdom. In *Firestone Tyre Co.* v. *Llewellin*,[63] an English subsidiary was held to be the means whereby the American parent company traded in the United Kingdom. A similar decision was arrived at in *DHN Food Distributors* v. *Tower Hamlets Borough Council*[64] which, however, was not followed by the House of Lords in the Scottish appeal of *Woolfson* v. *Strathclyde Regional Council*.[65] In *Lonrho* v. *Shell Petroleum*,[66] it was decided that documents could not be regarded as in the 'power' of a parent company when they were in fact held by a subsidiary. In *National Dock Labour Board* v. *Pinn & Wheeler Ltd and others*,[67] the court emphasised that it is only in 'special circumstances which indicate that there is a mere facade concealing the true facts that it is appropriate to pierce the corporate veil'. Similarly, the rule was approved and relied on in *J.H. Rayner (Mincing Lane) Ltd* v. *Department of Trade and Industry*.[68] This approach was upheld by the House of Lords in *Maclaine Watson & Co.* v. *DTI, Maclaine Watson & Co. Ltd, International Tin Council*[69] and applied in *Adams* v. *Cape Industries plc*.[70] The last case provides a particularly stark example of the application of the *Salomon* principle. Several hundred employees of the group headed by Cape Industries had been awarded damages for injuries received as a result of exposure to asbestos dust. The injuries had been received in the course of their employment. The damages had been awarded in a Texan court. The English Court of Appeal held that the awards could not be enforced against Cape even though one of the defendants was a subsidiary of Cape's and there was evidence that the group had been restructured so as to avoid liability. Slade J said:

Our law, for better or worse, recognises the creation of subsidiary companies, which, though in one sense the creation of their parent companies, will nevertheless under the general law fall to be treated as separate legal entities with all the rights and liabilities which would normally attach to separate legal entities . . . We do not accept as a matter of law that the court is entitled to lift the corporate veil as against a defendant company which is the member of a corporate group merely because the corporate structure has been used so as to ensure that the legal liability (if any) in respect of particular future activities of the group . . . will fall on another member of the group rather than the defendant company. Whether or not this is desirable, the right to use a corporate structure in this way is inherent in our law.

---

[63] [1957] 1 WLR 464.   [64] [1976] 1 WLR 852.
[65] (1978) 38 P & CR 521; see F. Rixon, 'Lifting the Veil Between Holding and Subsidiary Companies' (1986) 102 *LQR* 415.
[66] [1980] QB 358.   [67] [1989] BCLC 647.
[68] Court of Appeal judgment [1988] 3 WLR 1033.
[69] [1990] BCLC 102.   [70] [1990] BCLC 479.

And

If a company chooses to arrange the affairs of its group in such a way that the business carried on in a particular foreign country is the business of the subsidiary and not its own, it is, in our judgment, entitled to do so. Neither in this class of case nor in any other class of case is it open to this court to disregard the principle of *Salomon v Salomon* [1897] AC 22 merely because it considers it just so to do.[71]

As discussed earlier, although the court accepted the decision in *Jones v. Lipman*[72] as correct, the difficulty of distinguishing the two decisions is considerable. A similar approach to *Adams* was taken in *Re Polly Peck International Plc (in administration)*[73] where the court held that where companies were insolvent the separate legal existence of each within the group became more, not less, important and *Adams* v. *Cape Industries* was cited with approval in the recent cases of *Ringway Roadmarking* v. *Adbruf*[74] and *Yukong Line Ltd* v. *Rendsburg Investments*.[75] The courts seem increasingly to refuse to countenance the 'single economic unit' argument and confine the instances in which they are likely to interfere with the *Salomon* principle to subjective fraud by the controllers. A distinction made by Otto Khan Freund[76] between capitalist control in the sense of ownership of shares and functional control in the senses identified by Atkinson J in *Smith, Stone and Knight* v. *Birmingham Corp.* appears to be becoming increasingly irrelevant as the courts refuse to look behind the corporate veil in any circumstances other than actual dishonest fraud. Thus, in *Yukong*, Toulson J agreed with the Court of Appeal in *Adams* that some parts of the judgment in *DHN Food Distributors* had been too widely expressed and further considered that the same applied to *Smith Stone & Knight*:

I do not accept Mr Gross's submission that as a matter of general approach the court should ask whether the company was carrying on business as its owner's business or its own business, using as guidance the sub-questions posed by Atkinson J, and should determine the question of agency accordingly. On that approach, *Salomon's* case would surely have been decided differently . . . It was nothing to the point that [Salomon's company] acted on the direction of Mr Salomon and for his benefit. Something quite different would need to be established in order to show that the company, in law an entity independent of its owner, was acting in some respect as agent for its owner, the necessary requirement being to show that the relationship of agency was intended to be created. Ordinarily, the intention of someone who conducts trading activities through the vehicle of a one-man company will be quite the opposite.[77]

---

[71] *Ibid.* at 513.   [72] [1962] 1 WLR 832.   [73] [1996] 2 All ER 433.
[74] [1988] 2 BCLC 625.   [75] [1988] 2 BCLC 485.   [76] (1940) 3 *MLR* 226.
[77] Toulson J, in *Yukong Line Ltd* v. *Rendsburg Investments* [1998] 2 BCLC 485 at 496.

Similarly, in both *Ringway* and *Yukong* a passage from *Adams* cited with approval is arguably a very restrictive interpretation of the circumstances other than agency when the veil may be lifted in a group situation:

save in cases which turn on the wording of particular statutes or contracts, the court is not free to disregard the principle of *Salomon v Salomon & Co Ltd* merely because it considers that justice so requires. Our law, for better or worse, recognises the creation of subsidiary companies, which though in one sense the creatures of their parent companies, will nevertheless under the general law fall to be treated as separate legal entities with all the rights and liabilities which would normally attach to separate legal entities.[78]

The lower courts seem to be adopting a policy which would eliminate the agency route to lifting the veil and restrict any general doctrine to statute and cases of fraudulent misuse of the veil. Any concept of an 'enterprise doctrine' is losing ground.

Public or private law?

The courts seem to be moving away from the concept of lifting the veil in the interests of justice, i.e. imposing state control over the results achieved by the manipulation of the legal rules, and turning instead to a concept of lifting the veil only when the actual arrangements between the companies reveal day-to-day responsibility to lie in the hands of the parent. It may be seen as a movement towards private law notions of causation and thus be seen as a move in the direction of contractualism. Certainly, the result is to permit the exploitation of the free market by groups of companies free of state regulation and this concept of corporate responsibility across borders is a key problem for those seeking to regulate the giant corporations. In *Adams* a distinction was made between subjective factors such as fraudulent use of the corporate veil which was said to be an issue of 'should the veil be lifted' and issues of control or agency which went to whether there was a single economic unit. The difference is between a focus on the motive for establishing a controlled entity and the fact and degree of control. Where the corporate veil has been disturbed by the court, the conclusion reached at the end of the investigation is remarkably similar, although expressed in a variety of terms. Thus, in the subjective cases the subsidiary is said to be a 'fraud' or 'sham',[79] whereas in the objective cases the commercial reality of the situation is said to

[78] *Adams v. Cape Industries plc* [1990] BCLC 479 at 513 per Slade LJ.
[79] *Jones v. Lipman* [1962] 1 All ER 442; *Gilford Motor Co. Ltd v. Horne* [1933] Ch. 925; *Re Bugle Press Ltd* [1961] Ch. 270.

be that the subsidiary has no significant existence other than as an off-shoot of its parent[80] or that the interests of the related companies are so tied together that they should be regarded as one. The difference of approach is significant as the prevention of fraud approach may be seen as an application of the concession approach, i.e. the state permitting the use of its entrepreneurial tools within certain limits. The 'single unit' approach comes much closer to an application of single entity theories by recognising the power unit represented by the group as a whole. The rejection of the application of the single entity approach and thus the development of a law of the enterprise is to be found in *Salomon* itself, in the rejection of the contention that the company was not being used for a dishonest (subjective fraud) purpose but that the use of a company in a way authorised by the Act was contrary to the purposes envisaged by the statute. Thus, Lopes LJ:

> It would be lamentable if a scheme like this could not be defeated. If we were to permit it to succeed, we should be authorising a perversion of the Joint Stock Companies Acts. We should be giving vitality to that which is a myth and a fiction. The transaction is a device to apply the machinery of the Joint Stock Companies Act to a state of things never contemplated by that Act – an ingenious device to obtain the protection of that Act in a way and for objects not authorised by that Act, and in my judgment in a way inconsistent with and opposed to its policy and provisions.[81]

This analysis was roundly rejected by the House of Lords:

> It has become fashion to call companies of this class 'one man companies'. That is a taking nickname, but it does not help one much in the way of argument. If it is intended to convey the meaning that a company which is under the absolute control of one person is not a company legally incorporated, although the requirements of the Act of 1862 may have been complied with, it is inaccurate and misleading; if it merely means that there is a predominant partner possessing an overwhelming influence and entitled practically to the whole of the profits, there is nothing in that I can see contrary to the true intention of the Act of 1862, or against public policy, or detrimental to the interests of creditors. If the shares are fully paid up, it cannot matter whether they are in the hands of one or many.[82]

This may be an explanation of the paucity of UK case law treating the group as a whole and in particular imposing liabilities on related companies for the activities of others within the group.

---

[80] *DHN Food Distributors Ltd* v. *London Borough of Tower Hamlets* [1976] 3 All ER 462.
[81] *Broderip* v. *Salomon* [1895] 2 Ch. 323.
[82] *Salomon* v. *Salomon* [1897] AC 22 per Lord Macnaughten.

Agency and trust

Other cases that are often cited on this issue are sometimes put into categories such as 'agency' or 'trust' cases. This can give the impression that the reason for interfering with the corporate veil in those cases was because the court made a finding that an agency or trust relationship had developed between the company in question and some other body. In fact it may well be that, as in the *Malyon* and *Lee* cases, the interests of justice required the court to ignore the corporate veil. The argument failed to convince the court in *Adams* and *Yukong* (above) and there must be a suspicion that the future discretion of the court has been limited in this respect as well. In *Abbey Malvern Wells* v. *Minister of Local Government*,[83] the company owned a school which was managed by a board of trustees who were bound by the terms of the trust to use the assets of the company for educational purposes. The company applied to the Minister for Town and Country Planning for a ruling that the land they held was exempt from development charges because it was held for charitable (educational in this case) purposes. The Minister ruled against them but on appeal from that decision the court held (1) that the land was occupied by the company for the educational purposes of the school; (2) that the trusts in the trust deed were charitable; (3) that the company was controlled by trustees who were bound by the trust deed; so that (4) the property and assets of the company could only be applied to the charitable purposes of the trust deed. Accordingly, the company's interest in and use of the land were charitable and fell within the exemption provisions of the tax statute. In this case it was because the very strict control over the use of the land that was imposed by the trust deed bound the controllers of the company both as trustees and directors. In consequence the legally separate nature of the trust and the company could safely be ignored. Similarly, in *Littlewoods Stores* v. *IRC*,[84] it was held that a subsidiary company held an asset on trust for the holding company Littlewoods because Littlewoods had provided the purchase price. Littlewoods could therefore not take advantage of the separate legal identity of its subsidiary to avoid the tax consequences of ownership of the asset.

The decision in *Re F.G. Films*[85] is sometimes regarded as an instance of lifting the veil where the company concerned is acting as an agent for another. Although the judgment mentions agency, the true basis for the decision is that the interests of justice required the court to have regard to the realities behind the situation. The case concerned an application to

[83] [1951] Ch. 728.   [84] [1969] 1 WLR 1241.   [85] [1953] 1 WLR 483.

have a film registered as a British film. To succeed, the applicant company had to show that they were the 'makers' of the film. Vaisey J said:

The applicants have a capital of £100 divided into 100 shares of £1 each, 90 of which are held by the American director and the remaining 10 by a British one . . . I now understand that they have no place of business apart from their registered office and they do not employ any staff . . . it seems to me to be contrary, not only to all sense and reason, but to the proved and admitted facts of the case, to say or to believe that this insignificant company undertook in any real sense of that word the arrangements for the making of this film. I think that their participation in any such undertaking was so small as to be practically negligible, and that they acted, in so far as they acted at all in the matter, merely as the nominee of and agent for an American company called Film Group Incorporated . . . The applicant's intervention in the matter was purely colourable.

A similar motive lies behind the decision in *Daimler* v. *Continental Tyre Co.*,[86] where an English company was held to be an enemy alien because of the nationality of its shareholders.

In conclusion, the recent stance of the courts shows more sympathy for the contractualist viewpoint, refusing to impose notions of justice on the arrangements between the parties. This perspective favours the protection of the shareholder from risk even at the expense of tort victims. It is an attitude which is significant in creating difficulties for those seeking to hold corporations to account for their violations of environmental and human rights norms.

Deregulation, market failure, corporate governance and failures to fulfil human rights

The call for regulatory structures to rebalance the company's focus on shareholders so that it serves to deliver a more just economic outlook is in line with an understanding of human rights which moves away from a traditional focus on limiting the behaviour of the state and its officials and focuses instead on human rights as imposing duties on individuals to build institutions which lead to as full a delivery of human rights as possible.[87] One of these institutions is the capitalist market. There is a good case for applying the concept of institution-building to situations where there is market failure and making the case for regulations to try to correct the market failure so far as possible. Chapter 1 makes the case that the inequality seen in the international market is unjust and should be classified as market failure. This is in line with the concepts of

[86] [1953] 1 WLR 483.   [87] Pogge, *World Poverty*, p. 50 and see chapter 1.

neo-classical economic theorists who call for intervention when a market failure is identified but out of line with their often repeated calls for deregulation on the basis that markets will almost always function well. In truth, the identification of market failure provides us with yet another self-serving device; it tends to be identified only when those identifying it will benefit; the protection of intellectual property is often justified on this basis.

'But for the market economy to function well, there is a need for laws and regulations – to ensure fair competition, to protect the environment, to make sure that consumers and investors are not cheated'.[88] Stiglitz examines the ways in which deregulation in the USA in the 1990s was instrumental in assisting the economic 'bubble' to grow and then burst and the spectacular bankruptcies and revelation of fraud that followed:

> Regulations help restrain conflicts of interest and abusive practices, so that investors can be confident that the market provides a level playing field and that those who were supposed to be acting in their interests actually do so. But the flip side of this is that regulation restrains profits and so deregulation means more profits. And in the nineties, those who saw the larger profits that deregulation would bring were willing to invest to get it – willing to spend megabucks in campaign contributions and lobbyists.[89]

So far as corporate governance is concerned, market failure occurred by failure to regulate competition adequately, by permitting banks and accountancy firms to merge and take on tasks which inevitably involved conflicts of interest and by using perverse incentives as part of the rewards packages for chief executive officers (CEOs).[90] Competition regulation failure came partly from the argument that the 'New Economy' had arrived, that it provided new conditions where innovations would keep competition healthy so regulation was not necessary. Stiglitz was not convinced. Analysing the telecommunications market he writes:

> There were two reasons that I was suspicious of those who simply said 'Let competition reign'. The first [was] . . . everyone talked about the importance of being the first mover into a market. In doing so, they were, in effect, admitting that they did not anticipate *sustained* competition. There would be competition *for* the market, but not competition in the market. That, in fact, was why those who had a head start in the race were lobbying so hard: they thought they had the inside track, and the payoff, if they won, would be enormous . . . But secondly, why, if the local phone companies really thought that competition would break out, were they so resistant to efforts to make sure that there was strong anti-trust oversight?[91]

---

[88] J. Stiglitz, *The Roaring Nineties* (Allen Lane, London, 2003), p. 91.
[89] Stiglitz, *Roaring Nineties*, p. 90.   [90] *Ibid.*, ch. 4.
[91] *Ibid.*, pp. 97–8, emphasis in the original.

The second significant failure lay in permitting accountancy and banking firms to merge into huge giants carrying out activities which were clearly in conflict of interest. Thus, accountants were making huge profits by carrying on consultancies for firms whose accounts they were supposed to be auditing and banks were simultaneously lending money to firms such as Enron, while also undertaking the placing of initial public offers (IPOs) of shares with the public. The independent assessment of the lending branch of the bank as to the creditworthiness of the firm was likely to be undermined by the wish of the investment branch to do business issuing shares for the firm. This removed an important device for monitoring the solvency of the company and gave false signals. If the bank was still lending, investors would believe that the firm was still solvent. Loans were granted to Enron until the last moment before the scandal broke and such loans only increased the size of the eventual shortfall for employee pension schemes as well as investors.

A third significant failure was 'the strange corporate practice of giving corporate executives stock options – the right to buy company stock at below market prices – and then pretending that nothing of value had changed hands'.[92] These transactions were not adequately disclosed. The importance of this is clear to Stiglitz:

As a longtime student of the role of information in a well-functioning economy, I [understood that] . . . the executives are being paid too much partly because *it isn't widely known exactly how much they are really being paid.* And if no one knows how much the CEOs are being paid, that means no one knows how much profit (or loss) the company is making. No one knows how much the firm is really worth. Without this information, prices cannot perform the roles they are supposed to in guiding investment. As economists put it somewhat technically 'resource allocations will be distorted'.[93]

Further, compensation packages for CEOs ran out of control, with boards accepting huge increases and shareholders unable to prevent the packages going through. 'While senior executive compensation rose 36 percent in 1998 over 1997, the wages of the average blue-collar worker rose just 2.7 percent in the same period . . . Even in 2001, a disaster year for profits and stock prices, executive CEO pay increased twice as fast as the pay of the average worker'.[94] And you can be sure that it was not a percentage calculated from equivalent pay at the outset. Stiglitz understands the cause of the downturn of the American economy as being significantly caused by these factors which were all brought on by deregulation and a failure to understand the correct role of regulation in preventing or minimising market failures. And, as we shall also

[92] *Ibid.*, p. 115.   [93] *Ibid.*, p. 118, emphasis in the original.   [94] *Ibid.*, p. 124.

see in chapter 3, market failures impact most significantly on the poorest in the community and are likely to directly cause non-or underfulfilment of human rights. The imperative is to prevent perverse incentives and competition failures from so distorting the market that it fails. We must be on guard against the simplistic economic viewpoint which is analysed below since it is still endemic to many policy think-tanks and government advisers all over the world. There is, however, room for optimism:

> For almost a quarter century, beginning in the early seventies, the *rational expectations* school of economic thought dominated economic thinking. This portrayed the individual not only as a rational being, making consistent choices, but as someone capable of processing complex information and absorbing all the relevant knowledge. Its advocates focused on models in which everyone had the same information – there were no asymmetries. In fact, few people know enough math to process even the range of knowledge bearing on the simplest investment decision. (The rational expectations theorists conceded as much, yet asserted that, somehow, individuals acted *as if* they had processed it all.) Not content with upholding the rationality of individuals, they portrayed the economy itself as a rational mechanism – one in which, miraculously, prices reflect instantaneously everything that is known today, and prices today reflect a consistent set of expectations about what prices will be *infinitely far into the future*. The political agenda of this work often seemed barely beneath the surface: if the rational expectations school was right, markets were inherently efficient, and there would be little if any need, ever, for government intervention. The heyday of the rational expectations movement has ended, I am pleased to report.[95]

It is most notable that the most fervent believers of this creed have profited from it (at least until they have gone to prison), a clear example of Pogge's understanding that human beings prefer to take comfort from beliefs that will favour themselves. The analysis also makes it plain that building the market as an institution which will best deliver human rights is itself a human rights responsibility.

The nation state[96] as a moral deflection device

The primacy of nation states in international law creates obstacles to regulatory processes. It also acts as a moral and ethical barrier. As in the case of companies, the ethical barrier is a mirage. Just as creation of a company cannot lower minimum responsibilities, so creation of nation states, for whatever motive they were brought into existence, cannot have that effect. If the motive for the creation of nation states on the ending of

---

[95] *Ibid.*, pp. 151–2, emphasis in the original.
[96] The role of states is further discussed in the context of the international legal structure of human rights in chapter 4.

colonisation was a desire to exploit inequalities and perpetuate them, it is very clear that it has succeeded.

A belief common to 'many citizens of the affluent countries' is that the global economic order is not to blame for severe poverty and increasing global inequality; rather 'poverty is substantially caused not by global, systemic factors, but – in the countries where it occurs – by their flawed national economic regimes and by their corrupt and incompetent elites, both of which impede national economic growth and a fairer distribution of the national product'.[97] This comforting belief is accompanied by demands that the poor countries must first help themselves by giving themselves respectable political regimes. Since, until imposition of regime change in Iraq, it is not the responsibility of rich nations to impose regimes on others, nothing can be done. Aid, if given, would only be lost to corrupt elites. However, these comfortable beliefs 'are nevertheless ultimately unsatisfactory, because it portrays the corrupt social institutions and corrupt elites prevalent in the poor countries as an exogenous fact: as a fact that explains, but does not itself stand in need of explanation'.[98] The prevalence of bad regimes itself requires an explanation. By way of providing an explanation, Pogge focuses on the extraordinary double standards applied to a gang of thieves overpowering the guards at a warehouse and stealing the contents, as opposed to a group overpowering an elected government. The latter (but not the former) become owners of the contents, able to dispose of the natural resources of the country, transferring ownership to the buyers and are able to borrow freely (international resource privilege). Thus:

Indifferent to how governmental power is acquired, the international resource privilege provides powerful incentives toward coup attempts and civil wars in the resource-rich countries. Consider Nigeria, for instance, where oil exports of $6–$10 billion annually constitute roughly a quarter of GDP. Whoever takes power there, by whatever means, can count on this revenue stream to enrich himself and to cement his rule. This is quite a temptation for military officers, and during 28 of the past 32 years Nigeria has indeed been ruled by military strongmen who took power and ruled by force. Able to buy means of repression abroad and support from other officers at home, such rulers were not dependent on popular support and thus made few productive investments towards stimulating poverty eradication or even economic growth.[99]

The failure to alter the prevalence of corruption under Olusegun Obasanjo 'has provoked surprise. But it makes sense against the background of the international resource privilege: Nigeria's military officers know well that they can capture the oil revenues by overthrowing

[97] Pogge, *World Poverty*, p. 110.   [98] *Ibid.*, p. 112.   [99] *Ibid.*, p. 113.

Obasanjo. To survive in power, he must therefore keep them content enough with the status quo so that the potential gains from a coup attempt do not seem worth the risk of failure.'[100]

An expose of the way in which companies, states, codes of conduct and explanatory nationalism all work together has been provided by Global Witness.[101] They report that in Congo Brazzaville, Angola and Equatorial Guinea, huge sums of oil and extractive revenues have vanished from sight, paid as bribes by the companies to the local elites. This is despite the voluntary disclosure code launched by the UK government in 2003. A UK government spokesperson explained that it was for the governments of these countries to stamp out corruption. Global Witness had suggested preventing parent companies from listing on the FTSE, Dow Jones or Bourse (or any powerful country's Stock Exchange) unless companies were transparent about these sums of money. The UK government spokesperson explained that this was not possible since laws would have to be passed in all the countries where the mining companies were registered.[102] This is a manifest inaccuracy, since EU rules and American rules would cover most of the operations and the Stock Exchange of Angola has, to say the least, a low profile in world affairs. It displaces the burden to act on to the corrupt governments – manifestly a recipe of appeasement of the companies by smoke and mirrors while apparently 'tackling the problem'.[103] It is noteworthy in this context that 'corruption indices' always investigate countries where bribes are received, never the source of the bribes. The debt crisis and the imposition of structural adjustment plans and their successors, the badly-named poverty reduction strategy plans, are considered later in this chapter. The imposition of these devices by the international financial institutions are brought about by a number of factors. One is undoubtedly poor national economic policies (which themselves require explanation). Others are undoubtedly the onset of financial crises caused, as explained in chapter 3, to a considerable extent by capital market liberalisation and the short-term loans and herd behaviour of the Western banking community and what Pogge calls the 'international borrowing privilege'. The gang taking over the country also have the country's borrowing power at their disposal. This:

---

[100] Pogge, *World Poverty*, pp. 113–14.
[101] 'Time for Transparency: Coming Clean on Oil, Mining and Gas Revenues' (www.globalwitness.org), 24 March 2004.
[102] BBC 'Today' programme, 24 March 2004.
[103] In Angola one in four children die of preventable disease under five years old while US $1.7 billion goes missing each year. Companies involved in the scandal in the three states include Elf, Mobil and Chevron.

has three important negative effects on the corruption and poverty problems in the poor countries. First, it puts a country's full credit at the disposal of even the most loathsome rulers who took power in a coup and maintain it through violence and repression. Such rulers can then borrow more money and can do it more cheaply than they could do if they alone, rather than the entire country were obliged to repay. In this way, the international borrowing privilege helps such rulers to maintain themselves in power even against near-universal popular opposition. Second, indifferent to how governmental power is acquired, the international borrowing privilege strengthens incentives toward coup attempts and civil war . . . Third, when the yoke of dictatorship can be thrown off, the international borrowing privilege saddles the country with the often huge debts of the former oppressors. It thereby saps the capacity of its fledgling democratic government to implement structural reforms and other political programs, thus rendering it less successful and less stable than it otherwise would be. (It is small consolation that putchists are sometimes weakened by being held liable for the debts of their elected predecessors.)[104]

To that latter point can be added the conditionalities imposed on the nation. Brazil provides an excellent example with the high hopes for poverty reduction under President Lula frustrated to a considerable degree by the demands made on it to pay back its debts:

Antonio Paloccio, given the finance minister's post . . . [set] forth on a fiscal path that saw 14bn reals lopped off government spending and [negotiated] a new IMF agreement meaning a self-imposed budget surplus of 4.25% . . . Interest rates were high to curb inflation, the economy ground to a halt, and prized social programmes stumbled. Unemployment, already high in a country of 175million rose to around 13% and 20% in Brazil's biggest city, Sao Paulo. In Rio de Janeiro 160,000 people applied for only 1,000 jobs as rubbish collectors. The queue of applicants stretched miles.[105]

Add to these factors the formulation of international trade rules in the shape of *Rigged Rules and Double Standards*,[106] which make it extremely difficult for legitimate trade to provide sufficient funds for redistribution by democratic regimes and the role of international institutions in the creation and persistence of poverty becomes evident. Clearly the wickedness of some rulers is also a cause but the factors set out 'crucially affect what sorts of persons jostle for political power and then shape national policy in the poor countries, what incentives these persons face, what options they have, and what impact these options would have on the lives of their compatriots. These global factors thereby strongly affect the overall incidence of oppression and poverty'.[107] A moral debate focused

[104] Pogge, *World Poverty*, pp. 114–15.
[105] David Munk, 'Lula's Dreams for Brazil are Delayed as the Realities of Power Hit Home', *Guardian*, 31 December 2003.
[106] Oxfam, *Rigged Rules*.   [107] Pogge, *World Poverty*, p. 115.

on the degree to which affluent societies and individuals should help the poor lacks an important dimension. Both sides of the debate 'easily take for granted that it is as potential helpers that we are morally related to the starving abroad. This is true, of course. But the debate ignores that we are also and more significantly related to them as supporters of, and beneficiaries from, a global institutional order that substantially contributes to their destitution.'[108]

It is clear that the power of multinationals can overwhelm poor nations desperate to see inward investment[109] and that this can lead to the displacement of domestic production, dreadful labour conditions and environmental disasters,[110] but since the one concept which appears to be agreed on in international law is the primacy of nation states, it is very difficult to craft any form of solution. Traditionally, nation states have obligations to *respect, fulfil and protect* the human rights of their citizens[111] and the United Nations machinery is structured to call nation states to account for violations. However, some scholars argue that the international power of the corporations has entirely escaped from international mechanisms and nation states no longer have sufficient economic power or autonomy to be wholly responsible for the violations of human rights which happen on their territory.[112] This debate is further complicated by differences in the international human rights community between those whose primary motivation is the protection of civil and political rights and those who are principally concerned with economic, social and cultural rights, an unfortunate position since 'the denial of economic and social rights injures and kills more people than any denial of civil and political rights'.[113] Economic, social and cultural rights, for many years the 'poor relations' in the human rights field for a variety of reasons,[114] raise questions which tend to go beyond the model of nation state responsibility for wrongs such as torture or corruption which oppress their citizens. This is because the roots of poverty may rest not only in governmental actions but in the way in which the international community has long exploited differences in climate, resources, political and

---

[108] *Ibid.*, p. 117.
[109] Korten quotes a Philippine government advertisement (1995): 'To attract companies like yours . . . we have felled mountains, razed jungles, filled swamps, moved rivers, relocated towns . . . all to make it easier for you and your business here': Korten, *When Corporations Rule*.
[110] Dine, *Governance of Corporate Groups*, ch. 5.
[111] P. Hunt, *Reclaiming Social Rights* (Ashgate, Aldershot, 1996), p. 32.
[112] Anderson and Cavanaugh, *Global Corporate Power*.
[113] Solita Monsod, 'Human Rights and Human Development' in *Human Development and Human Rights* (Human Development Report Office, 1998).
[114] Dine, *Governance of Corporate Groups*, ch. 5.

economic power to structure a legal international system which systematically disadvantages some states.

The structure of international law relies on nation states as key players. Indeed, it was thought that they were the sole subjects. 'Since the law of nations is based on the common consent of individual States, and not individual human beings, States solely and exclusively are subjects of international law.'[115] It is true that states are no longer the sole players. Now, '[r]ecognised international organisations can make international agreements with other international organisations and individual countries'.[116] Even corporations now have access to international tribunals such as the International Center for the Settlement of Investment Disputes (ICSID).[117] However, it is also clear that states are still pre-eminent players. Two key factors are prominent: consent and equality. Oppenheim notes that *consent* is the basis of international law, while the United Nations Charter states that the United Nations is 'based on the principle of the sovereign equality of all its members'.[118] French notes that:

> The notion of sovereignty arose with the ascendancy of the independent nation state. As European countries began to shake off the influence of the Papacy, the concept of sovereignty provided those in authority with a dual justification for their position. Not only did sovereignty mean that a state was independent from the influence of other states (and arguably, to a lesser extent, the Church), but it also meant that the government-as-state had the right to impose its will on those who resided within its territory.[119]

Thus, the independence and equality of states arose as a philosophy of equality of value in reaction to the claims of powerful bodies of the right to interfere with autonomy. In this we can see a considerable parallel with the establishment of individualist philosophy. The trappings of sovereignty in international law include 'States are judicially equal' and that '[n]o State or group of States has the right to intervene, directly or indirectly, for any

---

[115] L. Oppenheim, *International Law: A Treatise* (2nd edn, 1912), p. 19.

[116] International Council on Human Rights, *Business Rights and Wrongs* (January 2000) (www.international-council.org) and see Rosalyn Higgins, *The Development of International Law Through the Political Organs of the United Nations* (Oxford University Press, London, 1963).

[117] The Washington Convention on the Settlement of Investment Disputes between States and Nationals of Other States was adopted by resolution of the Executive Directors of the World Bank on 18 March 1965.

[118] Article 2.1.

[119] D. French, 'Reappraising Sovereignty in Light of Global Environmental Concerns' (2001) *Legal Studies* 376 at 378, citing R. Anand, *Confrontation or Co-operation? International Law and Developing Countries* (Martinus Nijhoff, Dordrecht,1987).

reason whatever, in the internal or external affairs of any other State'.[120] Further, 'a State has a right to determine its own political, social, economic and cultural systems'. This culture of equality, autonomy and non-interference has had grafted on to it several more sinister attributes, in particular, the concept that a nation state has, as a primary justification for its existence, the duty to protect the perceived interests of its citizens at whatever cost to inhabitants of the rest of the world.[121] The responsibility to its citizens is reinforced by international law in the International Covenant on Civil and Political Rights which in 1966 declared that 'each State party to the present Covenant undertakes to respect and to ensure *to all individuals within its territory and subject to its jurisdiction* the rights recognised in the present Covenant'.[122] As Arambulo points out, the reporting procedure adopted to monitor aspects of human rights is clearly state-based, and focused on the way in which the state reporting treats its own citizens,[123] a situation which may well be satisfactory when rights of citizens against the state are the primary focus for protection. However, it is arguable that where economic, social and cultural human rights are concerned, the dangers of the doctrine of equality of consent present real problems. Both powerful corporations and other nation states have disproportionate bargaining power in relation to many developing countries. The attachment of international law to the primacy of nation states has made it extremely difficult to construct accountability mechanisms which might affect companies and inequalities of bargaining power and expertise have led to 'consent' being given to policies and treaties which have had a detrimental effect on the exercise of the economic, social and cultural rights of individuals, such as the right to food.[124] Hunt points to the distinction between *formal* equality *and structural* equality.[125] Many

---

[120] UN General Assembly's 1970 Declaration on Principles of International Law concerning Friendly Relations and Co-operation among States, UNGA Res. 2625 (XXV) (1970) Annex, see French, 'Reappraising Sovereignty'.

[121] K. Arambulo, *Strengthening the Supervision of the International Covenant on Economic, Social and Cultural Rights: Theoretical and Procedural Aspects* (Intersentia, Antwerpen, 1999), p. 66; P. Brown, 'Food as National Property' in H. Shue (ed.), *Food Policy: The Responsibility of the United States in Life and Death Choices* (Free Press, Macmillan, London, 1977).

[122] 1966, Article 2, emphasis added.

[123] Arambulo, *Strengthening the Supervision*, pp. 36–7, First General Comment of the UN Committee on Economic, Social and Cultural Rights, UN Doc. E/1989/22.

[124] This paper does not attempt to enter the individual rights/collective rights/ justiciability debate, taking rather the stance that it is difficult to dispute the concept that the right of an individual to adequate food is a basic right without which other rights cannot be exercised and so one which requires immediate fulfilment. See H. Shue, *Basic Rights* (2nd edn, Princeton University Press, 1996) p. 18; Arambulo, *Strengthening the Supervision* p. 114. A basic right is 'everyone's minimum reasonable demands on the rest of humanity'.

[125] P. Hunt, *Reclaiming Social Rights* (Dartmouth, Aldershot, 1996).

developing countries have had 'reforms' imposed on them (with consent?) by the World Bank and International Monetary Fund in return for
loans. Following the oil price rises imposed by the OPEC countries in
the mid-1970s, the foreign debts of developing countries increased enormously. From 1970 to 1980 the long-term external debt of low income
countries increased from US $21 billion to US $110 billion and that
of middle income countries rose from US $40 billion to US $317 billion.[126] With default on these loans an inevitability, the IMF and World
Bank were put into a position to impose structural adjustment packages
to ensure that payments were made. 'Each structural adjustment package called for sweeping economic policy reforms intended to channel
more of the adjusted country's resources and productive activity toward
debt repayment and to further open national economies to the global
economy. Restrictions and tariffs on both imports and exports were
reduced, and incentives were provided to attract foreign investors.'[127]
Cahn argues that the World Bank is a governance institution, it is exercising its power 'through its financial leverage to legislate entire legal regimens and even . . . [altering] the constitutional structure of borrowing
nations. Bank-approved consultants often rewrite a country's trade policy,
fiscal policies, civil service requirements, labor laws, health care arrangements, environmental regulations, energy policy, resettlement requirements, procurement rules, and budgetary policy.'[128]
      It is well documented that the consequent 'austerities' cause cuts in
all social and in particular health programmes, a move of the population away from rural areas into cities, the vicious-circle effects of poor
health and lack of proper food and education, and a consequent willingness of a population to work at any task however ill-paid and poorly
regulated.[129] It is true that the structural adjustment policies imposed
by the lending institutions now have a 'softer' face, as each of the Least
Developed Countries (LDCs) must prepare a Poverty Reduction Strategy
Plan (PRSP) as a condition of increased or continued finance or to bid for
forgiveness or rescheduling of debt. However, although these plans are

---

[126] *World Debt Tables 1992–3: External Finance for Developing Countries* (World Bank,
     Washington DC, 1992), p. 212.
[127] Korten, *When Corporations Rule*, p. 184.
[128] J. Cahn, 'Challenging the New Imperial Authority: The World Bank and the Democ-
     ratization of Development' (1993) 6 *Harvard Human Rights Journal* 160.
[129] Korten, *When Corporations Rule*, Chossudovsky, *The Globalisation of Poverty* (Pluto,
     Halifax, Nova Scofia, 1998); P. Harrison, *Inside the Third World* (3rd edn, Penguin,
     Harmondsworth, 1993); I. Wilder, 'Local Futures: From Denunciation to Revalorisa-
     tion of the Indigenous Other' in G. Teubner (ed.), *Global Law Without a State* (Dart-
     mouth, 1996); H. Heerings and I. Zeldenrust, *Elusive Saviours* (International Books,
     Utrecht, 1995).

often carefully prepared and considered there is still considerable emphasis on free trade solutions, including open markets and membership of
the World Trade Organisation (WTO).[130] Theoretically, the restructuring and poverty reduction plans are 'state owned', that is, they have been
drawn up by the impoverished state and contain the state's own solutions
to their poverty and trading dilemmas. There is little doubt that these
plans say what the IFIs and their rich donor nations wish to hear, as the
loans are conditional on their approval. In the end, the 'freeing' of markets is a precondition of loans or debt relief and the freedom of markets
is an aim pursued through the operation of regional trading areas and the
WTO.

The Washington consensus

The 'Washington consensus' has adhered to a rigorous programme of
liberalisation of trade, driven through by WTO rules and IMF and World
Bank conditionalities. It has become clear that this relentless liberalisation has not brought universal benefits and, in particular has exacerbated the conditions of those in most severe poverty. The imposition of a
'one size fits all' concept of economics, driven from rich economies, may
bear some responsibility. Rodrik has analysed government expenditures
in economies which differ in their exposure to the risks of trade. He found
that countries with small economies and large dependence on trade, like
Sweden, Belgium and Austria, developed expensive social support programmes to cushion the impact of trade risks on the population. What is
more, government expenditure increases almost precisely in proportion
to the risk posed by trade to a particular economy. Those with larger
economies (such as the USA and Japan) and less dependence on imports
had smaller social cushions.[131] Of course, cushions are not an option for
the smallest economies most exposed to trading shocks such as decline
in commodity prices. The poor of these countries are most at risk in the
international trading system. The doubts concerning the performance of
Washington consensus economics arises to a considerable extent from
the failure to identify the differing needs of very different economies.

Pogge also shows how discrimination is encouraged by turning the disadvantaged into foreigners by the creation of nation states. Discussing
this phenomenon in the context of a fictional creation of nation states on
the pattern of the South African 'homelands' policy he argues that, as

[130] For a sight of PRSPs, see World Bank website (www. worldbank.org); for an analysis of
the PRSP for Honduras, see chapter 3.
[131] D. Rodrik, *Has Globalisation Gone Too Far?* (Washington, DC, Institute for International
Economics, 1997), cited in I. Wilson, *The New Rules of Corporate Conduct: Rewriting the
Social Charter* (Quorum Books, Westport Connecticut, 2000), p. 21.

with the creation of companies, making others into foreigners by the creation of nation states cannot dilute the duties owed to those persons: 'Specifically, it should not allow such a group, by forming a social arrangement within the larger pattern of interaction, to bring a new moral standard into play that may outweigh, trump or cancel the minimal protections justice requires for those left out of this arrangement.'[132] In addressing the practical outcomes of this insight we need to consider whether the system of international law and the heavily state-based conception of international human rights has not achieved this object by creating barriers to ethical responsibility: 'when matters of common decency or basic justice are at stake, a morality must not be sensitive to changes that are consciously instituted in order to secure a more favourable evaluation, but are, by the lights of this morality itself, merely cosmetic'.[133]

We have already seen perceptions of the state as a moral deflection device working to comfort the rich and powerful by providing evil and corrupt regimes which can be blamed for the poverty of those within their borders. A further dimension is added by considering the failure of this 'explanatory nationalism' to address the relationship between the evil and corrupt regimes which are so deplored and the materials which underpin our standard of living. Because of the international borrowing and resource privileges:

> We authorise our firms to acquire natural resources from tyrants and we protect their property rights in resources so acquired. We purchase what our firms produce out of such resources and thereby encourage them to act as authorized. In these ways we recognize the authority of tyrants to sell the natural resources of the countries they rule. We also authorize and encourage other firms of ours to sell to the tyrants what they need to stay in power – from aircraft and arms to torture and surveillance equipment.[134]

In protecting and encouraging such tyrants by purchase of national resources we encourage the theft of national resources by tyrants and provide huge incentives for coups d'etat. Moral deflection devices become enshrined in laws, both national and international. The ineffectiveness of the human rights regime in tackling poverty also owes much to its perception of rights delivered by the rulers within their territories. The powerful role accorded to sovereignty in human rights interpretation has tended to reinforce the perception of each regime being solely responsible for the conditions within the border of the state. In chapter 4, this is examined together with a discussion on the role that should be played by the duty of international co-operation to be found in the Covenant on Economic, Social and Cultural Rights. Similarly, the WTO rules are

---

[132] Pogge, *World Poverty*, p. 81.   [133] *Ibid.*, p. 83.   [134] *Ibid.*, p. 142.

based on negotiations between nation states. As we shall see in chapter 3, the rules of the WTO also give a message of apparent equality between nation states which also acts as a moral deflection device, sending again the message that responsibility for trading conditions and their economic consequences are the 'fault' of the regime in power in each state, whereas the realities of differential bargaining power tell a different story.

Not only in matters of procedure but also at the substantive level is the deceptive appearance of equality important in the WTO. It works on the basis of unconditional most favoured nation treatment, i.e. that there can be no discrimination against other WTO members in allowing access to a home market.[135] Again, this is based on the equality principle. Social issues should figure prominently. The Preamble of the WTO Agreement stipulates that trade must:

> be conducted with a view to raising standards of living, ensuring full employment and a large and steadily growing volume of real income and effective demand, and expanding the production of and trade in goods and services, while allowing for the optimal use of the world's resources in accordance with the objective of sustainable development, seeking both to protect and preserve the environment and to enhance the means for doing so in a manner consistent with their respective needs and concerns at different levels of economic development.

However, although in international trade agriculture is central to the poverty debate because it is of vital importance in countries where most of the poor in the developing world can be found,[136] the WTO has failed to deliver a fair regime. Although the Uruguay Round attempted to integrate agriculture into the WTO rules by converting non-tariff barriers into tariff barriers and scheduling the barriers for reduction:

> with developed countries committing to deeper tariff cuts over a shorter time period. There is also a programme to reduce export subsidies (36% in six years) and to reduce the volume of subsidised exports. After four years of this scheme's operations, the developing countries' access to world markets should have increased. But it has not. What happened? First, most of those high sounding commitments are backloaded – that is to say, countries wait till the last possible minute to reduce the tariffs or subsidies. So the access to markets is still far from realised. Farmers in developing countries contend with low international prices, tariff barriers that still block countries' entry even if they can compete, or artificially cheap agricultural imports that reduce incentives for local production.[137]

---

[135] Article I of the General Agreement on Tariffs and Trade (GATT), Article II of General Agreement on Trade in Services (GATS).

[136] Monsod, 'Human Rights', p. 141, in particular noting that in the Philippines, 75 per cent of the poor are in agriculture.

[137] *Ibid.*, p. 142.

Similar patterns can be discerned in manufacturing, trade in services and trade-related intellectual property rights (TRIPS). Many factors contribute to the eventual emergence of rules favouring further polarisation of wealth, including the inability of poorer states to cushion themselves against unstable commodity prices and the sheer technical inability to negotiate the issues when resources and expertise are in short supply. These issues are discussed further in chapter 3,[138] but one of the fundamental difficulties faced by those concerned with the interface between free-trade values and other value systems is the reality that use by the international community of human rights law to admonish nation states in breach of their obligations to citizens may be seen as a protectionist move to keep off the market competing goods produced at low prices, for example by workers getting very low wages. This is a particularly acute problem where exclusionary mechanisms available under the WTO agreements are proposed but has resonance throughout the trading system:

As *exporters*, developing countries have traditionally been concerned that developed countries would use measures for health, environment or consumer protection as tools to protect their domestic industry with a consequent risk for developing country market access opportunities.

As *importers*, developing countries are facing a different risk in the biotechnology field – that of importing and utilising products which may prove to be harmful for human health or the environment.[139]

This issue amongst many others must be resolved if the objectives of the WTO are to be realised. The UN Committee of Economic, Social and Cultural Rights has expressed the following view:

It is the Committee's view that WTO contributes significantly to and is part of the process of global governance reform. This reform must be driven by a concern for the individual and not by purely macroeconomic considerations alone. Human Rights norms must shape the process of international economic policy formation so that the benefits for human development of the international trading regime will be shared equitably by all, in particular the most vulnerable sectors.[140]

---

[138] See generally F. Francioni (ed.), *Environment, Human Rights and International Trade* (Hart, Publishing, Oxford, 2001); J. Jackson, *The Jurisprudence of GATT and the WTO: Insights on Treaty Law and Economic Relations*; J. Weiler (ed.), *The EU, the WTO and the NAFTA: Towards a Common Law of International Trade* (Oxford University Press, Oxford, 2000).

[139] Simonetta Zarrilli, 'International Trade in Genetically Modified Organisms and Multilateral Negotiations: A New Dilemma for Developing Countries' in Francioni, *Environment, Human Rights*, emphasis in the original.

[140] Statement of the UN Committee on Economic, Social and Cultural Rights to the Third Ministerial Conference of the World Trade Organisation, 26 November 1999, E/C 12/1999/9.

Bending philosophies: oppressive equality – individualism, companies and states in the international trading system

Individualist philosophy initially served to enhance the status of human beings and argue against their oppression by concentrations of power in the hands of the wealthy, often represented by the nation state. Subsequent interpretation of the ideas inherent in such philosophy has, however, turned reality on its head and created a system which values power and wealth above individuals. The interpretations 'bite' at three levels: that of the individual, the corporation and, as we have seen, the nation state. In essence, what has occurred is that philosophy which values individuals as equals has been used to represent those same individuals as having equal power in market relationships. Thus, there has in all three spheres been an elision between equal *value* and equal power. At corporation level this slide of meanings has been exacerbated by theories which deconstruct companies and groups of companies into individual contractual relationships, a 'network of contracts', causing the aggregation of power in companies to disappear. Just as with individuals, at nation state level, the political equality of states has come to be mistakenly viewed as equality of bargaining power. Equality of power means that there is a true choice available in the market place. Thus, individuals and states that have 'chosen' options which lead to poverty may have their freedom and autonomy recognised by not interfering with those 'choices'. This further aspect of explanatory nationalism uses individualist philosophy to create distortions of the world trading system which, in producing huge disparities of wealth, undermines targets of poverty reduction and prevents many benefiting from the growth of international trade.

Individuals: sleight of hand – equality of value vs equality of power

The doctrine of individualism has been adopted in an exaggerated form that has led to detrimental results both for communities and individuals. The concept that it is the right of each individual to pursue a life plan and, short of the harm principle, be free from interference, has outgrown its undoubted utility in guaranteeing freedom from excessive state interference or societal disapproval and created a selfish concentration on individual pursuits regardless of their impact on others. Ironically, while Mill may be seen as one of the founding fathers of individualist philosophy, he was well aware of the dominant philosophy's tendency to favour those in power: '[w]herever there is an ascendant class, a large proportion of the morality of the country emanates from its class interests and its feelings of class superiority'[141] and Mill would very likely be horrified to realise that his notions of individual liberty were used to found a philosophy which allows rich Westerners to enjoy a quiet conscience while more than 1.3 billion people live in absolute poverty.[142]

Concepts of individual liberty are inextricably linked with the justice of equality. However, this principle has been open to significant corruption in the formation of methods of thought which are based on the concept of the equal *value* of individuals but posit policies which, because they ignore historical, geographical, social and economic inequalities of *power* which predate the commencement of the policy, continue to create a concentration of wealth in the hands of the few at the expense of the many.

Marx's understanding of the nature of reality was that real equality is determined not by theories of equal autonomy but is rooted in the position of each individual in relation to their material circumstances. Marx was concerned with debunking the Kantian and Hegelian notions of equality and autonomy. In Marx's view, these concepts were untrue and unreal attributions from outside the 'real' world. The way in which political equality and equality of autonomy were attributed to individuals in the Hegelian and Kantian perspectives was, to Marx, a denial of reality. The real world permitted great practical inequalities because actual equality is determined by an individual's place in the material world. Just like religion, Hegelian ideas served to disguise inequalities and the apparent attribution of equal autonomy served as a tool of the ruling class to oppress: MacIntyre writes[143] '[i]n the course of a discussion with Bruno Bauer over the political rights of the Jews, Marx brings out both the benefits of political equality and its limitations. The state may grant men equal political rights, but it ignores the basic inequalities of birth, occupation and property which render men in practice unequal.'

The 'speciousness' of this attribution of equal autonomy can be clearly seen in Marx's discussion of retributive justice:

From the point of view of abstract right, there is only one theory of punishment which recognises human dignity in the abstract, and that is the theory of Kant, especially in the more rigid formula given to it by Hegel. Hegel says, 'Punishment is the right of the criminal. It is an act of his own will. The violation of right has been proclaimed by the criminal as his own right. Punishment is the negation of

---

[141] J.S. Mill, *On Liberty* (Penguin, 1974), p. 65.

[142] UN Development Programme, *Human Development Report 1996* (Oxford University Press, New York, 1994); Third World Network, 'A World in Social Crisis: Basic Facts on Poverty, Unemployment and Social Disintegration', *Third World Resurgence* (No. 52, 1994).

[143] A. MacIntyre, *Marxism and Christianity* (Duckworth, London, 1969), p. 36.

this negation, and consequently an affirmation of right, solicited and forced upon the criminal by himself'. There is no doubt something specious in this formula, inasmuch as Hegel, instead of looking upon the criminal as a mere object, the slave of justice, elevates him to the position of a free and self-determined being. Looking, however, more closely into the matter, we discover that German idealism here, as in most other instances, has but given a transcendental sanction to the rules of existing society.[144]

Individualist philosophy has led Hayek to desire a 'Great Society' in which individual choice is maximised.[145] Hayek's thesis is that community is not founded on neighbourliness, shared goals, solidarity or a common good, and the limited consensus which binds society is about just processes. Thus, while it is unjust to intend to damage another human being's interests or person, if the damage is simply the unintended consequence of an impersonal transaction the issue of justice does not arise.[146] Provided the individual uses 'just' methods in pursuit of their interests, she has no responsibility for the outcome; it is meaningless to describe a factual situation as just or unjust.[147] This doctrine of individualism and the denial of collective rights is one of the major driving forces which has permitted a global free market to destroy community rights while removing any concept of responsibility for that result from those individuals who are causing the damage by pursuing their liberal goals:

to posit a society where people are bound together only by involvement in the market and observance of some simple rules of non-interference in other's private space is individualism run wild . . . The ideological nature of Hayek's theory of justice[148] is betrayed by the fact that it leaves the wealthy and powerful undisturbed and unchallenged provided that they obey the simple rules of fair dealing.[149] This very convenient philosophy absolves from blame the use of bargaining and trading mechanisms which are dictated by the rich and powerful and then followed by the letter so that the processes which are evident are 'just'. The consequences, however, are not.

---

[144] Karl Marx, 'Capital Punishment', *New York Daily Tribune*, 18 February 1853. For a commentary on this passage see J. Murphy, 'Marxism and Retribution' in *Marx, Justice and History* (Princeton University Press, 1980).

[145] F.A. Hayek, *Law, Legislation and Liberty* vol. III, *The Political Order of a Free People* (2nd edn, Routledge, London, 1982), p. 149.

[146] F.A. Hayek, *Law, Legislation and Liberty* vol. II, *The Mirage of Social Justice* (2nd edn, Routledge, London, 1982), p. 70, and see for commentary Duncan Forrester, *Christian Justice and Public Policy* (Cambridge University Press, 1997), esp. p. 142 *et seq.*

[147] Hayek, *Law, Legislation*, p. 32.

[148] For a powerful statement from a consequentialist perspective see P. Singer, 'Reconsidering the Famine Relief Argument' in H. Shue (ed.), *Food Policy: The Responsibility of the United States in Life and Death Choices* (The Free Press, Macmillan, London, 1977).

[149] D. Forrester, *Christian Justice and Public Policy* (Cambridge University Press, 1997), p. 151.

The concept of 'choice'

Individualist philosophers are also responsible for our understanding that choice is a good and leads to the possibility of choosing to live a good life, to have autonomy. The concept of choice has, however, been thereby elevated to a position where the original justification for considering choice to be good has been distorted into a method of avoiding moral truths. An excellent example of this is Pogge's 'explanatory nationality' which essentially blames the poor for choosing a corrupt and evil regime and decreeing that they must therefore bear the burden of whatever such a regime (or its predecessors) inflicts on them. Economics also assumes that persons make rational choices and it is this (and preferably this alone) that should govern the allocation or reallocation of resources. But the scope of many for making rational choices is severely restricted by their 'choice' of where to be born. Although both economic and sociological discourse contains much unreality there is some truth in the old chestnut 'Economics is the study of the choices that people make while sociology is the study of why people have no choices'.[150] As we shall see, the way in which individuals and states are said to have chosen their own circumstances is a central concern. Because of inequalities which predate the particular transaction under scrutiny, apparent equality and freedom of choice is undermined with the result that the cry for freedom of choice to contract becomes oppressive to those in the weaker position. The cry for freedom has become distorted into a legal vehicle for the oppression of the weak by the strong.

Economics and choice

Free market economists, while claiming moral neutrality for their theories,[151] use a discourse which has the effect identified above of causing a slide of perception from equality of value to equality of power. The theories rest on the concept of equal bargaining power (including equality of information) and the resultant 'efficiency'. The result of assuming equality of bargaining power means that there is no justification in intervening in the resultant property distribution. Such an intervention is an interference in the 'freedom to choose' to carry out a particular transaction. The defence of freedom may thus be prayed in aid

---

[150] Cited in N. Gilbert, *Researching Social Life* (Sage, 1993), p. 2 and attributed to Duesenenberry.
[151] According to D. Campbell, 'Reflexivity and Welfarism in the Modern Law of Contract' (2000) *Oxford Journal of Legal Studies* 477, a claim most powerfully made by F.A. Hayek in *The Road to Surfdom* (1986).

of a market system, which is then free to create enormous inequalities. This concept of freedom of choice has considerable resonance both at national and international levels, applying to individuals, corporations and states. Assertions of freedom and equality disguise the real power relations.

Every stable social system possesses an order of power and wealth, but unlike historically prior distributive schemes, the market order avoids the imposition of a detailed pattern. Instead of a structure of rank and privilege fixing entitlements to wealth and power, the distributive mechanism of the market allocates resources to those persons able and willing to pay the highest price for them . . . The market order avows blindness to claims of privilege or force, so it recognises no claims of an inherent right to govern or to possess superior wealth . . . The market order lets fly the centrifugal forces of radical individualism, permitting philosophers to celebrate the relative fluidity of its distributive outcome and to legitimate it by appeals to the impervious mask of market forces. No other order so successfully disguises the fact that it constitutes an order at all.[152]

Campbell agrees:[153] '*Laissez faire* is a social structure facilitating economic exchange, but one which, by virtue of its radical individualism, paradoxically denies that it is a social structure . . . *laissez faire* is a framework so characterised by unconscious asymmetries of power as to make choice "a very poor joke" for most citizens.'[154] Weber wrote: 'pure economics is a theory which is apolitical', which asserts 'no moral evaluations and which is "individualistic" in its orientation . . . The extreme free traders, however, conceived of it as an adequate picture of 'natural' reality, i.e., reality not distorted by human stupidity, and they proceeded to set it up as a moral imperative – as a valid normative ideal – whereas it is only a convenient ideal type to be used in empirical analysis.'[155] For Lukes, 'economics (including present-day neo-classical economics) is inherently normative, tending to present the core institutions of capitalism – private property, the market, free competition etc – as meeting the requirements of efficiency and equity'.[156]

Lukes cites Gunnar Myrdal's analysis of the mechanisms of the sleight of hand:

[152] H. Collins, *The Law of Contract* (1986), cited in Campbell, 'Reflexivity and Welfarism'.
[153] Campbell, 'Reflexivity and Welfarism', n. 32 at 490.
[154] *Ibid.* citing I.R. McNeil, 'Bureaucracy and Contracts of Adhesion' (1984) 22 *Osgoode Hall Law Journal* 5 at 6.
[155] M. Weber, 'The Meaning of "Ethical Neutrality" in Sociology and Economics' (1917) in E. Shils and H. Finch (eds), *Max Weber on the Methodology of the Social Sciences* (Glencoe, 1949), p. 44.
[156] S. Lukes, *Individualism* (Blackwells, Oxford, 1979), pp. 90–1.

Even when the claim is not explicitly expressed, the conclusions unmistakably imply the notion that economic analysis is capable of yielding laws in the sense of *norms*, and not merely laws in the sense of *demonstrable recurrences and regularities of actual and possible events.*

Thus the theory of 'free competition' is not intended to be merely a scientific explanation of what course economic relations would take under certain specified assumptions. It simultaneously constitutes a kind of proof that these hypothetical conditions would result in maximum 'total income' or the greatest possible 'satisfaction of needs' in society as a whole. 'Free competition' thus on logical and factual grounds becomes more than a set of abstract assumptions, used as a tool in theoretical analysis of the causal relations of facts. It becomes a political *desideratum*.[157]

Thus, Hayek calls for the 'abandonment of economic planning, the severe curbing of trade union powers, the dismantling of progressive taxation, the dropping of planning and rent controls, the withering away of the direct provision of education by the state, the restoration of wealth as a criterion for entry into higher education and the cessation of governmental conservationist policies'.[158] As Lukes points out:

These are the implications of present-day economic individualism at its strongest. They involve not a policy of laissez faire, but the demand that the government provide a framework within which competition and the price mechanism should be protected and promoted. In the context of monopoly capitalism with giant corporations increasingly controlling markets and consumer behaviour, this demand becomes ever more anachronistic.[159]

It is therefore important to examine closely foundation concepts to understand how norms have emerged from the analysis. A key concept is 'efficiency', a term which also has emotive power (distorted use of language is further discussed in the next section). Who has ever heard of a government asking advisers to formulate an inefficient economic policy? However, notions of the measurement of efficiency vary. Pareto efficiency requires that someone gains and no one loses. However, the Kaldor-Hicks test accepts as efficient 'a policy which results in sufficient benefits for those who gain such that potentially they can compensate fully all the losers and still remain better off'.[160]

---

[157] *Ibid.*, p. 91 citing G. Myrdal, *The Political Element in the Development of Economic Theory* (P. Streeten (trans.), London 1953), emphasis in the original.
[158] Lukes, *Individualism*, from F.A. Hayek *Individualism and Economic Order* (Routledge, London, 1949).
[159] Lukes, *Individualism*, p. 93.
[160] Explanation given by A. Ogus, *Regulation: Legal Form and Economic Theory* (Clarendon Press, Oxford, 1994), p. 24, who immediately points out that there is no requirement for the gainers to compensate the losers; see below in criticism section.

As explained above, the neo-classical economists believe that rational actors utilising perfect information will produce maximum allocative efficiency by making choices which exploit competition in the market. In plain English that means that everyone is assumed to be equally rational, have equal bargaining power and that there is no asymmetry of information. Stiglitz explains the theories thus:

One of the great intellectual achievements of the mid-twentieth century . . . was to establish the conditions under which Adam Smith's 'invisible hand' worked. These included a large number of unrealistic conditions, such as that information was either perfect, or at least not affected by anything going on in the economy, and that whatever information anybody had, others had the same information; that competition was perfect; and that one could buy insurance against any possible risk. Though everyone recognised that these assumptions were unrealistic, there was a hope that if the real world did not depart too much from such assumptions – if information were not too imperfect, or firms did not have too much market power – then Adam Smith's invisible hand theory would still provide a good description of the economy. This was a hope based more on faith – especially by those whom it served well – than on science. My research, and that of others, on the consequences of asymmetric information . . . has shown that one of the reasons that the invisible hand may be invisible is that it is simply not there.[161]

Since the invisible hand is not to be fettered, state regulations should be removed so that a 'free market' is permitted to reach maximum efficiency. As we shall see in the international context, deregulation distorts the concept of freedom by removing regulation which seeks to protect the vulnerable – trade union law, employment regulation, environmental legislation. Freedom to trade in this sense becomes someone else's lack of freedom. As we shall see in chapter 3, the slave traders defended their practices on the basis that they must be allowed 'free trade'.

It must be noted that any identified defect in the underlying assumptions tends to have a cumulative effect, each building block contributing to a picture which emphasises the necessity for a market free of regulatory interference, disguising the reality of imbalances of power which might be addressed by regulation. The basis of the theories on a pseudo-scientific notion of efficiency and the claim that creating wealth is beneficial for society as a whole means that the end result is a picture where interference with the freedom of markets needs to be justified by anyone who argues for any regulation of market behaviour.

Take first the Kaldor-Hicks notion of efficiency. The concept that net gains and losses need to be calculated and any net gain to any party is equivalent to efficiency is open to 'several powerful objections, at least

---

[161] Stiglitz, *Roaring Nineties.*

as a conclusive criterion of social welfare'.[162] Ogus points to the coercive imposition of losses on individuals, the assumption that one unit of money is of equal value whoever owns it and its hostility to the notion of distributive justice. Ogus gives the following example:[163]

Suppose that the policymaker had to choose between (A) a policy that increased society's wealth by $1 million and benefited the poor more than the rich, and (B) a policy that increased its wealth by $2 million, the bulk of which devolved on the rich? Many would argue for (A) on the grounds of fairness[164] but (B) would be considered to be superior in Kaldor-Hicks terms.[165]

Now, if we see this argument in the light of Marx's views on equality and the concept of freedom, we can see how the approach is based on the idea of 'notional equality' of the Kantian and Hegelian kind and how clearly Marx saw the reality that given real inequalities which predate the time of the transaction, inequalities will not only persist but become more and more accentuated. The Pareto-Hicks formula does not insist that the winning individuals and the losing individuals should be different in different transactions; in practice the powerful become more powerful, the poor more poor and disadvantaged. O. Lange writes:[166] 'let us imagine two persons: one who has learned his economics only from the Austrian School, Pareto and Marshall, without having seen or even heard a sentence of Marx or his disciples; the other one who, on the contrary, knows his economics exclusively from Marx and the Marxists . . . Which of the two will be able to account better for the fundamental tendencies of the evolution of Capitalism?', resolving the question in favour of the Marxists.[167] Lange also makes the contrast between Marx's theory of economic 'evolution' and the fact that 'for modern "bourgeois" economics the problem of economic evolution belongs not to economic theory but to economic history'.[168] This static nature may be seen as flowing from the essentially moral emptiness of current economic theory; unlike Marxism it is not driven by a desire to achieve freedom and fulfilment of a spiritual nature.[169]

---

[162] *Ibid.*, p. 25.   [163] *Ibid.*, p. 25.
[164] Ogus, *Regulation* and see J. Rawls, *A Theory of Justice* (Oxford University Press, Oxford, 1972).
[165] This argument has powerful resonance when the operation of transnational and global corporations is under scrutiny.
[166] 'Marxian Economics and Modern Economic Theory' in S. Horowitz (ed.), *Marx and Modern Economics* (Macgibbon and Key, London, 1968).
[167] *Ibid.* at p. 71.   [168] *Ibid.*, p. 73.
[169] A. Van Leeuwen, *Critique of Heaven* (Lutterworth, London, 1972), esp. ch. IV, 'Human Self-consciousness as the Highest Divinity'.

Benefit for all: the trickle down effect?

The foundation value of the economist's theory is that market forces will ultimately benefit all:

Economic analysis holds, on its normative side, that social wealth maximisation is a worthy goal . . . But it is unclear *why* social wealth is a worthy goal. Who would think that a society that has more wealth . . . is either better or better off than a society that has less, except someone who made the mistake of personifying society, and therefore thought that a society is better off with more wealth in just the way an individual is? Why should anyone who has not made this mistake think wealth maximisation a worthy goal?[170]

Dworkin answers this question[171] by considering the relationship between wealth and social value. An important distinction is that between social wealth as a component of social value, 'that is, something worth having for its own sake and social wealth as an instrument of social value i.e. valuable because the wealth may be used to promote other values by a distributive process either deliberate or "through an invisible hand process"'. Of social wealth as a component of social value, Dworkin identifies a modest and immodest claim. The former argues that social wealth is one component of social value: 'One society is *pro tanto* better than another if it has more wealth, but it might be worse overall when other components of value, including distributional components, are taken into account'. The immodest version holds that social wealth 'is the *only* component of social value'.[172] On social wealth as an instrument of social value, Dworkin makes three distinctions: (a) there may be a claim for a causal chain, i.e. that improvements in social wealth cause other improvements, 'improvements in wealth, for example, improve the position of the worst-off group in society by alleviating poverty through some invisible hand process', or (b) a claim that wealth is valuable because it provides the possibility of engineering such improvements, or (c) 'social wealth is neither a cause nor an ingredient of social value, but a surrogate for it. If society aims directly at some improvements in value, such as trying to increase overall happiness among its members, it will fail to produce as much of that goal than if it instead aimed at improving social wealth.' This he deems the 'false-target approach'.

The outcome

At the level of interaction between individuals, therefore, the current economic philosophy disguises real inequalities of bargaining power and

---

[170] R. Dworkin, 'Is Wealth a Value?' (1980) *Journal of Legal Studies* 191.
[171] In the negative.   [172] *Ibid.*, p. 195.

legitimates these inequalities as the outcome of freedom of choice. Further, it denies the legitimacy of government intervention to seek to redress a balance of bargaining power. When the individual comes into contact with a corporation, the problems are further exacerbated.

Corporations in the unequal society

Companies are central to this debate because the dominant philosophy underlying the most powerful transnational corporations is, at the same time, probably the purest form of the corruption of the 'equality' concept – the neo-classical economic analysis of corporations.[173] These theories inform much of Western government thinking about world economics and underpin the laws that structure the TNCs that play such a central role on the world economic stage.

The global free market is based on the neo-classical economic theories which are heavily individual-centric. Nowhere is this more noticeable than when they are applied to the analysis of companies. This analysis starts from the perspective that 'the company has traditionally been thought of more as a voluntary association between shareholders than as a creation of the state'.[174] Cheffins argues that 'companies legislation has had in and of itself only a modest impact on the bargaining dynamics which account for the nature and form of business enterprises. Thus, analytically, an incorporated company is, like other types of firms, fundamentally, a nexus of contracts.' For the purposes of economic analysis, individuals rather than the state are the legitimation for the operation of the commercial venture. Denial of a separate personality to the entity formed by the human group of actors[175] is a necessary foundation[176] for the application of market theories since the underlying assumption is the creation of maximum efficiency by individual market players bargaining with full information.[177] Taking the view that free markets are

[173] 'Greed is good'; M. Friedman, 'The Social Responsibility of Business is to Increase its Profits', *New York Times Magazine*, 13 September 1970.

[174] B. Cheffins, *Company Law: Theory, Structure and Operation* (Oxford, Clarendon, 1997), p. 41. Gower, *Principles of Company Law* disagrees: 'it is clear that without the legislative intervention, limited liability could never have been achieved in a satisfactory and clear-cut fashion, and that it was this intervention which finally established companies as the major instrument in economic development. Of this the immediate and startling increase in promotions is sufficient proof.'

[175] S.J. Stoljar, *Groups and Entities: An Enquiry into Corporate Theory* (ANU Press, Canberra, 1973), p. 40; and G. Teubner, 'Enterprise Corporatism: New Industrial Policy and the "Essence of the Legal Person"' (1988) 36 *American Journal of Comparative Law* 130.

[176] But S. Bottomley, 'Taking Corporations Seriously: Some Considerations for Corporate Regulation' (1990) 19 *Federal Law Review* 203 at 211, sees it as a way to 'submerge the tension that exists in making choices between individual and group values'.

[177] B. Cheffins, *Company Law: Theory, Structure and Operation* (Clarendon Press, Oxford, 1997), p. 6.

the most effective wealth creation system,[178] neo-classical economists
including Coase have analysed companies[179] as a method of reducing
the costs of a complex market consisting of a series of bargains among
parties.[180] Transaction costs are reduced by the organisational design
of the company.[181] 'Corporate law establishes a set of off-the-rack legal
rules that mimic what investors and their agents would typically contract to do. Most shareholders, it is assumed, would contract with
the business managers to ensure that the managers seek to maximise
profit.'[182]

This analysis has multiple tendencies, apart from the already noted
use of emotive terms such as (efficiency). Looking to the individual as
the legitimation for the corporation means that an appeal may be made
to 'free' the 'individual' from state oppression in their operation of the
nexus of contracts, hence the analysis is fundamentally anti-regulatory.
As well as a formal anti-regulatory foundation, the theory also has the tendency of making the company disappear and it is very difficult to regulate
the invisible. The consequences of unwise deregulation are addressed
above.

Linguistic devices: the invisible company and the determinist approach to globalisation

Analysis of a classic text is revealing. Easterbrook and Fischel[183] state by
way of introduction to their work: 'It may be helpful to recall what limited
liability is. The liability of "the corporation" is limited by the fact that
the corporation is not real. It is no more than a name for a complex set
of contracts among managers, workers and contributors of capital. It has
no existence independent of these relations.' This technique of discourse
sets up disparate actors as equivalent and begins the concealment of the
corporation as a seat of significant power which a state might seek to
control.[184] It implies that actors who have relationships with the corporation have equal power amongst themselves and denies an aggregation
of power within the corporation altogether. Further, the role of the state

[178] After A. Smith, *The Wealth of Nations* (J.M. Dent and Sons, London, 1910).
[179] And firms which are not always companies.
[180] Alice Belcher, 'The Boundaries of the Firm: The Theories of Coase, Knight and Weitzman' (1997) 17(1) *Legal Studies* 22.
[181] O.E. Williamson, 'Contract Analysis: The Transaction Cost Approach' in P. Burrows and C.G. Velanovski (eds), *The Economic Approach to Law* (Butterworths, London, 1981); O. Williamson, 'Transaction-Cost Economics: The Governance of Contractual Relations' (1994) 21 *Journal of Law and Society* 168.
[182] K. Greenfield, 'From Rights to Regulation' in F. Patfield (ed.), *Perspectives of Company Law I* (Klüwer, 1997), p. 10.
[183] 'Limited Liability and the Corporation' (1985) 52 *University of Chicago Law Review* 89.
[184] N. Fairclough, *New Labour, New Language* (Routledge, London, 2000), esp. p. 28.

in creating corporations (and therefore having a stake in its behaviour) disappears altogether. The corporation itself is in the process of disappearing.

The book continues with an extensive analysis of the roles of creditors, shareholders and managers from which the workers have entirely disappeared. They do not reappear until some fifteen pages later in a passage, which confirms the assumption of equal bargaining power: 'Employees, consumers, trade creditors and lenders are voluntary creditors. The compensation they demand will be a function of the risk they face.'[185] This list again equates the employee with the merchant bank and assumes that bargaining power is equal. Similarly, '[v]oluntary creditors receive compensation in advance for the risk that the firm will be unable to meet its obligations'.[186] Notice here also the shift from 'corporation' to 'firm' in order to background the common perception of corporations as powerful actors.

As we have seen, one interesting facet about many of the neo-classical economic models is the lowly place occupied by the doctrine of limited liability. The Easterbrook text analyses the situation: 'In the light of the ability of firms to duplicate or at least approximate either limited or unlimited liability by contract, does the legal rule of limited liability matter? The answer is yes, but probably not much.'[187] For Posner,[188] 'limited liability is a means not of eliminating the risks of entrepreneurial failure but of shifting them from individual investors to the voluntary and involuntary creditors of the corporation – it is they who bear the risk of corporate default. Creditors must be paid to bear this risk.' Note that the concept of 'creditor' covers the same categories as in the Easterbrook text but the power imbalances are even more hidden by the 'rolling up' of the disparate categories into the umbrella term. Similarly, 'if corporation law did not provide for limited shareholder liability, then in situations where the parties desired to limit that liability in exchange for a higher interest rate the loan agreement would contain an express provision to that effect'. Similarly, 'the wage rate can and in the long run will adjust to compensate the worker for the risk of non-payment of any compensation claim that he may have against his employer'.[189] Here the text combines the disappearance of the corporation into individual contractors with the disguise of disparate bargaining power amongst those actors. The backgrounding of the state role in the creation of companies gives it no legitimacy in seeking to remedy differential bargaining power, for example, by health and safety legislation. It further misrepresents the end

[185] Easterbrook and Fischel, 'Limited Liability', p. 104.
[186] Ibid., p. 105.   [187] Ibid., p. 102.
[188] Economic Analysis of Law (2nd edn, Little Brown, Boston, 1977), para. 14.3.
[189] Posner, Economic Analysis, p. 295.

result of limited liability in that an insolvency binds all transactors with the firm, not just those who have negotiated special deals. It leaves at risk those in no position to do so. Their position can only be alleviated by public regulation. Thus, although limited liability is seen as an incentive to investment,[190] the role of the state in providing this potentially 'market rigging' mechanism is generally played down, and the argument is made that if limited liability were not provided by the state as an available attribute of a company, participants would incorporate it into individual bargaining arrangements.[191] However, this belittles a mechanism which made a fundamental alteration to the structure of the market. The analysis represents it merely as a mechanism for removing transaction costs and recreating a more perfect market.[192]

The reluctance to accept a significant state role is thus a product of the contract/group realist theories, which reject state power as a source of legitimation for organisations. Linked with the conception that the state's role is solely an 'enabling' one rather than as a controlling power, it is anathema to suggest that the corporation should be used in any way as a form of social engineering. This is particularly noticeable in the characterisation of employees as voluntary creditors able to bargain sufficient compensation for the health and safety risks they may run. The state is excluded from a protective role.

The cumulative results of this discourse assumes equality of individuals and due to the deconstruction of firms disguises power imbalances which restrict choices. Once again, freedom for one party (the corporation) means absence of choice for those in a weak bargaining position. Thus, it depicts an employee contracting with a powerful corporate employer as two equal parties contracting, disguising the power of the company. This tendency is exacerbated at the international level. Although, as we have seen, the existence and enormous influence of companies in the international market place has generated much controversy,[193] remarkably,

---

[190] Posner, *Economic Analysis*, p. 292.

[191] See Cheffins, *Company Law*, pp. 41 and 502, but contra p. 250, pointing out the importance of the nineteenth century enabling legislation. See also Gower, *Principles of Company Law*, chs. 2 and 3.

[192] But for a contrary argument see H. Hazeltine, G. Lapsley and P. Winfield (eds), *Maitland Selected Essays* (Cambridge University Press, Cambridge, 1936), p. 392, arguing that limited liability would have come about by contract if not introduced by law; and J. Farrah and B. Hannigan, *Farrah's Company Law* (4th edn, Butterworths 1998), p. 21.

[193] See, for a small sample, J. Dine, The Governance of Corporate Groups (Cambridge University Press, Cambridge, 2000); Bottomley, 'Taking Corporations Seriously'; Greenfield, 'From Rights to Regulation'; J. Parkinson, *Corporate Power and Responsibility* (Clarendon Press, Oxford, 1995); D. Sugarman and G. Rubin, *Law, Economy and Society* (Professional Books, Abingdon, 1984); M. Stokes, 'Company Law and Legal Theory' in W. Twining (ed.), *Legal Theory and Common Law* (Blackwell, Oxford, 1986).

they are often absent from much writing and speech-making about issues in which their activities are central. Consider the following contrasting texts:

> In the increasingly global economy of today, we cannot compete in the old way. Capital is mobile, technology can migrate quickly and goods can be made in low cost countries and shipped to developed markets.[194]

> The poor nations are . . . exploited directly by the great multinational corporations which dominate a growing proportion of the economic and social life of the Third World . . . The global giants can exert a powerful influence over crucial aspects of development, such as trade balances, the direction of industrial growth, the choice of technology, the rate at which natural resources are extracted, even the culture, values and aspirations of ordinary people.[195]

Why are these so different? The first extract is analysed by Fairclough[196] who points to the absence of the agents involved in the actions portrayed. He exposes 'the ghost in the machine: the multinationals',[197] pointing out that many see the TNCs as dominating the global economy, yet the (apparent) description of their activities in this passage omits a specific reference to them. Thus:

> The second sentence is about processes that are often represented as actions on the part of multinationals. Yet that is not the way these processes are represented here . . . Two of them (*goods can be made in low cost countries*, (*goods can be*) *shipped to developed markets*) are indeed represented as actions but without any responsible agents. Another (*capital is mobile*) is not represented as an action at all, but as a relation of attribution . . . The fourth (*technology can migrate quickly*) is perhaps the most interesting: it is represented as an action but *technology* is represented as itself an agent in a process rather than something that is acted upon (i.e., moved) by the multinationals.[198]

The first passage hides the actors by use of language but the (nearly) invisible company is an entity which flows from the very foundations of the tenets of the neo-liberal economist representation of the corporation.

The systematic disappearance of the company from the neo-classical texts has a number of possible consequences, all of which would be welcomed by those theorists because each aspect conceals the aggregation of power in companies and corporate groups. The invisibility of this power makes companies seem less threatening and thus less likely to be a target for state or international regulation, a key facet of these theories which posit that the market place must be entirely free to regulate itself save for situations involving 'market failure'.[199] The emphasis on the

---

[194] Department of Trade and Industry, *White Paper on Competitiveness* (1998).
[195] Harrison, *Inside the Third World*.
[196] N. Fairclough, *New Labour, New Language?* (Routledge, London, 2000), pp. 23–4.
[197] *Ibid.*, p. 23.   [198] *Ibid.*, p. 23, emphasis in original.   [199] See Ogus, *Regulation.*

bargaining of individual actors also makes an appeal to individual autonomy and the right to freedom of contract and association so that the operation of the market becomes emotionally a 'right' of individuals, only to be interfered with if significant justifications can be found.[200] Corporations are simultaneously powerful wealth producers and have an immense destructive potential. However, the situation is extremely complex and is not amenable to 'easy solutions'. It is easy to sit on one or other side of the good thing/bad thing debate and call either for deregulation to 'free the market' for maximum wealth creation or to call for stringent control over powerful corporations. Voices recognising the complexity of the debate are less common. Francioni writes:

> at a time when humanity is reaching unprecedented levels of economic well-being, which still coexist with the abject poverty and environmental and social degradation of many nations, it may be helpful for international lawyers to reflect on what is the ultimate goal of economic freedom. There seems to be no dispute that the fundamental goals are wealth maximisation, growth and the material progress of peoples. The underlying idea in this chapter is that economic freedom is also a means for the moral and civil progress of the national and international society.[201]

Posnerian ideas of free markets and efficient profit maximisation means in this stream of thought an absence of state regulation.[202] In fact, corporations have escaped both from internal control by shareholders and state regulation.[203] The economic power of corporations is enhanced by a legal framework which has no international enforceable norms. This means that the jurisdictional exclusivity of nation states can be utilised by companies to 'escape' state control and to deny involvement in acts done by related but juridically separate entities (the parent/subsidiary problem).

Some argue that the free market philosophical foundation for the structure of corporations should be abandoned.[204] Where economic analysis is used as an ideology rather than a tool for analysis the danger is that:

> by maintaining that the only obligation of the individual is to honor contracts and the property rights of others, the 'moral' philosophy of market liberalism effectively releases those who have property from an obligation to those who do not. It ignores the reality that contracts between the weak and the powerful are seldom equal, and that the institution of the contract, like the institution of property, tends to reinforce and even increase inequality in unequal societies.

[200] *Ibid.*, and see S. Leader, *Freedom of Association* (Yale University Press, 1992).
[201] F. Francioni, 'Environment, Human Rights and the Limits of Free Trade' in Francioni, *Environment, Human Rights.*
[202] Dine, *Governance of Corporate Groups.*   [203] *Ibid.*
[204] Dworkin, 'Is Wealth a Value?'.

It legitimates and strengthens systems that institutionalise poverty, even while maintaining that poverty is a consequence of indolence and inherent character defects of the poor.[205]

Others reject any attack on free markets outright: Patrick Minford in *The World Turned Rightside Up*,[206] explains that the single European market was Thatcher's legacy but 'no sooner was the ink dry than he [Delors] brought in the raft of Social Charter proposals . . . Like a spreading poison, these proposals now inform and pollute most of the EU's activities; the latest terrifying idea embodied in the Social Chapter is that of pan-European union rights and bargaining.' This paper accompanies one by J. Hulsman arguing that an ethical stance must be taken against the statist German-French line on social responsibility because it interferes with the free market.[207]

While it is clear that there is no simple answer to curbing the destructive possibilities of corporations, solutions should urgently be sought if the equality and dignity of human beings is a true goal.

Determinist globalisation

The disappearance of the agents of change also predicates the inevitability of globalisation and contributes to the reification of the market.[208] The elevation of shareholders to the status of controllers in whose interests the managers must seek to maximise profits disguises the inability of shareholders to control and the consequent lack of control over managers. As Posner states: 'the coalescence of ownership and control is not a necessary condition of efficient management. What is necessary (and sufficient?) is that there be methods – the tender offer, the proxy fight, voluntary acquisition – by which investors (usually in this context, other large corporations) can obtain control of the board of directors and oust the present management'.[209] Note here that efficiency has been previously defined:[210] ' "efficiency" means exploiting economic resources in such a way that "value" = human satisfaction *as measured by aggregate consumer willingness to pay* for goods and services' – in other words, value has a solely monetary designation. The control function is wholly in the hands of the shareholders. The question mark following 'sufficient' is a precursor of, first, a defence against the unlikely events posited – 'it is unimportant whether these mechanisms are employed often; indeed, the

[205] Korten, *When Corporations Rule*, p. 83; and see Dworkin, 'Is Wealth a Value?'.
[206] Institute of Economic Affairs, 2001.   [207] *Ibid.*
[208] Fairclough, New Labour, p. 28.   [209] Posner, *Economic Analysis*, para. 14.6.
[210] *Ibid.*, para. 1.2.

more effective a threat is as a deterrent, the less often it has to be carried out' – and then an attack on the regulatory mechanisms of the Securities and Exchange Board and the competition laws. Note that the 'large corporation' has made a come-back here. The author wishes us to assume that there is a powerful regulatory mechanism available to replace those he is attacking. The text fully disguises the fact that the state might prefer goals other than profit maximisation to be pursued.[211]

Conclusion

This analysis has only scratched the surface of the many ways in which the people of the rich nations comfort themselves with deflection devices in order to see less clearly the injustice that is being daily perpetrated. Vigilance in spotting other devices is required.

---

[211] Dworkin, 'Is Wealth a Value?'.

3   The institutional framework

This chapter looks briefly at the major international institutions which create the framework for world trade: the International Monetary Fund (IMF), the World Bank and the World Trade Organisation (WTO). Although in the case of all three institutions the negotiations and agreements are made between nation states, there is considerable evidence that the negotiations are driven by what is perceived to be for the benefit of transnational corporations (TNCs), in particular because the most powerful nation, the USA, has consistently pressed for outcomes which benefit their giant corporations. The most obvious example is the Trade Related Intellectual Property (TRIPS) Agreement which was extremely beneficial for big pharmaceutical companies,[1] but there are numerous other examples, including the absence of real progress on agricultural issues, the World Bank's insistence on large infrastructure projects which can only be undertaken by the multinationals and the assistance rendered to the large private banks by IMF bail-outs of countries in crisis. There are many other significant organisations involved in the international trading system. Space does not permit a study of them here.[2] This chapter deals briefly with the role of the three institutions and then seeks to show how complex their operations in international finance and trade actually are. In particular, these case studies seek to show how impossible it is to trivialise or sloganise international trade issues and come up with simple solutions. It also seeks to show that actions by the international financial institutions (IFIs) may have far-reaching and sometimes unexpected effects.

[1] See P. Cullett, 'Patents and Medicines: The Relationship between TRIPS and the Human Right to Health' (2003) 79 *International Affairs* 139–60 and P. Drahos, 'Bilateralism in Intellectual Property', paper prepared for Oxfam (2003).
[2] See Hans van Houtte, *The Law of International Trade* (2nd edn, Sweet and Maxwell, London, 2002); A. Qureshi, *International Economic Law* (Sweet and Maxwell, London, 1999); P. Kenen, *The International Economy* (4th edn, Cambridge University Press, 2000); D. Kennedy and J. Southwick (eds), *The Political Economy of the World Trading System* (Cambridge University Press, 2002).

The international financial system

Between 1 and 22 July 1944, the International Monetary Fund was established at the United Nations International Monetary and Financial Conference held in Bretton Woods, New Hampshire. The Articles of Agreement were signed by forty-four nations.[3] According to its Articles of Agreement:

the purposes of the IMF are to promote international monetary cooperation, facilitate the expansion of international trade for the sake of high levels of employment and real income, promote exchange-rate stability and avoid competitive depreciation, work for a multilateral system of current international payments and for elimination of exchange controls over current transactions, create confidence among member nations and give them the opportunity to correct balance of payments maladjustments while avoiding measures destructive of national and international prosperity, and make balance of payments disequilibriums shorter and less severe than they would otherwise be.[4]

Essentially, the role of the IMF was seen as limited; it remains the case that '[t]here is no international monetary convention which comprehensively deals with the monetary sphere'.[5] The IMF acts as a 'central bank of central banks', acting as a lender of last resort, but it also 'creates liquidity through the SDR [Special Drawing Right] facility, it manages the international monetary system, it is engaged in information collection and dissemination, and it has regulatory powers over national monetary policy'.[6] The regulatory power is exercised on a continuous basis through the scrutiny of national and international monetary systems under Article IV of its Articles of Agreement as well as when there is a balance of payments issue causing a member to seek assistance. The Bank for International Settlements (BIS) also has a significant role in the international economic system: 'The BIS in many respects performs competing functions as that of the IMF. It acts essentially as an institution for central banks, and as a forum for international monetary co-operation. The BIS has been instrumental in the crafting of codes of conduct in the monetary field – a notable example of which is the Basle Concordat relating to banking supervision.'[7]

However, the membership of the IMF is much wider. Its membership is exclusively comprised of states and in 2003 comprised 184 states – 'nearly universal' membership.[8] The following extract from the IMF webpage explains the basic functioning of its surveillance role:

[3] L. McQuillan and P. Montgomery (eds), *The International Monetary Fund: Financial Medic to the World?* (Hoover Institution Press, Stanford, California, 1999).
[4] *Ibid.*, p. 6.   [5] Quereshi, *International Economic Law*, p. 106.
[6] *Ibid.*, pp. 107–8.   [7] *Ibid.*, p. 108 (www.bis.org).
[8] See the IMF website (www.imf.org).

The IMF was given a mandate under Article IV of its Articles of Agreement to exercise surveillance over the exchange rate policies of its members in order to ensure the effective operation of the international monetary system. The principles of surveillance were set out in further detail in a 1977 decision, which established that the IMF's appraisal of exchange rate policy requires a comprehensive analysis of the general economic situation and policy strategy of each member country. The decision also stressed that the ultimate objective of surveillance is to help member countries achieve financial stability and sustainable economic growth.

IMF surveillance today
The objectives of surveillance remain the same today as in 1977, but the framework for surveillance has evolved significantly since then. During the past decade in particular, the IMF has sought to respond to the challenges of globalization, including the dramatic expansion of international capital flows. Surveillance today covers a wide range of economic policies, although the emphasis given to each policy area varies according to each country's individual circumstances.

Exchange rate, monetary and fiscal policies remain at the center of IMF surveillance. IMF economists provide advice on issues ranging from the choice of exchange rate regime, to ensuring consistency between the exchange rate regime and the stance of fiscal and monetary policy.

Structural policies were added to the IMF's surveillance agenda in the 1980s as economic growth slowed in many industrial countries in the wake of the second oil price shock. The debt crisis in the developing world and the fall of communism further underlined the need for structural change in many countries. Today, structural issues are included in the IMF's policy dialogue with its member countries when they have an important impact on macroeconomic performance. Examples include international trade, labor market issues, and power sector reform.

Financial sector issues were added to IMF surveillance in the 1990s following a series of banking crises in both industrial and developing countries. In 1999, the IMF and the World Bank decided to create a joint Financial Sector Assessment Program (FSAP) specifically designed to assess the strengths and weaknesses of countries' financial sectors. When available, FSAP findings provide important input into IMF surveillance.

Institutional issues, such as central bank independence, financial sector regulation, corporate governance, and policy transparency and accountability, have also become increasingly important to IMF surveillance in the wake of financial crises and in the context of member countries undergoing transition from a planned to a market economy. In recent years, the IMF and the World Bank have taken a central role in developing, implementing and assessing internationally recognized standards and codes in areas that are crucial for the efficient functioning of a modern economy.

Assessment of risks and vulnerabilities
Crisis prevention has always been central to IMF surveillance. In recent years, coverage has expanded beyond the traditional focus on the current account position and external debt sustainability to encompass risks and vulnerabilities stemming from large and volatile capital flows.

How IMF surveillance works in practice

Article IV consultations, as IMF surveillance discussions are known, usually take place once a year. IMF economists visit the member country to collect data and hold discussions with government and central bank officials, and often private sector representatives, members of parliament, civil society, and labor unions as well. Upon its return, the mission submits a report to the IMF's Executive Board for discussion. The Board's views are subsequently summarized and transmitted to the country's authorities.

In recent years, surveillance has become increasingly transparent, and the IMF's assessment of its members' policies are now in most cases made available to the public. A public information notice, which summarizes the report and the Board's views, is published in four out of five instances, and the report itself in two out of three instances (March 2002–February 2003 data).

Multilateral and regional surveillance

The IMF also continuously reviews global economic trends and developments in what is known as multilateral surveillance. In its bi-annual World Economic Outlook (WEO), IMF staff discusses prospects for the world economy and provides in-depth analysis of specific issues and challenges. The IMF furthermore publishes a bi-annual Global Financial Stability Report (GFSR), which provides assessments of the stability of global financial markets and identifies potential systemic weaknesses that could lead to crises. Both the WEO and the GFSR provide important input into IMF surveillance of its member countries, and vice versa.

Finally, the IMF regularly examines economic developments and policies pursued under regional arrangements such as the euro area and the West African Economic and Monetary Union.[9]

It can be seen from this that the role of the IMF has expanded over the years. The surveillance role is supported by an obligation on the part of member states to co-operate with the fund.[10] The IMF role in 'structural adjustment' is one of the most controversial areas of operation.[11] However, this chapter deals with the crisis management role of the IMF and its relationship with the major TNCs involved in financial deals, the major private banks. The human rights issues relevant to the IFIs are dealt with in chapter 4.

The IMF and its relation to private banks: risk free banking?

It is a strange aspect of the 'globalisation debate' that multinational companies are in the forefront of the debate but some of the biggest of all tend to escape scrutiny. Attention focuses on companies which produce tangible items which end up with a consumer. This lends an extra veil of invisibility to the operations of giant banks. Thus, despite the total assets

[9] IMF website, 21 February 2003.   [10] Article IV, s. 1.   [11] See chapter 1.

of the top five banks being estimated at US$4,807,294 million,[12] their
activities have frequently been left off the globalisation agenda. However,
the way in which the global financial architecture has managed financial crises in a number of recent events has given rise to unprecedented
opportunities for banks to make huge profits while running virtually no
risks. This is, in part, because of the response that the IMF has made to
those crises. Underhill and Zhang see the rise of multinational banks as
a threat to domestic political legitimacy by weakening states' authority
over macroeconomics and social policy and by being significant in the
formulation of national economic policy: 'integration with global financial structures has strengthened the position of private market actors over
public authority. Powerful private actors come to dominate the formulation of national economic policies which, in their attempts to extract
benefits from global integration, tend increasingly to serve the interests
of market agents.'[13]

However, the IMF has largely (rightly) been vilified for the conditionality policies which it pursues, demanding severe cutbacks in social services
in return for its loans,[14] rather than the financial policies which it has pursued. Recently, however, the financial policies behind its activities have
been questioned as well as the effect that its structural adjustment policies and their successors have had on the poorest within creditor nations.
Stiglitz writes:

The IMF is pursuing not just the objectives set out in its original mandate of
enhancing global stability and ensuring that there are funds for countries facing a threat of recession to pursue expansionary policies. It is also pursuing the
interests of the financial community . . . Simplistic free market ideology provided
the curtain behind which the real business of the 'new' mandate could be trans-
acted. The change in mandate and objectives, while it may have been quiet, was
hardly subtle: from serving global *economic* interests to serving the interests of
global *finance*.[15] Capital market liberalisation may not have contributed to global
economic stability, but it did open up vast new markets for Wall Street.[16]

This reassessment of the IMF turns partly on the 'bail-out' policies it
has pursued. The allegation is that loans to risky areas are encouraged
and underpriced because it is known that the IMF will support the country's currency when a crisis threatens (see below). Eichengreen and Ruhl
describe the 'moral hazard' thus:

[12] Figures issued by Bank of America and reported in the *Guardian*, 28 October 2003.
[13] G. Underhill and X. Zhang, 'Global Structures and Political Imperatives: In search of
Normative Underpinnings for International Financial Order' in *International Financial
Governance under Stress* (Cambridge University Press, 2003), p. 78.
[14] See chapter 1 and for a study of a PRSP, the World Bank section of this chapter.
[15] Emphasis in original.
[16] J. Stiglitz, *Globalisation and its Discontents* (Allen Lane, London, 2002), pp. 206–7.

102 Companies, International Trade and Human Rights

Investors, it is argued, have been able to escape the financial costs of crises through the extension of international rescue loans. These 'bailouts' (as they are described by their critics) give governments the funds they require to pay off their creditors, who are then able to exit the country free of losses. Not being subject to the cost of crises, investors disregard the risks of lending, and the consequent lack of market discipline allows feckless governments to set themselves up for a painful fall.[17]

The allegation that the IMF is in the service of international finance essentially flows from the insistence by the IMF on liberalisation, in particular capital account liberalisation. The intended result of this is to permit capital flows to take place freely across the world. However, while this may be good for the financial community, it is not necessarily good for developing countries. 'The cocktail of free capital flows, floating exchange rates, domestic financial liberalisation in G3 countries, and unregulated innovations in financial instruments and institutions such as derivatives and hedge funds has dramatically increased financial instability after the collapse of the Gold-Dollar standard.'[18] The instability is a result of a system of liberalisation based on neo-classical assumptions, including perfect information flows.

If one asks which of the neo-classical assumptions fail in a way that permits [financial] crises to develop, it is the information structure on the basis of which lending decisions are made. Rather than each investor deciding individually his or her expectations on the basis of their estimate of the fundamentals, investors make their decisions on the basis of what others are expected to do, resulting in herd behaviour.[19]

This assessment is based on Keynes' beauty contest analysis, referring to a game in the UK tabloid press in the 1930s in which readers were asked to assess from pictures which women would be judged as the most beautiful by the entire readership:

in other words, readers would not win by giving their own opinion about the women's beauty, not even by assessing what others' personal opinions would be, but by guessing what people would, on average, believe average opinion to be. In financial markets, a trader will not bid a price according to what he or she believes an asset's fundamental value to be, but according to what he or she assesses average opinion to be about average opinion of the asset's value. The beauty contest analogy helps understand why market participants tend to

---

[17] B. Eichengreen and C. Ruhl, 'The Bail-in Problem: Systematic Goals, Ad Hoc Means' (http://emlab.berkeley.edu/users/eichengr/).

[18] L. Taylor and J. Eatwell, *Global Finance at Risk* (New Press, 2000), cited in Oxfam, *Global Finance*, 26.

[19] J. Williamson, 'Costs and Benefits of Financial Globalisation' in Underhill and Zhang, *International Financial Governance*, p. 44.

engage in 'momentous trading' (i.e. herd behaviour) and why market valuations are subject to sudden shifts in 'market sentiment'.[20]

Underhill and Zhang point out that 'more than seventy financial and monetary crises of different proportions and characteristics have occurred in both developed and developing countries over the past two decades'.[21] They see as '[a] common background to these developments . . . the intensifying process of global financial liberalisation and integration . . . As financial crises have become more frequent and more severe over the past two decades, this has raised the question of whether the growing frequency and severity of crises correlate with the emergence of this liberal and transnational financial order.'[22]

While domestic policies have a large part to play in countries' financial crises, many studies now show that two other factors have great significance. One is the role of speculators, and the second is ' "crony capitalism" at the global level, in the form of IMF bailing out Wall Street'.[23] Opportunities for speculators increase every time markets are opened, as do opportunities for the most powerful multinational banks. The role of the 'bail-out' mechanism is discussed below. Following the Asian crisis of 1997–8 a flurry of reports sought to identify the root causes.[24] Story identifies two distinct interpretations: an internalist explanation which sought to blame the governments suffering the crises and an externalist argument focused on the international financial markets.[25] It is important to be aware of the possibility of 'explanatory nationalism' leading the IFIs to the most convenient explanation, exonerating them from blame. A classic proponent is Moore: 'most of the responsibility for these [Asia 1997, Argentina 2002] collapses lies with domestic policy-makers, of course' despite, in the same paragraph, admitting that the very magnitude of money flows create forces so great that 'they are difficult for all but the most powerful nations to resist'.[26]

[20] Oxfam, *Global Finance Hurts the Poor* (Oxfam America, 2002), p. 26.

[21] Underhill and Zhang, *International Financial Governance*, p. 1.

[22] Underhill and Zhang, *International Financial Governance*, p. 1.

[23] Oxfam, *Global Finance*, p. 28.

[24] IMF, *International Capital Markets* (IMF, Washington DC, 1998); IMF, *World Economic Outlook* (IMF, Washington, 1998); Group of 7, Declaration of G-7 Finance Ministers and Central Bank Governors (G7, 1998) (www.imf.org/external/np/g7/103098dc.htm); Group of 22, *Report of the Working Group on International Financial Crises*, (G-22, Washington, 1998); *Report of the Working Group on Transparency and Accountability* (G-22, Washington, 1998); United Nations Executive Committee on Economic and Social Affairs, *Towards a New International Financial Architecture* (Economic Commission for Latin America and the Caribbean, Santiago, 1999).

[25] J. Story, 'Reform: What has been Written?' in Underhill and Zhang, *International Financial Governance*, p. 27.

[26] M. Moore, *World Without Walls* (Cambridge University Press, 2002), p. 32.

The 'internalist' explanation of the Asian crisis sees the cause of the collapse:

as lying in the close connections established within the states between politics and bank-centred financial systems. The states provided implicit guarantees to banks, encouraging the banks to lend to corporations with good political contacts. As capital controls were eased, foreign creditors lent to the banks and credit exploded, despite multiple warning signals ahead of June 1997. Externally, the inflow of capital to the east Asian countries was stimulated by the near zero interest rates prevailing in a moribund Japan, and by continued investor pessimism about business prospects in Europe. Consumption and imports boomed, just as volume export growths plummeted. With China's accelerated move into world markets, foreign investors switched their attention to opportunities on the mainland, so that east Asian balance of payments' dependence on short-term capital flows increased. When the Thai 'wake-up call' came, alerted investors withdrew in haste from one currency after another.[27]

As we shall see, the externalist explanation focused more sharply on the instability inherent in liberalisation followed by 'herd behaviour'.[28]

Economists now identify three types of currency crisis.[29] 'First generation crises, such as the Mexican crisis of 1982, involve excessive budget deficits yielding unsustainable current account deficits, depletion of reserves and eventually devaluation. The culprit here is thus clearly the national government.'[30]

Second generation crises are caused by temporary macroeconomic difficulties which may be responded to in two different ways, either by maintaining fixed interest rates and incurring short-term losses of output and employment or by devaluation and decreasing interest rates.[31] 'Both solutions may make sense depending on the government's overall development strategy and priorities. But financial markets may bet on one response . . . Speculation then forces the government to increase rates higher than otherwise necessary, which increases the cost of maintaining fixed exchange rates. Eventually the government is led to devalue against its will – generating profits for the successful speculators. In such a scenario the government is the victim and speculators the villains.'[32] Let us not forget two things here: first, it is very difficult to distinguish

---

[27] Story, 'Reform', p. 27.
[28] George Soros, *The Crisis of Global Capitalism: Open Society Endangered* (Public Affairs, New York, 1998).
[29] P. Krugman, 'Currency Crises' in M. Feldstein (ed), *International Capital Flows* (University of Chicago Press, 1999).
[30] Oxfam, *Global Finance*, p. 28.
[31] For a discussion of the role of capital controls in the international monetary system, see P. Athukorala, *Crisis and Recovery in Asia: The Role of Capital Controls* (E. Elgar, Cheltenham, 2003).
[32] Oxfam, *Global Finance*, p. 28.

between 'speculation' and 'hedging' and it may well be that banks, as the most powerful financial institutions, are involved in both. We also need to remember the analysis of increased financial volatility which cited both the invention of the speculators' tools of derivatives and the freedom of finance to flow across the world, the latter being an article of faith for the 'Washington consensus'.

The 'third generation' of crises involve twin banking and financial crises.[33] 'They were initially attributed to poor financial regulation and supervision as well as poor monetary policy, thereby putting the blame back on national governments and their "crony capitalist" clientele . . . It is now recognised that third generation crises are more complex, and may also include multiple equilibria effects, originate from abroad due to contagion effects or involve "crony capitalism" at the global level, in the form of IMF bailing out Wall Street.'[34] The 'bail-out effect' will be examined below as the IMF policies and the response of the banking sector will be examined in chronological order from liberalisation to crisis to imposition of structural adjustment. Here, it is important to note the multifactorial cause of 'third generation' crises which include macroeconomic policies of G3 countries. Reinhart and Reinhart link currency crises to the volatility of G3 exchange rates.[35] Other studies show links to dollar interest increases.[36] However, analysing the East Asia crisis, Stiglitz writes: 'in retrospect, it became clear that the IMF policies not only exacerbated the downturns but were partially responsible for the onset: excessively rapid financial and capital market liberalisation was probably the single most important cause of the crisis, though mistaken policies on the part of the countries themselves played a role as well'.[37] The most significant of IMF policies is the liberalisation of capital flows.

Liberalisation

According to Jagdish Bhagwati, 'a dense network of like-minded luminaries among the powerful institutions – Wall Street, the Treasury Department, the State Department, the IMF, the World Bank most prominent amongst them – have hijacked the argument in favour of free trade markets and applied it to promote free capital mobility

[33] S. Sharma, *The Asian Financial Crisis* (Manchester University Press, 2003).
[34] Oxfam, *Global Finance*, p. 28.
[35] C. Reinhart and V. Reinhart, 'What Hurts Most: G3 Exchange Rate or Interest Rate Volatility' in S. Edwards and J. Frenkel (eds), *Preventing Currency Crises in Emerging Markets* (University of Chicago Press, 2001), p. 73.
[36] J. Frankel and N. Roubini, 'The Role of Industrial Policies in Emerging Market Crises' (National Bureau of Economic Research Working Paper 8634, 2000).
[37] Stiglitz, *Globalisation*, p. 91.

everywhere'.[38] The embrace of liberalisation of capital markets and the acceptance of 'pushed' (see below) incoming capital flows is difficult to understand without an understanding of the central role that the IMF plays in credit rating. It has the power to alter the domestic policies of states simply by a suggestion that the credit rating of a country should be downgraded, making credit of any sort either impossible to obtain or very expensive. While a country might prefer limited credit controls it is unlikely to wish to be cut off entirely from access to credit. The naked power of the IMF becomes clear. Why, then, do they insist on capital market liberalisation? Stiglitz claims that the push for liberalisation was driven by arguments that it would enhance economic stability by diversification of sources of funding, increase efficiency by dismantling 'inefficient' capital controls and belief in the ultimate efficiency of markets and inefficiency of government controls on market activities.[39] These arguments he finds false on the grounds that it is clear that liberalisation decreases global stability, that capital controls used properly can prevent 'hot money' flowing rapidly into a country at boom times and leaving it in times of recession and that sensible government intervention in markets can protect fragile local industries until they are ready to compete globally. The World Bank agrees that capital inflows can have a negative effect by creating increased volatility but argue that there are three potential benefits: they permit the financing of trade deficits allowing countries to invest more than they save and thus accumulate capital faster; they permit the import of technology which is essential to build a productive capacity; and they may improve the working of the financial sector.[40] Support for liberalisation is based on the belief that the benefits outweigh the effect of the increase in volatility. Oxfam identifies a further disadvantage of capital flows: 'the interest payments and profit repatriation that can represent an unsustainable drain on a country's resources'.[41] Although discussed in a different context, the increase in avoidance or evasion of taxes is also identified by Oxfam as a mechanism which costs developing countries US$15 billion a year.[42] Although correlation between lower tax rates and capital liberalisation cannot be shown,[43] 'capital account liberalisation is probably correlated with the administrative capacity to collect taxes on capital, which is hard to control for in econometric regressions'

---

[38] Jagdish Bhagwath, 'The Capital Myth: The Difference Between Trade in Widgets and Dollars' (1998) 77(3) *Foreign Affairs* (May–June) cited in Story, 'Reform', p. 32.

[39] Stiglitz, *Globalisation*, pp. 100–2.

[40] World Bank, *Global Development Finance 2001* (World Bank, Washington, 2001).

[41] Oxfam, *Global Finance*, p. 38.

[42] Oxfam, 'Tax Havens: Releasing the Hidden Billions for Poverty Eradication' (Oxfam Policy Papers, 2000).

[43] Oxfam, *Global Finance*, p. 35.

and 'international tax evasion would simply be impossible under strict international control of capital flows'.[44]

Do the benefits outweigh the disadvantages, contrary to Stiglitz's view? A wide-ranging literature review by Oxfam of the studies that attempt to measure the long-term effect of capital flows on investment concludes that:

> The empirical studies summarised in this section leave the reader with a sense of confusion. In the past decades, capital account liberalisation may have, on average, had an independent and causal positive effect on growth – or maybe not . . . The lack of robust correlation between capital inflows and growth, together with the weak correlation between capital account liberalisation and capital inflows, sheds some doubt about the causality of the relationship between capital account liberalisation and growth.[45]

There are two factors here, capital flows and capital account liberalisation. The studies show that there is no *causal* proof that capital flows increase growth and further no strong evidence that capital account liberalisation increases capital flows. Many of the attempts to measure effects identify correlation rather than causation and are therefore suspect as relevant variables affecting growth may be omitted. Choice of country may also be significant as other studies indicate that 'success breeds success' and capital is attracted to already booming economies. The only clear result is that a 'one size fits all' policy is most unlikely to work – the effect of capital flows is critically dependent on individual factors within the country concerned including an adequate 'absorptive capacity'. In particular it may be that 'a certain threshold of development needs to be reached before liberalisation becomes beneficial'.[46]

If the overall effect of both capital flows and liberalisation of those flows is in doubt, it may be useful to consider the benefits and disadvantages studied individually. It will be remembered that the first benefit identified by the World Bank was the increase in investment causing capital accumulation. The World Bank shows that an increase in private capital inflows equal to 1 per cent of GDP has increased domestic investment by an average of 0.72 per cent of GDP in the South over the past three

---

[44] *Ibid.*   [45] Oxfam, *Global Finance*, p. 42.

[46] Oxfam, *Global Finance*, p. 41, citing five recent (2001) papers: G. Bekaert, H. Campbell and C. Lundblad, 'Does Financial Liberalisation Spur Growth?' (National Bureau of Economic Research Working Paper 8245, 2001); S. Edwards, 'Capital Mobility and Economic Performance: Are Emerging Economies Different?' (National Bureau of Economic Research Working Paper 8076, 2001); C. Arteta, B. Eichengreen and C. Wyplotz, 'When Does Capital Account Liberalisation Help More than it Hurts?' (National Bureau of Economic Research Working Paper 8414, 2001); D. Quinn, C. Inclan and A. Maria Toyoda, 'How and Where Capital Account Liberalisation Leads to Economic Growth,' paper presented at the 2001 American Political Science Review, 30 August 2001.

decades.[47] However, this trend significantly weakened in the 1990s compared with the 1970s and 1980s[48] due to the rise of merger and acquisitions following privatisation programmes and the significant outflows of capital occurring at the same time.[49] While it is clear that increases in investment occur, they do so differently in different countries. The reasons are unclear, although the World Bank finds some evidence that 'absorptive capacity' of foreign direct investment (FDI) increases with better education and that the impact of short-term debt on investment increases with political stability.[50] In a study of nearly one hundred countries Rodrik found no correlation between open capital accounts and long-term economic performance once the other determinants of growth are controlled for.[51] Stiglitz contends that instability has a negative effect on economic growth.[52] Studies by Quinn, Klein and Olivei appear to find a positive and statistically significant association between international financial openness and long-term financial growth.[53] Williamson asks:

Are these findings in conflict or is it possible to reconcile them? . . . The first three studies [that found no impact] use a variable which measures whether the capital account was open or closed, whereas Quinn and Olivei sought to construct a measure of the *degree* to which the capital account was open . . . Now most countries liberalised FDI relatively early on, and most also liberalised long-term before short-term capital . . . we have strong reasons for believing that liberalisation of FDI, portfolio equity and other long-term capital should be beneficial for growth; it is what is usually the last stage – of opening up to unlimited flows of short-term money – that is problematic.[54]

Williamson concludes, therefore, that the studies thus show that opening to long-term capital is helpful whereas exposure to short-term capital mobility is harmful. Further the Quinn, Klein and Olivei studies included developed countries, whereas the Rodrik and Stiglitz studies focused on developing countries.

---

[47] World Bank, *Global Development Finance 2001*.   [48] *Ibid.*, Figure 3.3.

[49] Oxfam, *Global Finance*, p. 43. Mergers and acquisitions consist of the transfer of ownership of existing capital and thus may be contrasted with 'greenfield' foreign direct investment which involves creation of physical capital.

[50] World Bank *Global Development Finance 2001*, cited in Oxfam, *Global Finance*, p. 44.

[51] D. Rodrik, 'Who Needs Capital Account Convertibility?' (1998) *Princeton Essays in International Finance* 55.

[52] J. Stiglitz, 'Capital Market Liberalisation, Economic Growth and Instability' (2000) 28 (6) *World Development* 1075.

[53] D. Quinn, 'The Correlates of Change in International Financial Regulation' (1997) 91 (3) *American Political Science Review* 531; M. Klein and G. Olivei, 'Capital Account Liberalisation: Financial Depth and Economic Growth' National Bureau of Economic Research Working Paper 7384, 1999.

[54] Williamson, 'Costs and Benefits', p. 48.

The second benefit identified by the World Bank is the import of technology by FDI. This is analysed in chapter 1. In summary, the ability of countries to benefit from FDI in this or other ways is country and industry specific. It appears to depend on a country's 'absorptive' capacity which grows strongly with better education. The poorest countries have the least absorptive capacity and are most likely to suffer the social and environmental dangers which come with FDI.

The third identified benefit is improvement in the capacity and efficiency of domestic financial systems. The World Bank states that:

> Greater financial sector development is expected with faster economic growth, and larger international capital flows are associated with improvements in financial sector depth and liquidity. However, an inflow of foreign capital does not, in itself, guarantee improvements in the financial sector. The short-term consequences may well be unfavourable, given the volatility of capital flows, which can have negative implications for output and employment.[55]

This less than glowing endorsement is greeted with some further doubts by Oxfam. Accepting the link between financial sector development and growth in most cases, Oxfam cites Durham whose study shows that 'the relationship between stock market development and growth does not hold with samples including only low-income countries and that interacting stock market development with the level of GDP produces very significant results, suggesting that promoting financial development through stock markets is not a very good idea in low-income countries'.[56] Further, while a correlation between capital inflows and financial development is accepted, the World Bank accepts that this also only holds good for middle-income countries.[57] The Stiglitz and Rodrik studies noted above indicate no or negative correlation between openness of financial markets and growth. For Williamson this 'raises an important question; why open capital accounts may not provide the same benefits to developing countries as they often do to industrial nations. One plausible answer . . . is that developing countries need a constellation of economic, legal and social institutions that are normally present in industrial countries in order to minimise the costs associated with capital account liberalisation and to translate financial openness into greater economic growth.'[58] This is similar to the absorptive capacity issue noted above. Oxfam believes

[55] World Bank, *Global Development Finance 2001*, p. 70, cited in Oxfam, *Global Finance*, p. 48.
[56] Oxfam, *Global Finance*, p. 48, citing J. Durham, 'Econometrics of the Effects of Stock Market Development on Growth and Private Investment in Lower Income Countries' (Queen Elizabeth House Working Papers 53, Oxford).
[57] World Bank, *Global Development Finance 2001*.
[58] Williamson, 'Costs and Benefits', p. 49.

that even where correlation can be shown, 'the direction of causality is again problematic, as global capital is likely to flow into countries with well-developed financial markets'.

The link between inflows and growth depends on the ability of financial systems to improve the allocation of capital across industries but there are many reasons why this link may break down, not least the absence of strong regulatory frameworks and the consequent rise of criminal activity on stock markets.[59] Thus, there is good evidence that financial development improves the allocation of capital across industries and enterprises, and hence boosts economy-wide productivity and growth. However, the evidence supporting the view that openness to foreign capital increases financial development is much weaker. According to Williamson, '[g]rowing income inequality, associated with capital account liberalisation and global market integration, may prove deleterious to long-term economic growth'.[60] Thus, there are reasons to believe that capital account liberalisation can worsen the allocation of resources in low and middle-income countries, including the lack of adequate financial supervision, the existence of price distortions, or the narrowness of capital markets. Macroeconomic instability can also harm the allocation of financial resources.[61]

What about the disadvantages? Tax issues are much neglected in this debate, but increased possibilities of tax evasion must be taken into account as a factor. However, the major disadvantage identified by most, with the notable exception of the IMF, is the increase in volatility. 'In a neo-classical world, capital mobility would bring gains in the efficiency of allocation of capital without any offsetting costs. In fact most economists are convinced that there are several important costs, the most obvious of which is that foreign borrowing exposes countries to an increased risk of financial crisis.'[62] Dismissing claims that capital account liberalisation was not a cause of the Asian crises, Williamson analyses the structure of those markets in the countries which were affected, comparing them with those untouched by the crises and concludes that the major difference between affected and non-affected countries is:

whether or not they had liberalised the capital account of the balance of payments. All the crisis countries had essentially opened themselves to uncontrolled inflows of short-term funds, and allowed foreign borrowing of their domestic currency such as occurred in Thailand. None of the non-crisis countries had opened their capital accounts, except Singapore, and even Singapore still retained control over foreign borrowing Singapore dollars, which minimised foreign speculation against its currency.[63]

[59] Oxfam, *Global Finance*, p. 49.   [60] Williamson, 'Costs and Benefits', p. 47.
[61] Oxfam, *Global Finance*.   [62] Williamson, 'Costs and Benefits', p. 44.
[63] *Ibid.*, p. 46.

For Oxfam, '[t]he questions are whether the effect is transitory or permanent and, in the latter case, whether it outweighs the positive impacts of capital inflows on growth'.[64] While studies can be found to support both optimistic (no long-term effects) and pessimistic (permanent effects) views,[65] many are intent on an aggregate analysis. The World Bank makes the point that financial crises have a disproportionate effect on the poor due to their impact on health, schooling and nutrition and that this is often not regained by a simple improvement in growth.[66] The inequality impact should not be lost sight of in considering overall growth rates (see below). Eatwell and Taylor put forward a hypothesis that links lower growth rates since the late 1970s and the increased volatility which emerged following the collapse of the Gold-Dollar Exchange Standard system in 1971.[67] In other words, increased liberalisation inducing volatility is hurting worldwide. They argue that:

- Flexible exchange rates are prone to major misalignments in the medium term. It is hard or impossible to hedge currency exposures in the medium term and enterprises' investment decisions can be misguided, which harms growth. Short-term exchange rates fluctuations can be hedged, but at a cost.
- Volatile exchange rates feed the volatility of interest rates.
- The volatility of both exchange rates and interest rates increases long-term real interest rates . . . debtors must pay higher risk premia to cover the increased likelihood of financial crisis, financial crisis contagion, or mere over or undershooting of exchange rates. This happens not only in the South, but also in the North (e.g., Scandinavia, Japan and the European currency zone in the late 1980s and early 1990s).
- High and volatile interest rates reduce investment and hurt enterprises, particularly firms with high debt ratios and small companies that do not have easy access to credit. This results in high rates of corporate bankruptcies, which dampen economic growth. High default rates on corporate bonds justify high long-term interest rates, generating a vicious cycle.[68]

While not accepting this thesis completely and citing other factors which might be of significance such as the oil shocks of 1974 and 1979, the end of Europe's 'catch-up' potential vis-à-vis the USA in the 1970s,

[64] Oxfam, *Global Finance*, p. 50.
[65] For an analysis of a range of studies see Oxfam, *Global Finance*, ch. 11; S. Sharma, *The Asian Financial Crisis* (Manchester University Press, 2003).
[66] World Bank, *Global Economic Prospects* (World Bank, Washington, 1999), p. 48.
[67] J. Eatwell and L. Taylor, *Global Finance at Risk* (New Press, New York, 2000).
[68] As summarised in Oxfam, *Global Finance*, p. 51. I have omitted references to further supporting studies.

the slowing of technological progress in the 1970s and social conflicts and unrest in the South, and while conceding that much research still needs to be done, Oxfam writes: 'Eatwell and Taylor's thesis should concentrate the minds of researchers and policy-makers who consider reforming the global financial architecture. It implies that global finance has decreased long-term growth in both South and North.'[69] It also means that comparative studies of individual nations do not provide the best research methodology since '[a]t best, further research along the cross-country methodology might robustly establish that capital account liberalisation is good for growth given the post Bretton Woods global financial architecture, for example because attempting to control capital movements when major financial centers let them move freely may prove counterproductive'.[70] Even if this hypothetical study established such a correlation it could only mean that liberalisation is a 'second best' solution. In order to improve growth, the global financial architecture needs to control fluctuations between the major currencies.

The role of private banks

Given the advent of liberalisation, how do banks operate within it? The first impact of liberalisation of capital flows on poorer countries is often the overshadowing or disappearance of local banks, which may well be displaced by the multinational giants. Of course, this has the advantage of capital stability; absent a regulatory outrage it is most unlikely that the bank will default. 'The advantages are clear: the increased competition can lead to improved services. The greater financial strength of the foreign banks can enhance stability.'[71] However, as we shall see, the inflow of money into the developing country is at the choice of the Northern institution, looking for a good return, and this may leave out the small businesses looking for small loans which take a considerable amount of administration on the part of the bank. Further, the temptation from the foreign bank's perspective is to reduce risk by opting for short-term loans which greatly increase the volatility factor. What is clear is that expansion of credit follows liberalisation.

There is evidence that investment is 'pushed' into developing countries by the search for new investment markets, rather than 'pulled' into the South by genuine desire or need for capital.[72] Studies show that there are significant correlations between money flows from North to South and periods of easing of American monetary policy. 'The effect is striking

[69] Oxfam, *Global Finance*, p. 55.   [70] *Ibid.*, p. 55.
[71] Stiglitz, *Globalisation*, p. 69.   [72] Oxfam, *Global Finance*, p. 13.

for bank lending. Periods of monetary easing usually correspond to the bottom of the business cycle, and banks have two reasons to expand their foreign lending activity: domestic interest rates are low and creditworthy domestic lending operations are few.'[73] The terms of these loans, as well as their duration, have been criticised as being heavily influenced by IMF behaviour at times of financial crisis. In several significant instances the IMF has reacted to a crisis by pushing in large amounts of money to stabilise the exchange rate. Critics argue that this has two major effects: knowledge that it will happen creates a 'moral hazard' in the setting of the terms of loans; risk is not estimated in the absence of the understanding that this will happen so the risk to foreign investors is significantly lower. Secondly, when the crisis in fact occurs the money pushed in enables foreign investors and very rich locals to remove the greater part of their money:

Moral hazard is increasingly seen as a problem in international financial markets, and private-sector burden sharing is increasingly seen as the solution. Investors, it is argued, have been able to escape the financial costs of crises through the extension of international rescue loans. These 'bailouts' (as they are described by their critics) give governments the funds they require to pay off their creditors, who are then able to exit the country free of losses. Not being subject to the costs of crises, investors disregard the risks of lending and the consequent lack of market discipline allows feckless governments to set themselves up for a painful fall.[74]

Solutions are not easy to find. Eichengreen and Ruhl discuss the problems of designing a 'bail-in' system which would involve the private sector in solving the crisis. They criticise the limited initiatives adopted by the IMF following the Asian crises.

Eatwell shows how countries lose control over fiscal policies on the opening of markets. Long-term interest rates are affected by market sentiment. Because long-term bond yields are simply the market's understanding of what will happen to short-term interest rates plus a risk premium and maturity calculation, if the market (i.e. the banks) believe that attempts by a central bank to lower short-term rates are unlikely to succeed, long-term interest rates will remain high to the benefit of creditors.[75] However, if the central bank increases short-term interest rates, the markets see this as an appropriate move to pre-empt inflation above the long-term yields forecast, economic activity slows, inflation is

---

[73] *Ibid.*, p. 13 citing in particular Reinhart, and Reinhart, 'What Hurts Most?'.
[74] Eichengreen and Ruhl, 'The Bail-in Problem'.
[75] J. Eatwell, 'International Capital Liberalisation: The Impact on World Development' (Center for Economic Policy Analysis, New York, Working Paper Series III), p. 8.

kept low and real long-term interest rates remain high, to the benefit of creditors.[76] The danger of this lack of control is that:

the more market-orientated and transnational financial order which has emerged in the past three decades has increasingly aligned economic policy and regulatory processes with the preferences of powerful private interests and [has] crucially altered the nature of public policy objectives in monetary and financial governance. If the financial sector and regulatory policy become unduly dominated by private interests, we risk not only the legitimacy deficit but also economic instability and crisis, as has been so forcefully revealed through the recent episodes of economic turmoil and socio-political unrest in Asian and Latin American countries.[77]

Increasing inequality

Low, or no risk, banking bears more heavily on small economies. As Oxfam observe:

the sheer size of large economies protects them from the most severe forms of capital flight simply because the capital has nowhere else to go: if all European investors wanted to move their wealth to the United States, they would simply not find enough profitable investment opportunities. The South is much more vulnerable to sudden and steep capital flight which greatly reduces the scope for expansionary monetary policy.[78]

The fear of volatility keeps interest rates high, to the benefit of investors. The ability of governments to conduct expansionary policies at time of recession is also weakened by market reactions to growing budget deficits and higher inflation. In both situations banks will quickly demand higher yields, slowing economic activity.

Underhill and Zhang point out that liberalisation of financial markets is often discussed without any understanding of the likely effects on social policy: 'the difficulties which the transformation of financial market structures might present for the achievement of major policy commitments of democratically elected governments are given little attention'.[79]

The IMF prescriptions for high interest rates and balanced budgets support Stiglitz's claim that it works primarily in the interests of the international financial community rather than in the interests of developing countries, and the claim here that between them the IMF and the international banks have invented risk-free banking. The insistence on reserve building by the IMF and by national governments which fear volatility

---

[76] *Ibid.*   [77] Underhill and Zhang, *International Financial Governance*, p. 6.
[78] Oxfam, *Global Finance*, p. 58.
[79] Underhill and Zhang, *International Financial Governance*, p. 7.

also fuels the net flow of resources from South to North (see chapter 1 on 'measuring FDI'): 'A substantial part of South-North capital outflows consists of the purchase of foreign exchange reserves by central banks aiming at cushioning the domestic economy from sudden capital flow reversals. This practice is thus equivalent to an insurance policy purchased by national governments to protect national and global investors'.[80] As we have seen in chapter 1, this effect, with others, means that very often the cost of FDI is actually higher than its benefits.

The emphasis on market forces by the IMF has not rendered it free from criticism for distorting the market, both by the terms of its loans and the 'moral hazard' effect of its rescue operations:

IMF loans, then, actually offered extraordinarily generous rebates of about 10% below market rates. On the $117 billion lent to East Asia under IMF auspices thus far, the region is saving about $12 billion a year in interest payments. Over three years, South Korea, Thailand and Indonesia will have received a direct wealth transfer of at least $35 billion, mostly from US and Western European taxpayers.

But this $35 billion figure actually understates the true scale of the transfer. Investors priced South Korea's debt at a yield of 14.5 percent only because there was a good chance the IMF would come in sooner or later and rescue them. Absent the market-distorting activities of the IMF, the risk premium on this sovereign debt would have been even greater.

More specifically, much of the $35 billion will amount to a wealth transfer from middle-class Westerners to East Asian Governments, Banks, and their rich equity owners and from there to wealthy Western and Japanese investors who risked capital in foolish ways (or perhaps not so foolish since there was a good chance they would be bailed out in the end). The whole series of transactions amounts to a remarkably regressive tax.[81]

The danger of failing to reform this system is 'that if the policy mix is simply left to the dictates of financial market pressures and to dominant private interests, the legitimacy and much-trumpeted benefits of financial openness may prove politically unsustainable over time . . . [there is a] widely perceived conflict between the globalisation of finance and democratic forms of governance'.[82]

Response to crises

Analysing the East Asia crises, Stiglitz notes that the IMF's response was to provide:

[80] Oxfam, *Global Finance*, p. 61.
[81] D. Sacks and P. Thiel, 'The IMF's Big Wealth Transfer' in. McQuillan and Montgomery, *IMF: Financial Medic*, pp. 32–3.
[82] Underhill and Zhang, *International Financial Governance*, p. 6.

huge amounts of money (the total bailout packages, including support from G-7 countries was $95 billion) so that the countries could sustain the exchange rate. It thought that if the market believed that there was enough money in the coffers, there would be no point in attacking the currency, and thus 'confidence' would be restored. The money served another function: it enabled the countries to provide dollars to the firms that had borrowed from Western bankers to repay the loans. It was thus, in part, a bailout to the international banks as much as it was a bailout to the country; the lenders did not have to face the full consequences of having made bad loans. And in country after country in which the IMF money was used to sustain the exchange rate temporarily at an unsustainable level, there was another consequence: rich people inside the country took advantage of the opportunity to convert their money into dollars at the favourable exchange rate and whisk it abroad.[83]

Louis Uchitelle agrees:

Much of the $55billion that has been pledged by the international community for South Korea – like the $40billion for Indonesia and the $17billion for Thailand before it – will ultimately go to lenders who dished out huge sums for risky projects that failed to pay off. The rescue plan centers on shaky Korean banks. The nation's industrialists, who borrowed billions of dollars from them for new factories and such, have not made enough profit to repay their debts. The banks, of course, got their money in part from Korean depositors. Other money came from foreigners, big European, American and Japanese banks, for example – that lent enthusiastically to the Korean banks, in hopes of sharing in the profits. The bailout money, from the International Monetary Fund, the World Bank and individual countries, will be channelled through the Korean government and its central bank in great measure to the private banking system. In some cases, foreign creditors may be paid off directly. Mostly, the money will go to salvage some institutions and to close others while paying off creditors. The bailout will, in effect, repay the depositors and the foreign lenders. At the end of last year [1996], South Korean banks owed nearly $60billion to foreign banks, according to the Bank for International Settlement.[84]

Finally, the loans from either the IMF or World Bank come, not only at a financial price but at the cost of agreement to 'structural reforms'. While the IMF denies absolutely that it has any role in political matters (see below), many have argued the contrary case. Stiglitz puts the matter succinctly: 'The IMF took rather an imperialistic view . . . since almost any structural issue could affect the overall performance of the economy, and hence the government's budget or the trade deficit, it viewed almost

---

[83] Stiglitz, *Globalisation*, p. 95.
[84] L. Uchitelle, 'A Bad Side of Bailouts: Some Go Unpenalized' in McQuillan and Montgomery, *IMF: Financial Medic*, pp. 28–9.

everything as falling within its domain.' Loans came with a Structural Adjustment Plan (SAP) attached.

Both the IMF and the World Bank claim that the imposition of conditions for loans – 'conditionality' – are designed by the countries themselves, usually include measures to 'foster greater efficiency in government spending' and come with advice on how best to design social safety nets, since '[a]djustment programs typically have an impact on income distribution, employment and social services'.[85] Underhill and Zhang chart the tension between democratically elected regimes, accountable to their electorate, and financial openness: 'the process of global financial integration and opening of domestic economic space have constrained in important ways (though not eliminated) the autonomy of national governments in managing their macroeconomic variables, deploying social welfare policies and making strategic choices about the character of their respective societies'.[86]

IMF loans and growth

As we have seen, the effect on growth of the inflow of FDI is by no means a simple matter to assess. Do loans from IMF achieve macroeconomic objectives and/or encourage growth? Again, the measurement methodologies are problematic since it is impossible to observe the country in question as it would have been without the assistance. However, a review of studies undertaken by the IMF itself in 1990 concluded that:

a summary of the results obtained by the various studies that have evaluated the effects of fund-supported adjustment programs on the principal macroeconomic objectives . . . yield three conclusions. First, there is frequently an improvement in the balance of payments and the current account, although a number of studies show no effects of programs. Second, inflation is generally not affected by programs. Finally, the effects on the growth rate are uncertain, with the studies showing an improvement or no change being balanced by those indicating a deterioration in the first year of a program.[87]

Other studies are more forthright:

In addition to weakening much of the world economy generally, IMF lending has hurt less-developed countries specifically. For example, a review of IMF loan

[85] IMF, 'Conditionality: Fostering Sustained Policy Implementation' in McQuillan and Montgomery, *IMF: Financial Medic*, pp. 68–71.
[86] Underhill and Zhang, Normative Underpinnings, pp. 77–8.
[87] M. Khan, 'The Macroeconomic Effects of Fund-Supported Adjustment Programs' in McQuillan and Montgomery, *IMF: Financial Medic*, p. 51.

recipients indicates that most are no better off economically today (measured in per capita wealth) than they were before receiving those loans. In fact, many are poorer; forty-eight of the eighty-nine less-developed countries that received IMF money between 1965 and 1995 are no better off economically than they were before; thirty-two of these forty-eight countries are poorer than before; and fourteen of these thirty-two countries have economies that are at least 15 percent smaller than they were before their first IMF loan.[88]

These studies are all problematic since the number of variables that need to be considered are enormous, from the fluctuation of commodity prices to the change in WTO rules and other conditions of trade. Nevertheless, it is far from clear that the IMF loans, despite conditionality, achieve either macroeconomic objectives or encourage growth.

What effect on inequality?

Underhill and Zhang find that there is evidence that, even in the absence of a financial crisis, financial integration has led to growing income inequality and to the reversal of welfare policies traditionally associated with social democracy.[89] Increased economic uncertainty leads to demands for enhanced welfare spending which cannot be delivered due to the financial goals of exchange rate and monetary stability imposed by market sentiment. These tensions create a crisis for democracy, heightened by inequality: 'although financial integration tends to benefit mobile asset holders and enhances their ability to hedge against market volatility, it generally leads to welfare losses of internationally immobile factors of production, such as domestically orientated firms, labour and agriculture. This, together with reduced government intervention in market activities has contributed to growing income inequality among different social groups within countries.'[90] The pressure to cut back on public services spending is, they argue, partly caused by the 'risk of speculative panic' which holds 'national economic policies hostage to financial market sentiment'.

The effects of financial volatility on inequality stem from multiple factors. Since, by definition, the poor have few assets, fluctuations in value of assets will not directly affect them. However, the loss to governments is huge: 'The severest crises have cost governments between 20% and 50% of GDP with a cumulated fiscal cost of $662 billion in 1995.'[91]

---

[88] Johnson and Schaefer, 'Why the IMF is Ineffective' in McQuillan and Montgomery, *IMF: Financial Medic*, p. 56.
[89] Underhill and Zhang, 'Normative Underpinnings', p. 80.
[90] *Ibid.*   [91] Oxfam, *Global Finance*, p. 35.

Essentially, this is the cost incurred by defence of currency and represents an 'astounding transfer from taxpayers and users of public services to banks' depositors, creditors and shareholders'.[92] These figures relate to currency defence. Other effects are:

- increased government debt;
- decrease of government revenue;
- lower creditworthiness causing increased interest rates.

All of these make governments poorer and less able to provide services, even before 'conditionality' bites demanding decreases in government spending:

It is hardly necessary to make the case in detail that financial crises are extremely costly to the countries that experience them: it is sufficient to cite recent events in east Asia. One reason that these costs are so high is a phenomenon to which little attention is paid, namely 'redlining' (something that never happens in a neoclassical model). That is, developing countries in crisis find themselves completely unable to borrow voluntarily from international capital markets, on any terms. Nothing similar happens to developed countries . . . This is one of the few ways in which there appears to be a systematic difference between developing and developed countries.[93]

Another difference is the inability of developing countries to borrow in their own currency, 'sometimes referred to as "original sin". This means that a currency collapse undermines the net worth of agents that have borrowed abroad, to a point where it can threaten large-scale bankruptcies, as we saw in several east Asian countries'.

Moreover, taxes in developing countries tend to be regressive so increased taxation will bite into the poor's income disproportionately.[94] UNCTAD shows that in Latin America in the 1980s and 1990s and Asia in the 1990s, even after a two-year recovery period, wages remained lower and unemployment higher than before the respective financial crises.[95] Diwan argues that labour has been the 'shock absorber' of financial crises, allowing firms to recover profitability after crises and, moreover, since labour shares of GDP remain low after a crisis that 'terms of trade and financial shocks induce an initial decline of the labor share, which fails to be offset by subsequent corrections because industrial relations are permanently transformed'.[96] For thirty-two developing countries this effect

---

[92] Oxfam, *Global Finance*, p. 35.
[93] Williamson, 'Costs and Benefits', p. 44.   [94] Oxfam, *Global Finance*, p. 35.
[95] UNCTAD, *Trade and Development Report 2000: Global Economic Growth and Imbalances* (UN, Geneva, 2000).
[96] I. Diwan, *Labor Shares and Financial Crises* (World Bank, Washington, 1999), cited Oxfam, *Global Finance*, p. 34.

amounts to a loss to labour of US$27billion a year on average, two-thirds of which will be a permanent loss.[97]

Further drivers of inequality are:

- unskilled labour loses to skilled labour;
- small firms may experience credit-rationing as a result of capital account liberalisation since large loans are administratively more efficient;
- small farmers and firms are more vulnerable to exchange rate fluctuations which they cannot hedge;
- tax evasion can only be carried out by the wealthy at the expense of governments;
- only the wealthy have access to sophisticated hedging mechanisms.

Oxfam concludes:

Worldwide financial instability generates massive transfers of income and wealth from the general public in the South, including the poor, to the rich in both South and North. As summarised in Table 1, three redistribution channels together account for a transfer of an order of magnitude that exceeds the benefits of capital inflows derived from spurred growth: falling labor shares of GDP, the fiscal cost of banking crises, and tax evasion. Although the part of these transfers born by the poor themselves is unknown, it is likely to be high. Taxes tend to be regressive or at least not very progressive in developing countries, and fiscal deficits are often reduced by cutting spending which harms the poor.[98]

Williamson draws attention to the erosion of the tax base as a consequence of capital mobility: 'there is no doubt that tax evasion is a significant motivation for foreign investment. Unlike risk diversification, the gain to the investor comes in this instance at a cost to society . . . Since those who own capital tend to be relatively well off, the consequence is a more unequal income distribution.'[99] Williamson concludes that this effect will be felt especially in the richer countries but the transfer of wealth abroad from poor countries may also be significant as disparities of wealth grow there.

Reform

George Soros[100] writes 'In spite of its shortcomings, I am an avid supporter of globalisation. I support it not only because of the extra wealth it produces, but even more because of the freedom it can offer. What I call a global open society could ensure a greater degree of freedom than

---

[97] *Ibid.*   [98] Oxfam, *Global Finance*, p. 77.
[99] Williamson, 'Costs and Benefits', p. 47.
[100] G. Soros, *Soros on Globalisation* (Public Affairs, New York, 2002).

Table 1. *Growth vs. redistribution*

Benefits of capital mobility for the poor (all developing countries, 1980–98)	
Cumulated income due to capital inflow-induced growth;	$1,198bn[a]
Part of this income that benefited the poorest 20% of each country's population:	$36 ~ 120bn[b]
Costs of capital mobility for the poor (all developing countries, 1980–98)	
Cumulated transfers from all taxpayers and workers to the rich due to capital flows:	$947bn
Tax evasion:	$285bn[c]
Bailing out of bankrupt banks after currency crises:	$662bn
Part of these transfers that was born by the poorest 20% of each country's population:	$6 ~ 47bn[d]
Cumulated transfers from all wage-earners to the rich due to falling labor share after currency crises:	$545bn[c]
Part of this transfer that was born by the poorest 20% of each country's population:	?

Source: J. Williamson, 'Costs and Beregits of Financial Globalisation' in G. Underhill and X. Zhang, *International Financial Governance understress* (Cambridge University Press, 2003).

Notes: All figures in 1995 dollars. a. Based on the estimate of capital inflow-induced per capita growth rate of 0.6 per cent, derived from the World Bank, *Global Development Finance 2001* (World Bank, Washington, 2001). This figure covers the 1990–98 period only, because the partial correlation coefficient between capital inflows and growth is insignificant (and actually negative) for the 1980s. Applying this insignificant coefficient to the 1980–89 period would dwarf the total benefits over the 1980–1998 period to $155bn. b. The poorest 20% of the population receive between 3% and 10% of total income in most developing countries. c. Estimate for 1990 multiplied by 19 (1990 dollars). d. Assuming that (i) the whole fiscal cost is eventually paid for by extra taxes without reducing spending, (ii) the ratio of consumption taxes in total government revenues remains unchanged, (iii) consumption inequality remains unchanged, and (iv) the poorest 20% of the population only pay taxes on consumption, in the same proportion as the rich. This is a conservative estimate as tax and spending systems in developing countries are often regressive. e. This figure is underestimated because the data end in 1994, before the Mexican and Asian crises, and because it excludes many developing countries due to lack of data, including Argentina and Brazil. On the other hand, it is overestimated because it does not take into account the increase in labor share that is likely to precede a currency crisis.

any individual state. I consider the present arrangements, in which capital is free to move around, but social concerns receive short shrift, as a distorted form of a global open society.' Soros and Moore call for:

Institutional reforms in the following areas

- to contain the instability of financial markets;
- to correct the built-in bias in our existing international trade and financial institutions (IFIs) that favors the developed countries that largely control them;
- to complement the World Trade Organisation (WTO), which facilitates wealth creation, with similarly powerful international institutions devoted to other social goals, such as poverty reduction and the provision of public goods on a global scale; and
- to improve the quality of public life in countries suffering from corrupt, repressive or incompetent governments.

Moore states:

The IMF's prescription . . . in Indonesia to abolish food and kerosene subsidies, looked good on paper. But the impact on the poor was devastating. The riots, deaths and communal violence were predictable. Global economic policy must pay careful attention and focus on political, social and ethnic stability. This is not to say we should do nothing: rather to look at *sequencing* before abruptly sentencing societies to violent disruption. Theories, beloved in the safety of marble institutional palaces, can have deadly implications for fragile societies. Radical reforms are frequently necessary, but without basic civil and political infrastructures, many recent reforms have allowed oligarchies to plunder economies as they moved from command systems to more open and free societies . . .[101]

Although free trade and fair markets are very good things, they are not an end in themselves; it is not, as some free marketers seem to suggest, a case of abolishing all taxes and the role of government and thus ending poverty overnight. There are public goods – be it in heritage, health or housing for the poor – that the market on its own cannot provide. Justice systems, policing, defence and security are and must remain the basic responsibilities of the state . . . we need economic and political safety nets and systems, not only to protect the poor and each of us from the other, but to preserve the market from itself. The open market on Monday can be a monopolised market by Friday, and then all the virtues of open markets are under siege. It is the natural tendency of business to seek more and bigger market share. That's why antitrust, competition, transparency policies are necessary.[102]

Moore also believes that 'public goods are better paid for together, because on our own we will never have the parks, the museums, the art galleries, clean air, education facilities or police necessary to make life worthy of its promise'.[103]

[101] Moore, *World Without Walls*, p. 228.   [102] *Ibid.*, p. 239.
[103] Moore, *World Without Walls*, p. 239.

The role of insolvency

The net effect of the system that has been created is to reduce countries to the same position as companies operating within a single jurisdiction but with one absolutely vital legal institution missing. That missing ingredient is insolvency. Many states are insolvent in any understanding of the term yet they are denied the mechanisms that have been established by national laws to spread the risk of entrepreneurial activity amongst participants. States are obliged to take part in free trade activities and prevented from using risk-reducing protectionist mechanisms. At the same time, the international financial community prevents them from declaring bankruptcy, thus revisiting the risk on those who financed these risky trading activities. There is no reason why an international bankruptcy regime should not be established as a way to permit a state to 'start again' free of all debt, and every reason why this should be the case. Usually, in companies the risks taken have been assented to by the participants in the enterprise. The consent of some states is very much in doubt, either because of the imposition of free trade by IMF, World Bank or WTO pressure or by bilateral arrangements imposed by powerful states, or because corrupt or unrepresentative governments have imposed the risks on their populations. The possibility of state insolvency is canvassed in chapter 6.

The World Trade Organisation

Introduction[104]

The WTO is the successor of the General Agreement on Tariffs and Trade (GATT) but it is substantially different. In particular, '[i]n the sense of being an international organisation, GATT never had any legal foundation. With its small Secretariat in Geneva, it was only a *de facto* international organisation, with neither regulatory nor jurisdictional powers.'[105] All that changed in 1994 when the Marakesh Agreement of 15 April

---

[104] The following is a brief introduction to the WTO; consideration of WTO jurisprudence of relevance to human rights issues can be found in chapter 4. More detailed descriptions of the working of the WTO can be found in Quereshi, *International Economic Law*; B. Hoekman and M. Kostecki, *The Political Economy of the World Trading System* (2nd edn, Oxford University Press, 2001); C. Arup, *The New World Trade Organisation Agreements: Globalising Law through Services and Intellectual Property* (Cambridge University Press, 2000); D. Kennedy and J. Southwick (eds), *The Political Economy of International Trade* (Cambridge University Press, 2002); John Jackson, *The Jurisprudence of the GATT and the WTO* (Cambridge University Press, 2000) and at www.wto.org/.

[105] Hans van Houtte, *The Law of International Trade* (2nd edn, Sweet and Maxwell, London, 2002).

1994 was signed, establishing the WTO. The Preamble to the Marakesh Agreement reads:

The *Parties* to this Agreement:

Recognising that their relations in the field of trade and economic endeavour should be conducted with a view to raising standards of living, ensuring full employment and a large and steady volume of real income and effective demand, and expanding the production of and trade in goods and services, while allowing for the optimal use of the world's resources in accordance with the objective of sustainable development, seeking both to protect and preserve the environment and to enhance the means for doing so in a manner consistent with their respective needs and concerns at different levels of economic development,

Recognising further that there is a need to ensure that developing countries, and especially the least developed among them, secure a share in the growth in international trade commensurate with the needs of their economic development,

Being desirous of contributing to these objectives by entering into reciprocal and mutually advantageous arrangements directed to the substantial reduction of tariffs and other barriers to trade and to the elimination of discriminatory treatment in international trade relations,

Resolved, therefore, to develop an integrated, more viable and durable multilateral trading system encompassing the General Agreement on Tariffs and Trade, the results of past liberalisation efforts and all the other results of the Uruguay Round of Multilateral Trade Negotiations,

Determined to preserve the basic principles and to further the objectives underlying this multilateral trading system

Agree as follows . . .

To set up the WTO to 'provide the common institutional framework for the conduct of trade relations among its Members in matters related to the agreements . . . referred to as the Multilateral Trade Agreements',[106] four principles underpin the framework: non-discrimination, reciprocity, enforceable commitments and transparency. Non-discrimination comes in the shape of the Most Favoured Nation (MFN) concept and the national treatment rule. The former requires that a product made in one member country be treated no less favourably than a 'like' good that originates in another country.[107] The national treatment rule requires that

---

[106] The Agreements adhered to by all members are: the Agreements are General Agreement on Tariffs and Trade 1994; Agreement on Agriculture; Agreement on the Application of Sanitary and Phytosanitary Measures; Agreement on Textiles and Clothing; Agreement on Technical Barriers to Trade; Agreement on Trade-Related Investment Measures; Agreements on Implementation of Article VI and Article VII of the General Agreement on Tariffs and Trade 1994; Agreement on Pre-shipment Inspection; Agreement on Rules of Origin; Agreement on Licensing Procedures; Agreement on Subsidies and Countervailing Measures; Agreement on Safeguards; General Agreement on Trade in Services; Agreement on Trade-related Aspects of Intellectual Property Rights; Understanding on Rules and Procedures governing the Settlement of Disputes; Trade Policy Review Mechanism.

[107] For discussion of the interpretation of this provision, see chapter 4.

foreign goods that have satisfied border requirements must be treated no
less favourably than like or directly competitive domestically produced
goods so far as the imposition of taxes and charges are concerned. Reciprocity is a vaguer concept which seeks to 'sell' liberalisation by ensuring
that industries which lose protective tariffs may also gain from a *quid
pro quo* reduction of barriers to other markets.[108] Enforceable commitments are the subject matter of the dispute resolution mechanisms and
a degree of transparency comes with the requirements on member states
to publish their trade regulations and with the establishment of Trade
Policy Reviews under the Trade Policy Review Mechanism whereby
periodic country-specific reports are prepared by the Secretariat and
discussed by the WTO General Council. Of course, the general rules
have exceptions which are sometimes referred to as 'safety valves'.[109]
These permit the erection of trade barriers to protect national health
or public safety, where there are serious balance of payments problems
or to ensure 'fair competition'. It is often the ambit of these exceptions which causes controversy. This is because the imposition of WTO
rules, allowing only very narrowly defined exceptions, impinges severely
on the ability of member states to achieve social objectives. Some relevant cases are discussed in chapter 4. Within the WTO rules there is
a wide range of exceptions for developing countries, although compliance with the MFN rules is an ultimate goal. The existence of exceptions
and the situation which arises as full compliance with MFN approaches
creates immense complexities and is the subject of the study on sugar
preferences granted by the EU to former slave-trade economies which
follows.

The WTO has 146 member states,[110] has international legal personality and a large number of internal councils overseeing the operation of the
component Treaties as well as the plenary General Council. Importantly,
there is also a dispute resolution mechanism whereby disputes between
the member states may be heard by a panel appointed to hear the matter.
There is the possibility of appeal to an Appellate Body. The dispute settlement mechanism may result in permission being given for the imposition
of trade sanctions on a defaulting country by a successful complainant
country. Most decision-making on WTO issues is taken by consensus.

---

[108] There is evidence that this principle is weakened by the ability of strong countries to
obtain benefits by bilateral agreement. See J. Finger, 'The GATT as International
Discipline over Trade Restrictions: A Public Interest approach' in R. Vaubel and
T. Willett (eds), *The Political Economy of International Organisations: A Public Choice
Approach* (Westview Press, Boulder, Colorado, 1991); P. Drahos, 'Bilateralism in Intellectual Property' (Oxfam, 2003).
[109] Hoekman and Kostecki, *Political Economy*, p. 36.   [110] April 2003.

This means that no delegation physically present in the Council has a fundamental objection on an issue. Absent or abstaining members do not count. While the promotion of 'free trade' does not appear in the Marakesh Treaty, '[t]he representatives and supporters of the Organization convey a strong sense of a mission to promote open trade across the world and free markets in every locality'.[111] This 'mission' raises the question once again of what is meant by 'free trade' since any legislation imposing social standards to be attained can be seen as a 'disguised barrier to trade'. This gives us the first clue as to the nature of the major dispute surrounding the WTO. Its officials argue that removing tariff barriers increases world trade and that such an increase is likely to be for the benefit of all. While there are major questions as to the statistics used to support these claims (see chapter 1), the rhetoric disguises the possibility of including in the concept of a 'barrier to trade' such issues as labour standards as well as environmental and human rights protections. The opposite positions adopted are often talking about wholly different conceptions of 'free trade'. It is useful to remember here that those opposing the abolition of the slave trade used as an argument interference with their right of free trade and an attack on property.[112]

Mike Moore (Director-General of WTO, 1999–2002) argues that the basis of free trade is reciprocity: 'you treat others as you would like to be treated yourself' and adds to that the theory of comparative advantage, concluding '[t]here is no great mystery as to why free trade, democracy and good governance work. Economic liberty, which allows choice, rewards enterprise and allows the creators of wealth to enjoy the results of their work and risk, means a more efficient allocation of resources, labour and capital.'[113] This analysis assumes many things, not least that there is some form of choice available to be exercised. As we have seen, in countries ravaged by colonialism and slavery, with geographical disadvantages compounded by this exploitation, choices are very few. Further, it is plain that the rise of the industrial world was built on the back of complete protectionism – instant free trade benefits the powerful. The rewarding of risk is also highly problematic since economic power can be used to create a virtually risk-free way of making money, as shown by the behaviour of the banking community. It further glosses over the development of

---

[111] C. Arup, *The New World Trade Organisation Agreements: Globalising Law through Services and Intellectual Property* (Cambridge University Press, 2000), p. 42.

[112] Boswell spoke of abolition as 'robbery to an innumerable class of our fellow subjects': Hugh Thomas, *The Slave Trade* (Papermac, London, 1997), pp. 475–6; and see the account of evidence given to a Committee of the Privy Council p. 495 *et seq*. For a discussion of 'property' rhetoric, see chapter 6.

[113] Moore, *World Without Walls*, p. 52.

states such as China, where economic development and democracy do not go conveniently hand-in-hand. Citing as success stories the provision of micro-credit in Bangladesh, Moore ignores the tendency of liberalisation to push precisely in the opposite direction, by opening to the big multinational banks only interested in mega-finance. Conditionality is portrayed as a method of getting aid to where it is needed, ignoring the reality of social programme cuts, increases in regressive taxes and fuel prices which are demanded by the IMF and impact so cruelly on the poor.[114]

So far as corporations are concerned, they are formally excluded from the decision-making process at the WTO. However, it is clear (see chapter 4) that trade negotiators will have clearly in mind benefits to the major TNCs when negotiating at the WTO. Another significant dispute concerning the working of the WTO is the extent to which the negotiations and the outcomes favour the powerful trading nations. On the face of it, the WTO has highly democratic decision-making processes where one objection could prevent a decision being reached.

Moore argues that:

The undemocratic claim is based upon a basic fallacy. The WTO is not imposed on countries. Countries choose to participate in an open, rules-based multilateral trading system for the simple reason that it is overwhelmingly in their interest to do so. The alternative is a less open, less prosperous, more uncertain world economy – an option few countries would willingly choose. It is difficult to conceive of a system that could be more democratic . . . The multilateral trading system works precisely because it is based on persuasion, not coercion – rules, not force.[115]

Further:

All decisions – from the creation of the GATT to 2001's launch of the Doha Development Agenda – have been taken collectively by the Member governments themselves in the numerous councils and committees, the most important of which is the Ministerial Meeting. Each WTO Member has equal rights and an equal vote under the agreements. Because no decision is taken unless all Member governments agree, effectively every country – from the largest to the smallest – has the power of veto.[116]

There are considered claims that this is not the case: 'The outcome of the Uruguay round was tainted by threats. The US, in particular, frequently expressed (and demonstrated) its readiness to use "Special 301" against countries whose intellectual property regimes it judged

---

[114] *Ibid.*, p. 57.   [115] *Ibid.*, pp. 103–4.   [116] *Ibid.*, p. 105.

to be weak. Such threats played a role in producing the strong TRIPS agreement.'[117]

Moore insists that developing countries are active participants in the WTO dispute settlement system:

Developing countries are increasingly active participants; in 2001 they filed about 80% of all complaints, of which 20% were against developed countries and the balance against developing countries. These figures show that, contrary to the widespread disinformation of the WTO's critics, the organisation provides justice for all countries and do not just work for the rich and powerful.[118]

This is not a universal assessment: 'compared to what they received, the concessions of developing countries in the Uruguay Round seem very large. During the round, the question of what developing countries were going to get in exchange for what they were being asked to give up . . . was answered by "textiles and clothing". It didn't seem persuasive then, and it seems even less persuasive now.'[119]

Ostry asks of the Uruguay Round: 'How was such a lopsided bargain achieved?', stressing that neither 'side' in the negotiations had thought through the full implications.[120]

Moore's claim that WTO provided justice is backed by reference to the establishment in 2001 of the Advisory Centre for WTO Law which provides legal assistance concerning WTO rules. However, this minor assistance is dwarfed by the possible outcome of disputes which, if the violator does not comply with the ruling, permits the imposition of trade sanctions. Now, the possibility of a small developing country hurting the USA or the EU by the imposition of trade sanctions needs to be balanced against the certainty that imposition of trade sanctions by either of those trading blocks against a developing country will be ruinous. The narrower the economic base, the easier it is to target sanctions to really hurt. Moore partially addresses this problem by suggesting that a useful reform would be to permit the winner of a trade dispute to demand compensation in the form of demanding a reduction of trade barriers by the loser in a product area of the winner's choice.[121] Amina Mohamed, Kenya's WTO envoy who speaks for the African group, told WTO negotiators: 'We do find quite objectionable the manner that the WTO dispute settlement system

[117] B. Hindley, 'What Subjects are Suitable for WTO Agreement?' in D. Kennedy and J. Southwick, *The Political Economy of World Trade* (Cambridge University Press, 2002), p. 164. The special 301 law enables the USA to impose unilateral trade sanctions.
[118] Moore, *World Without Walls*, p. 107.
[119] Kennedy and Southwick, *Political Economy*, p. 164.
[120] S. Ostrey, 'The Uruguay Round North-South Grand Bargain' in Kennedy and Southwick, *Political Economy*, p. 288.
[121] Moore, *World Without Walls*, p. 108.

is uncritically hailed as a resounding success, when more than half the WTO membership have been sidelined by the system.'[122] Just over ninety disputes 'about one-third of the 270-odd cases brought to the WTO in its eight-year history – have been filed by developing countries, roughly half against industrialised nations. However, a dozen developing countries in Latin America and Asia, led by Brazil and India, account for almost all the 90-plus filings.'[123]

There is further evidence that Moore paints only part of the picture. Kwa interviewed developing country delegates to the Doha Ministerial Round and discovered a very different picture.[124] The report paints a picture of divide and rule tactics by powerful countries, of pressure put on individual negotiators and threats to withdraw aid or tariff preferences if support for the rich countries' agendas are not forthcoming:

The usual practice is to make promises to a developing country so that it will defend the interests of a developed country, with the result that the developing countries are pitted against each other. Apart from that, developed countries use pressure tactics, for example, political pressures, threatening to withdraw some type of tariff preferences and trying to discredit the people in charge of small country delegations in Geneva.[125]

Reports of secret meetings in 'the Green Room' by the powerful and subsequent imposition of the agreements on the majority are also common: 'it often proves difficult to re-open the debate in formal meetings, for Chairpersons are invariably eager to move on after being party to informal consultations'.[126] The lack of capacity to maintain a presence at the continuous negotiations is also a problem.

On the 'Green Room' negotiations, Moore dismisses charges of bullying at Doha:

At every Ministerial, after everyone has expressed their view, facilitators and key representative ministers then get down to the nitty-gritty of negotiations in smaller groups, coming back to the Green Room on discussions on how each subject folded into the wider picture. These have often been, correctly in the past, criticised as being untransparent; as being an opportunity for the big players to bully the small; as being the scene of secret negotiations. The reality at Doha was that developing countries were always in the majority in the room, and could report back swiftly to their groupings.[127]

[122] F. Williams, 'WTO Minnows Cry Foul on Mediation', *Financial Times*, 24 October 2002.
[123] *Ibid.*
[124] A. Kwa, *Power Politics in the WTO*, Focus on the Global South (January, 2003 www.focusweb.org).
[125] Kwa, *Power Politics*, p. 12.   [126] *Ibid.*, p. 15.
[127] Moore, *World Without Walls*, pp. 128–9.

In fact, developing country delegates felt that attempts to ensure wider participation, especially by General Council Ambassador Kare Bryn of Norway, had met with some limited success between Seattle and Doha:

> in the initial phase of preparation for Doha, some delegates in Geneva felt that the process was becoming somewhat more inclusive. This does not mean that there was total transparency or that negotiators of the politically weaker countries always knew what negotiations were going on. But delegates of the small economies would be invited to some consultations when before they were totally excluded. However, the moment the powerful countries felt the pressure, the same secretive, non-democratic and exclusive negotiating practices re-emerged.[128]

Moore praises the work of US Trade Representative Bob Zoellick and EU Trade Representative Pascal Lamy at Doha: 'Without their leadership we would have failed.'[129] Other 'constituencies' were represented by facilitators who were awarded a 'specific allocation of two hours every day (morning and afternoon) when facilitators could report back and allow regional and other groupings to meet and coordinate'.[130]

At Doha, the developing countries felt that, although they were given limited participation rights (and they severely criticised the work of 'facilitators'), their views were marginalised, particularly on the inclusion of the 'new' or 'Singapore' issues (investment, competition, transparency in government procurement and trade facilitation). By far the majority of developing countries were against the inclusion of these issues and felt aggrieved when this view was not taken account of. 'In Doha they created a process where Ministers could go the Committee of the Whole and discuss and raise issues, but nobody was taking into account what they said . . . Those managing Doha kept Ministers in a semblance of being involved in the process, when they were not, because what was discussed in the Committee of the Whole was not reflected in the Declaration.' The passionate endorsement of these issues by the then Director-General throws some doubt on his claims of impartiality. On the 'new issues' Moore writes: 'investors go to where the rules are predictable and transparent and corruption is low . . . [therefore] The new issues are integral to a coherent Doha Development Agenda strategy'. Moore argues strongly for WTO competition law, which would '*not* require the creation of an international competition agency, nor . . . involve harmonisation of national approaches . . . WTO rule-making would focus, rather, on the adoption of broad principles relating to non-discrimination, transparency and procedural fairness in addition to the prohibition of private cartels.'[131] While the abolition of price-fixing cartels is an

---

[128] Kwa, *Power Politics*, p. 19.   [129] Moore, *World Without Walls*, p. 123.
[130] *Ibid.*, p. 124.   [131] *Ibid.*, p. 154.

admirable aim, it appears to be secondary to non-discrimination aims. The perceived danger is that non-discrimination will benefit large TNCs as against smaller local providers. Hindley argues that with the likelihood of coercion being used to negotiate on these issues, independent criteria should be established to evaluate their utility – relying on consent is no longer viable. This issue is further discussed in chapter 6.[132]

On trade and investment, Moore is unequivocal in support of the benefits of FDI:

Attracting more FDI has become a key economic policy objective for many WTO members, particularly developing countries, to help them integrate further and faster into the world economy. It brings an attractive foreign capital inflow, one that is comparatively stable, that has no fixed interest payments attached to it, and that contributes directly to productive investment. It also brings entrepreneurship, technology, managerial skills and marketing know-how – assets that are in short supply in many countries and difficult for them to acquire, yet which are vital to helping them raise productivity and accelerate their growth and development.[133]

Moore thus argues for a multilateral framework to lower perceived investment risk. Moore sees the 'mind-set' of developing countries who oppose any such agreement as being based in the imperialist extraction of minerals and resources as well as rich country double standards 'wanting to invest in their forests, but then putting tariff escalator clauses on to penalise local added value and local jobs'.[134]

Transparency in government procurement is another issue with two facets. It appears to be a simple matter of the elimination of corruption, but increased competition in government procurement will (as well as saving money for governments as Moore points out) also lead to further privatisation of utilities with the TNCs at the forefront. The consequent dangers to health of, for example, the privatisation of water supplies in a country unable to regulate effectively the distribution networks are clear.

The cumulative result of the frustration felt by developing countries led to the breakdown of negotiations at Cancun. Nevertheless, Moore is right in his assessment that:

The fact remains that the multilateral trading system – for all its imperfections – gives even the smallest and poorest countries far greater leverage and security than they would ever have outside the system. Multilateral negotiations allow weaker countries to pool their collective influence and interests – as opposed to bilateral or even regional negotiations in which they have virtually no negotiating clout.[135]

---

[132] Hindley, 'What Subjects'.   [133] Moore, *World Without Walls*, p. 155.
[134] *Ibid.*, p. 157.   [135] *Ibid.*, p. 109.

The problem with this assessment is that the multilateral route is not exclusive and a multilateral agreement can be levered by the threat of disadvantages or advantages in a 'side' bilateral deal. In this way the powerful trading blocks are able to 'buy' or threaten in order to obtain the votes of the smaller nations, a classic divide and rule strategy. There is evidence that withdrawal of the EU Conotou preferences which are the subject of the detailed study in this chapter was one device used to bring developing countries into line at Doha.[136] Moore refutes this analysis:

Those who accuse the WTO's more powerful members of riding roughshod over the less developed world have a limited grasp of the reality of international diplomacy within the WTO, especially given the surge in new members in recent years; over *eighty* new Members have joined since the launch of the Uruguay Round, mostly from the developed world or economies in transition. Those governments, ministers and ambassadors will not be bullied or bought.[137]

However, Moore was writing prior to the events at Cancun in September 2003 which exposed the intransigence of the developed world when an alliance of developing countries could not be prised apart. Moore's assessment of the trading system is that there are significant improvements to be made, especially in respect of the agricultural protectionism of the EU and USA.

Also encouraging were EU Agriculture Commissioner Franz Fischer's proposals announced in July 2002, to reform the EU's Common Agricultural Policy (CAP) which, . . . swallows around $46billion per annum, or half the EU's budget. European subsidies make food prices 44% higher than they should be, according to OECD estimates . . . The latest proposals take on board, for the first time, the principle of supporting *farmers*, not *farming*.[138]

Essentially, the WTO supports free trade, which is trade without tariff barriers and subsidies, and fails to secure it because of the power imbalance in the world. But it is a different animal from the free trade promoted by some economists which is trade free of regulation, i.e trade which is not counterbalanced by obligations to ensure environmental sustainability or decent labour conditions etc. In defining 'free trade' one needs to be very careful of which animal one speaks. It is perhaps this dichotomy which makes the debate so confusing and explains the contradictory aims of many of the NGOs which engage in anti-WTO rhetoric:

---

[136] Kwa, *Power Politics*, p. 32; and P. Drahos, 'Bilateralism in Intellectual Property', paper prepared for Oxfam (2003).
[137] Moore, *World Without Walls*, p. 111.   [138] *Ibid.*, pp. 181–2.

The reality is that a new kind of international politics is emerging, its agenda set by organised, media-savvy groups of NGOs, activists and protestors, not just by politicians and bureaucrats. The drama is no longer played out in meeting rooms and conference halls, but on the streets.[139] . . . Fuelling much of this NGO anger are perceptions of rich country, multinational dominance . . . Many NGOs seem to feel that corporates are totally motivated by maximising returns to shareholders.[140]

Creditably, Moore feels that engagement and transparency is the way forward: 'Wider debate can only benefit internationalism by demystifying globalisation. Better, more informed engagement, can lift the discussion out of a virtual world of slogans and sound bites, and into the real world of difficult problems and tough choices.'[141] The difficulty of creating an equitable system is immense but calls for abolition of the WTO are a simplistic response to the problem: reform of the WTO is much more likely to assist the poor of both developing and developed countries. This issue is discussed in chapter 6. What follows here is a detailed analysis of the relationship between Barbados and England/the EU, tracing the development of the sugar industry from its inception to the present day, highlighting the difficulty of determining a 'just' outcome in matters of trading relations. As this book goes to press the regime is still attracting headlines: 'Sugar Lobby Defends "Scandalous" Regime.'[142] According to the *Guardian*:

Britain's sugar industry is conducting a last-ditch lobbying campaign to prevent Brussels from removing its lucrative virtual monopoly in the high priced European market in favour of more competitive farmers from the developing world . . . Robert Sturdy, the Conservative MEP for East Anglia, the stronghold of the sugar beet production, will begin a campaign to water down the reforms, backed by British Sugar, which has a monopoly on processing beet sugar in the UK. Oxfam estimates that British Sugar made a profit of £77 million in 2002 from its position as the only processor in a market where prices are fixed.[143]

The African, Caribbean and Pacific States (ACP) countries are also opposing the reforms for reasons which should become clear later:

Clare Wenner, of British Sugar, said the company was on the side of poor countries . . . But aid agencies are afraid that the sugar lobby will succeed in preventing other poor countries getting access to Europe's market. 'The British Sugar lobby is pretending to be the friend of the developing world in a desperate attempt to preserve their own highly lucrative interests' said Matt Griffith, a trade policy advisor at the Roman Catholic aid agency at Cafod. 'We've got a system which provides very limited opportunities to a small group of countries, that generates

---

[139] *Ibid.*, p. 193.   [140] *Ibid.*, p. 195.   [141] *Ibid.*, p. 199.
[142] Guardian, 23 February 2004.   [143] *Ibid.*

vast surpluses which destroy international markets, at huge cost of farmers in the poor world and all for the greater good of British Sugar and the sugar beet lobby' said Kevin Watkins, head of trade at Oxfam. The agencies fear that opposition from the highly organised sugar lobby, which has formed an alliance of convenience with a small group of developing countries, will stymie the reform attempts. 'This is the most powerful agro-industrial lobby group attempting to systematically mislead public opinion to maintain their monopoly' Mr Watkins said.[144]

How has the issue arisen? The complexities of this issue show how detailed knowledge of the history of trade is important before equity is a possibility.

Rigging the trade rules: the history of sugar production

'Sugar and tobacco production . . . developed hand-in-hand with coerced and degraded labor: grasping for wealth, profit-maximising English planters relentlessly sought overseas markets, ruthlessly exploited fellow humans, accumulated narrowly concentrated power, and resonated very little to liberal ideas and higher values.'[145] This section shows that small jurisdictions have always been at the mercy of the rules governing international trade and that, in that respect, little has changed. In the light of the discussion relating to 'free trade' above it is worth reiterating the point that one of the key points made by those who opposed abolition of the slave trade was that such an abolition interfered with the 'freedom of trade' of the merchants involved. It is also interesting to note that the slave trade was 'free' from regulation but protected by a network of law, including company, contract and insurance law, as well as 'international' laws such as the Navigation Acts.

One of the great difficulties in unravelling the rights and wrongs of the globalisation debate is that 'the devil is in the detail'. International trade laws are complex, not only because the text itself is complex, but also because the *effects* of their application are complex. In order to assess the operation of any of the rules, it is necessary to be familiar both with the rules that apply to a given situation and the way in which those rules impact on particular countries. It is exceedingly difficult, therefore, to make sweeping generalisations about the fairness or otherwise of any particular rule of trade law and even more difficult to distil any perceived unfairness into a slogan suitable for protest banners. To illustrate the difficulties, what follows is a detailed analysis of a tiny area of international

[144] *Ibid.*
[145] G. Nash, 'Forward' in R. Dunn, *Sugar and Slaves: The Rise of the Planter Class in the English West Indies, 1624–1713* (University of North Carolina Press, 1972 and 2000).

trade rules relating to sugar as they impact on the African, Carribean and Pacific group of countries, and in particular, Barbados.

These jurisdictions started to profit greatly from the trade in sugar when they became slave economies. Before 1640, settlers on Barbados grew and exported to England, tobacco and cotton. However, around 1640 'a superior grade of tobacco which originated in Trinidad was being produced in Virginia. As a result, the value of West Indian tobacco was reduced and the cultivation of tobacco was no longer viable in Barbados.'[146] The settlers turned to sugar production:

Once the English colonists in the Caribbean learned how to grow and process sugarcane in the 1640s, they developed a life-style all their own. They turned their small islands into amazingly effective sugar-production machines, manned by armies of black slaves. They became far richer than their cousins in the North American wilderness . . . They lived fast, spent recklessly, played desperately, and died young. And although they persuaded the merchants and politicians at home that the sugar colonies were more valuable than the North American colonies, they could not persuade themselves to live in the Indies any longer than necessary. Indeed, they made their beautiful islands almost uninhabitable.[147]

Barbados is 166 square miles in area, 21 miles long and 14 miles wide.[148] As late as 1972 sugar accounted for 90 per cent of the island's exports[149] although the first crops grown by the settlers were cotton and tobacco.[150] Barbados was totally transformed by the sugar business: 'Between 1640 and 1660 the Barbados planters switched from tobacco and cotton to sugar and from white servants to black slaves.'[151] This switch was a matter of emphasis – white indentured servants and convicts continued to be exported: 'between 1654 and 1685 ten thousand [indentured servants] sailed from Bristol alone, chiefly for the West Indies and Virginia'.[152] Kidnappers called 'spirits' flourished in London and Bristol and:

The political and civil disturbances in England between 1640 and 1740 augmented the supply of white servants. Political and religious nonconformists paid for their unorthodoxy by transportation, mostly to the sugar islands . . . So thoroughly was this policy pursued that an active verb was added to the English language – to 'barbadoes' a person.[153] However, the advantages of Negro slave labour became evident to the planters. These included racial differences which made it 'easier to justify and rationalize Negro slavery, to exact the mechanical

[146] www.geocities.com/The Tropics/Shores/3392/history.htm, 8 October 2003.
[147] Dunn, *Sugar and Slaves*, p. xxiii.   [148] *Insight Guide Barbados* (London, 2001).
[149] Dunn, *Sugar and Slaves*, p. 28.   [150] *Ibid.*, p. 49.   [151] *Ibid.*, p. 59.
[152] E. Williams, *Capitalism and Slavery* (1944; University of North Carolina Press, 1994), p. 10.
[153] Williams, *Capitalism and Slavery*, p. 12.

obedience of a plough-ox or cart-horse, to demand that resignation and that complete moral and intellectual subjection which alone made slave labor possible'.[154] The decisive factor was economics. Finally, and this was the decisive factor, the Negro slave was cheaper. The money which procured a white man's services for ten years could buy a Negro for life.[155]

Sugar production developed with great speed between 1640–3. Sugar was a 'very scarce and much desired commodity'.[156] Once able to process the cane the crop proved immensely valuable. The land was fertile and one acre of cane could yield 'upwards of two tons of sugar, twice the yield obtained in most West Indian Islands (including Barbados) later in the century'.[157] Since sugar production required a large injection of capital, small planters were squeezed out.[158] 'Barbados in 1645 had 11,200 small white farmers and 5,680 Negro slaves; in 1667 there were 745 large plantation owners and 82,023 slaves.'[159] The system of huge plantations supported by slave labour was fully established by the 1680s.[160] The profits were huge: 'The Barbados crop in 1650, over a twenty month period, were worth over three million pounds, about fifteen million in modern money.'[161] The rush to cultivate the valuable cane meant that the forests were cut down, leading to a timber shortage and the desire to grow cane meant that no land was available to grow food for the increasing population. Barbados became heavily dependent on supplies of food, clothing and slaves from outside.[162] Thus grew up the notorious 'triangular trade', imports of food, clothing and slaves into Barbados and other colonies in return for sugar and rum. 'The slave ship sailed from the home country with a cargo of manufactured goods. These were exchanged at a profit on the coast of Africa for Negroes, who were traded on the plantations, at another profit, in exchange for a cargo of colonial produce to be taken back to the home country.'[163] In comparison with the trade to India, which 'drained Britain of bullion to buy unnecessary wares . . . The Slave trade . . . was ideal in that it was carried out by means of British manufactured goods and was, as far as the British colonies were concerned, inseparably connected with the plantation trade which rendered Britain independent of foreigners for her supply of tropical products'.[164] The trade was immensely lucrative: 'About 1730 in Bristol it was estimated that on a fortunate voyage the profit on a cargo of about 270 slaves reached £7,000 or £8,000 . . . An eighteenth century writer has estimated the

---

[154] *Ibid.*, p. 19.   [155] *Ibid.*, p. 19.   [156] Dunn, *Sugar and Slaves*, p. 62.
[157] Dunn, *Sugar and Slaves*, p. 65.   [158] *Insight Guide Barbados*, p. 37.
[159] Williams, *Capitalism and Slavery*, p. 23.   [160] Dunn, *Sugar and Slaves*, p. 69.
[161] Williams, *Capitalism and Slavery*, p. 25 – note that Williams was writing in 1944.
[162] *Insight Guide Barbados*, p. 37; Dunn, *Sugar and Slaves*, p. 59.
[163] Williams, *Capitalism and Slavery*, p. 52.   [164] *Ibid.*, p. 37.

sterling value of the 303,737 slaves carried in 878 Liverpool ships between 1783 and 1793 at over £15 million.'[165] In 1798, Pitt assessed the annual income from West Indian plantations at £4 million as compared with £1 million from the rest of the world.[166] At all points, the lucrative traffic was supported by trading laws and protectionist and monopolist measures. The legal trading framework which supported the trade consisted of three categories of rules: rules governing trade in goods, including slaves; rules governing the treatment and disposal of the slaves themselves; and the rules supporting the system which prevailed in English law. In the first category are the Navigation Acts which restricted foreign imports to English-owned colonies and the monopoly granted to the Royal African Company to trade slaves in the islands, a protectionist measure. In the second category are the laws enacted on the island itself and accepted in England, these latter starting with the concept of property rights over people, extending this to property rights over descendants, extending that to the concept of humans as real property so that they could be traded or inherited with the estate. The defence of property rights meant that any punishment meted out to a slave was permissible. In the third category are a whole raft of contractual, property rights, insurance rights etc. which were regularly applied by the English courts, which rarely sought to distinguish between slaves and other goods.

International trade rules

The Company of Royal Adventurers trading to Africa was incorporated in 1663 but failed to prosper due to conflict with the Dutch. The Royal African Company was formed in 1672 to take over the monopoly in the slave trade. However, in 1698 in accordance with economic thinking of the time, the company lost its monopoly and 'the right of a free trade in slaves was recognised as a fundamental and natural right of Englishmen'.[167] In accordance with this freedom, in 1755, 237 slave traders operated from Bristol, 147 from London and 89 from Liverpool.[168] The volume of the slave trade hugely increased: 'The Royal African Company, between 1680 and 1686, transported an annual average of 5,000 slaves. In the first nine years of free trade Bristol alone shipped 160,000 Negroes to the sugar plantations . . . it has been estimated that the total import of slaves into all the British colonies between 1680 and 1786 was over two million.'[169]

[165] *Ibid.*, p. 36, citing to E. Donnan (ed.), *Documents Illustrative of the History of the Slave Trade to America* (Washington DC, 1930–35).
[166] Williams, *Capitalism and Slavery*, p. 53.   [167] *Ibid.*, p. 32.   [168] *Ibid.*, p. 32.
[169] *Ibid.*, pp. 32–3.

Relevant Treaties include the Treaty of Utrecht in 1713 which conceded trade in Negroes to the Spanish colonies (the Asiento) to the English.[170]

One of the most important parts of the legal framework was the Navigation Acts. The triangular trade was supported by a rigid monopoly system. The Navigation Acts of 1651, 1670, 1685 and 1696 required the use of English ships and crew in trade with the Caribbean, and the loading and unloading of Caribbean cargo in English ports. The colonies could buy only British products, use English ships and refrain from any manufacture. In return, colonial products were given a monopoly in the home market. The ban on manufacturing in the colonies meant that the triangular trade was a terrific stimulus to the woollen and cotton manufacturers, and it gave rise to sugar refining – an order of the Privy Council in England prohibited aliens from erecting sugar houses or practising the art of refining sugar in England.[171] It was also a boost to the production of glass artefacts, either for use as bottles or as 'pacotille', items of small value to exchange for slaves, as well as metal items such as fetters and chains, branding irons, nails, sugar stoves and rollers, guns and brass, copper and lead items.[172] Williams shows how the great wealth generated by this trade was invested in the agricultural and industrial revolutions, in particular helping to found some of the powerful banking houses which have turned into the great banking TNCs of today.[173] The wider consequences of the slave trade are further discussed below.

The laws governing the slaves

Although the nature of the relationship between masters and slaves was not clearly defined in legislation, '[b]y 1650 certainly and probably a good bit earlier, slavery in Barbados had become more than a lifetime condition. It extended through the slave's children to posterity.'[174] Of the legislation on the island itself, Dunn identifies the 1661 'Act passed by the Barbados Assembly "for the better ordering and governing of Negroes" [as] the most important surviving piece of legislation issued in the English islands during the seventeenth century'. It was re-enacted several times[175] and copied in Jamaica, Antigua and North Carolina.[176] The Preamble clearly indicates the chattel status of slaves, since its object is 'to protect them as wee doe men's other goods and Chattles'. Negroes are 'an heathenish, brutish and an uncertaine, dangerous kind of people', unfit to be governed by English law. This reinforced the concept

[170] *Ibid.*, p. 40.   [171] *Ibid.*, p. 73.   [172] *Ibid.*, pp. 65–84.   [173] *Ibid.*
[174] Dunn, *Sugar and Slaves*, p. 228.   [175] 1676, 1682 and 1688.
[176] Dunn, *Sugar and Slaves*, p. 239, Public Record Office, Barbados Laws 1645–82, Acts of Assembly, Barbados, 1648–1718 (London, 1738).

of the colonies as being 'beyond the line', or outside the reach of the influence of European law and culture. In recognition of this, and the chattel status of slaves, the master was permitted to punish slaves as he saw fit and 'if while beating a Negro for a misdemeanour he happened to maim or kill him ("which seldom happens"), he suffered no penalty. To be sure, the master could be stiffly fined (three thousand pounds of sugar or about £25) for wantonly killing his slave; the fine was a good deal stiffer for wantonly killing someone else's slave. But since the master could always claim to be correcting a slave for a misdemeanour, this fine was easy to evade.'[177] In contrast to the provisions applicable to servants, no minimum food requirements were applicable to slaves, although the master was obliged to give his Negroes new clothing once a year – a pair of drawers and a cap for every male, a petticoat and cap for every female. Again, in contrast to servants, slaves had no access to courts to complain of mistreatment. However, a master could be charged with murder if a servant died at his hands.[178] But offences committed by the slaves were tried by his master for petty offences and by two justices of the peace and three freeholders (all of whom would be slave masters) for major crimes. Murder, rape, arson, assault and theft of anything beyond a shilling in value were all capital offences. Not surprisingly, in a small island where the slave population substantially outnumbered the white masters, rebellion was the most serious charge. A master of a rebel slave received compensation from the Island Treasury when his Negro was executed. Although the Barbados Act for the good governing of servants fixed minimum food and clothing allotments for servants, permitted servants to sue in court if mistreated and provided for fines if the master failed to take proper care of a sick servant, there is some doubt about whether their conditions were any better than those of the slaves. Indeed, Williams points out that '[s]ince they were bound for a limited period, the planter had less interest in their welfare than in that of the Negroes, who were perpetual servants and therefore the most useful appertenances of a plantation'.[179] However, the limited rights accorded to servants and the fact that their loss of liberty was finite distinguished the servant from the slave. Further, 'the conception of the servant as a piece of property never went beyond that of personal estate and never reached the stage of a chattel or real estate'.[180]

---

[177] Dunn, *Sugar and Slaves*, p. 239.
[178] Barbados Act for the Good Governing of Servants, 27 September 1661; Dunn, *Sugar and Slaves*, p. 240.
[179] Williams, *Capitalism and Slavery*, p. 17, citing Calendar of State Papers, Colonial Series V, 229, Report of Committee of Council for Foreign Plantations, August 1664.
[180] Williams, *Capitalism and Slavery*, p. 18.

English jurisprudence

Bingham has argued that 'The Law Favours Liberty',[181] arguing that the judges developing the common law made significant inroads on the institution of slavery. If true, the statement must be set against the strict nature of the slavery regimes found in the English colonies when contrasted with the more humane treatment afforded to slaves in the Spanish colonies.[182] However, Bingham's analysis appears very much to be 'special pleading' on behalf of the judges and he selects particular issues for discussion. In general 'prior to 1793 . . . all classes in English society presented a united front with regard to the slave trade. The monarchy, the government, the church, public opinion in general, supported the trade.'[183] Slavery thrived in the colonies despite Blackstone's analysis of the constitutional position of the colonies:

the common law of England, as such, has no allowance or authority there, they [the colonies] being no part of the mother country, but distinct (though dependent) dominions. They are subject however to the control of the parliament . . . But it is particularly declared by statute 7 & 8 Will.III.c22. That all laws, by-laws, usages and customs, which shall be in practice in any of the plantations, repugnant to any law, made or to be made in this kingdom relative to the said plantations, shall be utterly void and of no effect.[184]

Attempts by colonial governors to impose taxes on the import of slaves to lessen the fear of rebellion due to the overwhelming majority of Negroes, were met with frustration by the Board of Trade and subsequently by Parliament.[185] Slaves could be sold by contracts made in England and the only controversy before the courts for many years was the status of slaves which had actually been brought to England. Bingham describes the 'confused and contradictory nature of the law' up to 1765, with the courts variously declaring (in 1569) that 'England was too pure an air for slaves to breathe in',[186] then in *Butts* v. *Penny* (1677)[187] that 'Negroes being usually bought and sold among merchants as merchandise and also being infidels, there might be a property in them sufficient to maintain trover.' In 1697, the court in *Chamberlain* v. *Harvey*[188] held

---

[181] 'The Law Favours Liberty: Slavery and the English Common Law', Essex Law Lecture 2003.
[182] A. Watson, *Slave Law in the Americas* (University of Georgia Press, 1989).
[183] Williams, *Capitalism and Slavery*, p. 39.
[184] Blackstone, *Commentaries on the Laws of England* 1:105 (1765), cited in Watson, *Slave Law*, p. 64.
[185] Williams, *Capitalism and Slavery*, p. 41.
[186] Bingham, 'The Law Favours Liberty', p. 5.
[187] *Butts* v. *Penny* (1677) 2 Lev. 201, 83 ER 518.
[188] (1697) 1 Ld Raym 146, 91 ER 994.

that a sale contract concluded in London in respect of a slave would be valid if the slave was in Virginia but that 'as soon as a Negro comes into England he becomes free'.[189] In 1729, the Solicitor-General and Attorney-General issued a joint opinion asserting that not only did arrival on English soil not make a slave free, but neither would baptism.[190] This conclusion was flatly contradicted in *Shanley* v. *Harvey* (1762):[191] 'As soon as a man sets foot on English ground he is free: a Negro may maintain an action against his master for ill-usage, and may have a *Habeus Corpus* if restrained of his liberty.' There followed a number of cases where determination of the question was avoided.[192] The *Sommersett* case of 1772 was a case where a slave had absconded from his master in England. Subsequently recaptured he was sent by force to a ship about to sail for Jamaica. Lord Mansfield concluded that 'the black must be discharged', a decision often hailed as the beginning of abolition of slavery in the British Empire. However, subsequent cases restricted the ratio of *Somersett* to the situation where a slave is removed by force to a colony. Where a slave has stayed in England for a year but voluntarily returned to Antigua, the stay in England was held to have had no effect on her slave status.[193] The 'beginning of abolition' argument is dismissed by Williams as 'merely poetic sentimentality translated into modern history',[194] showing that two years after the *Sommersett* decision Jamaican Acts restricting the slave trade were disallowed. The issue in *Somersett* and the other cases discussed here, was, in any event only whether the condition of slavery could be tolerated in England – out of sight in the colonies it was clear that the Negroes were property. Further, in *Gregson* v. *Gilbert*,[195] where the captain had thrown 132 slaves overboard because the ship *Zong* was short of water, the issue calmly decided by the court was whether the cost of the slaves came within the relevant clause of the marine insurance policy. Lord Mansfield held 'the case of the slaves was the same as if horses were thrown overboard'. Apart, therefore, from the 'NIMBY'[196] attempts of the English courts to sweep slavery back 'beyond the line', the full commercial back-up of contract and insurance laws covered and protected the traders, and there was no attempt to prevent the sale of these goods on the grounds that enforcement of such a contract would be contrary to public policy. Indeed, Williams shows how the earliest development of

---

[189] Cited Bingham, 'The Law Favours Liberty', p. 7.
[190] Williams, *Capitalism and Slavery*, p. 45; Bingham, 'The Law Favours Liberty', p. 8.
[191] (1762) 2 Eden 126, 28 ER 844.
[192] Bingham, 'The Law Favours Liberty', pp. 9–13.
[193] *The Slave Grace* (1827) 2 Hag. 94.   [194] Williams, *Capitalism and Slaves*, p. 45.
[195] (1783) 3 Dougl. 233, 99 ER 629.   [196] 'Not in my back yard'.

Lloyds depended on marine insurance covering the trade of slaves to the West Indies.[197]

Consequences of the slave trade

Eric Williams famously showed how the capital amassed by the slave traders financed the Industrial Revolution, tracing the huge fortunes made by slaving into the banking, heavy industry and insurance sectors of the eighteenth century: 'The industrial expansion required finance. What man in the first three-quarters of the eighteenth century was better able to afford ready capital than a West Indian sugar planter or a West Indian slave trader?'.[198] Family by family he traces the fortunes of the planters and traders into more 'respectable' occupations. Notable among the banking families that owed its foundation to slaving was the Barclay family, which combined with other Quaker families of Gurney and Freame gave rise to Barclay's Bank.[199] Williams traces the financing of some of the great inventions of the age to capital accumulated via the triangular trade:

Boulton and Watt received advances from Lowe, Vere, Williams and Jennings – later the Williams Deacons Bank. Watt had some anxious moments when the West Indian fleet was threatened with capture by the French. 'Even in this emergency,' wrote Boulton to him hopefully, 'Lowe, Vere and Company may yet be saved, if ye West Indian fleet arrives safe from ye French fleet . . . as many of their securities depend on it.[200]

Nor were the benefits confined to England: Rolston shows how Belfast also prospered:

There were many benefits for towns such as Belfast from involvement in provisioning the Caribbean, and these were not confined to agriculture. The importation of sugar encouraged the development of a sugar-refining industry. Such industries as rope-making, meat packing, flour milling and the salting of beef and fish were highly dependent on West Indian trade. And, of course, linen production benefited; cheap Belfast linen was exported to clothe the slaves.[201]

One of the slave traders, Waddell Cunningham, made enormous wealth from the slave trade, returning to Belfast in 1765 to run a diverse and powerful trading empire with 'business contacts from Antigua to Jordan, and from St Petersburg and Danzig to Holland and Spain'.[202] He also

---

[197] Williams, *Capitalism and Slavery*, p. 105.   [198] *Ibid.*, p. 98.
[199] *Ibid.*, pp. 43 and 101.   [200] *Ibid.*, p. 103.
[201] B. Rolston, '"A Lying Old Scoundrel": Waddell Cunningham and Belfast's Role in the Slave Trade' (www.historyireland.com/magazine/features/11.1Feat.html, 8 October 2003).
[202] Rolston, 'A Lying Old Scoundrel', p. 3.

set up a bank and became involved in the insurance business. Building on Williams' work, Inikori shows how the cotton textile industry grew so dramatically in the eighteenth century.[203] Analysing the development as import substitution industrialisation (ISI) he shows how imports of East India cotton goods from 1613 developed a taste for dyed and printed cotton goods. Partly as a result of agitation from the wool and silk trades, protection was provided against 'all silk goods and painted, dyed, printed or stained calicoes imported into England from China or the East Indies',[204] in the form of a prohibition against wearing them. Later import duties on white calicoes and excise duties on those printed in England were imposed.[205] Finally, from 25 December 1722, Parliament prohibited the consumption in England of 'printed, painted, stained, and dyed calicoes. Muslins, neckcloths, fustians and calicoes dyed all blue were excepted. Printed East India calicoes could still be imported for re-export, and plain calicoes were allowed to be imported for export. But the home market was closed for these goods.'[206] The effect of this was a huge expansion of the protected English cotton industry. However, ISI analysis shows that once the domestic market reaches saturation point, stagnation sets in. One solution to this problem is exporting. Inikori shows that:

The crisis of stagnation was resolved through the exploitation of export opportunities in the transatlantic slave trade from Africa and in the slave-based economy of the Atlantic system. These early export opportunities were crucial to the subsequent transformation of the industry for a number of reasons. First, the larger market offered by export demand helped to enlarge the total number of firms in the industry at an early stage, which contributed to the development of its competitiveness. Second, the operation of the export producers outside the protected domestic market exposed them to stiff competition with cheap and high-quality Indian goods in West Africa, and this induced them to adopt innovations that reduced costs and raised quality.[207]

Inikori argues that it was this which laid the foundation for successful invasion of the major European and American markets from the late eighteenth century: 'The rapid expansion of exports which followed, together with the multiplier effects on the domestic market for cottons and other manufactures, provided the favourable environment for the rapid transformation of the industry's technology and organisation between the late eighteenth and mid-nineteenth centuries.'[208] Thus, the cotton trade was developed by protection from imports into England, by protection of the

[203] J. Inikori, 'Slavery and the Revolution in Cotton Textile Production in England' in J. Inikori and S. Engerman (eds), *The Atlantic Slave Trade* (Duke University Press, 1992), p. 145.
[204] Inikori, 'Slavery and Cotton Textile', p. 154.   [205] *Ibid.*, p. 154.
[206] *Ibid.*   [207] *Ibid.*, pp. 146–7.   [208] *Ibid.*, p. 147.

export trade to West Africa via the monopoly of the Royal African Company in the triangular trade to the West Indies,[209] and the protection of English cottons on the West Indian Islands themselves. It was not until the limited size of these markets was evident that cotton manufacturers were forced to sell to markets outside the protected slave trade. Once the Royal African Company lost its monopoly, the slave trade was open to all nations and competition in West Africa became intense. The competition was only overcome by means of the series of inventions which industrialised the cotton industry:

The evidence . . . shows that the rate of growth of domestic consumption of cotton, after the completion of the first-stage import-substitution, was decidedly low. Such slow growth could not have provided the market conditions for the production of cotton textile machinery. The rapid growth of cotton exports from the middle decades of the eighteenth century created pressures which stimulated the inventions.[210]

We need also to remember that turning the inventions from the drawing board into real functioning machines was greased by capital, some of which, as with the Watt steam engine, was amassed from the slave trade. There is a very credible claim, then, that while the slave trade has been dismissed as a significant base for the industrial expansion of British industry,[211] '[t]his curiosity contrasts sharply with the perspective of eighteenth century strategists who, on the eve of the industrial revolution, placed great stock in both the trade and the colonial plantations as vital instruments for British economic progress'.[212] In a critical overview of the attitudes of economic historian's viewpoints on the importance of the slave trade to British industry, Darity considers the strange invisibility of human cargo from the debate and the dismissal of the 'Williams hypothesis':

The polite explanation is, of course, that the historians of the industrial revolution have a valid reason for not mentioning arguments that assign a leading role in British industrial expansion to the foreign sector and, more specifically, to the slave trade and plantation slavery. The modern economic historians, ostensibly, have considered the case for the Williams hypothesis in careful, deliberate fashion and have simply found it wanting. For them, commerce with the colonial plantations and with the African coastal regions was no more than a handmaiden to the British process of industrialization, and a minor handmaiden at that.[213]

---

[209] The Royal African Company could carry only English cottons to trade for slaves; slaves could only be imported into the West Indies via the Royal African Company.

[210] Inikori, 'Slavery and Cotton Textile', p. 171.

[211] W. Darity, 'British Industry and the West Indies Plantations' in Inikori and Engerman, *Atlantic Slave Trade*, p. 247.

[212] *Ibid.*, p. 248.   [213] *Ibid.*, p. 250.

This was certainly not the view of many of those giving evidence before the enquiry ordered by George III when, in 1788, he ordered the Lords of the Committee in Council to produce a report on the 'state of trade to Africa' in all its dimensions.[214] John Shoolbred, on behalf of the Company of Merchants Trading to Africa, gave evidence that:

the Effects of this Trade to Great Britain are beneficial to an infinite Extent. In its immediate Effect it employs about 150 Sail of Shipping which carry annually from this Country upwards of a Million of Property, the greatest Part of our own Manufactures; and in its more remote Effects, there is hardly any Branch of Commerce in which the Nation is concerned that does not derive some Advantage from it. But the beneficial Effects of this Trade have been no where so eminently striking as in the Sugar Colonies in the West Indies . . . it is therefore fair to include every Advantage which this Country enjoys by Means of its West India Colonies, among the benefits of the African trade, more particularly that for Slaves; and if their Lordships will take the Trouble to look back to the Condition of the British Nation at the Time of commencing this Trade, and observe its Progress in Navigation, in commerce, in Manufactures, Opulence and Power, they will find its Acquirements of those great national objects in pretty exact Proportion to its pursuits in the African Trade, and the consequent Improvement of the British colonies and Settlements in America.[215]

A substantial body of scholarship throws doubt on the claim that Williams' work was mistaken and it is evident that the slave trade played a major part in the industrialisation and booming economies of both Britain and the USA.[216] A particular insight into the controversy is provided by Inikori who has analysed 112 years of scholarship on the causes of the Industrial Revolution. His thesis is that scholarship on this issue falls generally into three phases:

Between 1884 and the late 1940s historians generally identified the growth of English overseas trade as the principal cause of the Industrial Revolution, what I refer to as the 'Commercial Revolution' thesis. Above all, this thesis of the early historiographical epoch gave the pride of place to trans-Atlantic commerce. But between the 1950s and early 1980s there was a shift from external to independent

---

[214] House of Commons Sessional Papers of the Eighteenth Century; George III, *Report of the Lords of Trade on the Slave Trade 1789.*

[215] House of Commons Sessional Papers, cited by W. Darity, 'Economic Aspects of the British Trade in Slaves: A Fresh Look at the Evidence from the 1789 Report of the Lords of Trade (Committee of Council)' in H. Cateau and S. Carrington (eds), *Capitalism and Slavery: Fifty Years Later* (Peter Lang Publishing, New York, 2000).

[216] See especially the contributors to Part II of Inikori and Engerman, *Atlantic Slave Trade*, especially J. Inikori, R. Bailey and W. Darity; D. Richardson, 'Slavery, Trade and Economic Growth in Eighteenth Century New England' in B. Solow (ed.) *Slavery and the Rise of the Atlantic System* (Cambridge University Press, 1991); Cateau and Carrington, *Capitalism and Slavery*, the contrary case is put (unconvincingly) by H. Thomas, *The Slave Trade* (Picador, London, 1997).

natural forces – internally derived agricultural progress, population growth, progressive socio-political structures, exogenous (accidental) development of science and technological innovation, and the chance endowment of abundant mineral energy resources (coal) and metallic ores. Then another turning point came in the mid-1980s, shifting the explanation back again to the 'Commercial Revolution' thesis.[217]

Considering a wide range of sources, Inikori shows how the pendulum swung from a comprehensive acceptance of the central importance of trade, particularly the Atlantic slave trade, to the concept that internal factors were paramount. At the end of this second period he places the work of Ronald Findlay, who 'in his 1982 paper . . . faintly supported the supply side technological argument . . . But this is qualified so strongly, with much emphasis on the role of overseas trade, that it not only mellowed the uncompromising tone of the "manna from heaven" technological argument, as Findlay characterised it, but virtually amounted to a rejection of the thesis.'[218] Findlay wrote:

The analysis of the trade-growth nexus in the formative period of the Industrial Revolution given here seems to imply that the causal growth runs from growth (in the form of technological change in the manufacturing sector) to trade rather than in the reverse direction that the literature appears to have emphasized. However, the 'manna from heaven' nature of technical progress as it appears in simple formal models needs to be supplemented with common sense. To begin with imagining that the doubling of efficiency in the manufacturing sector . . . took place in a closed economy makes no sense . . . Under these circumstances it is difficult to imagine the crucial innovations being diffused as rapidly and pervasively as they were, particularly since the dynamic cotton industry was much more export-orientated than any other . . . Trade and growth, like trade and the flag, are inextricably intertwined in the first take-off.[219]

Inikori, having charted the changes, seeks to explain them. One factor he identifies is the appropriation of Williams' work by anti-colonial scholars, making it extremely unpopular 'among Western scholars, who, understandably, sprang to the defence of the moral foundation of Western civilization'.[220] The reversal to the modern acceptance of the 'Commercial Revolution' thesis could thus be explained by the increasing distance

---

[217] J. Inikori, 'Capitalism and Slavery, Fifty Years After: Eric Williams and the Changing Explanations of the Industrial Revolution' in Cateau and Carrington, *Capitalism and Slavery*, pp. 51–2.

[218] Inikori, 'Changing Explanations', pp. 60–1.

[219] R. Findlay, 'Trade and Growth in the Industrial Revolution' in C. Kindleberger and G. di Tella (eds), *Essays in Honour of W.W. Rostow*: vol. I, *Models and Methodology* (New York University Press, 1982), pp. 186–8, cited in Inikori, 'Changing Explanations', p. 61.

[220] Inikori, 'Changing Explanations', p. 67.

from colonialism. However, Inikori regards such an explanation as inadequate and is persuaded that the international economy is more important:

It would seem that other more powerful factors were at play. Here we must
turn to the collapse of the international economy arising from the devastating
impact of two world wars and the Great Depression. The collapse of world
trade that resulted forced both scholars and administrators to lose confidence in
the ability of international trade to operate as the propelling force for long-term
development.[221]

'Export pessimism' was the result of the collapse and the existence of
non-market led economies in the Soviet Union and China. The effects of
economic pessimism and the dominance of formal growth theories were
reinforced by the advent of a new breed of economic historians armed
with formal models of growth which treated technological innovation
as accidental and 'computed gains from international trade in terms of
Ricardo's static comparative advantage theory, which enabled them to
argue that the resources employed in producing for export between 1650
and 1850 could have been employed to produce for the home market
in England without much loss of growth'.[222] When the international
economy began to grow at about 8 per cent per annum as a result of
international trade, perceptions switched again:

just as postwar export pessimism and the neoclassical formal growth theory to
which it gave rise were largely responsible for inward-looking interpretations of
the Industrial Revolution in the 1950–1980 period, so also the disappearance
of postwar export pessimism and the construction of relatively more realistic
growth theories by economists are the main factors driving the new trend in
the historiography of the Industrial Revolution. And the new rising tide of the
'Commercial Revolution' thesis is pulling *Capitalism and Slavery* along with it,
the same way that it dragged it down between the 1950s and 1980s.[223]

In view of the support now accorded to this part of Williams' work, it
would be foolish to dismiss the further insight of Williams that abolition
came about only when the trade had become unprofitable. This must
also be taken seriously and may hold a key to suggested solutions to
today's unfair trading practices: the chances of change may depend less
on altruistic motives and more on an economic analysis which tends to
show that such practices may be self-destructive in the long term. Such
an analysis could stem from the import substitution analysis examined
above. The protected markets and subsidised products of the West will
hit a ceiling in the market which will require any growth to be fuelled by
selling abroad. If impoverishment of large parts of the world continues,

[221] *Ibid.*, p. 69.   [222] *Ibid.*, p. 71.   [223] *Ibid.*, p. 73.

and continues to accelerate, there will be few with the dollars to purchase the goods which the Western nations wish to sell.

Sugar and trade in Barbados in the twenty-first century

The history of the slave trade shows a convincing picture of laws made to suit the economic interests of the powerful. Are matters different now? 'Food's production, storage and global distribution is a fascinating study of the best and worst aspects of globalisation over the ages. As a worst case example, take sugar, one of the first industrialised food products, the lure for some of the world's cruellest colonial exploitation. Today, sugar is an egregious example of how trade subsidies and tariffs keep developing countries poor.'[224]

Today, the world sugar market contains some of the largest and most blatant forms of trade protection. Having exploited these countries for generations, now the North keeps their products out of their markets and betrays the principles of free trade they expound in fine speeches.[225]

Consider the following facts:

- Over 90 per cent of world sugar supplies are sold at prices above the 'world price'. Excess prices are paid for by taxes on consumers.
- On average, prices in developed countries are over double the world price.
- 40 per cent of the world production is highly subsidised.
- Japan, Western Europe and the USA are among the most protected.
- Some small exporters receive export subsidies as aid.
- Producer subsidies are paid for by taxes on consumers.
- For over 300 years, most national sugar industries have been maintained behind high trade barriers.
- Removal of price protection would see prices fall by around 65 per cent in Japan, 40 per cent in Western Europe and 25 per cent in the USA, Mexico, Indonesia and Eastern Europe, and by around 10 per cent in China and the Ukraine.[226]

American producers, who developed their own sugar beet industry, as well as controlling vast sugar cane plantations, have benefited hugely from protectionism. The USA assists the domestic sugar industry through price supports and import restriction in the form of a tariff rate quota, under which sugar-exporting countries are given a tiny quantity that they

[224] Moore, *World Without Walls*, p. 44.   [225] *Ibid.*, p. 45.
[226] *Ibid.*, pp. 45–6, citing to Brent Borrell and David Pearce, *Sugar: The Taste Test of Trade Liberalisation* (1999).

can sell in the USA at the regular tariff, with exports beyond that subject to a tariff rate of nearly 150 per cent. These sugar import restrictions and price supports cost domestic users of sweeteners US$1.6 billion in 1998, while benefiting domestic sugar beet and sugar cane producers to the tune of US$1 billion. Moreover, 42 per cent of the total benefits to sugar growers went to just 1 per cent of all farms.[227]

The sugar programme is not just economically and politically inequitable – it prevents desperately poor sugar-producing countries from exporting to the USA. Countries such as Columbia and Guatemala are deprived of valuable foreign exchange earnings that could be spent on food, fuel and medicine. A number of observers have warned that Andean, as well as Caribbean, farmers are more likely to turn to illegal drug crops because they are being prevented from selling their sugar in the world market place, where they would be globally competitive were it not for rich country subsidies. And it is not just the USA. Australian Trade Minister Mark Vaile told the IFAP Family Farmer's Summit on International Trade: 'The EU's out-of-quota tariffs for barley, sugar and beef are well over 100 per cent; their mean out-of-quota tariff on agricultural items is 45 per cent.'[228]

Barbados belongs to the trading group known as the African, Caribbean and Pacific States (ACP). Relations between forty-six ACP states and the European Union were, after the accession of the United Kingdom to the Community, governed by the first Lomé Convention, signed in 1975. This was followed by Lomé II in 1979 (fifty-eight ACP countries), Lomé III in 1984 (sixty-five ACP countries) and Lomé IV in 1989 (sixty-eight ACP countries, extended in 1995 to seventy ACP countries).[229] (For the special sugar regime see below.) The current relationship is under negotiation, outlined by the ACP-EU Partnership Agreement which was signed on 23 June 2000 (the Cotonou Agreement) in accordance with which, on 27 September 2002, the EU and ACP countries officially opened negotiations on Economic Partnership Agreements (EPAs). The negotiations are scheduled to take place over five years. The talks face the difficult task of creating a system which is compatible with the WTO agreements and still provides some real possibility of development for the ACP countries. The Lomé system of non-reciprocal trade preferences which was set up with the benefit of a GATT waiver 'was supposed to increase ACP competitiveness and promote the diversification of those countries' economies through privileged access for the

---

[227] Moore, *World Without Walls*, p. 46, citing to Douglas A. Irwin, *The Case for Free Trade* (2002).
[228] Moore, *World Without Walls*, p. 47.   [229] See the Europa website (www.eutopa.eu.int).

majority of their products to the European market'.[230] Karl's assessment is that the results are disappointing: 'Only a handful of ACP countries – 10 at the most – have had the know-how or have been able to profit from these advantages. The overall share of the ACP countries in total EU imports has systematically fallen – from 6.7 per cent in 1976 to 2.8 per cent in 1999'.[231] This result is attributed to '[t]he structural problems inherent in the ACP economies which limit their competitiveness, the lack of investment and under-industrialisation, combined with economic difficulties arising out of the international environment, and the existence of sophisticated mechanisms of disguised protectionism at the very gateways to the European market'.[232] The international problems are combined with the effect of increased liberalisation: as tariff barriers fall, generally the preferential margin is lowered to 'barely 2 per cent'.[233]

One outcome of the Uruguay Round of Multilateral Trade Negotiations was to bring agriculture into the international regime dealing with trade in goods, specifically the Multilateral Agreement on Trade in Agriculture. Under the general provisions, developed countries agreed to cut their tariffs by 36 per cent over six years; developing countries agreed to cut their tariffs by 24 per cent over ten years. Non-tariff barriers were to be tariffied and the resulting tariff cut by the same amount. The developed countries agreed to reduce export subsidies to agriculture by 36 per cent over six years; developing countries agreed to reduce their export subsidies by 24 per cent over ten years. On domestic support, developed countries agreed to a 20 per cent reduction over six years; developing countries agreed to a 13.3 per cent reduction over ten years. Developed countries are not required to include in the calculation income support for farmers. As a direct result of the Round and despite the survival of the Sugar Protocol in the Lomé Convention, sugar prices were predicted to fall by 10 per cent.[234] Prior to the Uruguay Round, export subsidies were permitted in the agricultural sphere so long as 'they were not used by a country to receive a more than equitable share of the world market'.[235] However, the concept of an 'equitable market share' proved problematic and:

countries which could afford to pay export subsidies enjoyed almost complete licence in applying them to stimulate their exports of agricultural products. Export subsidies on agricultural products became a serious problem in the 1980s when

---

[230] K. Karl, 'Economic Partnership Agreements: Hopes, Fears and Challenges' (2002) 195 *Courier ACP-EU* (November-December).

[231] *Ibid.*, p. 21, using European Commission figures.   [232] *Ibid.*, p. 21.   [233] *Ibid.*

[234] F. Rampersad, *Critical Issues in Caribbean Development, No. 2* (Ian Randle Publishers, Jamaica, 1997), p. xiv.

[235] Rampersad, *Critical Issues*, p. 130.

commodity prices declined precipitously. The rich countries, to sustain their national agricultural output, greatly increased their export subsidies, thus driving prices down and severely affecting agricultural production, especially in the developing countries.[236]

Despite this, the final agreement reflected the power of the EU by 'securing agreement that the Union should be allowed to amend the CAP before reaching any agreement at the international level on agriculture'.[237] UNCTAD has estimated the tariffs applied by the EU, Japan and the USA on tropical agricultural produce pre-Uruguay at 162.4 per cent, 589 per cent and 536.9 per cent respectively.[238] This means that the proposed reductions of 36 per cent over six years 'makes little difference in opening the markets of the industrialised countries to imports from developing countries since the tariffs prevailing at the end of the six-year transitional period will still be prohibitive'.[239]

The sugar regime

In respect of sugar, the Caribbean Community (CARICOM) retained both the Sugar Protocol in respect of the EU and the quota arrangements with the USA. In respect of the EU, the quota for Barbados stood at 54,000 tonnes in 1998.[240] Barbados was unable to fulfil its quota: only 48,000 tonnes was shipped to the EU. None was shipped to the USA. For EU-ACP sugar there are two preferential import schemes: at the time of the United Kingdom's accession to the EU in 1973, the United Kingdom imported annually about 2 million tonnes a year under the British Commonwealth Sugar Agreement. This was turned into a preferential import arrangement with the EU and embodied in the Lomé Convention arrangements made in 1975. There is also a parallel agreement with India. Both agreements permit the import of 1.3 million tonnes of raw sugar annually. The tonnage is not subject to import duties and is paid for at a guaranteed price at the level of the EU support for raw sugar (euro 52.37/100 kilo).[241] The amounts under the ACP-India Protocol (now embedded in the Cotonou Agreement and under negotiation at the European Partnership Agreement talks)[242] are fixed, although if any

---

[236] *Ibid.*, pp. 130–1.   [237] *Ibid.*, p. 132.
[238] UNCTAD, *Trade and Development Report 1994*, p. 148.
[239] Rampersad, *Critical Issues*, p. 136.
[240] Ministry of Agriculture and Rural Development, Barbados, *Agriview 1998*: these were the latest figures available in January 2003.
[241] International Sugar Organisation, 'Everything But Arms Iniative (EBA): Implications for the World Sugar Market' (MECAS (02) 18, 11 November 2002), p. 23.
[242] 'EU and ACP Countries Negotiate Economic Partnership Agreements' (2002) *Courier ACP-EU* (July–August).

country fails to fulfil its agreed quantities the quota may be permanently reduced by the quantity it fails to deliver. Shortfalls are redistributed by the EU Commission in consultation with the ACP.

The Special Preferential Sugar Scheme (SPS) provides access for a variable amount of sugar, depending on EU production quotas and sugar provided under the Everything But Arms Initiative (EBA, see below) up to the Maximum Supposed Needs (MSN) of the sugar-refining countries. The MSN varies according to EU production quotas. The amount allocated to SPS is the MSN minus the ACP-India quotas, the EBA sugar and imports from two other special regimes (one concerning Cuba and Brazil and a further one with Balkan states). The impact of the EBA on the ACP countries is clearly negative (with the exception of LDC-ACP countries):

In the *short* to *medium run* (up until 2009), the negative effect of the EBA on the ACP countries is rather obvious. The EBA sugar will gradually replace most if not all the SPS with corresponding losses in sugar export earnings of LDP countries excluding ACP-LDCs (Madagascar, Malawi, Tanzania, Zambia). In the *longer run*, the impact of the EBA on the ACP countries will depend on the negotiations on Economic Partnerships Agreements . . . the list of possible options includes the severe deterioration of the ACP sugar protocol.[243]

The aim of the EPA talks is the progressive abolition of both tariff and non-tariff barriers between the EU and the ACP, since in 2008 the waiver obtained from WTO rules will lapse. Under the new regime, special treatment will be reserved for the Least Developed Countries (LDCs) in the ACP which already benefit from the 'Everything But Arms' Initiative[244] which, in March 2001, sought to extend duty and quota free access to all products originating in the LDCs except arms and ammunition. The EBA originated in the 1996 Singapore Declaration by which Trade Ministers committed themselves to address the problem of marginalisation of LDCs and adopted a Plan of Action, 'including provision for taking positive measures, for example duty-free access, on an autonomous basis, aimed at improving their overall capacity to respond to the opportunities offered by the trading system'.[245]

The adoption of the Plan of Action and its attempted implementation by the EBA is one clear example of the complexity of the tangled politics and economics of the international trade law rules, because of its potential impact on countries which already had Lomé preferential treatment, the impact on EU prices to which the Lomé preferential sugar is tied, and the impact on LDCs themselves.

[243] International Sugar Organisation, 'EBA: Implications', p. 5.
[244] Governed by Council Regulation 416/2001 of 28 February 2001.
[245] WTO Ministerial Conference, Singapore, 9–13 December 1996, see WTO website (www.wto.org).

The impact of the Everything But Arms Initiative on Barbados is unclear since the UN list of LDCs does not include Barbados.[246] Parties to the Lomé Convention which are not LDCs are excluded from the EBA.[247] As explained above, the EC-ACP Sugar Protocol (surviving from the Lomé Convention) admits a quota of sugar from Lomé Convention countries at a fixed price. There is therefore a complex calculation to be made as to how the LDCs access to the EU will affect the non-LDC-ACP countries, although, as the International Sugar Organisation (ISO) points out, the impact is certain to be negative.

Disquiet over the possible effects was widespread.[248] In November 2000 the EU Agriculture Commissioner, Franz Fischler, released an internal study on the EBA.[249] The report anticipated that sugar exports from LDCs to the EU could amount to 2.7 million tonnes. Sugar is the largest exportable good affected by the EBA.[250] The risk to the European sugar industry was estimated at over one billion euros, not including the possibility of paying compensation to EU producers if the production quota were to be reduced.[251] The non-LDC-ACP countries which were:

enjoying a preferential access to the lucrative EU sugar market with prices 2–2.5 times higher than those in the world market . . . also expressed their concerns about the EBA initiative. The ACP countries insisted that any move by the EU to abandon decades of preferential treatment for their traditional exports would devastate their economies. In the words of Brian Webb, chief executive officer of the Guyana Sugar Corporation, 'they have robbed the poor to give to the poorest'.[252]

---

[246] They are ACP countries: Sudan, Mauritania, Mali, Burkino Faso, Niger, Chad, Cape Verde, Gambia, Guinea-Bissau, Guinea, Sierra Leone, Liberia, Togo, Benin, Central African Republic, equatorial Guinea, Sao Tome and Principe, Democratic Republic of Congo, Rwanda, Burundi, Angola, Ethiopia, Eritrea, Djibouti, Somalia, Uganda, Tanzania, Mozambique, Madagascar, Comoros, Zambia, Malawi, Lesotho, Haiti, Solomon Islands, Tuvalu, Kiribati, Vanuatu and Samoa. Non-ACP countries: Yemen, Afghanistan, Bangladesh, Maldives, Nepal, Bhutan, Myanmar, Laos and Cambodia. Source: UNCTAD, *Least Developed Countries Report 2002* (UN, Geneva, 2002).

[247] 'EU Trade Concession to Least Developed Countries Possible Impacts on the Agriculture Sector' (www.europa.eu.int/comm/trade/miti/devel/eba.htm, visited 10 October 2003).

[248] 'Everything But Arms Initiative Threatens European Sugar Producers', *Ag Journal*, 14 October 2002 (www.agjournal.com, 14 October 2003).

[249] Everything But Arms Proposal: First Remarks on the Possible Impacts on the Agricultural Sector, European Commission DG-AGRI, November 2000.

[250] US$67 million according to Danish Research Institute of Food Economics: 'Is the 'Everything But Arms' Initiative All Good News and Everything the EU Can Do for the LDCs?' (www.FODLK, Policy Brief, 8 June 2003).

[251] Sugar beet growing covers 1.8 million hectares in the fifteen member state Community (1.2 per cent of utilised agricultural area): 'Reforming the European Union's Sugar Policy' (Commission Staff Working Paper, Brussels, SEC, 2003).

[252] International Sugar Organisation, 'Everything But Arms Initiative (EBA): Implications for the World Sugar Market' (MECAS (02)18, 11 November 2002), p. 2.

These concerns led to the introduction of exceptions to the EBA in respect of bananas, rice and sugar. For these commodities, free access is being phased and the implementation of duty reductions was delayed until 2002 (bananas) and 2006 (rice and sugar). The full duty free access in respect of sugar is delayed until 2009 and until then annual duty free quotas are being allocated. Under the EBA, tariff quotas for LDCs will rise from 74 thousand tonnes in 2001/2 to 197 thousand tonnes by 2008/9.[253] Imports under EBA are not subject to quantitive restrictions but to rules of origin. This means that partly processed products originated in other countries do not benefit.

In the case of sugar, custom duties will be reduced starting in 2006, and will be phased out over three years. Until 2009, duty free quotas are allocated. These are based on the exports by LDCs during the 1990s plus 15 per cent, growing by 15 per cent annually. The quotas are for raw sugar only. There will be no duty free access for white sugar until 1 July 2009.[254] Nevertheless, the International Sugar Organisation calculates that the advantage to LDCs taking advantage of EBA initiatives is 'US$271.36/tonne or 127 per cent of world prices'.[255] The full quota was fulfilled in 2001/2. The ISO expects that '[i]n the *short to medium run* (up until 2006) no impact of the EBA sugar on the EU market is expected'.[256] In any event, the EU can apply safeguard measures if exports by LDCs are likely to increase by 25 per cent over the previous year. The implications for ACP countries are not so bright: 'Impact on the world market appears to be limited to a redistribution of exports to the EU market between LDCs and ACP countries. The EBA sugar will gradually displace the Special Preferential Sugar.'[257] Inevitably, '[t]he effect of removing trade barriers to one group of countries, leaving others unchanged, is to increase imports from the favoured group'.[258] The longer term outlook is extremely difficult to predict as the number of complex factors considered in the following passage make evident:

In the *longer run*, the impact of an unlimited access to the EU market granted for the LDCs starting from 2009 will depend on the shape of the future sugar regime,[259] which, in its turn, will influence the volume of sugar entering under the EBA. If the EU prices remain significantly higher than those of the world

---

[253] Council Regulation 416/2001 of 28 February 2001 [2001] OJ L60, 1 March 2001. See also ISO, 'EBA: Implications'.

[254] For details of the quotas, tables and prices see ISO, 'EBA: Implications'.

[255] *Ibid.*, p. 3.   [256] *Ibid.*, p. 4.   [257] See www.isosugar.org, 3 December 2002.

[258] S. Page and A. Hewitt, 'The New European Trade Preferences: Does 'Everything But Arms' (EBA) Help the Poor' (2002) 20(1) *Development Policy Review* 91, at 95.

[259] For proposals for reform see Communication from the Commission to the Council and the European Parliament, Accomplishing a Sustainable Agricultural Model for Europe through the Reformed CAP: the Tobacco, Olive Oil, Cotton and Sugar Sectors (SEC

market, the export-orientated sugar producers in the least developed countries will be attracted to the lucrative EU market. Sugar from LDCs could easily surpass the 'maximum supposed needs'[260] (MSN), and solutions for balancing the sugar trade in the EU have to be found . . . The EU will face a difficult task to find ways to accommodate this additional sugar.[261] Possible options include a combination of cuts in quotas and prices, which can make the EU market a less attractive export outlet for developing countries, on one hand, and sugar beet a less attractive crop for European farmers on another hand; cessation of cane raw sugar tolling and white sugar re-export as well as the severe deterioration of the ACP Sugar Protocol.[262]

Without the Sugar Protocol the non-LDC countries may not be able to export sugar viably: 'Caribbean countries could live with the gradual decrease in European prices but not with competition from Asian least developed countries.'[263]

There is also doubt about the real benefits of EBA for developing countries. The likelihood of the preferences being eroded by eventual liberalisation under multilateral agreements means that 'relying on trade preferences might be a dangerous route for the LDCs . . . Moreover, such preferences are insecure due to the attached safeguard clauses and rules of origin[264] which may result in potential poverty-creating adjustment costs for the LDCs.'[265] Although there have been significant gains (estimated at US$117 million for sub-Saharan Africa)[266] the likelihood of reform of the Common Agricultural Policy under pressures from WTO and the EU enlargement process means that the gains are perilously insecure. If the EU reduces market access barriers by 50 per cent and reduces domestic support by 35 per cent it is estimated that sub-Saharan Africa would 'suffer a loss of over half a billion dollars from the EU reforms alone, thereby turning the gains from the EBA to losses of nearly

---

(2003) 1022 and 1023, Brussels, 23 September 2003, COM (2003) 554 final): the options for discussion are extension of the present regime, reduction of internal price and full liberalisation.

[260] I.e. the estimated needs of the four countries with refining industries, United Kingdom, France, Portugal and Finland.

[261] For the European Commission study on reform see 'Reforming the European Union's Sugar Policy' (Commission Staff Working Paper, Brussels, SEC, 2003).

[262] ISO, 'EBA: Implications', p. 4.

[263] Page and Hewitt, 'Does EBA Help the Poor', p. 98.

[264] For a good analysis of the reasons for underutilisation of preferences see Paul Brenton, 'Integrating the Least Developed Countries into the World Trading System: the Current Impact of EU Preferences under Everything But Arms' (World Bank, Washington, 27 February 2003).

[265] Danish Research Institute of Food Economics, 'Is the "Everything But Arms" Initiative All Good News and Everything the EU Can Do for the LDCs?' (www.FODLK, Policy Brief, 8 June 2003).

[266] Danish Research Institute, 'Is EBA Good News'.

$400 million . . . In contrast the world gains from such a scenario (estimated at nearly $15 billion with the EU itself being the biggest beneficiary of nearly $13 billion).'[267] The dilemmas for policy-makers are evident and severe. At present the EU sugar regime is under challenge at the WTO – Australia, Brazil and Thailand have requested the setting up of a panel under the dispute resolution mechanism. The ACP Consultative Group on Sugar describes the move as 'utterly disappointing'.[268] The Group sees the move as pursuit of interests by 'large multi-commodity producers/exporters . . . a further demonstration of the use of legal rules in the context of the WTO to further marginalize the interest of the small and vulnerable economies'.[269] The EU characterises the complaint as 'nothing less than an attack on the EU's trade preferences for developing countries'.[270] The EU points out that Brazil's sugar cane production 'has quadrupled since the mid-1970s' and claims that this would have been impossible without substantial government aid; that the Australian market is closed but exports have substantially increased since the early 1990s; and imports to Thailand are 'essentially nil whilst Thailand is one of the biggest sugar exporters in the world'.[271]

The Cotonou Agreement sets out the framework for future ACP-EU trade co-operation. Part III of the Agreement sets out 'Co-operation Strategies' together with 'Development Strategies' and emphasises that development strategies and economic and trade co-operation are 'interlinked and complementary and that the efforts undertaken in both areas must be mutually reinforcing'.[272] Article 34.4 specifies that economic and trade co-operation must be 'in full conformity with the provisions of the WTO, including special and differential treatment'. Special deals may only be obtained in defence of the countries' special interests. Adjustments in favour of the weakest trading nations are provided for in GATT rules but 'ACP countries judge them insufficient, poorly defined and not rigorous enough, particularly in their application, and believe that they pay only lip service to development needs'.[273] Although the official EU line is that development needs are a primary concern, the negotiations are viewed with all the suspicions inherent in trade negotiations between the rich countries and impoverished nations, ranging from the belief that

[267] *Ibid.*
[268] ACP Consultative Group on Sugar, 'ACP Response to Australia, Brazil and Thailand's Request for a Panel in the EU Sugar Regime Challenge in WTO' (Brussels, July 2003) (www.acpsec.org, visited 10 October 2003).
[269] ACP Group, 'ACP Response', p. 1.
[270] 'WTO Challenge against Sugar will Hurt Developing Countries' (www.europa.eu.int/comm/trade/issues/respectrules/dispute/pr110703'en.htm, Brussels, 10 July 2002, visited 15 October 2003, quoting, Franz Fischler).
[271] *Ibid.*   [272] *Ibid.*   [273] Karl, 'Economic Partnership Agreements', p. 22.

the motive behind liberalisation is to open up ACP countries to EU companies, to real anger at the protectionist measures adopted by the EU in agriculture.[274]

Implications for Barbados

The Country Strategy Paper for Barbados (concluded March 2002) for the period 2002–7 sets out an agreement between the government of Barbados and the European Commission.[275] Sugar exports account for around 3 per cent of GDP. The response to the threat to these exports is to attempt to diversify into other food crops including 'onions, hot peppers, tomatoes, paw paws and mangoes'.[276] Development aid of 17 million euros is supporting the Caribbean rum sector to limit the damage caused by liberalisation of the spirits market. 'Barbados, being the location of some important distilleries, is likely to benefit substantially from this programme. Bearing in mind the decline of cane sugar, this programme may play an important role in diversifying into higher value added products.'[277] The paper draws a picture of a hitherto robustly developing country with excellent life expectancy rates (79 for women, 74 for men), good social security, health and education provision, but 14 per cent of the population falling below the poverty line of BDS$5,502 per annum and 9.9 per cent unemployment (2001). However:

The Caribbean region is currently facing huge challenges on the external front as it grapples with the effects of globalisation and international trade commitments under the World Trade Organisation (WTO) alongside pressures arising from economic groupings such as the Free Trade Area of the Americas (FTAA) . . . The EPA, as envisaged under the Cotonou Agreement will progressively eliminate barriers to trade between the parties and enhance cooperation in all areas relevant to trade. By virtue of deeper trade liberalisation imperatives and being signatories to hemispheric and multilateral trade-related disciplines in particular, trade strategies and policy governing trade relations with countries outside the Caribbean must now evolve.[278]

The World Bank

The World Bank was founded at the same time as the IMF as the International Bank for Reconstruction and Development. Its role is supported by regional development banks such as the European Bank for Reconstruction and Development. Other institutions forming part of the group

---

[274] *Ibid.*
[275] European Commission DG Development 1: \ Barbados \ CSP \ CSSdraft7a.EDF.doc.
[276] *Ibid.*, p. 14.   [277] *Ibid.*, p. 21.   [278] *Ibid.*, p. 19.

are the International Finance Corporation (IFC, established 1956), the International Development Association (IDA, established 1960), the International Centre for the Settlement of Investment Disputes (ICSID, 1966) and the Multilateral Investment Agency (MIGA, 1988). The objectives of the Bank are stated as:

(i) To assist in the reconstruction and development of territories of members, including the restoration of economies destroyed or disrupted by war, the reconversion of productive facilities to peacetime needs and the encouragement of the development of productive facilities and resources in less developed countries.
(ii) To promote in the long run the balanced growth of international trade and the maintenance of equilibrium in balance of payments, and to assist in raising productivity, the standard of living and conditions of labour.[279]

The development aims are to be achieved through:

(1) the facilitation of investment of capital;
(2) the promotion of private investment by means of guarantees or participation in loans and other investments made by private investors;
(3) the supplementing of private investment by the Bank, out of its own capital, through funds raised by it, and through other resources on suitable conditions;
(4) the encouragement of international investment.[280]

Of the other agencies in the group, the most notable for our purposes are the IFC and MIGA which are dedicated to private investment. IFC is to 'further economic development through the encouragement of productivity of private enterprises in member countries'.[281] The purpose of MIGA is to encourage the flow of private investments for productive purposes.[282] Given these objectives it is perhaps not surprising that the Bank has been accused of rendering assistance to companies, but how did an institution founded with such laudable aims come to be pilloried along with the IMF as the creator of great social misery?

The IMF-World Bank reforms brutally dismantle the social sectors of developing countries, undoing the efforts and struggles of the post-colonial period and reversing 'with the stroke of the pen' the fulfilment of past progress. Throughout the world, there is a consistent and coherent pattern: the IMF-World Bank reform package constitutes a coherent programme of economic and social collapse.[283]

[279] Article 1 of the Articles of Agreement.   [280] Article 1 of the Articles of Agreement.
[281] IFC Articles of Agreement, Article 1.
[282] MIGA, Articles of Agreement, Article 2; for a more detailed study see Quereshi, *International Economic Law*, p. 345 *et seq.*
[283] M. Chossudovsky, *The Globalisation of Poverty* (Zed Books, 1998), pp. 68–9.

Even on the free market economic model criteria adhered to by these institutions any success is elusive: 'On the basis of existing studies, one certainly cannot say whether the adoption of programs supported by the Fund led to an improvement in inflation and growth performance. In fact it is often found that programs are associated with a rise in inflation and a fall in the growth rate.'[284]

Even without the assistance of the IMF/World Bank packages, TNCs were on a winning ticket as their vertical integration and relatively small overhead costs, as well as global mobility and huge reserves enable them to cushion any sudden market movement. However, the IMF/World Bank packages for developing nations assist TNCs in a number of ways.

The sequence works like this. Large amounts of corporate debt in developed countries have been transferred to the state because countries were lent money to reimburse the private sector banks.[285] In more than 100 debtor nations,[286] the IMF and World Bank work together to impose 'structural adjustment programmes' which appear to directly benefit TNCs. How does it work? Following the oil price rises imposed by the OPEC countries in the mid-1970s, the foreign debts of developing countries increased enormously. From 1970 to 1980 the long-term external debt of low-income countries increased from US$21 billion to US$110 billion and that of middle income countries rose from US$40 billion to US$317 billion.[287] With default on these loans an inevitability, the IMF and World Bank were put into a position to impose structural adjustment packages to ensure that payments were made.

Each structural adjustment package called for sweeping economic policy reforms intended to channel more of the adjusted country's resources and productive activity toward debt repayment and to further open national economies to the global economy. Restrictions and tariffs on both imports and exports were reduced, and incentives were provided to attract foreign investors.[288]

The contents of these packages have become clearer over recent years. Palast revealed the contents of the Ecuador Interim Country Assistance Strategy which contained instructions to Ecuador to raise the price of cooking gas by 80 per cent by 1 November 2000. Also required was the elimination of 26,000 jobs and a cut in real wages for remaining workers 'in a timetable specified by the IMF. By July 2000, Ecuador had to transfer ownership of its biggest water system to foreign operators,

[284] M. Khan, 'The Macroeconomic Effects of Fund Supported Adjustment Programs' (IMF Staff Papers vol. 37, No. 2, 1990), pp. 196–222.
[285] Chossudovsky, *Globalisation of Poverty*, p. 22.
[286] World Bank, *World Debt Tables 1994–5* (Washington DC, 1994).
[287] World Bank, *World Debt Tables 1992–3*, 'External Finance for Developing Countries' (Washington DC, 1992), p. 212.
[288] Korten, *When Corporations Rule*, p. 184.

then Ecuador would grant British Petroleum's ARCO unit rights to build and own an oil pipeline over the Andes.'[289] Honduras was forced by the IMF/World Bank to open rice markets to heavily subsidised rice and 'tens of thousands' of small farmers became destitute.[290] In Jamaica, the IMF insisted on the removal of tariffs on imported goods and dairy farmers poured their milk down the drain as they could not compete with subsidised American milk: 'Jamaica's high unemployment, lawlessness and social turmoil have to be seen against the background of IMF/World Bank policies that governments of both the left and the right have been forced to pursue for well over two decades.'[291] Argentina has half of its population below the poverty line but the IMF was insisting on a US\$3.1 billion payment to itself as well as renegotiation of more than US\$90 billion owed to private banks. Cahn argues that the World Bank is a governance institution, it is exercising its power:

through its financial leverage to legislate entire legal regimens and even . . . [altering] the constitutional structure of borrowing nations. Bank-approved consultants often rewrite a country's trade policy, fiscal policies, civil service requirements, labor laws, health care arrangements, environmental regulations, energy policy, resettlement requirements, procurement rules, and budgetary policy.[292]

It is well documented that the consequent 'austerities' have in the past caused cuts in all social and in particular health programmes, a move of the population away from rural areas into cities, the vicious-circle effects of poor health and lack of proper food and education, and a consequent willingness of a population to work at any task however ill-paid and poorly regulated.[293] The structural adjustment policies imposed by the lending institutions now have a 'softer' face as each of the LDCs must prepare a Poverty Reduction Strategy Plan (PRSP) as a condition of increased or continued finance or to bid for forgiveness or rescheduling of debt. However, although these plans are often carefully prepared and

[289] G. Palast, *The Best Democracy MoneyCan Buy* (Pluto Press, London, 2002).
[290] J. Vidal, 'Hewit Joins Angels on Farm Visit, Agriculture Minister Blames IMF for Problems in Honduras', *Guardian*, 13 September 2003.
[291] L. Kwesi Johnson, 'Jamaica Uncovered', *Guardian*, 28 February 2003, reviewing 'Life and Debt', a film by Stephanie Black. See also J. Pilger, *The New Rulers of the World* (Verso, London, 2002).
[292] J. Cahn, 'Challenging the New Imperial Authority: The World Bank and the Democratization of Development' (1993) 6 *Harvard Human Rights Journal* 160.
[293] Korten, *When Corporations Rule*; Chossudovsky, *Globalisation of Poverty*; P. Harrison, *Inside the Third World* (3rd edn, Penguin, Harmondsworth, 1993); I. Wilder, 'Local Futures: From Denunciation to Revalorisation of the Indigenous Other' in G. Teubner (ed.), *Global Law Without a State* (Dartmouth, 1996); H. Heerings and I. Zeldenrust, *Elusive Saviours* (International Books, Utrecht, 1995).

considered there is still considerable emphasis on free trade solutions, including open markets and growth as creating the answer to the nation's poverty.[294]

As we have seen, free trade policies are tailor-made for a TNC seeking to locate its plant at the least expensive site globally. Negative externalities in the form of health, safety and environmental regulations will either be minimal or can be negotiated in that direction with a government which needs the transnational investment in order to be able to repay its debts. At the end of the day, however, the result is a huge disparity in income within the developing countries between those who were 'in on the act' of development and associated with the incoming TNCs, and the majority whose conditions worsen. Further, the export of profits to the developed world and the repayment of debt amounts to a huge subsidy by the poor nations of the rich ones,[295] and leads to the growing disparity of incomes and living conditions between nations. While TNCs base their *raison d'etre* on profit maximisation they will remain an integral part of this process unless it can in some way be regulated.

While it is early days for an overall assessment of PRSPs, some light can be thrown on their operation by looking at one such document in some detail. The World Bank's operations in Honduras have been chosen for this purpose. Honduras has a population of 6.6 million and is part of the Heavily Indebted Poor Countries (HIPC) programme which, in theory, should entitle it to relief from some outstanding debt. In the words of the World Bank, 'Honduras has launched an ambitious strategy to break a long cycle of poverty and inequality. Nearly two-thirds of Hondurans live in poverty and close to half are extremely poor. Anti-poverty efforts were making steady progress in the 1990s but the devastating effects of Hurricane Mitch in 1998 reversed the country's gains.'[296] In other words, the country is worse off than it was in 1990. This is despite the fact that a PRSP was agreed in 2000 and on 10 July 2000 the World Bank and IMF announced that they had 'agreed to support a comprehensive debt reduction package for Honduras under the enhanced HIPC initiative'.[297] HIPC is described by the World Bank in the following terms:

The HIPC Initiative was launched by the IMF and the World Bank in 1996 as the first comprehensive effort to eliminate unsustainable debt in the world's poorest, most heavily indebted countries. In October 1999, the international community

---

[294] For a sight of PRSPs see World Bank website (www.worldbank.org).
[295] Estimated variously but probably in the region of US$200 billion. See M. Hertsgaard, *Earth Odyssey* (Abacus, London, 1999), p. 307.
[296] World Bank website (www.worldbank.org) accessed 24 February 2004.
[297] World Bank Press Release No. 2001/002/LAC.

agreed to make the Initiative broader, deeper and faster by increasing the number of eligible countries, raising the amount of debt relief each eligible country will receive, and speeding up its delivery. The enhanced Initiative aims to reduce the net present value (NPV) of debt at the decision point to a maximum of 150 per cent of exports and 250 per cent of government revenue, and will be provided on top of traditional debt relief mechanisms (Paris Club debt rescheduling on Naples terms, involving 67 per cent debt reduction in NPV terms and at least comparable action by other bilateral creditors).

Eligible countries will qualify for debt relief in two stages. In the first stage, the debtor country will need to demonstrate the capacity to use prudently the assistance granted by establishing a satisfactory track record, normally of three years, under IMF- and IDA-supported programs. In the second stage, after reaching the decision point under the Initiative, the country will implement a full-fledged poverty reduction strategy, which has been prepared with broad participation of civil society, and an agreed set of measures aimed at enhancing economic growth. During this stage, the IMF and IDA grant interim relief, provided that the country stays on track with its IMF- and IDA-supported program. In addition, Paris Club creditors, and possibly others, are expected to grant debt relief on highly concessional terms. At the end of the second stage, when the floating completion point has been reached, the IMF and IDA will provide the remainder of the committed debt relief, while Paris Club creditors will enter into a highly concessional stock-of-debt reduction operation with the country involved. Other multilateral and bilateral creditors will need to contribute to the debt relief on comparable terms.

Thirty-six countries are expected to qualify for assistance under the enhanced HIPC Initiative, of which 29 are sub-Saharan African countries. By the end of July, 16 countries will have been reviewed under the enhanced framework, for packages amounting to some $25 billion in debt service relief over time. Eight countries have already reached their decision point under the enhanced framework (Honduras joins Bolivia, Burkina Faso, Mauritania, Mozambique, Senegal, Tanzania and Uganda), with total committed assistance estimated at roughly US$15 billion, representing an average NPV stock-of-debt reduction of about 45 per cent on top of traditional debt relief mechanisms. In addition, in the coming days Benin is expected to qualify for assistance under the enhanced HIPC framework.[298]

The plan agreed for Honduras was to save Honduras US$900 million in debt service. At the end of 1999, Honduras' total external public debt was 'about US$3.1 billion . . . This equalled about 135% of exports and more than 300% of the country's central government revenue.' The relief was to be spread over twenty years. The eligibility for relief is 'a recognition by the international community of the country's progress in implementing reforms in macroeconomic, structural and social policies. The 25% debt service reduction enabled by the framework will help sustain this progress through the next decade'.[299]

---

[298] *Ibid.*   [299] Both quotes from *ibid.*

The centrepiece of the Poverty Reduction Strategy is the PRSP which was prepared in August 2001 and gained the approval of the Bank and IMF. It has a number of striking features:

- it shows clear evidence of wide participation by civil society in Honduras;
- it delivers a detailed picture of poverty in the country;
- it sets up clear strategies to reduce poverty and measurable targets to be reached;
- it has a clear budget and institutional framework for delivery of the strategies;
- sources of funding are identified.

Nevertheless, as we shall see, the plan is not succeeding. Some more detail on the characteristics identified above: the participation in the formulation of the plan is impressive, involving the direct participation of 3,500 representatives of Honduran civil society[300] between January 2000 and May 2001. A wide range of organisations were represented and 'many participants brought with them mandates based on grassroots consultations carried out by their organisations with their members'.[301] Groups represented included 'small farmers, blue-collar workers, market and ambulatory salespeople, teachers, media representatives, businessmen and women, farmers and ranchers, ethnic groups and women's organisations' as well as representatives of professional and employers' associations, community organisations, service clubs, co-operatives, churches, NGOs and universities.[302] These groups were joined by political representatives and members of the international community. The suggestions and recommendations were judged according to compliance with six criteria. They must:

- have a clear focus or impact on the poor population;
- promote a more equitable access to basic public services;
- strengthen or clarify policy measures, programmes and projects;
- develop important activities not included in previous versions;
- strengthen non-economic dimensions related to the wellbeing of the population;
- demonstrate that the activities suggested have a favourable cost-benefit relationship.[303]

With these criteria in mind the authors sought to reach the 'broadest possible accord'.[304]

---

[300] Honduras PRSP (www.worldbank.org).
[301] *Ibid.*, p. 6.   [302] *Ibid.*, p. 4.   [303] *Ibid.*, p. 5.   [304] *Ibid.*, p. 5.

The PRSP contains a forty-two page sophisticated analysis of poverty in Honduras. The multidimensional nature of poverty is recognised. 'Poverty is an economic and social condition with multiple causes and expressions. Although the most common and simplest way to present it is as the lack of sufficient income to reach a certain minimum standard of living, the concept of poverty also includes the degree to which a series of basic human needs are met.'[305] The simple 'Poverty Line' methodology showed 66 per cent of households in poverty, and 49 per cent in extreme poverty, 47 per cent suffering at least one unsatisfied basic need. 40.6 per cent of the total school population were undernourished, 14 per cent severely so. Basic needs were:

- water: access to water within the property (urban) or from a piped system or well (rural);
- hygiene: have a toilet other than a simple pit latrine (urban); have at least a simple pit latrine (rural);
- primary education: children of primary school age enrolled in school;
- subsistence capacity: head of family has more than three years primary education and is employed; if not, at least one employed person for each three members of the household;
- crowded quarters: no more than three persons per room (excluding bathrooms);
- housing status: not improvised or built from scrap materials and does not have an earth floor (urban); not improvised or built from scrap materials (rural).[306]

The incidence of poverty is considered in the context of difference between urban and rural regional differences, by municipality, by ethnic and gender group, by age group and in respect of disabilities. Housing, employment and income are analysed together with the devastating effect of Hurricane Mitch on poverty in 1999. Exchange rate liberalisation, liberalisation of domestic trade, financial sector liberalisation and trade liberalisation were all found to have variable effects on poverty, benefiting some groups while disadvantaging others, although the most positive effect on poverty was found to have come from trade liberalisation, although much of this was due to the maquila assembly operations in San Pedro Sula, operations which have attracted criticism for the treatment of workers. Between 12 and 15 per cent of children between 10–14 are employed.

The strategy for poverty reduction and targets to be reached are also clearly addressed. The targets are:

---

[305] *Ibid.*, p. 9.   [306] *Ibid.*, p. 10.

- reduce by 24 per cent the incidence of poverty and extreme poverty;
- double the net pre-school educational coverage for five-year-old children;
- achieve 95 per cent net coverage in access to the first two cycles of basic education;
- achieve 70 per cent net coverage in the third cycle (seventh to ninth grades) of basic education;
- achieve completion of secondary education by 50 per cent of new entrants to the labour force;
- reduce infant mortality rates by half;
- decrease malnutrition in children under five to not more than 20 per cent;
- reduce maternal mortality rates by half, from 147 to 73 per 100,000 live births;
- achieve 95 per cent access to potable water and sanitation;
- achieve parity and raise by 20 per cent the Human Development Index related to gender;
- implement a strategy for sustainable development.

While, at first reading, these sound like ambitious goals, the PRSP still envisaged 42 per cent of households living below the poverty line in 2015.

The macroeconomic framework which is to achieve these targets is the subject of the Poverty Reduction and Growth Facility (PRGF), the IMF equivalent of the PRSP. As could be expected, this requires a low fiscal deficit, the maintenance of international monetary reserves of approximately four months of imports, firm control over fiscal expenditures and further liberalisation of trade, some privatisation measures as well as the introduction of legal reform and anti-corruption laws. The plan calls specifically for the facilitation of the development of agro-business, 'including developing incentives for restructuring production, based on market forces and consistent with WTO regulations'.[307]

The detailed costing of the strategy leads to the conclusion that the two plans leave 'a resource gap that will have to be closed with additional funding or postpone and reduce the targets'.[308] Sadly, the First Progress Report on the PRSP shows that 'poverty reduction has not yet accelerated decisively'.[309] To a considerable extent this was due to the projection that 35 per cent of the funding for the programme was to come from debt relief which was not forthcoming, since the debt relief by both the World Bank and the IMF was conditional on maintaining the economic

---

[307] *Ibid.*, p. 67.   [308] *Ibid.*
[309] *Honduras Poverty Reduction Strategy First Progress Report* (December 2003), para. 8 (www.worldbank.org).

discipline imposed by the PRGF, which was not achieved – the PRGF consequently had to be renegotiated.

The fiscal problems that arose when the PRGF Agreement with the IMF was suspended caused significant delays in the Culmination Point of the HIPC, which was originally anticipated for 2002 and now for June 2004. This situation, combined with the normal precepts of responsible fiscal management, made it imperative to postpone the new programs financed with HIPC funds.[310]

Only 58.5 per cent (2001) and 34 per cent (2002) of the projected HIPC funds were forthcoming. Growth stalled, due in part to the drop in coffee prices worldwide, and the end result was that only about 50 per cent of the funding was available for any of the strategies to be implemented. In 2002, thirteen of the PRSP's twenty impact indicators were not met: GDP growth, per capita growth, pre-basic education coverage, water coverage, sanitation coverage, the two gender indices and the three environmental goals. It is probable that the goals for infant and under-five mortality were not met.[311] While there is a new Country Assistance Strategy agreed with the World Bank (24 June 2003) to provide a US$296 million loan interest free, the goals of the PRSP have had to be redefined in a less ambiguous way and children will continue to die unnecessarily.

[310] *Ibid.*, para. 93, p. 20.   [311] *Ibid.*, p. 14.

4   Relationship between companies and human rights law

This section of the book turns from looking at the problems within the international trading system to considering solutions which have been suggested. One growing debate suggests that human rights law might provide some control over the power wielded by companies and provide some answers to the abuses of human rights which occur within the trading system, such as poor labour standards.[1] This has triggered a debate in which companies seek to claim rights as well as be subjected to duties to respect rights. This chapter considers the possibility of using human rights law to control companies, either by imposing direct duties on them or by subjecting them to control via states' obligations or obligations on the international financial institutions (IFIs). It also looks at the complexities of claims to rights by companies.

There are a number of significant problems in choosing human rights law to impact on companies. They are:

- the civil and political rights versus economic and social rights controversy;
- reaching a proper understanding of 'rights';
- the international legal systems and international institutions which are heavily state-orientated; and consequently
- the ways in which corporations can (or cannot) be seen as duty holders and as human rights violators;
- direct and indirect routes to the imposition of human rights obligations on companies;
- the possibility of human rights standards being inserted into the decision-making of the IFIs and the IMF;
- can companies claim rights?

---

[1] For an excellent discussion of these issues see S. Bottomley and D. Kinley (eds.), *Commercial Law and Human Rights* (Dartmouth, Aldershot, 2002). Unfortunately, I acquired a copy of this work too late to incorporate references in the text, it is, however, highly recommended reading. See, e.g., J. Woodroffe, 'Regulating Multinational Corporations in a World of Nation States' in M. Addo (ed.), *Human Rights Standards and the Responsibility of Transnational Corporations* (Kluwer, The Hague, 1999); S. Skolgy and M. Gibney, 'Transnational Human Rights Obligations' (2002) *Human Rights Quarterly* 781.

Perhaps the most obvious difficulty is that companies have no place in international law, including international human rights law, as the primacy of nation states is so important. Some argue that companies should be made accountable as players on the international stage[2] since international law may grant personality to organisations other than states. The attributes of personality are then open for discussion: would companies have rights as well as duties? Could either be enforced and how? Would the grant of rights outweigh the imposition of duties? What would happen to the responsibility of states within which corporations operate? Given the hidden power of corporations, is it at all likely that they wish to have a formal voice? The complexity of the argument as to whether companies should be able to claim human rights is considered in a detailed study of cases in which the right not to self-incriminate has been considered by various courts in a corporate context.

The importance of the primacy of the nation state both in international human rights law and in the context of the membership of the IMF, World Bank and WTO cannot be underestimated. It means that there is a further strand to the 'invisibility' of companies which was discussed in chapter 2 in that, although they may provide the impetus behind decisions made within the international institutions, they are, for the most part, the invisible power behind the negotiators. The imposition of human rights duties on states as the principal if not the sole duty holder also carries with it the major possibility of engendering an 'explanatory nationalism' cast of mind, and blaming the poor states and their citizens for the poor human rights record, which has causes wider than such a narrow vision would allow. The direct route to imposing obligations on companies can be supplemented by arguing that a state has a duty to control the operations of the companies operating within their jurisdictions and/or subsidiaries operating abroad over which a resident company exercises control. This argument is based on a state's responsibility to *protect* human rights, i.e. prevent violations of rights by private individuals. In respect to the Covenant on Economic, Social and Cultural Rights, the duty of international co-operation can be seen as spelling out the obligation to ensure no violations by companies abroad which are controlled by resident parents. The relationship between states and companies is of particular importance as the international human rights structures normally focus solely on the accountability of nation states, mostly to their citizens. To argue that private bodies may be bound by responsibilities imposed by international or human rights law is a recent departure from that original framework, opening up the question: in what way do

[2] See n. 1.

corporations violate human rights? The question is, of course, complicated by the perception that states are the primary obligation holders for
human rights responsibilities so that it can be argued:

- that companies can never violate human rights as they are not obligation
  holders;
- that violations can only occur if a company is conspiring/aiding/inciting
  a state and/or an IFI to commit human rights violations;
- that, even if it were possible to impose human rights obligations in the
  case of complicity etc., only violations of civil and political rights are
  justiciable;
- that violations of economic, social and cultural rights are committed,
  for example, by mass displacements of people to build large projects
  (e.g. dams) either by companies as obligation holders or by companies
  in association with IFIs or states or by violations of rights to property
  communally held in items over which intellectual property rights are
  claimed by multinational enterprises (MNEs);
- that the operations of companies, because of their profit maximisation
  aim and their tendency to export profit from developing countries to the
  rich world affect economic, social and cultural rights by the systematic
  impoverishment of poor countries and that this should be acknowl-
  edged by the international human rights system.

Primacy of nation states also means that companies have no presence
in the decision-making of the IFIs or the WTO. Other routes to indirect
control of companies are to argue that these organisations have human
rights obligations or that states when they vote in their capacity as members of those organisations cannot 'leave their human rights obligations
at the door' and vote for activities that will lead to human rights violations, including those by companies, and that systems to monitor the
delivery of decisions made at this level should be sufficiently robust to call
attention to any such violations. Here again, the duty of international co-
operation could be prayed in aid. Some argue that this latter route would
lead to human rights clauses being embedded in trade treaties and in the
jurisprudence of the WTO. There have even been arguments that WTO
jurisprudence should contain a 'right to trade'. The issue of whether such
incorporation of rights would be beneficial is examined in the last part of
this chapter.

The question of the potential role of human rights law and standards is
thus a complex one, involving the investigation of both direct and indirect
routes to holding companies to account.

Civil and political rights and economic, social and cultural rights

This debate continues to create a significant divide within the human rights community and is important for defining the place of companies within the trading system since a number of the rights which they might be considered to have violated are economic, social and cultural rights, not least by the net export of capital from the poorer countries to the rich. The championing of privatisation, liberalisation and foreign direct investment by the Washington consensus, together with plans for large infrastructure improvements in poor countries, have favoured large companies. The authors of those plans open up the possibility that human rights abuses violations by those benefactors will occur (if indeed companies can violate human rights, see below) and monitoring the results of their interventions should not be too much to ask. The lowly status still accorded to economic, social and cultural rights tends to affect the debate as to the nature of corporate violations. There are numerous detailed considerations of the issue which are not duplicated here. The following brief summary appeared first in *The Governance of Corporate Groups*. Economic, social and cultural rights are indisputably the 'junior branch' of human rights law.[3] The disparity was made clear by the UN Committee on Economic, Social and Cultural Rights in its statement to the Vienna World Conference of 1993:

The shocking reality . . . is that states and the international community as a whole continue to tolerate all too often breaches of economic, social and cultural rights which, if they occurred in relation to civil and political rights, would provoke expressions of horror and outrage and would lead to concerted calls for immediate remedial action. In effect, despite the rhetoric, violations of civil and political rights continue to be treated as though they were far more serious, and more patently intolerable, than massive and direct denials of economic, social and cultural rights.[4]

While significant progress has been made in freeing individuals from state oppression, the concentration of the human rights community on civil and political rights in a world where hundreds of thousands of children die of preventable diseases may itself be seen as a moral deflection device, especially where it is coupled with explanatory nationalism.

---

[3] See A. Eide, C. Krause and A. Rosas (eds), *Economic Social and Cultural Rights* (2nd edn., Martinus Nijhoff, Dordrecht, 2001), p. 15.
[4] UN Doc. E/C.12/1992/2,82. See D. Beetham, 'What Future for Economic and Social Rights?' (1995) *Political Studies Association* 43.

Alston[5] has shown that the rejection by the American Reagan administration of the concept of social, economic and cultural rights as having
the status of rights at all was influenced by a number of factors. One
was the influential arguments of Secretary of State Abrams,[6] invoking
the distinction between public rights (i.e. civil and political rights) and
social, economic and cultural rights which, he argued, were 'left in the private sphere'. This public/private dichotomy has significant impact on the
thinking about the nature and place of companies and is closely linked to
the individualism which Alston identifies as part of the American psyche:
this country has chosen individualism as a central value. It has sustained
its complex multicultural and multireligious diversity, and avoided con-
frontations by separating church from state and keeping national government out of the family.[7]

As we shall see, adherence to this concept of private individualism has
heavily influenced company law jurisprudence, giving great credence to
legal and economic contractualists.

The political divide

Partly because of the perception of economic, social and cultural rights
as impinging on private freedoms, they became pilloried in the USA as
an attempt to introduce 'uneconomic, socialist and collective rights',[8]
which in turn led to the perception of the introduction of such rights as
an issue of a 'hidden agenda' to destroy capitalism: 'To put it bluntly: the
effect of the hidden agenda was to help delegitimise the market economy
(capitalism) that is an indispensable precondition of a traditional liberal
(bourgeois) society.'[9]

Thus grew a perception of Western thought prioritising political rights
set against Soviet/Third World thought prioritising social, economic
and cultural rights. That this was a false perception is explained by
Alston, citing the adherence of Western governments to the Covenant

---

[5] P. Alston, 'US Ratification of the Covenant on Economic, Social and Cultural Rights:
The Need for an Entirely New Strategy' (1990) 84 *Am. J International Law* 365.

[6] Review of State Department Country Reports on Human Rights Practices for 1981,
Hearing before the Subcommittee on Human Rights and International Organisations of
the House Committee on Foreign Affairs, 97th Congress, 2d Sess 7 (1982).

[7] E. Erikson and K. Fritzell, 'The Effects of the Social Welfare System on the Well-being of
Children and the Elderly' in A. Palmer, T. Smeeding and E. Torrey (eds), *The Vulnerable*
(University of Chicago Press, 1988); cited in Alston, 'US Ratification', p. 384.

[8] Alston,'US Ratification', p. 366.

[9] Irving Kristol, 'Human Rights: the Hidden Agenda' (1986/7) *National Interest* (winter)
3; and Alston, 'US Ratification', p. 391.

on Economic, Social and Cultural Rights, and identifying the problem as American rather than Western.[10]

The original division between civil and political rights on the one hand and economic, social and cultural rights on the other stemmed from 'a controversial and contested'[11] decision of the UN General Assembly in 1951 which was based on the underlying assumption that civil and political rights were absolute, immediate and justiciable, whereas economic, social and cultural rights were programmatic and would be costly to implement. Even where the rights are formulated as creating legally binding obligations on contracting states, individuals have no right of enforcement: 'traditionally, whereas civil and political rights were seen as justiciable, i.e. rights which could be invoked by the individual against the public authorities, economic and social rights were generally regarded as "programmatic".'[12] While one must accept[13] that this 'neat distinction' is now too simplistic,[14] it is nevertheless true that the rights built into economic, social and cultural treaties are less well known generally and less easy to enforce. For example, labour rights are 'quite far from reaching a reasonable degree of their juridization'.[15]

From the perspective of the detractors of economic, social and cultural rights, their nature has provided two apparently contradictory arguments. On the one hand, the rights would be too costly and burdensome to implement; on the other, their vague nature and lack of exact standards means they are not rights at all, mere ephemera. Thus, on the one hand, Alston cites J.P. Anderegg[16] as arguing that acceptance of the Covenant would 'bring with it an enormous and incalculable commitment to an expanding, centralised welfare state with reduced liberties for the individual'; and on the other hand, exhorting those seeking to persuade the American administration towards ratification not to pursue the line that 'the Covenant could convincingly be portrayed as being devoid of any substantive practical or legal significance. Metaphorically speaking, it could be characterized as being the ultimate toothless tiger.'[17]

---

[10] Alston, 'US Ratification', p. 387.
[11] Eide, Krause and Rosas, *Economic Social and Cultural Rights*, p. 22.
[12] L. Betten and N. Grief, *EU Law and Human Rights* (Longman, 1998), p. 10.
[13] As do Betten and Grief, *ibid.*.
[14] See, e.g., Michael K. Addo, 'Justiciability Re-examined' in R. Beddard and D. Hill (eds), *Economic Social and Cultural Rights: Progress and Achievements* (Macmillan, 1992), pointing out that justiciability may be achieved through 'inquisitorial justiciability' using the investigative processes built into many of these provisions; and see Eide, Krause and Rosas, *Economic Social and Cultural Rights*, chs. 1, 2 and 3.
[15] K. Drzewicki, 'The Right to Work and Rights at Work' in Eide, Krause and Rosas, *Economic Social and Cultural Rights*, p. 172.
[16] Adjunct Professor, Columbia Law School, in hearings before the Senate Committee on Foreign Relations, 1979.
[17] Alston, 'US Ratification', p. 366.

Positive and negative enforcement

The distinction between civil and political rights on the one hand and economic, social and cultural rights on the other has often been seen to lie in the distinction between positive and negative categories of rights. This distinction has again led to two arguments against the adoption of the economic, social and cultural category. Enforcement of positive obligations to create a programme of reform is much more difficult than enforcement of an individual right to non-interference.[18] This difficulty has fuelled concerns that acknowledging the existence of social, cultural and economic rights will in some way dilute civil and political rights: 'Without so labelling them Abrams used the distinction between positive and negative categories of rights and concluded that the rights that no government can violate [i.e., civil and political rights] should not be watered down to the status of rights that governments should do their best to secure [i.e. economic, social and cultural rights].'[19] Arguing that these assumptions were simplistic and have now been shown to be ill-founded, Eide points out that: 'Some civil rights require state obligations at all levels – also the obligation to provide direct assistance, when there is a need for it. Economic and social rights, on the other hand, can in many cases best be safeguarded through non-interference by the State with the freedom and use of resources possessed by the individuals.'

Because of the understanding of civil and political rights as 'more important' than economic, social and cultural rights, studies of the possible violations by companies have tended to focus on violations of these rights – complicity in violence by the state is an example. The role of companies and institutions in creating destitution is less studied as a human rights issue.

Understanding of 'rights'

The human rights systems are complex and operate at various levels and across different disciplines. Here, we are concerned with human rights law but a question must first be raised as to whether human rights should be embedded in a 'legal' framework at all, since legal thinking tends to make for a certain rigidity. Pogge's understanding of human rights as compelling the construction of institutions to deliver rights[20] is clearly at odds with 'rights' as understood in a legal context. Where *legal* 'rights' exist it is difficult to justify violations of those rights on the basis of any concept

---

[18] For a consideration of this issue in the field of criminal sanctions, see J. Dine, *Criminal Law in the Company Context* (Dartmouth, 1995).
[19] Alston, 'US Ratification', p. 373.   [20] See chapter 2.

of the 'greater good' or on an intergenerational basis, i.e. that violations now are justified for the good of later generations. With a proliferation of rights, some of which must sometimes be in conflict, a complex systems of trade-offs is inevitable and some question whether this is a more suitable area for political negotiation rather than a 'legal' system. It is also arguable that the lack of enforcement mechanisms at the international level means that international human rights law is less a legal system than a formalised political negotiation. This cannot be argued at the domestic level where an increasing number of countries have adopted human rights norms into domestic law and are generating a significant body of jurisprudence over its interpretation.

There are also difficulties in understanding the concepts inherent in 'rights'. The World Bank claims that it is promoting rights by encouraging economic development. However, this misses the 'rights' point that enjoying a right to something implies a reasonable guarantee that the substance of the right should be available. An example is that food should not just be available but that the obligation holder should as far as possible guarantee the availability of food.[21] The differences in the international human rights community between those whose primary concern is the protection of civil and political rights and those who are principally concerned with economic, social and cultural rights further complicates the debate. The latter raise questions which tend to go beyond the model of nation state responsibility for wrongs such as torture or corruption which oppress their citizens and point to wider causes of poverty, including not only governmental actions but the way in which the international community has long exploited differences in climate, resources, political and economic power to structure a legal international system which systematically disadvantages some states. Others argue that such concerns excuse or justify corrupt or violent regimes, an argument that does not perhaps take account of the myriad of concurrent causes which can lead to human disasters.

Are states the only players on the international law field?

The status of MNEs in the international arena and their rights and responsibilities under international law are a subject of considerable concern. The structure of international law relies on nation states as key players. Indeed, it was thought that they were the sole subjects. 'Since the law of nations is based on the common consent of individual States,

[21] S. Anderson and J. Cavanaugh, *The Rise of Global Corporate Power* (Institute for Policy Studies, Washington DC, 1996).

and not individual Human beings, States solely and exclusively are subjects of international law'[22] but they are no longer the sole players: 'Recognised international organisations can make international agreements with other international organisations and individual countries.'[23] Corporations now have access to international tribunals such as the International Center for the Settlement of Investment Disputes (ICSID)[24] so that 'no theoretical obstacle . . . prevents commercial enterprises from 'participating in international law'.[25] However, it is also clear that states are still pre-eminent players. Two key factors are prominent: consent and equality. Oppenheim notes that *consent* is the basis of international law, while the United Nations Charter states that the United Nations is 'based on the principle of the sovereign equality of all its members'.[26] French notes that:

The notion of sovereignty arose with the ascendancy of the independent nation state. As European countries began to shake off the influence of the Papacy, the concept of sovereignty provided those in authority with a dual justification for their position. Not only did sovereignty mean that a state was independent from the influence of other states (and arguably, to a lesser extent, the Church), but it also meant that the government-as-state had the right to impose its will on those who resided within its territory.[27]

Thus, the independence and equality of states arose as a philosophy of equality of value in reaction to the claims of powerful bodies of the right to interfere with autonomy. The trappings of sovereignty in international law include 'States are judicially equal' and that '[n]o State or group of States has the right to intervene, directly or indirectly, for any reason whatever, in the internal or external affairs of any other State'.[28] Further, 'a State

[22] L. Oppenheim, *International Law: A Treatise* (2nd edn, 1912), p. 19.
[23] International Council on Human Rights, 'Beyond Voluntarism' (www.internationalcouncil.org) and see Rosalyn Higgins, *The Development of International Law Through the Political Organs of the United Nations* (Oxford University Press, London, 1963).
[24] The Washington Convention on the Settlement of Investment Disputes between States and Nationals of Other States was adopted by resolution of the Executive Directors of the World Bank on 18 March 1965.
[25] International Council on Human Rights, 'Beyond Voluntarism', p. 58, and see W. Friedmann, *Law in a Changing Society* (2nd edn, Penguin Books, London, 1971), p. 6: 'Private corporations must now be regarded as – in a limited but important sense – participants in the development of public international law'; see also L. Henkin, *International Law: Policies and Values* (Martinus Nijhoff, Dordrecht, 1995); Rosalyn Higgins, *Problems and Process: International Law and How We Use It* (Clarendon Press, Oxford, 1994), p. 49.
[26] Article 2.1.
[27] D. French, 'Reappraising Sovereignty in Light of Global Environmental Concerns' (2001) *Legal Studies* 376 at 378, citing R. Anand, *Confrontation or Co-operation? International Law and Developing Countries* (Martinus Nijhoff, Dordrecht, 1987).
[28] UN General Assembly, 1970 Declaration on Principles of International Law concerning Friendly Relations and Co-operation among States, UNGA Res. 2625 (XXV)(1970) Annex, see French, 'Reappraising Sovereignty'.

has a right to determine its own political, social, economic and cultural systems'. This culture of equality, autonomy and non-interference has had grafted on to it several more sinister attributes. In particular, the concept that a nation state has, as a primary justification for its existence, the duty to protect the perceived interests of its citizens at whatever cost to inhabitants of the rest of the world.[29] The responsibility to its citizens is reinforced by international law in the International Covenant on Civil and Political Rights which in 1966 declared that 'each State party to the present Covenant undertakes to respect and to ensure *to all individuals within its territory and subject to its jurisdiction* the rights recognised in the present Covenant'.[30] As Arambulo points out, the reporting procedure adopted to monitor aspects of human rights is clearly state-based, and focused on the way in which the state reporting treats its own citizens,[31] a situation which may well be satisfactory when rights of citizens against the state are the primary focus for protection. However, it is arguable that, particularly where economic, social and cultural human rights are concerned, the dangers of the doctrines of equality and consent present real problems. As we have seen, powerful corporations, other nation states and the IFIs have disproportionate bargaining power in relation to many developing countries. The attachment of international law to the primacy of nation states has made it extremely difficult to construct accountability mechanisms which might affect companies, and inequalities of bargaining power and expertise have led to 'consent' being given to policies and treaties which have had a detrimental effect on the exercise of the economic, social and cultural rights of individuals, such as the right to food.[32] Hunt points to the distinction between *formal* equality *and structural* equality.[33]

As discussed in chapter 3, the structural adjustment policies imposed by the lending institutions now have a 'softer' face as each of the Least

---

[29] K. Arambulo, *Strengthening the Supervision of the International Covenant on Economic, Social and Cultural Rights: Theoretical and Procedural Aspects* (Intersentia, Antwerpen, 1999), p. 66; P. Brown, 'Food as National Property' in H. Shue (ed), *Food Policy: The Responsibility of the United States in Life and Death Choices* (Free Press, Macmillan, London, 1977).

[30] 1966, Article 2, emphasis added.

[31] Arambulo, *Strengthening the Supervision*, pp. 36–7; First General Comment of the UN Committee on Economic, Social and Cultural Rights, UN Doc. E/1989/22.

[32] This chapter does not attempt to enter the individual rights/collective rights/justiciability debate, taking rather the stance that it is difficult to dispute the concept that the right of an individual to adequate food is a basic right without which other rights cannot be exercised and so one which requires immediate fulfilment. See H. Shue, *Basic Rights* (2nd edn., Princeton University Press, 1996), p. 18, Arambulo, *Strengthening the Supervision*, p. 114. A basic right is 'everyone's minimum reasonable demands on the rest of humanity'.

[33] P. Hunt, *Reclaiming Social Rights* (Dartmouth, Aldershot, 1996).

Developed Countries (LDCs) must prepare a Poverty Reduction Strategy Plan (PRSP) as a condition of increased or continued finance or to bid for forgiveness or rescheduling of debt. However, although these plans are often carefully prepared and considered there is still considerable emphasis on free trade solutions, including open markets and membership of the World Trade Organisation (WTO).[34] As with the Honduran plan considered in chapter 3, they also rely on compliance with a Poverty Reduction Growth Facility (PRGF) which must be approved by the IMF, and any poverty reduction is dependent on debt forgiveness which will be withheld if the terms of the PRGF are not fulfilled. Theoretically, the restructuring and poverty reduction plans are 'state-owned', that is, they have been drawn up by the impoverished state and contain the state's own solutions to their poverty and trading dilemmas. There is little doubt that these plans say what the IFIs and their rich donor nations wish to hear, as the loans are conditional on their approval. In the end, the 'freeing' of markets is a precondition of loans or debt relief and the freedom of markets is an aim pursued through the operation of regional trading areas and the WTO.

With the consequent decline in the reality of the notion of sovereignty, a number of scholars argue that it is time to rethink the fundamentals of international law to reflect the reality of where the power lies. This might well include constructing accountability mechanisms to control corporations, including the imposition of human rights responsibilities on them.[35]

In what ways can companies be subject to human rights responsibilities?

Beyond Voluntarism[36] starts from the question: 'Do private companies have a responsibility to respect human rights?'.[37] The purpose of the report is to examine 'the extent to which international rules for the protection of human rights create binding obligations on companies'.[38] Arguing that voluntarism and market forces are not enough to prevent the growth in human rights abuses perpetrated by companies, the report argues that 'a function of law is to balance power and obligations by establishing enforceable rights and corresponding duties'.[39] The rising power of the

---

[34] For PRSPs generally, see the World Bank website (www.worldbank.org); for a detailed consideration of a PRSP see chapter 3.
[35] See citations in n. 1.
[36] International Council on Human Rights Policy, 2002 (www.international-council.org).
[37] International Council on Human Rights, 'Beyond Voluntarism', Summary, p. 1.
[38] *Ibid.*, p. 2.   [39] *Ibid.*, p. 9.

multinational companies makes the exclusive emphasis of the international human rights system on state behaviour appear too narrow in its focus. And the report makes the point that many transnational corporations (TNCs) are out of control, in the sense that individual states are unable to regulate them effectively. Consequently, international legal solutions are required. The report contains an innovative analysis of the relationship between international human rights law, states and companies on which the following draws extensively.

Direct and indirect routes to the imposition of human rights obligations

Direct

Arguing from the limited instances where 'participation' of companies in the international arena already exists, and the grant of certain rights to companies by the ECHR,[40] the International Council conclude that while it is early days, 'one can see a conscious and gradual evolution of international law towards clear, binding norms that are directly applicable to companies'. One may ask if this assessment does not underestimate the power of companies to resist any such development. Arguing from the perspective of the gradual expansion of the grant of international legal personality, Nicola Jagers reaches a conclusion similar to that of the International Council.[41] Citing the International Court of Justice in *Reparations for Injuries Suffered in the Service of the United Nations*[42] to the effect that '[t]he subjects of law in any legal system are not necessarily identical in their nature or in the extent of their rights, and the nature depends on the needs of the community',[43] she concludes that, while there has been an emphasis on the rights of companies in international law (for example to be compensated for expropriation), too little concern has been paid to control over TNCs and the international community now requires this development. Although the International Council's report musters some evidence of direct applicability, it is clear that the development of this jurisprudence is very much in its infancy and the use of the

---

[40] For example, protection under Article 10 of the ECHR (freedom of expression): *Autronic AG v. Switzerland* (1990) EHRR 485.

[41] N. Jagers, 'The Legal Status of Multinational Corporations under International Law' in M. Addo (ed.), *Human Rights Standards and the Responsibility of Transnational Corporations* (Kluwer, 1999).

[42] [1949] ICJ Rep. 174.

[43] *Ibid.*, although later in the piece she follows Higgins in rejecting international personality and subjects and objects of international law as 'an intellectual prison': Higgins, *Problems and Process*, pp. 49–50.

OECD Guidelines for Multinational Companies is less than a convincing support for the concept. There is, of course, a further significant problem with the international human rights framework and that is that there are no enforcement mechanisms.

Indirect responsibility

However, the direct involvement and imposition of legal responsibility on MNEs at the international level remains largely a theoretical debate. What is of immediate interest is the possibility of indirect legal accountability of corporations for abuses of international norms via the responsibility of nation states under international law, in particular international human rights law.[44] States have the obligation to *respect, fulfil and protect*[45] human rights of individuals. The obligation to 'protect' requires a state to 'protect people by stopping private actors from abusing rights'. It is at this level of indirect enforcement that codes of practice such as those considered in chapter 5 may have some legal effects. The grave difficulty in giving substance to any possible effects is to merge the understanding of international lawyers of states' obligations with the detailed substantive knowledge of corporate laws and regulation which is necessary in order to create effective national enforcement mechanisms at national level. The state's duty to *protect* human rights could be an effective vehicle for arguing that a number of human rights treaties specifically require states to regulate private actors to prevent violations of rights protected by the treaties and that these rights have, on occasion, been upheld in regional human rights courts, including the European Court of Human Rights (ECtHR). For example[46], in *Z and others* v. *United Kingdom*,[47] the ECtHR 'concluded that authorities in the United Kingdom had violated the right of four children not to be ill-treated when it failed to take reasonable steps to prevent them being horrifically abused over a four-year period by their parents'. The International Council ventures rather tentatively a question: 'If international law requires that states prohibit certain conduct by private actors, is that conduct itself a violation?'.[48] This would be a step too far for many human rights lawyers and would make the companies direct violators. The growing recognition that the 'private' sector is of increasing importance because of the privatisation of services, particularly essential utilities, is very welcome.

---

[44] And see the discussion on the duty of international co-operation, chapter 6.
[45] International Council on Human Rights, 'Beyond Voluntarism', para. 52.
[46] *Ibid.*, p. 50.   [47] 10 May 2001.
[48] International Council on Human Rights, 'Beyond Voluntarism', p. 51.

Indirect liability of companies would be imposed by holding states responsible for the behaviour of corporations. This requires states to ensure that proper national laws are in place to control corporations, in this way states fulfil their duty to protect human rights. This indirect obligation must be enforced by the monitoring of national laws in two ways:

- By ensuring that rights enshrined in international treaty obligations are present in national law together with a functioning legal system to enforce them. This can be illustrated by *Z and others* v. *United Kingdom* (above n. 47) and *X and Y* v. *The Netherlands*.[49] In that case, a sixteen-year-old mentally handicapped girl was sexually abused by the son-in-law of the director of a private nursing home situated in the Netherlands. The Dutch criminal law did not extend to cover the case. The ECtHR found that the Dutch government had violated the girl's right to privacy by not ensuring that a criminal prosecution could be brought.
- By ensuring that the legal system is indeed functioning, i.e. that it does not contain loopholes which corporations can exploit to behave in a way which violates human rights. This approach requires an examination of the corporate law mechanisms existing in national laws. The target is to ensure that states do not permit or encourage the violation of rights by private actors, acting directly or via control of other corporations.

This latter point would not be served by focusing simply on the translation into national law of specified rights but through an understanding of the corporate mechanisms that enable companies and multinationals in particular to evade obligations by utilising national law to insist on their technical separation from entities which they control. There are significant difficulties in enforcing corporate obligations in poor host states and a more profitable route may be to explore the possibility of forcing rich host nations to improve their record on 'lifting the veil' so that parent companies would become liable for the way in which they exercise control over their foreign subsidiaries.

Thus, although the international legal structures for direct accountability are at an early stage of development, the content of the duties which may apply directly to companies or, more likely, should be imposed by nation states may give us valuable clues as to the emerging norms on which any international regulatory theory could be based. In pointing out the value of the human rights framework, the International Council

---

[49] 91 ECHR Series A (1985), para. 23.

point out that it provides 'a common and universal standard'.[50] However, this claim must be met with a degree of scepticism as there is certainly a real possibility that human rights norms could be used as an instrument of oppression, not least when coupled with trading agreements (see below).

In the human rights context, and, indeed, in the context of corporate social responsibility, by far the most attention has been paid to the manifest abuses which impact directly on individuals. Thus, the International Council include in their text[51] a survey of human rights guarantees which may impact on the way in which businesses conduct themselves. These possible impacts are extremely important and will be examined here. However, hidden beneath these obvious impacts is a more fundamental problem relating to the way in which groups of companies operate. Their structure and operation is such that the effect of their trading is to export money from the poor to the rich. Of course, impact on individual employees or citizens is of vital importance, but this export of resources is one of the root causes of the impoverishment of many. This effect must also be examined to see if international human rights law has anything to provide possible redress.

Human rights and direct impacts

According to the International Council the following are among the rights which are likely to be directly violated by companies:

- non-discrimination;
- women's rights;
- life, liberty and physical integrity of the person;
- civic freedoms;
- employees' rights;
- child labour;
- slavery, forced and bonded labour;
- right to food, health, education and housing;
- environmental rights[52] (see chapter 5).

The following section considers a number of these impacts, in particular with reference to the concerns of international trade and the consequences of using international trade as a possible enforcement mechanism for human rights abuses.

---

[50] International Council on Human Rights, 'Beyond Voluntarism', p. 15.
[51] *Ibid.*, p. 23 *et seq.*   [52] *Ibid.*, pp. 23–43.

Non-discrimination and women's rights

Discrimination is prohibited by the Universal Declaration of Human Rights[53] (UDHR) and the International Covenant on Civil and Political Rights (ICCPR)[54] on the grounds of 'race, colour, sex, language, religion, political or other opinion, national or social origin, property, birth or other status'. The list of prohibited grounds is not closed, recent treaties include an expanded list including marital status, nationality, ethnic origin and economic position.[55] Specifically in the case of gender equality, human rights law in the form of the Convention on the Elimination of All Forms of Discrimination Against Women 1979 (CEDAW), the International Covenant on Economic, Social and Cultural Rights (ICESCR)[56] and numerous International Labour Organisation (ILO) instruments. Many of the obligations imposed by these instruments oblige states to ensure these rights exist by enforcing them against private employers.[57] It would seem, then, that non-discrimination is a prime candidate for inclusion in an international concession theory. Companies are clearly able to have a significant impact on implementing this aspect of human rights law. Similarly, non-discrimination comes high in the list when corporate social responsibility is under consideration (see chapter 5). The Global Compact, the OECD Guidelines, the European Commission Green Paper, *Promoting a European Framework for Corporate Social Responsibility*[58] and the UK *Corporate and Social Responsibility Report,*[59] all deal with the issue. Non-discrimination must be high on the list of values for an international regulatory theory. It must be emphasised that this does not mean adherence to the view that refusing to trade with countries where there is discrimination affords a way forward. With Blair, we need to be tough not only on discrimination but on the complex, often trade-related causes of discrimination.

Life, liberty and physical integrity of the person

These rights are to be found principally in UDHR[60] and ICCPR as well as more detailed instruments derived from them such as the Convention

---

[53] Article 2.   [54] Articles 22(1) and 26.
[55] See the International Convention on the Rights of All Migrant Workers and Members of Their Families 1990.
[56] Article 7(a)(i), recognising the right of everyone to the enjoyment of just and favourable conditions of work.
[57] See Convention No. 111 concerning Discrimination in respect of Employment and Occupation 1958, and Convention No. 100 concerning Equal Remuneration for Men and Women Workers for Work of Equal Value 1951, examples given in International Council on Human Rights, 'Beyond Voluntarism', p. 25.
[58] Brussels 17 July 2001, COM (2001) Final.
[59] Department of Trade and Industry, 2002.
[60] Prohibition of arbitrary killing: Article 3 UDHR, Article 6 ICCPR.

Against Torture and other Degrading Punishments[61] and various anti-slavery Conventions.[62] These rights are, of course, relevant to employee treatment which is also covered by a raft of other measures (see below).

Apart from employee treatment, violations of these rights may occur where private security forces are engaged either wholly by the company or by the company and the state, or where penal functions such as imprisonment have been privatised.[63]

The International Council argues that such rights may also be violated by:

direct or indirect support for Government policies. For example, a company's presence in conflict areas may aid one side that is committing abuses. Companies engaged in resource extraction (oil, mining etc.) may open up areas and, through the transport links and infrastructure they create, give armed forces access to what were once remote communities. Extracting the resource – where benefits are not shared equally – may itself help to create or perpetuate conflict.[64]

This masterpiece of understatement leaves out the more extreme allegations that companies have been complicit in revolutions and other political violence.[65] *Beyond Voluntarism*[66] also makes a tentative link with these rights and the right to life, although their caution seems unjustified, particularly in the light of significant disasters such as the Bhopal explosion[67] and the vast literature on environmental degradation by companies which now exists.[68]

---

[61] Prohibition against torture and other cruel, inhuman or degrading treatment or punishment: Article 5 UDHR, Article 7 ICCPR and the Convention Against Torture.

[62] Including the Slavery Convention, 25 September 1926, Supplementary Convention on the Abolition of Slavery, the Slave Trade, and Institutions and Practices Similar to Slavery, adopted by a Conference of Plenipotentiaries convened by UNGA Res. 608 (XXI), 30 April 1956, see International Council on Human Rights, 'Beyond Voluntarism', p. 26.

[63] Amnesty International, Human Rights Principles for Companies: An Introductory Checklist, AI Index: ACT 70/01/98, January 1998.

[64] International Council on Human Rights, 'Beyond Voluntarism', p. 26.

[65] G. Palast, 'Pat Robertson, General Pinochet, Pepsi-Cola and the Anti-Christ: Special Investigative Reports' in G. Palast, *The Best Democracy Money can Buy* (Pluto, London 2002).

[66] International Council on Human Rights, 'Beyond Voluntarism', pp. 26–27.

[67] *Ibid.*, p. 13, J. Paust, 'Human Rights Responsibilities of Private Corporations' [2002] *Vanderbilt Journal of Transnational Law* 801.

[68] See also the report of the Sessional Working Group on the working methods and activities of transnational corporations to the Commission on Human Rights E/CN.4sub.2/2002/13, 15 August 2002, which calls for transnationals to ensure equality of opportunity and treatment for the purpose of eliminating discrimination based on race, colour, sex, religion, political opinion, nationality, social origin, social status, indigenous status, disability, age (except for children who may be given greater protection) or other status of the individual unrelated to the individual's ability to perform his or her job.

These rights are so fundamental that they often appear in the corporate social responsibility literature as simply a duty or commitment to human rights. This is true even of the Global Compact which exhorts companies to support and respect the protection of international human rights within their sphere of influence (Principle 1) and make sure their own corporations are not complicit in human rights abuses (Principle 2).

The OECD Guidelines are perhaps stronger, stating that '[enterprises should] respect the human rights of those affected by their activities consistent with the host government's international obligations and commitments'. Although the Guidelines are voluntary and the formulation of the obligations vague, what this makes clear is that companies must look to the international obligations of the state, not to national rules or standards and are not expected to hide behind national laws and practices. This is also consistent with the General Policies set out in the Guidelines that companies should '[r]efrain from seeking or accepting exemptions not contemplated in the statutory or regulatory framework related to environmental, health, safety, labour, taxation, financial incentives, or other issues'. As explained in chapter 5, this contrasts with the OECD Principles of Corporate Governance which rely heavily on national laws.[69]

Employees' rights, child labour, forced and bonded labour

The principal body dealing with these issues is the International Labour Organisation (ILO) which operates on a tripartite structure of representatives of governments, employers and employees. The constitution of the ILO contains a number of principles, such as freedom of association and non-discrimination, but less general standards are enshrined in Conventions and Recommendations. By the ILO Constitution, Article 19(5)(d), a state ratifying a Convention must take 'such action as may be necessary to make effective its provisions'. Recommendations provide soft law guidance on the detailed implementation of Conventions or exhort the adoption of higher standards.[70] Adoption of a new Recommendation or Convention occurs by a two-thirds majority vote in the International Labour Conference. This consists of delegations from member states, each comprising two government representatives, one employers' delegate and one employees' delegate, the latter nominated in agreement with the most representative organisations within the relevant member state. The ILO Constitution provides for jurisdiction over disputes relating to the interpretation of the Constitution or a Convention to belong to the

---

[69] See chapter 5.
[70] See K. Ewing, 'Britain and the ILO' in K. Ewing, C. Gearty and B. Hepple (eds), *Human Rights and Labour Law* (Mansell, London, 1994); S. Deakin and G. Morris, *Labour Law* (3rd edn, Butterworths, London, 2001), p. 115.

International Court of Justice. However, only one dispute has followed this course. It is more common for the standing Secretariat of the ILO, the International Labour Office, to be consulted on the meaning of the Conventions.[71] There is no possibility of enforcement of standards by individuals but states must submit reports at regular intervals (two or four years). The reports are examined by a Committee of Experts and submitted to the Committee on the Application of Conventions and Recommendations. Although these procedures bear some similarity to that under the European Social Charter, the tripartite nature of all the bodies of the ILO makes it a more credible operation. Further, there is a system of complaints which may be instigated by member states against each other, by the Governing Body or by employers' or employees' organisations. At European level, labour issues are covered by the European Social Charter, first signed in 1961 by eleven Council of Europe members. Amending Protocols were adopted in 1988 (First Additional Protocol), 1991 (Amending Protocol) and 1995 (Second Additional Protocol). In 1996, a revised Charter was adopted. The First Additional Protocol first contained the right of workers to information and consultation, and to take part in the determination and improvement of working conditions;[72] and these provisions are now contained in the 1996 consolidation. Because the rights enshrined in the Charter cannot be invoked by individuals in either national or international courts, and owing to the perception of economic, social and cultural rights as second-class rights, the European Social Charter has a much lower profile than the parallel European Convention on Human Rights. Only in exceptional cases can it be invoked by individuals, either in national courts or before an international body.[73] The enforcement mechanism is a rather elaborate reporting procedure set out in Articles 21–29. Reports are submitted by contracting parties on a regular basis, examined by the Committee of Independent Experts, and subsequently by the Committee of Governmental Representatives and the Parliamentary Assembly. The reports and comments of all these bodies come together before the Committee of Ministers, which issues Recommendations to contracting parties which fail to comply with the Charter's requirements. Significant weaknesses in the procedure include the reluctance of the Committee of Ministers to issue Recommendations.[74]

---

[71] Opinions are communicated to the third body of the ILO, the Governing Body, and published in the Official *Bulletin*.

[72] Articles 1–4.

[73] Betten and Grief, *EU Law and Human Rights*, p. 47, cite the right to strike in the Netherlands as a possible exception.

[74] None were issued until 1993. According to Betten and Grief, this is partly because of a reluctance by politicians to criticise each other and partly because of the composition of

The Global Compact has, as Principle 6, the elimination of discrimination in respect of employment and occupation. The OECD Guidelines repeat many of the human rights/ILO norms and provide for
non-discrimination against employees on similar terms as the UDHR
and ICCPR, i.e 'on such grounds as race, colour, sex, religion, political opinion, national extraction or social origin'. There is an exception
intended to excuse positive discrimination – 'unless selectivity concerning employee characteristics furthers established governmental policies
which specifically promote greater equality of employment opportunity' –
and one relating to specific employments – 'or relates to the inherent
requirements of a job'.[75]

Failure to protect workers

Companies are seen as in the private sphere and worker participation
has been pilloried simultaneously as too burdensome and too vague, and
collective rights were seen as a 'hidden agenda' for destroying capitalism.
It is perhaps at this level of the failure to incorporate substantive rights
into the corporate structure that the phobia against economic, social and
cultural rights is most clearly seen in its corporate context. Its expression
has robbed corporate law of a vital element of control over management,
which has systematically been destroyed by the adherence to contractualist theory.

There is a tendency to portray [labour] legislation as conferring 'rights' upon
workers . . . It is probably more accurate to view labour legislation as a form
of legal regulation of business activity which . . . explicitly or implicitly strike
a balance between the interests of management autonomy and the interests of
workers' protection.[76]

The relationship between regulation and the rights of participants in
company operations is explored in chapter 6.

The culmination of the failure of the economic, social and cultural
rights' approach to protect labour rights and the consequent rise of individualist philosophies has left companies with an imbalance. The absence
of shareholder control of management and the absence of employees from

---

the Committee of Ministers which contained representatives from states which had not
ratified the EU Social Charter. Understandably, they were reluctant to criticise those
who were at least on paper committed to the Charter. See *EU Law and Human Rights*,
p. 48.
[75] OECD Guidelines Part IV, para. 1(d). See also C. Chatterjee, 'The OECD Guidelines for Multinational Enterprises: An Analysis' (2002) *Amicus Curiae* 18; J. Karl, 'The
OECD Guidelines for Multinational Enterprises' in M. Addo (ed.), *Human Rights Standards and the Responsibility of Transnational Corporations* (Kluwer, 1999).
[76] Steven D. Anderman, *Management Decisions and Workers' Rights* (3rd edn, Butterworths,
London, 1998), p. 1.

the decision-making structure of the company leaves us with management power but an absence of responsibility. How has this happened? The free market individualist theories have been given too much credence, enough to prevent the introduction of widespread high standards in the workplace, the harmonisation of company law because of fear of 'outsiders' such as employees gaining access to the workplace, and the downgrading of economic, social and cultural rights, including labour rights.

Right to food, education and housing (and other ESC rights)

Principally set out in the ICESCR, these rights are perhaps the most neglected in the companies/human rights debate because the effects that companies and their allies, the IFIs, have is indirect and therefore less easy to put into a legal framework. However, General Comment No. 14 UN Economic and Social Council requires 'the World Bank and the International Monetary Fund [to] pay greater attention to the protection of the right to health in their lending policies, credit agreements and structural adjustment programmes'. As we have seen, these programmes contribute to the ability of companies within the international trading system to export money from the poor world to the rich, thus having a devastating effect on the possibility of delivery of economic, social and cultural rights. We have seen in chapter 2 how poverty has multiple causes but the unfair trading system and the conditions imposed on countries by the IFIs contribute.

Obstacles to enforcement

These are too well known to require a detailed review. Even the attempts to enforce indirect obligations, i.e. bring pressure to bear on states, are hamstrung by the lack of sanctions and the system of state accountability which, in the corporate world, would seek to place obligations on the poorest states to control the richest corporations. The record of success against parent companies is negligible in both the USA (where attempts to use the Alien Tort Claims Act have not yet yielded a final success)[77] and in the United Kingdom, with the landmark case of *Adams* v. *Cape Industries* standing as a huge brick wall to prevent any recovery.[78]

---

[77] Paust, 'Human Rights Responsibilities'; P. Muchlinski, 'Corporations in International Litigation: Problems of Jurisdiction and the United Kingdom Asbestos Case' (2001) ICLQ 1.

[78] For a detailed study see J. Dine, The *Governance of Corporate Groups* (Cambridge University Press, 2000); P. Muchlinski, *Multinational Enterprises and the Law* (Blackwell, Oxford, 1995); International Council on Human Rights, 'Beyond Voluntarism'.

Relationship between human rights norms and the IFIs and WTO

Once again, human rights norms might impact on international organisations either directly or indirectly. Direct impact would mean that the organisations were bound by the norms *as organisations*; indirect impact might happen in two ways, which are not mutually exclusive. The first is that the impact would be felt by the obligations on states to abide by those norms when voting or using a voice within the organisation.[79] Hunt takes this line, explaining the approach of the UN Committee on Economic, Social and Cultural Rights: 'If they wish, relevant state parties, such as Least Developed Countries (LDCs) may argue that it is impermissible for any international or other policy maker to push the most vulnerable members of their societies below the basic international threshold represented by the Covenant's[80] provisions.'[81] This approach may also have implications at national level: the prescriptions of the IMF are being challenged as unconstitutional in Argentina where some economic, social and cultural rights are granted by the Constitution.[82] A second approach would embed the norms in the jurisprudence of the organisation, either by way of including them in the assessment criteria for decision-making (i.e. by making sure that any initiative or project has a human rights impact assessment before it can go ahead) or in the case of the WTO in the jurisprudence of the dispute resolution mechanism. So far as companies are concerned, this would mean that initiatives which were likely to lead to corporate exploitation of labour or the environment would not go ahead unless sufficient guarantees were extracted from them; it would probably be necessary to insist that the company provide a fund in case of non-compliance as the sanction of not pursuing a project which had already started might be worse for human rights than failing to start it in the first place. Skolgy has argued strongly for the first two options with respect to the IMF and World Bank,[83] but the arguments for direct impact have met with short shrift from the IMF, although the duties of individual states meet with no challenge.

[79] This approach is adopted by the Committee on Economic, Social and Cultural Rights; for a discussion of that approach see J. Tooze, 'Aligning States' Economic Policies with Human Rights Obligations: The CESCR's Quest for Consistency' (2002) *Human Rights Law Review* 129 and see chapter 6.

[80] I.e. the Covenant on Economic, Social and Cultural Rights.

[81] P. Hunt, 'Relations between the UN Committee on Economic, Social and Cultural Rights and International Financial Institutions' in W. Genugten, P. Hunt and S. Mathews, *World Bank, IMF and Human Rights* (Wolf Legal Publishers, Nijmegan, 2003).

[82] I am grateful to my colleague Sabine Michalowski for this insight.

[83] S. Skolgy, *The Human Rights Obligations of the World Bank and IMF* (Cavendish Publishing, London, 2001).

The IMF strongly rejects any claim to be directly bound by international human rights norms. Mr Gianviti, General Counsel to the IMF, argues:[84]

First, at the most general level, the Fund and the Bank saw themselves (and continue to see themselves) as international organizations separate from their members, governed by their respective charters. Unlike States, international organizations are established to achieve limited objectives and they are equipped with financial and human resources to achieve only the objectives assigned to them. This division of labor among international organizations is required not only for reasons of efficiency but also because the members of international organizations have agreed to cooperate within the framework of their respective charters without necessarily sharing other objectives or values outside these charters. And, in the event that some or all members of an international organization adhere to a treaty containing such other objectives or values, this in itself does not result in these objectives or values becoming part of the organization's mandate unless and until agreement is reached to amend the organization's charter.[85]

Secondly, and more specifically, the Fund and the Bank saw themselves as purely technical and financial organizations, whose Articles of Agreement enjoined them (explicitly in the case of the Bank, implicitly in the case of the Fund) from taking political considerations into account in their decisions. Their role as financial institutions was to provide economic assistance, not to dictate political changes.

Thirdly, as was the case of the Bank, but unlike the United Nations, decision-making power in the Fund was vested in organs whose decisions were taken by weighted voting, rather than on a one-country, one-vote basis. These factors led to concerns over the possibility of inconsistent decisions between the United Nations and the Fund or the Bank.

Fourthly, the importance of maintaining the independence of the two Bretton Woods organisations was further highlighted by the provisions of their respective Articles of Agreement which required that they co-operate with what became the United Nations. The Articles made it clear, however, that arrangements for such co-operation could not indirectly amend the Articles. Any such arrangement that would involve a modification of any provision of the Articles would be effected only after amendment in accordance with the Articles.[86]

---

[84] Statement at Committee on Economic and Social Rights, international consultation, 7 May 2001.

[85] E.g., the European Community is not bound by the provisions of the ECHR, although its members are party to the Convention (see the advisory opinion of 28 March 1996 of the European Court of Justice on Accession by the Community to the European Convention for the Protection of Human Rights and Fundamental Freedoms, reviewed by Giorgo Gaja in (1996) *Common Market Law Review* 973; Jean-François Renucci, *Droit européen des droits de l'homme* (2nd edn, 2001), p. 339; see also, decision of 20 February 2001 of the EC Court of First Instance, reviewed by J.C. Fourgoux in *Gazette du Palais*, 25–26 April 2001).

[86] Article X of the Articles of Agreement of the Fund, and Article V, section 8(a) of the Articles of Agreement of the IBRD. As it was finally adopted in 1966, the Covenant contains a 'symmetrical' provision to the effect that 'nothing in the present Covenant is

Fifthly, the Relationship Agreements that the Fund and the Bank had entered into with the United Nations in 1947 stated clearly the need, based on their respective Articles of Agreement, for the Fund and the Bank to function as independent international organisations.

In addition to these common elements, the Fund's own mandate was even more remote than the Bank's from the issues the Commission on Human Rights would debate. The Fund was not a project lender, and was not involved in sectoral activities: it did not finance health or education. It was a monetary agency, not a development agency. Its financial role was limited to providing foreign exchange to help its members overcome temporary balance of payments problems. In a formal interpretation of its Articles of Agreement in 1946, the Fund's Executive Board had interpreted them 'to mean that the authority to use the resources of the Fund is limited to use in accordance with its purposes to give temporary assistance in financing balance of payments deficits on current account for monetary stabilization operations'.[87] The Fund had no authority over its members' domestic policies, and economic growth was not a recognised factor in the Fund's decisions. Moreover, the Fund's Articles did not authorise any distinction among the members of the Fund based on their status as developing or otherwise, and access to the Fund's resources was a matter of entitlement, subject to conditions specified in the Articles, leaving little scope for introducing differentiation among members based on economic or social rights considerations.

However, '[w]hile the Covenant has no legal effect on the Fund, it does not follow that the Fund may not, on the basis of its Articles of Agreement, take into account the relationship between its activities and the achievement of the social rights contained in the Covenant'.[88]

Further, the obligations of members of the IMF to take account of their international obligation to protect human rights is not the subject of significant challenge. The Fund merely argues that it cannot enforce those obligations: States parties would be under a general obligation to seek, in the international organizations in which they are members, the adoption of policies conducive to the achievement of the rights set out in the Covenant in the territories of all states parties. Such a duty would fall particularly on the states parties that are thought to have some influence on the policies of the international organisations.[89]

---

to be interpreted as impairing the provisions . . . of the constitutions of the specialized agencies . . . in regard to the matters dealt with in the . . . Covenant'.

[87] Decision No. 71-2, 26 September 1946, *Selected Decisions and Selected Documents of the International Monetary Fund* (25th Issue, 31 December 2000), p. 129.

[88] *Ibid.*

[89] See, e.g., the Committee's Concluding Observations on Belgium: 'The Committee encourages the Government of Belgium, as a member of international organizations, in particular the International Monetary Fund and the World Bank, to do all it can to ensure that the policies and decisions of those organizations are in conformity with the obligations of States parties to the Covenant, in particular the obligations contained in article 2.1 concerning international assistance and cooperation' (E/C.12/1/Add.54, 1 December 2000, para. 31). Similar observations have been made with respect to Italy (E/C.12/1/Add.43, 23 May 2000, para. 20). Since these countries do not make use of

The problem with the limitation to indirect effect is two-fold. First, it requires a generous approach to the duty of international co-operation (see chapter 6) and, more practically, the states representatives who carry out their duties at the World Bank are unlikely to be experts on human rights obligations. An international finance expert who has also expertise in human rights obligations is, sadly, a rare find. The World Bank is more sympathetic to a rights approach to development, although it is not clear that its reports distinguish between provision of the 'good' itself and provision of the 'right to the good' (see above). States' representatives at the World Bank have not made it clear that they are determined to fulfil human rights obligations in determining the design and scope of projects, although the functioning of the Inspection Panel might provide a glimmer of light. Its procedural rules do not expressly draw on human rights norms.[90]

Human rights responsibilities of the WTO

The World Trade Organisation is different from the IMF and World Bank because of its structure and the nature of its operations (see chapter 3 above). While it would deny any direct obligations to comply with human rights norms on the basis that it is merely a forum for member state negotiation, there are two ways in which an indirect route to the enforcement of human rights norms might be part of the operation of the multilateral trading system. One is by inserting human rights norms into trade Treaties. The other is by including human rights norms in the jurisprudence of the dispute resolution mechanism. The former route has not been the subject of extensive studies to determine what impact, if any, these clauses will have on human rights standards. There appears to be an element of blind faith that the insertion of human rights clauses will have a positive effect. Since no state has an unblemished human rights record, there is a danger of further empowering powerful nations by giving them an option to pull out of the deal at any time, so that there must be careful design of any sanctions for failure to live up to human rights conditionality. Such sanctions run the risk of making matters worse, particularly for the delivery of economic, social and cultural rights.

On the other hand, there have been a number of studies of the jurisprudence of the WTO dispute resolution mechanism and the possibility

the Fund's resources, there is no conditionality to which questions related to human rights could be attached.

[90] I am obliged to Sanae Fujita, Ph.D student at Essex University, for this insight.

of using the jurisprudence of the WTO to create a method of enforcing human rights (and other social) norms as the pressure to create
'fair trade'[91] grows. Here again, the debate is confused by competing
objectives. The proponents of this course of action point to the treatment
by the Panels and Appellate Body of environmental protections and argue
that human rights issues could be treated in an analogous way. However,
as we shall see, taking the environment seriously is not a speciality of the
Panels or the Appellate Body.

The WTO and human rights issues

The WTO works on the basis of non-discrimination, i.e. that there can
be no discrimination against other WTO members in allowing access to
a home market.[92] This imposes two 'categories of obligations on member states of the WTO. One category requires that member states treat
all other member states on a Most Favoured Nation (MFN) basis with
respect to any border restrictions. The other, the principle of national
treatment, requires member states to treat like products of other member states as favourably within their domestic markets as they treat
domestic products.'[93] Article XI prohibits the imposition of quantitative
trade restrictions. In some important cases, member states have imposed
restrictions which would be banned under Article XI and sought to justify them under Article XX which permits exceptions to Article XI on the
grounds that the restriction of trade is 'necessary to protect human, animal or plant life or health'[94] or 'relating to the conservation of exhaustible
natural resources if such measures are made effective in conjunction with
restrictions on domestic production or consumption'.[95] However, these
exceptions are restricted by the first part of Article XX which reads:

Subject to the requirements that such measures are not applied in a manner which
would constitute a means of arbitrary or unjustifiable discrimination between
countries where the same conditions prevail, or a disguised restriction on international trade, nothing in this agreement shall be construed to prevent the adoption
or enforcement by any contracting parties of [restrictive] measures.

---

[91] In accordance with its mandate. For an argument urging the insertion of human rights
norms into WTO jurisprudence, see S. Bal, 'International Free Trade Agreements and
Human Rights: Reinterpreting Article XX of the GATT' (2001) 10 *Minn. J Global
Trade* 62.
[92] Article I of the General Agreement on Tariffs and Trade (GATT), Article II of General
Agreement on Trade in Services (GATS).
[93] F. Macmillan, *WTO and the Environment* (Sweet and Maxwell, London, 2001), p. 69.
[94] Article XI(b).   [95] Article XI(g).

It is on this restrictive paragraph that some measures have failed.

In principle, environmental issues figure prominently.[96] The Preamble of the WTO Agreement stipulates that trade must:

be conducted with a view to raising standards of living, ensuring full employment and a large and steadily growing volume of real income and effective demand, and expanding the production of and trade in goods and services, while allowing for the optimal use of the world's resources in accordance with the objective of sustainable development, seeking both to protect and preserve the environment and to enhance the means for doing so in a manner consistent with their respective needs and concerns at different levels of economic development:

However, the case law of the WTO does not reflect these aims. Part of the problem is the duality of approach to the environmental issues involved, reflected also in the approach of human rights groups to the WTO. Writing from the latter perspective, Caroline Dommen explains:

Some groups would like to see Trade, or the WTO's enforcement mechanisms used to ensure Western Human Rights standards are enforced on other countries . . . Other human rights groups . . . are concerned that WTO rules or the application of those rules will incidentally harm human rights. The political will to consider these two different types of human rights is very different . . . Because . . . [a]ctivists have so far not clearly distinguished between the two, the WTO has, in a sense been able to throw the baby out with the bathwater.[97]

The same problem faces environmental concerns. A major problem that has been thrown up by this regime is the difficulty inherent in permitting states parties to use domestic environmental issues as a reason for raising barriers against the entry of certain products *because of the way in which they had been produced or obtained*. Of course, this can be seen as an attempt to impose Western standards on others and simultaneously gain a protectionist advantage. On the other hand, 'throwing the baby out with the bathwater' runs a grave risk of a 'race to the bottom' on environmental standards.

The case law of the WTO appears in the form of findings of a Panel (and sometimes an appeal to the Appellate Body) convened as part of the dispute resolution mechanism of the WTO. The report of the Panel (if not appealed) must now be accepted unless all parties to the dispute

[96] For a detailed study see Macmillan, *WTO and the Environment*; G. Marceau, 'A Call for Coherence in International Law: Praises for the Prohibition Against "Clinical Isolation" in WTO Disputes' (1999) *Journal of World Trade* 87.
[97] C. Dommen, 'Raising Human Rights Concerns in the World Trade Organisation: Actors, Processes and Possible Strategies' (2001) *Human Rights Quarterly* 30.

veto the report (including the victor). This reverses previous practice where any party could veto the report.[98] The finding of the Panel may be appealed to an Appellate Body. Many of the relevant issues were considered in three Panel reports and a subsequent Appellate Body report in two cases concerning tuna and dolphins and one concerning shrimp. All three cases concerned the importation of fish which had been obtained in a way which endangered other species, in the first cases dolphin, in the second, an endangered species of sea turtle. The latter case (*Sea Turtles*) is widely seen as moving the jurisprudence of the WTO forward and it is therefore more likely to have laid the foundation for future determinations.[99] In *Sea Turtles*,[100] the USA enacted legislation in 1989 which provided that shrimp harvested with technology harmful to sea turtles could not be imported into the USA unless one of two certification regimes were satisfied. Either the certification could confirm that the fishing environment of the exporting country posed no threat to sea turtles or that country provided evidence that it had a regulatory programme governing the incidental taking of sea turtles that was comparable to that of the USA and that its rate of incidental taking of sea turtles was comparable to that of American fishing ships.[101] The President certified to Congress that the country of origin had a regulatory programme equivalent in effect to the American programme in respect of the incidental taking of turtles.

Two issues arose for consideration. First, did the American measure amount to a 'prohibition or restriction' contrary to GATT 1994, Article XI.I? Secondly, if it did so could the legislation be saved by the environmental exceptions? The first question is of vital importance not only to this case but also to any consideration of national exclusion of products produced in an environmentally unfriendly way or in a way which violates human rights, for example by the use of slave labour. As Joanne Scott points out,[102] the issue turns on what the definition of 'like' product is in the interpretation of Article III.4 GATT, which reads:

The products of the territory of any contracting party imported into the territory of any other contracting party shall be accorded treatment no less favourable

---

[98] WTO Understanding on Rules and Procedures Governing the Settlement of Disputes (Dispute Settlement Understanding (DSU)), in force 1995.

[99] Robert Howse, 'The Early Years of WTO Jurisprudence' and J. Scott, 'Trade and Environment in the EU and WTO' both in J. Weiler (ed.), *The EU, the WTO and NAFTA* (Oxford University Press, 2000).

[100] *United States – Import Prohibition of Certain Shrimp and Shrimp Products*, Panel Report WT/DS 58/R, 15 May 1998, Appellate Body Report WT/DS 58/AB/R, 12 October 1998, adopted.

[101] Macmillan, *WTO and the Environment*, p. 89.

[102] Scott, 'Trade and Environment', p. 134.

than that accorded to like products of national origin in respect of all laws, regulations and requirements affecting their internal sale, offering for sale, purchase, transportation, distribution or use.

Scott distinguishes two issues: the construction of the legislation in terms of the motive behind it, i.e. was it passed for a protectionist motive (on which more later) and the textual construction issue which is clearly driven by the dominance of free trade values over other competing values.[103] The consistent conclusion of GATT Panels has been that:

products which are intrinsically comparable will . . . be considered as 'alike', regardless of differences in the manner in which they have been produced or harvested. One batch of shrimps is like any other, regardless of how many turtles died in the course of their capture . . . The concept of national treatment has been construed in such a way as to permit the application of domestic *product* standards to imported goods. However, the application of domestic *process* standards to imported goods will amount to less favourable treatment.[104]

Could the American legislation be saved by the environmental exceptions?

The first instance report of the Panel, while not excluding the possibility that such measures would *always* fall foul of GATT, nevertheless adopted a highly restrictive approach:

if an interpretation . . . of Article XX were to be followed which would allow a Member to adopt measures conditioning access to its market for a given product upon the adoption by the exporting Members of certain policies, including conservation policies, GATT 1994 and the WTO agreement could no longer serve as a multilateral framework for trade among Members as security and predictability of trade relations under those agreements would be threatened . . . if one WTO Member were allowed to adopt such measures, then other Members would also have the right to adopt similar measures on the same subject but with differing, or even conflicting requirements . . . Market access for goods could become subject to an increasing number of conflicting policy requirements for the same product, and this would rapidly lead to the end of the WTO multilateral trading system.[105]

This approach was dismissed by the Appellate Body:

We . . . find that when considering a measure under Article XX, we must determine not only whether the measure *on its own* undermines the WTO multilateral trading system, but also whether such type of measure, if it were to be adopted by other Members, would threaten the security and predictability of the multilateral trading system.[106]

[103] See Howse, 'The Early Years', esp. pp. 38–9.
[104] Scott, 'Trade and Environment', p. 135.
[105] *United States – Import Prohibition of Certain Shrimp and Shrimp Products* (www.wto.org), para. 45.
[106] Appellate Body Report, para. 7.44 (emphasis in original).

On the face of it, this would exclude most, if not all, exclusion on the basis of process of production. However, the GATT Panel did not conclude that the legislation was extra-territorial, i.e. it accepted that the USA had a legitimate interest in the protection of creatures beyond its borders. Secondly, the Appellate Body, in coming to the conclusion that sea turtles could be regarded as 'exhaustible natural resources', referred to a range of international environmental agreements including the 1982 United Nations Convention on the Law of the Sea, the Convention on Biological Diversity and the Convention on the Conservation of Migratory Species of Wild Animals.[107] Thirdly, the Appellate Body, while coming to the same conclusion on the facts, relied far more heavily on the way in which the restriction had actually operated, rather than the blanket categorisation approach adopted by the Panel. This relates back to the motive behind the legislation. Thus, the Appellate Body relied on the arbitrary way in which the certification regime had been administered which had resulted in the exclusion of shrimp caught in a comparable way with that permitted in the USA merely because the importer state had not been certified. The Appellate Body concluded that the measures in question were aimed at producing a change in policy in exporting states rather than with the conservation of sea turtles. Critics may discern a wafer thin distinction here. The other major ground found by the Appellate Body was that the USA had failed to negotiate on a multilateral basis with a view to reaching a compromise position. The reference to other international law instruments was less happy here (from the sea turtles' point of view) since the reference to Principle 12 of the Rio Declaration calls for the avoidance of unilateral measures. This reinforced the GATT's own preference for multilateral negotiation. However, the 'Appellate Body took a fresh look at the policy objectives that should be served by the *chapeau* to Article XX.'[108] This is the first paragraph of the Article set out above, relating to unjustifiable or arbitrary discrimination. The Appellate Body 'took the view that the *chapeau* should be read in the light of the preamble to the WTO Agreement and in the context of the decision of the WTO to establish the Committee on Trade and the Environment (CTE)'.[109] The CTE has terms of reference which require it to recommend changes to the WTO system if required to 'ensure responsiveness of the multilateral trading system to environmental objectives set forth in Agenda 21 and the Rio Declaration'.[110]

---

[107] Dommen, 'Raising HR Concerns', points out the marked contrast with the Appellate Body's failure to agree that the 'precautionary principle' was applicable in the *Hormones* case: *European Communities – Measures Affecting Meat and Meat Products (Hormones)*, Report of the Appellate Body, 19 February 1998.
[108] Macmillan, *WTO and the Environment*, p. 93.   [109] *Ibid.*
[110] WTO Ministerial Decision on Trade and the Environment, Marakesh, April 1994.

Since the final decision was the same it may be argued that the approach of the Appellate Body was more concerned with establishing the legitimacy of the WTO dispute resolution process by a less rigid approach to prioritising the free market values which underpin GATT,[111] rather than any fundamental shift in policy.

Indeed, the policy has powerful supporters. 'There is, after all, an argument that exempting protectionist measures under the guise of the conservation exception is the worst of all possible worlds, especially where the measure is taken by a developed country and primarily affects developing countries.'[112] Roessler[113] dismisses the two principal arguments used by environmentalists against the WTO regime, i.e that '[t]he obligations under the WTO agreements prevent the attainment of legitimate domestic environmental policy goals and environmental policies should therefore be exempted from WTO obligations' and '[t]he principle of open markets leads to a race to the bottom, forcing all WTO members to lower their environmental standards'[114] or suffer competitive disadvantages. Roessler argues that the adoption of unilateral measures would wholly destabilise the trading system, the argument adopted by the panel in *Shrimps*. He believes that the competitive advantage argument can be addressed by domestic subsidies (ignoring prohibitions which prevail in EU and NAFTA) or multilateral agreement on differential tariffs. A different scheme of border tax adjustment for process-based environmental taxes is suggested by Petersmann.[115]

Once again, it can be seen that the argument is extremely complex. The WTO dispute settlement mechanism has the delicate task of stopping protectionist measures while ensuring sustainable development and not putting obstacles in the way of members fulfilling their other obligations. The same difficulties would surely arise if the WTO dispute settlement mechanism were to be used to attempt to enforce human rights norms. Once again a simple solution is not the right one. However, some scholars, including Roessler, Howse and Weiler[116] argue that until the DSM of the WTO pays more than lip service to environmental values as embodied in the international law of the environment, its jurisprudence will continue

---

[111] See Howse, 'The Early Years', arguing that the Appellate Body has significantly increased the legitimacy of the process.

[112] Macmillan, *WTO and the Environment*, p. 86.

[113] F. Roessler, 'Environmental Protection and the Global Trade Order' in Revesz, Sands and Stewart (eds), *Environmental Law, the Economy, and Sustainable Development* (Cambridge University Press, 2000).

[114] *Ibid.*, p. 109.

[115] E. Petersmann, 'International Trade Law and International Environmental Law: Environmental Taxes and Border Tax Adjustment in WTO and EC Law' in Revesz, Sands and Stewart, *Environmental Law*.

[116] Roessler 'Environmental Protection'; Howse 'The Early Years'; J. Weiler, 'Epilogue: Towards a Common Law' in Weiler, *The EU, the WTO and NAFTA*.

to lack credibility. The fact remains that the dispute resolution process has a dismal record when the application of the environmental exceptions have been in issue[117] and the fundamental definition of 'like' goods as excluding the process by which they are produced or captured remains a significant limitation on the possibility that environmental standards can be seriously considered in this theatre. However, it is clear that a simple acceptance of protectionist measures is not a viable solution.

Other suggested solutions come from a different perspective and essentially advocate 'pricing' the damage so that companies would pay for environmental degradation either directly or by being required to use enhanced technology which would prove less harmful to the environment. Voices seeking less production and/or a redistribution of resources find it difficult to be heard. Because no country has a perfect human rights record, the insertion of human rights conditionality into trade agreements is likely to give a more powerful trading nation *carte blanche* to end the agreement when it becomes inconvenient. As with any legal system, the laws do not operate in a vacuum and it is necessary to monitor the actual effect of the enforcement of those laws before sitting too comfortably on a moral 'high horse'. Throughout the ages, law has been used as a method of oppression of the weak – it is imperative in constructing a fair international law framework that human rights are not hijacked to have this effect.

Developing countries are deeply suspicious (with good cause) of human rights involvement in trade issues. The fear is that imposition of high labour/environmental standards as a condition of trade will keep them and their goods out of markets (this may particularly be the case where it is suggested that WTO exclusion mechanisms be used). Any trade sanctions bear disproportionately on poor nations which may be dependent on a small range of export goods and have no slack in the economy. It is difficult to devise any enforcement mechanism involving human rights which would be more likely to improve conditions rather than invite sanctions

---

[117] List taken from Petersmann, 'International Trade Law' pp. 128–32 includes: 1982 Panel report on American imports of tuna – import embargo inconsistent with GATT; 1987 Panel report on American taxes on petroleum – the taxes discriminated against imports; 1988 GATT Panel report on Canada's restrictions on herring and salmon – not justified as 'not primarily aimed at the conservation of salmon and herring stocks'; 1991 and 1994 GATT Panel reports on importation of tuna into USA – restrictions not 'necessary' for the protection of dolphins; 1996 Panel and Appellate Body report on American standards for reformulated and conventional gasoline – certain regulations of the Clean Air Act (the aim of which was to reduce air pollution caused by motor vehicles) were held to be contrary to GATT: 'Members are free to set their own environmental objectives but they are bound to implement those objectives through measures consistent with [GATT] provision.' Most recently, see the *Shrimp* case referred to in the text.

or a withdrawal of preferences or access to markets which is more likely
to deprive citizens of human rights.

Human rights for corporations? the content of a 'right to trade'

Another way of achieving the insertion of human rights norms into the
WTO process has been to suggest that there is a 'right to trade' or a
right to free trade. On analysis it appears that this method might well be
counterproductive. One problem is the disputed meaning of 'free trade'.

'Free trade': two disparate meanings

The General Agreement on Tariffs and Trade (GATT) had the original aim, as its title suggests, of progressively reducing tariffs which affect
trade. The purposes of the WTO seem to have gone substantially beyond
this aim and appears to espouse an enlarged vision of 'free trade' which is
in tension with the imposition of regulations providing social protection.
This deregulatory approach, espoused by the economic contractualists,
seeks to destroy any rule which can conceivably be seen as a 'barrier to
free trade'. There has thus grown up two disparate meanings of 'free
trade'. One reflects the original GATT aim of reducing obvious barriers
to the exchange of goods (and services) across boundaries and, at the
other end of a sliding scale, 'free trade' means the dismantling of as many
as possible of the regulations governing business. This dual meaning may
explain some of the ferocious divisions evident in the discourse surrounding 'globalisation'. There is considerable agreement about the beneficial
effects of 'free trade' in the first sense (provided that the freedom is reciprocal rather than rigged in favour of the powerful)[118] and fierce arguments
about the second, expanded, meaning as is evidenced by the opposition to
the introduction of the Multilateral Agreement on Investment (MAI) and
the disquiet about the Trade Related Investment Measures (TRIMS). In
this context, calls for a 'right to trade' need to be carefully analysed to
determine its parameters. Is it merely an attempt to allow multinational
enterprises to conduct their affairs without submitting to state control?

A 'right to trade'?

Petersmann has made a number of claims about a 'right to trade',
contending (i) within the Community legal order there is either a

[118] Oxfam Report, *Rigged Rules and Double Standards* (Oxfam, 2002).

fundamental right to trade with third states or that such a right should be recognised[119] and (ii) that such a right (together with others) should be integrated into the work of the WTO by way of a 'global compact'.

Steve Peers comprehensively addresses the issue as to whether a right to trade exists within the Community legal order and, after an exhaustive search of possible sources, concludes that there is no evidence for such a claim.[120] On the issue of whether such a right *should* exist, Peers leaves us with a range of questions unanswered by Petersmann's analysis: 'should a *free-standing* "right to trade" be developed? What would its relationship be with WTO rules? How should conflicts between the right to trade and other rights be reconciled? What "derogations" would be allowed and how should they be interpreted? What legal form would recognition of the right to trade take?'.[121] Pointing out that 'derogations' to any right to trade would exist for the purpose of protecting other human rights such as the right to development and so could not be narrowly interpreted, Peers concludes that:

The way forward to any international recognition of a 'right to trade' is to place it firmly in the framework of the World Trade Organisation, on condition that the grave concerns about the legitimacy of that organisation and the issues of derogations and relationship with other rights can be fully addressed. But if the WTO agreements contained an enforceable 'right to trade' independent of their specific provisions, the result would be a substantial transfer of power to an international 'judiciary', with considerable legal uncertainty and even further doubts about the legitimacy of the Dispute Settlement Body's decisions. It would be preferable rather to recognise 'the right to trade' freely as a non-justiciable principle underlying the framework of the WTO decisions, with due recognition to the 'derogations' from that right set out in the WTO agreements and parallel consideration of the development of an international right for individuals to *move* freely.[122]

Peers has neatly encapsulated some of the difficulties associated with the establishment of a 'right to trade'. Philip Alston offers a wide-ranging and wholly credible critique of Petersmann's methodology and

---

[119] E. Petersmann, 'Constitutional Principles Governing the EEC's Commercial Policy' in M. Maresceau (ed.), *The European Community's Commercial Policy After 1992: The Legal Dimension* (Martinus Nijhoff, Dordrecht, 1993), p. 21; 'The EEC as a GATT Member: Legal Conflicts between GATT Law and European Community Law' in M. Hilf, F.G. Jacobs and E. Petersmann (eds), *The European Community and GATT* (Kluwer, Deventer, 1986), p. 23; 'Time for a United Nations 'Global Compact' for Integrating Human Rights into the Law of Worldwide Organisations: Lessons from European Integration' (2002) 13 EJIL 621.

[120] S. Peers, 'Fundamental Right or Political Whim? WTO Law and the European Court of Justice' in G. de Burca and J. Scott (eds), *WTO and the European Court of Justice* (Hart, Oxford, 2001).

[121] Peers, 'Fundamental Right', p. 129.   [122] *Ibid.*, p. 130.

analysis.[123] Robert Howse engages with both methodology and the detail of his interpretation of some WTO decisions.[124] There are others which only become apparent on a detailed analysis of Petersmann's arguments. Because the author's principal concern is with trade by corporations, to which the 'global compact' is addressed, this analysis will concentrate on the Petersmann call for a global compact encompassing (*inter alia*) a right to trade. Most fundamentally, both Howse and Alston point to the primacy that Petersmann would accord to 'property and free trade rights' and the incompatible (Alston)[125] linking of this primacy with the attainment of social rights. Howse notes:

At one point in his essay, Petersmann suggests that the effect of giving property and contractual rights the status of fundamental rights at the international level would be to constrain that democratic balancing by imposing a requirement of necessity whenever a government seeks to limit such rights.[126] In Petersmann's ideal world, a citizen could directly challenge social, environmental or other public policies and the government that had enacted those policies would be required to show that they are necessary limits on freedom of trade (or property rights). To the extent that the public policies in question themselves happen to be based on human rights (for example social rights), we can see clearly the hierarchy of rights Petersmann is proposing. Social and other positive human rights may only be pursued by governments to the extent that they can be shown as 'necessary' limits on market freedoms. But why not the reverse? . . . Petersmann's implicit answer to this question entails recourse to the standard faith of the ideological free traders that trade restrictions are only rarely an efficient instrument for correcting 'market failures' and supplying 'public goods', (at 645). Precisely *because* of this faith, trade-restricting market interventions to fulfil social or other human rights obligations are likely to be viewed with great scepticism if one sees trade liberalisation rules as economic rights – the free trader can always imagine, in the abstract, an alternative policy instrument to trade restrictions, which is less trade restrictive and supposedly more efficient.[127]

Given that these three texts provide powerful critiques of Petersmann's work, what more is there to say? Both Howse and Alston note the lack of definitions available in Petersmann's work, although it is most elegantly put by Howse: 'It is impossible to disagree with many of Petersmann's propositions, stated at the high level of abstraction that characterises much of this text.'[128] One instance in which this is most evident to a

---

[123] P. Alston, 'Resisting the Merger and Acquisition of Human Rights by Trade Law: A Reply to Petersmann' (2002) 13 EJIL 815.
[124] R. Howse, 'Human Rights in the WTO: Whose Rights, What Humanity? Comment on Petersmann' (2002) 13 EJIL 651.
[125] Alston, 'A Reply', p. 817.
[126] Howse, 'Whose Rights', cites to p. 641, the reference actually appears on p. 645.
[127] Howse, 'Whose Rights', p. 655, emphasis in the original.
[128] The reference is to Petersmann, 'Global Compact': Howse, 'Whose Rights', p. 651.

corporate lawyer is his discussion of the way in which property rights and freedoms are represented as individual rights whereas the rights proposed will be of most value to the 'individuals' that own and trade most of the property on the planet, the giant corporations. Where they belong in the 'human rights' debate is discussed below.

Forum shifting

Both Howse and Alston have identified the attempt to give primacy to free trade values. The Petersmann method of achieving this by praising the WTO and denigrating other UN agencies would seem to be a prime example of 'forum shifting' as described by Drahos and Braithwaite. One method of using this technique, often used by the USA, involves the move of 'a regulatory agenda from one organisation to another . . . strong states forum-shift to fora that embed the principles most valued by them for the relevant regulatory problems. For example, the principle that knowledge is the "common heritage of mankind" was defeated by shifting intellectual property issues from UNESCO and UNCTAD to the World Intellectual Property Organisation and GATT, where knowledge was treated as property subject to trade principles.'[129] A human rights agenda subjected to WTO dispute settlement would look very different.

The content of Petersmann's 'right'

As Peers, Howse and Alton have explained, the content of the 'right' promoted by Petersmann is surprisingly hard to identify.[130] He starts from the view that '[t]he neglect for economic liberty rights and property rights in the UN Covenant on economic and social human rights reflects an anti-market bias which reduces the Covenant's operational potential as a benchmark for the law of worldwide economic organisations and for a rights-based market economy and jurisprudence, for example, in WTO dispute settlement practice'.[131] What does the Covenant say? Article 1 of both the International Convention on Civil and Political Rights (ICCPR) and the International Convention on Economic, Social and Cultural Rights (ICESCR) provide: 'All peoples have the right of self-determination. By virtue of that right they freely determine their political status and freely pursue their economic, social and cultural development.' Article 1(2) of both Covenants provides that: 'All peoples may, for their

---

[129] J. Braithwaite and P. Drahos, *Global Business Regulation* (Cambridge University Press, 2000), p. 29.
[130] As Alston says, there is a 'fundamental lack of clarity': Alston, 'A Reply', p. 814.
[131] Petersmann, 'Global Compact', pp. 628–9.

own ends, freely dispose of their natural wealth and resources without
prejudice to any obligations arising out of international economic co-
operation.' Article 3 ICESCR provides for the 'equal right of men and
women' to the enjoyment of all of the rights in the Covenant. What is
missing? According to Petersmann, 'European integration confirms the
insight of "functional theories", namely that citizen-driven market integration can provide strong incentives for transforming "market freedoms"
into "fundamental rights" which – if directly enforceable by producers,
investors, workers, traders and consumers through courts (as in the EC) –
can reinforce and extend the protection of basic human rights (e.g. to liberty, property, food and health.'[132] Food and health appear specifically
in the ICESCR,[133] so the 'missing' rights must be 'liberty' and 'property'. What is the content of these? Both Covenants are full of 'liberty'
statements: Article 9 ICCPR grants 'the right to liberty and security of
person', Article 12 'liberty of movement'. And these and other liberties
are to be granted without discrimination.[134] The ICESCR grants liberties to join trade unions, to be free from hunger, to take part in cultural
life etc.[135] Together with the right freely to pursue economic development it is difficult to see what is missing. What does Petersmann mean
by a right to 'property'? It sits strangely with a plea for market freedoms.
Does it presuppose a claim by all people to some property? Or to an
equitable or equal distribution of property? Note that the right claimed
by Petersmann is a right *to* property. This wording changes in the next
paragraph: 'Wherever freedom and property rights are protected, individuals start investing, producing and exchanging goods, services and
income.'[136] Here, the emphasis seems to be not on a right *to* property,
which might indicate a distributive notion, but on a right to *protect* property, which seems to indicate preservation of a status quo, even if there is
highly unequal distribution of property. Which interpretation is correct?
Later, 'property rights and liberty rights' are described as 'such as freedom of contract and transfers of property rights'.[137] This is yet another
dimension. What is meant by 'freedom' in this passage and the 'property' emphasis is on 'transfers' rather than on ownership or aspiration to
'property'. What can 'freedom' mean in this context? There are many
things I am confident it *cannot* mean: freedom to make a contract with a
hit man, or freedom to buy and sell atom bombs or people. All property
rights are subject to constraints. The plea for freedom here means little.
As Howse notes 'a moment's reflection on phenomena such as conflict
diamonds and sex tourism suffices to remind us that the markets and

---

[132] *Ibid.*, p. 629.   [133] Articles 11 and 12.   [134] Article 26.
[135] Articles 8, 11, 15.   [136] Petersmann, 'Global Compact', p. 629.   [137] *Ibid.*, p. 630.

trade are entwined with some of the most horrific human rights abuses, and on a massive scale'.[138]

Petersmann argues that '[t]he moral "categorical imperative" of max-imising personal autonomy and equal liberties across frontiers[139] cor-responds with the economic objective of maximising consumer welfare through open markets and non-discriminatory competition'.[140] But does it? What many have shown is that, since the distribution of advantages is geographically and historically uneven and further unbalanced as a legacy of colonial domination and various forms of discrimination, what open markets tend to do is increase the divide between the richest and the poorest. What Kant abhorred was treating a person as a means to an end and this is precisely what is happening in the export processing zones where women produce clothes for rich consumers at subsistence (or less) wages. Further the 'personal autonomy' most likely to be enhanced by a 'right to trade' and emphasis on 'property rights' is, as noted above, that of the giant multinational corporations.

Human rights and corporations

One extra problem, therefore, with the analysis is Petersmann's under-standing of a 'right to trade' as a 'human right' when trade is normally carried out by corporate bodies. There is a complex and wide-ranging controversy about whether corporations should be viewed as individuals and thus be able to claim 'human' rights and privileges. From an eco-nomic and political perspective, it has been strongly argued that such an approach runs a grave risk of disguising accumulations of political and economic power.[141] This is true both of single corporations and, even more so, of groups of corporations. Although companies are 'legal' individuals, an approach that does not differentiate them from single humans gravely distorts perception. The approach is evident both in the work of 'classical' economics and in the more recent 'nexus of contracts' approach. As we have seen, both approaches disguise the power that is

[138] Howse, 'Whose Rights', p. 651.
[139] Petersmann, 'Global Compact', cites Kant in support.
[140] Petersmann, 'Global Compact', p. 630.
[141] S. Bottomley, 'Taking Corporations Seriously: Some Considerations for Corporate Reg-ulation' (1990) 19 *Federal Law Review* 203; D. Sullivan and D. Conlon, 'Crisis and Transition in Corporate Governance Paradigms: The Role of the Chancery Court of Delaware' (1997) *Law and Society Review* 713; D. Korten, *When Corporations Rule the World* (Kumarian Press, Connecticut, 1995); D. Campbell, 'Why Regulate the Mod-ern Corporation? The Failure of Market Failure' in J. McCahery, S. Picciotto and C. Scott (eds), *Corporate Control and Accountability* (Clarendon Press, Oxford, 1993); Dine, *Governance of Corporate Groups*.

available to an organisation and the aggregation of power available to a group of companies which may freely transfer funds between separate component companies within the group, thus evading state control by switching between jurisdictions. Legal controls over companies become useless if the money has gone and the presence within a jurisdiction is reduced to a legal 'shell'. Of course, viewing companies in the same light as individuals and thus concealing their economic power has the effect of rendering them less threatening and so less likely to be subjected to controlling regulations. Since the proponents of the 'nexus of contracts' viewpoint believe that markets should only be regulated in a small number of instances where there is 'market failure', this invisibility of power is a useful side-effect.[142]

From a human rights perspective, the foundation concept of rights would seem to prevent the extension of human rights to corporations since '[h]uman rights are recognised for all on the basis of the inherent human dignity of all persons'.[143] Furthermore, Petersmann makes it clear that he considers that 'the core of human rights consists of inalienable "birth rights" deriving from the inherent dignity and basic needs of every human being, as universally recognized today in numerous human rights treaties'.[144]

Can companies claim rights?

So far from controlling companies, a right to trade is likely to enable companies either to directly enforce a right to 'free trade' or to influence governments to exercise their power on behalf of companies. The former possibility is discussed here.

The major issues are (a) whether corporations may claim rights at all, and (b) whether they may claim rights, but with a more limited scope than those available to individuals.

Under the ICCPR, the Human Rights Committee, until 1993, denied that corporate bodies can claim to be victims of violations of any rights under the Covenant for the purpose of founding a right of individual petition under the Optional Protocol.[145] In 1993, it accepted that

---

[142] See chapter 2.
[143] Alston, 'A Reply', p. 814 and see the discussion of the right not to self-incriminate (below), despite American jurisprudence to the contrary effect.
[144] E. Petersmann, 'Taking Human Dignity, Poverty and Empowerment of Individuals More Seriously: Rejoinder to Alston' (2002) 13 EJIL 846.
[145] D. Feldman, 'Corporate Rights and the Privilege Against Self-incrimination' in D. Feldman and F. Meisel (eds), *Corporate and Commercial Law: Modern Developments* (Lloyds of London, 1996), p. 365; M. Novak, *UN Covenant on Civil and Political Rights: CCPR Comentary* (Engel, Kehl, 1993).

corporations may have rights under Article 19 of the Covenant which is concerned with freedom of expression. As Feldman notes:

> Corporate bodies have a more restricted claim than natural persons to many rights, because corporate claims cannot be directly founded on the essentially human needs and aspirations which underpin numerous rights in many settings . . . On the other hand, corporations, although artificial and non-human entities, are created to serve the purposes of humans and are staffed by them . . . If the corporation is the defendant and suffers a large fine or, in civil proceedings, a huge award of damages (such as the $5 billion awarded in September 1994 to 10,000 plaintiffs by a jury in Alaska against the Exxon Corporation in respect of liability for the *Exxon Valdez* oil spill), it might affect the viability of the corporation, putting at risk employees' pay rises and shareholders' investments and dividends. The corporate veil should not lead us to ignore the effect of corporate liabilities on real people when considering whether corporations should be treated as having procedural rights in contesting those liabilities.[146]

From the rights perspective, then, it may be argued that a corporation should have procedural rights, as damage to the corporation may damage the human individuals involved in it. From the more utilitarian perspective, corporations may have procedural rights to prevent a distortion of justice. Such an argument is not rights-based as Dworkin has argued[147] as it is not concerned with a right to equal treatment and respect but 'has the potentially valuable effect of reaffirming the state's general commitment to fair and more or less rational decision-making'.[148] However, as Feldman points out, if the process rights of corporations are instrumental, supported by public interest arguments rather than individual moral rights, they are more readily outweighed by countervailing public interest considerations than are the process rights of individuals, at least in those areas where the corporations rights claims do not overlap with the interests of an individual litigant or potential litigant.

Thus, Petersmann's 'right to trade', as well as the obvious effects of giving primacy to trade values over 'social' values, may also have the hidden agenda of seeking to widen the claim of corporations to 'human rights' from procedural rights to a substantive 'right to trade', a move clearly in opposition to those seeking to use the 'rights' framework to control companies. In any event, forum shifting the human rights issue to the WTO would greatly increase the power of large corporations since large companies would undoubtedly seek to influence states to use the disputes resolution mechanism to contest social legislation, such as labour standards, which affects their 'human' right to trade.

---

[146] Feldman, 'Corporate Rights', pp. 366–7.
[147] R. Dworkin, *Taking Rights Seriously* (Duckworth, London, 1977), p. 272.
[148] Feldman, 'Corporate Rights', p. 371.

The first hurdle to overcome in establishing a 'right to trade', therefore is to determine in what circumstances it can be viewed as a 'human right' and the extent to which countervailing public interest considerations may displace it. The 'derogations' to which Steve Peers refers begin to look even wider if this corporate context is taken into account.

Companies and rights: a European case study

As discussed above, the extension of the human rights framework to corporations is unlikely to result in their being subject only to restrictions and debates have already arisen about what rights companies may have under human rights instruments. The complexities do not end at the consideration of the rights and liabilities of companies but extend to those of their managers, as the complex European case law concerning the right against self-incrimination shows. This part of this chapter contains a detailed study of one small part of that debate in order to emphasise the complexities of the issue. The right in question is the right not to self-incriminate.

Spielmann places the issue of the right not to give evidence against oneself in the category of 'open conflict' between the European Court of Justice (ECJ) and European Court of Human Rights (ECtHR)[149] In interpreting Article 6 of the European Convention on Human Rights (ECHR), the relevant part of which is in virtually identical terms to the EU Social Charter,[150] Spielman[151] contrasts *Orkem*[152] with *Funke*[153] concluding that 'the decision of the ECJ is now inconsistent with the Strasbourg case law in so far as the applicability of Article 6 of the Convention is concerned, even though the ECJ concluded that the impugned right is part of the rights of the defence'. The issue has been the subject of lengthy litigation in the United Kingdom.[154] The issues are complex and

---

[149] D. Spielman, 'Human Rights Case Law in the Strasbourg and Luxembourg Courts: Conflicts, Inconsistencies and Complementarities' in P. Alston, M. Bustelo and J. Heenan (eds), *The EU and Human Rights* (Oxford University Press, 1999).

[150] The relevant part of Article 6(1) reads: 'In the determination of his civil rights and obligations or of any criminal charge against him, everyone is entitled to a fair and public hearing within a reasonable time by an independent and impartial tribunal established by law.'

[151] Spielman, 'Human Rights Case Law'.

[152] [1989] ECR 3283.   [153] (1993) 16 ECHR 297.

[154] *Saunders v. United Kingdom* (1996) 23 EHRR 313; *R v. Lyons and others* [2002] UKHL 44. The House of Lords avoided the substantive issue of compatibility of the regime with human rights law by holding that international law obligations could not override an express and applicable provision of statutory law in force at the time of the conviction: see Lord Bingham of Cornhill, para. 12. See also S.H. Naismith, 'Self-incrimination – Fairness or Freedom?' [1997] *European Human Rights Law Review* 229.

the apparent disparities in the case law have far-reaching consequences, as does the possibility that the EU Charter of Fundamental Rights may provide a means for a more harmonious relationship.[155]

In *Orkem*,[156] the ECJ addressed the question as to whether the Commission was entitled, in the course of investigating possible infringements of EC competition law, to require an undertaking to answer questions which might amount to an admission of infringement of competition rules. The court held that the relevant rules[157] empowered the Commission to obtain all necessary information from undertakings, if necessary requiring by decision[158] that information be supplied to it where an undertaking does not supply the information requested or supplies incomplete information.[159] No express right to remain silent appeared in the relevant Regulation, so the court held that it was therefore:

appropriate to consider whether and to what extent the general principles of Community law, of which fundamental rights form an integral part and in the light of which all Community legislation must be interpreted, require . . . recognition of the right not to supply information capable of being used in order to establish, against the person supplying it, the existence of an infringement of the competition rules.[160]

In determining this question two factors were fundamentally important:

(1) A comparative analysis of the laws of member states showed that the right not to give evidence against oneself generally applied only 'to a natural person charged with a criminal offence'.[161] The same restriction applied to Article 14(g) of the ICCPR. Thus it was not possible to find a general principle of Community law, derived from this source, to cover the situation on two grounds (a) that the proceedings were not criminal proceedings and (b) that the defendant was an undertaking not a natural person.

(2) Article 6 of the European Convention may be relied on by an undertaking subject to an investigation relating to competition law but 'neither the wording of that article nor the decisions of the European Court of Human Rights indicate that it upholds the right not to give evidence against oneself'.[162]

The conclusion was that Article 6 (and only Article 6) provides limited rights for a corporate defendant in a competition or other administrative

---

[155] S. Gless and H. Zeitler, 'Fair Trial Rights and the European Community's Fight against Fraud' (2001) *European Law Journal* 219; A. Riley, 'The ECHR Implications of the Investigative Provisions of the Draft Competition Regulation' (2002) ICLQ 55.
[156] See n. 152.   [157] Article 11(1) of Regulation 17.   [158] Article 11(5).
[159] *Orkem* judgment (see n. 152), paras 23, 24.   [160] *Ibid.*, para. 28.
[161] *Ibid.*, para. 29.   [162] *Ibid.*, para. 30.

investigation. These rights amount essentially to a right not to answer leading questions.[163] Applied to the facts in *Orkem* it meant that any question to elicit facts were permissible but where the questions related to the 'purpose of the action taken and the objective pursued by [the] measures',[164] they could be left unanswered. A specific example given by the court was 'sub-question 1(c), which seeks clarification on "every step or concerted measure which may have been envisaged or adopted to support such price initiatives"[165] which the court held was 'such as to compel the applicant to acknowledge its participation in an agreement whose object was to fix selling prices and which was capable of preventing or restricting competition, or to state that it intended to achieve that objective.'[166]

Is this finding and subsequent case law upholding and relying on *Orkem*[167] wholly contrary to the jurisprudence of the ECtHR or previous finding of the ECJ? Is it wrong in principle?

Asserting that the ECJ jurisprudence and the ECtHR jurisprudence are at odds requires showing that competition investigations are 'criminal' in nature and that the privilege applies equally to companies as to natural persons.

In *Funke* v. *France*,[168] the ECtHR held that there had been a violation of the right to a fair trial in violation of Article 6(1) of the ECHR in circumstances where Strasbourg customs officers had made a search and seized documents at the applicant's house in order to obtain particulars of overseas assets held by the applicant and his wife. Although the search and seizures did not result in any criminal proceedings under the relevant financial dealings regulations, they did lead to parallel proceedings for disclosure and for interim orders. As a result of these disclosure proceedings the applicant was convicted and fined by the Strasbourg police court for failing to provide the customs authorities with statements of his overseas bank accounts. The relevant part of the judgment reads:

> The Court notes that the customs secured Mr Funke's conviction in order to obtain certain documents which they believed must exist, although they were not certain of the fact. Being unable or unwilling to procure them by some other means, they attempted to compel the applicant himself to provide the evidence of offences he had allegedly committed. The special features of customs law

---

[163] C. Kerse, *EC Antitrust Procedure* (4th edn, Sweet and Maxwell, London, 1998), para. 3.44; Riley, 'ECHR Implications', p. 63.

[164] *Orken* judgment (see n. 152), para. 38.   [165] *Ibid.*   [166] *Ibid.*

[167] Case T-34/93 *Societe Generale* v. *Commission* [1995] ECR II-545; Case T-112/98 *Mannesman Werke AK* v. *Commission*, 20 February 2001 (not yet reported); Case C-294/98P *Metsa Serla Org Y*, 6 November 2000 (not yet reported); Joined Cases C-238/99P, C-244/99P, C250/99P to C252/99P and C-254/99P, Judgment of the ECJ on appeal from the Court of First Instance, 15 October 2002 (not yet reported).

[168] (1993) 18 EHRR 297.

cannot justify such an infringement of the right of anyone 'charged with a criminal offence' within the autonomous meaning of this expression in Article 6, to remain silent and not to contribute to incriminating itself. There has accordingly been a breach of Article 6(1).

As Butler notes,[169] this 'curt handling' of the right to silence and the right against self-incrimination leaves the true reach of the judgment in some doubt. Analysing the judgment in the light of the facts in *Funke*, Butler concludes that there are five main implications of the judgment:[170]

(a) that the right extends to documentary material;
(b) that it extends to *pre-existing* documents,[171] i.e. documents existing prior to the order to produce;
(c) the right applies at the investigation stage;
(d) the right protects all of those subject to investigation, regardless of their co-operation; and
(e) the right cannot be trumped by considerations as to the nature of the legislation which imposes the obligation to incriminate.

This analysis shows the breadth of the decision and Butler analyses its potentially damaging effect on the ability of states to investigate financial wrongdoing. This approach is very much shared by Sedley[172] who assesses the impact of *Funke* and the subsequent case of *Saunders*[173] by examining amendments to UK legislation made in their wake:

How serious is the problem? How many areas of public administration and personal activity does it affect? . . . The Youth Justice and Criminal Evidence Act 1999 amends eleven important pieces of primary legislation passed between 1982 and 1992 together with their Northern Ireland counterparts, most of them designed to detect financial malpractice before innocent people lose their savings or investments . . . One has only to look at the purposes of the amended provisions to see what a swathe this has cut through the financial regulatory system: general investigations into insurance companies; documents obtained from insurance companies; documents and evidence produced to inspectors conducting investigations into companies; insolvent' statements of affairs; statements made by directors facing disqualification; answers given to inspectors investigating building societies' affairs; investigations of persons carrying on investment businesses; investigations into insider dealing; information required from and investigations into banking institutions; statements required by the Director of the Serious Fraud Office; powers for assisting overseas regulatory authorities; inspections

---

[169] A. Butler, '*Funke* v. *France* and the Right Against Self-Incrimination: A Critical Analysis' (2001) *Criminal Law Forum* 461.
[170] *Ibid.*, p. 466.   [171] Emphasis in original.
[172] S. Sedley, 'Wringing Out the Fault: Self-Incrimination in the 21st Century' (2001) *Northern Ireland Legal Quarterly* 115.
[173] (1996) 23 EHRR 313.

required by the Friendly Societies Commission; statements required in Scotland by a nominated officer.[174]

Sedley also points out that legislation is now 'tailored to fit', including the Financial Services and Markets Act 2000, and concludes that in many cases those undertaking regulated activities may not be called upon to explain their activities and have their answers put before a jury where illegality comes to light.[175]

Both Sedley and Butler are clear that *Funke* and *Saunders* give rights to the accused which are too extensive. Both also see *Orkem* as out of step with these decisions. Sedley cites *Orkem* as authority for the proposition that '[t]he Court of Justice of the European Communities, despite its policy of protecting human rights, has declined to include the privilege in the rights it considers to be protected by Article 6'[176] and Butler questions whether *Orkem* can be considered to remain good law in the light of *Funke*.[177] There are two issues which suggest that these assessments of conflict may be somewhat overstated. One is the jurisprudence of the ECtHR subsequent to *Funke* and the other is one of the key findings of the ECJ in *Orkem*, which was that Article 6 of the ECHR could be relied on by an *undertaking* but that the rights given to it were limited.[178] Has enough attention been paid to the fact that *Orkem* concerned an undertaking and *Saunders* and *Funke* concerned individuals? A further question, implicitly raised by Lord Justice Sedley's conclusion, is whether (at least) Saunders ought to have been given full-blooded individual status or whether he should have been considered as acting in his capacity as a director of an enterprise owing its existence to the state?

In *Saunders*,[179] the point at issue was statements given by Saunders to Department of Trade Inspectors appointed[180] to investigate a take-over bid by Guinness during which the defendant was alleged to have operated an illegal share support scheme, essentially causing Guinness shares to

---

[174] For the relevant legislation see Sedley, 'Wringing Out the Fault', n. 60.

[175] *Ibid.*, p. 126.

[176] Sedley, *ibid.*, p. 122, despite para. 30 of the *Orkem* judgment which stated that Article 6 of the ECHR may be relied on by an undertaking subject to an investigation relating to competition law and para. 35 which precludes the Commission from compelling 'an undertaking to provide it with answers which might involve an admission on its part of the existence of an infringement which it is incumbent upon the Commission to prove'.

[177] Butler, '*Funke* v. *France*', p. 494.

[178] An approach subsequently adopted by Advocate-General Mischo in interpreting Article 8 of the ECHR as it related to competition investigations. He interpreted the words 'private life' and 'home' to include *certain* professional or business activities or premises but concluded that states' entitlement to interfere 'might well be more far-reaching where professional or business activities or premises were involved than would otherwise be the case': Case C-94/00 *Roquette frères SA* [1980] ECR 3333, Opinion of 20 September 2001.

[179] (1996) 23 EHRR 313.   [180] Under Companies Act 1985, s. 432.

be purchased by 'supporters', using money provided by Guinness. Such a scheme was criminally illegal under s.151 of the Companies Act 1985. Saunders was required to give answers to the inspectors since if he refused to do so he could be found to be in contempt of court and fined and/or be imprisoned for up to two years.[181] The ECtHR seemed to row some way back from *Funke*. Paragraphs 67–69 of the judgment read:

> 67. The Court first observes that the applicant's complaint is confined to the use of the statements obtained by the DTI inspectors during the criminal proceedings against him. While an administrative investigation is capable of involving the determination of a 'criminal charge' in the light of the Court's case law concerning the autonomous meaning of the concept, it has not been suggested in the pleadings before the Court that Art. 6(1) was applicable to the proceedings conducted by the inspectors or that these proceedings themselves involved the determination of a criminal charge within the meaning of that provision (see, *inter alia, Deweer* v. *Belgium* (A/35) (1980) 2 EHRR 439 at 457–460 (paras 42–47)). In this respect the Court recalls its judgment in *Fayed* v. *UK* (A/294-B) (1994) 18 EHRR 393 where it held that the functions performed by the inspectors under s. 432(2) of the Companies Act 1985 were essentially investigative in nature and that they did not adjudicate either in form or in substance. Their purpose was to ascertain and record facts which might subsequently be used as the basis for action by other competent authorities – prosecuting, regulatory, disciplinary or even legislative (see 18 EHRR 393 at 427–428 (para. 61)). As stated in that case, a requirement that such a preparatory investigation should be subject to the guarantees of a judicial procedure as set forth in Art. 6(1) would in practice unduly hamper the effective regulation in the public interest of complex financial and commercial activities (18 EHRR 393 at 428 (para. 62)). Accordingly, the Court's sole concern in the present case is with the use made of the relevant statements at the applicant's criminal trial.
>
> 68. The right not to incriminate oneself, in particular, presupposes that the prosecution in a criminal case seek to prove their case against the accused without resort to evidence obtained through methods of coercion or oppression in defiance of the will of the accused. In this sense the right is closely linked to the presumption of innocence contained in Art. 6(2) of the Convention.
>
> 69. The right not to incriminate oneself is primarily concerned, however, with respecting the will of an accused person to remain silent. As commonly understood in the legal systems of the contracting parties to the Convention and elsewhere, it does not extend to the use in criminal proceedings of material which may be obtained from the accused through the use of compulsory powers but which has an existence independent of the will of the suspect such as, *inter alia*, documents acquired pursuant to a warrant; breath, blood and urine samples and bodily tissue for the purpose of DNA testing.

---

[181] Companies Act 1985, s. 436. Note that the answers given would not now be admissible in any criminal proceedings other than for making false statements on oath (amendment of Companies Act 1985, s. 434 by the Youth Justice and Criminal Evidence Act 1999, Sch. 3, para. 5, inserting s. 434(5A) and (5B) in the Companies Act 1985). They are not retrospective.

This analysis of the right not to incriminate oneself relies heavily on actual statements by the accused, the overbearing of the defendants 'will to remain silent' and exempts (*inter alia*) 'documents acquired pursuant to a warrant', surely a significant departure from *Funke* where the conviction was obtained to discover precisely such documents, records of overseas bank accounts. Even if *Funke* and *Orkem* are at odds, the obtaining of documents in *Orkem* and subsequent cases looks much more consonant with this later ruling of the ECtHR.

Dennis traces differences in the way the cases have developed in different jurisdictions to different perceived foundations of the rule, with the ECtHR developing a principle based on the presumption of innocence and the protection of human rights and English jurisprudence developing a utilitarian approach based on the protection of certain interests of the defendant in criminal proceedings.[182] He further points out the distinction between a privilege against self-incrimination and a right to silence.[183] *Funke* and *Saunders* seem to take different viewpoints on the latter while being at one on the former. Thus, both courts regarded the right as fundamental and unable to be overborne by the special nature of legislation, but the court in *Saunders* emphasised the right to silence rather than the wider right not to incriminate oneself, basing the existence of the right on the effect that questioning would have on the 'will' of the defendant. This appears to be based on a concept of invasion of mental privacy, permitting the utilisation of other sources of evidence such as pre-existing documentation or physical samples. Dennis comments on this approach: 'Is it really true that personal privacy is more deeply or significantly infringed by questions, say, about a person's movements on a particular day, than by a strip search or the taking of a urine sample?'.[184] If the answer is no, the distinction lacks justification. *Orkem*, while also accepting a rights-based foundation for the application of the privilege, appears to be based on a different approach in which the presumption of innocence 'makes a political statement about the relationship between the state and the citizen. The statement is to the effect that the state, which has greater resources for the purpose, must prove its case without help from the suspect.'[185] While capable of founding a very wide approach, including the *Funke* finding, such a base is also capable of limitation to a prohibition against demanding answers to leading questions. These rights-based approaches differ fundamentally from approaches which seek to protect against unfair practices by prosecution authorities since such protection,

---

[182] I. Dennis, 'Instrumental Protection, Human Right or Functional Necessity? Reassessing the Privilege Against Self-Incrimination' (1995) *Cambridge Law Journal* 342.
[183] *Ibid.*, p. 345.   [184] *Ibid.*, p. 357.   [185] *Ibid.*, p. 353.

it is argued, can be provided by other procedures such as those set out in the Police and Criminal Evidence Act 1984. Sedley argues against the 'absolute right' viewpoint in favour of the more utilitarian approach. However, either approach must define its field of operation and *Saunders* certainly seems to limit the broad approach taken in *Funke*. In relation to the *Orkem/Funke* discussion, if the competition proceedings were criminal,[186] a requirement to provide 'information' which has an independent existence might well be in line with *Saunders* and it will be recalled that the ECJ rules inadmissible questions which called upon the defendant to 'construct their own guilt', i.e. questions which sought to elicit more than the facts. Even if competition proceedings are to be classified as criminal, and without recourse to the arguments concerning the status of undertakings, it may be seen that while the ECtHR may have departed from consistency with *Orkem* in *Funke* the jurisprudence in *Saunders* may have restored harmony between the two courts. If the competition proceedings in *Orkem* were not criminal according to the autonomous definition adopted by the ECtHR, it may be that the ECJ extends more generosity to the defendant than the ECtHR would countenance, because in *Orkem* the ECJ held that 'Article 6 of the European Convention may be relied on by an undertaking subject to an investigation relating to competition law'[187] whereas the ECtHR held in *Saunders*, following *Fayed*,[188] that the inspectors were carrying out an investigation and that a 'requirement that such a preparatory investigation should be subject to the guarantees of a judicial procedure as set forth in Art. 6(1) would in practice unduly hamper the effective regulation in the public interest of complex financial and commercial activities'.[189]

What of the ECJ's emphasis on the rights available to *undertakings* and the treatment of Saunders as an accused individual? How does this sit with the argument propounded by Sedley that 'an unscrupulous financier can cause just as much human misery as a drunk driver, and a good legal system is entitled . . . to offer both prospective drivers and prospective financiers a deal: this is a regulated activity; undertake it by all means, but be prepared to answer to the authorities for what you do, and to have your answers put before a jury if they show that you've broken the law'.[190]

---

[186] A matter of considerable controversy: see Joined Cases 100-103/80 *SA Music Diffusion Franchise et al* v. *EC Commission* [1983] ECR 1825; *Society Stint* v. *France* (1992) 14 EHRR 509; Spielman, 'Human Rights Case Law', p. 770; S. Gless and H. Zeitler, 'Fair Trial Rights and the European Community's Fight Against Fraud' (2001) *European Law Journal* 219. Riley considers that for ECHR purposes competition investigations are criminal in nature: Riley, 'ECHR Implications'.

[187] *Orkem* judgment (n. 152), para. 30.   [188] (A/294-B) (1994) 18 EHRR 393.

[189] *Saunders* judgment (n. 179), para. 67.

[190] Sedley, 'Wringing Out the Fault', p. 126.

There are a number of assumptions implicit in this statement. One is that the creation of corporations is something achieved by the state, the classic concession theory of company existence.[191] This approach was well expressed in *Re Rolus Properties Ltd* and *another*:[192]

The privilege of limited liability is a valuable incentive to encourage entrepreneurs to take on risky ventures without inevitable personal total financial disaster. It is, however, a privilege which must be accorded upon terms and some of the most important terms that Parliament has imposed are that accounts be kept and returns made so that the world can, by referring to those, see what is happening. Thus, a total failure to keep statutory books and to make statutory returns is significant for the public at large and a matter which amounts to misconduct if not complied with and is a matter of which the court should take account in considering whether a man can properly be allowed to continue to operate as a director[193] of companies, or whether the public at large is to be protected against him on the grounds that he is unfit, not because he is fraudulent but because he is incompetent and unable to comply with the statutory obligations attached to limited liability. In my view that is a correct approach and the jurisdiction does extend and should be exercised in cases where a man has by his conduct revealed that he is wholly unable to comply with the obligations that go with the privilege of limited liability.

Of course, this interpretation is disputed by those who espouse an economic analysis of companies by which 'the company has traditionally been thought of more as a voluntary association between shareholders than a creation of the state'.[194] Thus, individuals, rather than the state, provide the legitimation for corporations. That this analysis is both flawed in conception and has dangerous results has been argued elsewhere.[195] The concession approach would certainly support the limitations expressed by the ECJ in *Orkem* but would it extend to *Saunders?* That issue depends on whether undertakings and individuals are equally entitled to protection during investigations, and if not, on what basis could Saunders be equated to an undertaking for the purpose of determining the breadth of the privilege.

The first question raises again the complex and wide-ranging controversy about whether corporations should be viewed as individuals and thus be able to claim 'human' rights and privileges. From an economic

---

[191] See Dine, *Governance of Corporate Groups.*   [192] (1988) 4 BCC 446.
[193] The case concerned disqualification under the Company Directors (Disqualification) Act 1986.
[194] B. Cheffins, *Company Law: Theory, Structure and Operation* (Clarendon, 1997), p. 41.
[195] Dine, *Governance of Corporate Groups*; Bottomley, 'Taking Corporations Seriously'; D. Sullivan and D. Conlon, 'Crisis and Transition in Corporate Governance Paradigms: The Role of the Chancery Court of Delaware' (1997) *Law and Society Review* 713; Korten, *When Corporations Rule*; Campbell, 'Why Regulate the Modern Corporation?' and see chapter 2.

and political perspective it has been strongly argued that such an approach runs a grave risk of disguising accumulations of political and economic power.[196] Certainly, if the *Saunders* approach is adopted and the right to be protected is concerned with the mental privacy of the accused, it makes no sense to extend the privilege to undertakings. Some jurisdictions, including the United Kingdom, have done so, however.[197] The USA and Canada have not extended the right to corporations.[198]

Three issues arise:

(a) whether corporations may claim rights at all;
(b) whether they may claim rights, but with a more limited scope than those available to individuals;
(c) whether the right at issue, not to self-incriminate, should be available to corporations.

In determining these questions it is important to bear in mind the difference between the approach of the ECtHR and ECJ which focus on the nature of the right, and the more pragmatic approach identified by Dennis[199] as representing English jurisprudence which seeks to safeguard the defendant so that a conviction is the result of a fair trial. As already noted, a rights-based approach, particularly that in *Saunders* which is concerned with the mental autonomy of the defendant, would be very reluctant to grant this privilege to corporations.

As we have seen, concerns about whether or not companies can claim rights revolve around the denial that a company has human dignity but acknowledgement that it may claim limited rights to protect the human actors involved from neither perspective should corporations have available rights as wide as those set out in either *Funke* or *Saunders* since pre-existing documents are good evidence and the mental distress of the corporation is not a real issue. Indeed, such an analysis puts in doubt the ECJ's *Orkem* decision outlawing leading questions. It is, at any event, surely sufficient to stop at *Orkem* to achieve a fair trial. In conclusion, if the EU Social Charter were to impose *Funke* or *Saunders* jurisprudence

---

[196] See sources cited in n. 65; R. Peritz, *Competition Policy in America* (Oxford University Press, 1996).

[197] *Rio Tinto Zinc Corporation* v. *Westinghouse Electric Corporation* [1987] AC 547; D. Feldman, 'Corporate Rights and the Privilege Against Self-Incrimination' in D. Feldman and F. Meisel (eds), *Corporate and Commercial Law: Modern Developments* (Lloyds of London, 1996).

[198] *Hale* v. *Henkel* 201 U.S. 43 (1906); *Bellis* v. *United States* 471 U.S. 85 (1974), Butler, '*Funke* v. *France*, pp. 484–92. For the confused Australian position see *Environment Protection Authority* v. *Caltex Refining Co. Pty Ltd* (1993) 68 ALJR 127. For a general survey of common law jurisdictions see Feldman, 'Corporate Rights'.

[199] Dennis, 'Instrumental Protection', n. 52.

on investigations into the behaviour of corporations because it is said to import an ECtHR analysis, it would be inconsistent with the principles set out above. However, my argument is that it will not do so as the ECJ and ECtHR are not in conflict.

Another concern, clearly raised by Sedley is the position of individual 'financiers' caught up in corporate misbehaviour. Is their situation different, as Feldman suggests by claiming that corporate claims to rights are different 'at least in those areas where the corporations' rights claims do not overlap with the interests of an individual litigant or potential litigant'[200] or is their claim to protection in some way limited by their position within the corporation? Overlap will occur when the individual seeks to raise the privilege to protect the corporation. *Orkem* would grant a limited privilege in this case. The American courts would deny the privilege altogether as they view it as entirely personal to the individual and it therefore cannot be raised in circumstances where that individual might incriminate a third party.[201] As Feldman notes 'this effectively bars the corporation from claiming the privilege on its own account, because a corporation can only ever perform a testimonial act through its agents'.[202] The situation in Canada is similar, with the Supreme Court of Canada basing its reasoning on the perceived purpose behind the privilege – the protection of the intrinsic dignity of human beings.[203] In line with *Saunders*, the US Supreme Court has also held that no officer or agent of a corporation can claim the privilege in respect of the corporation's records, even if they incriminate the officer or agent personally.[204] Sedley appears to call for a greater restriction on the privilege than these cases impose, calling for 'answers' to be admissible.[205]

What boundaries can be suggested for denying the privilege when the sole issue at trial is the criminal liability of the individual? One possible way forward would be to look at the position held by the defendant. This would be in line with Sedley's concessionary approach. The argument would be that the privilege not only of incorporation but of (say) being a director is one extended by the state on terms that include inroads into human dignity as a consequence. The countervailing public interest arguments relate to the human rights dignity argument, the pragmatic procedural arguments concerning the possibility of wrong outcomes, as well as the familiar concerns about the cruel trilemma in which a defendant may be, of 'perjury (if they lied), contempt (if they stayed silent)

---

[200] *Ibid.*   [201] *Braswell* v. *United States* 487 U.S. 99 (1988).
[202] Feldman, 'Corporate Rights', p. 373; see also Butler, '*Funke* v. *France*', p. 486.
[203] *R* v. *Amway Corp.* (1989) 56 DLR (4th) 309.
[204] *United States* v. *White* 322 U.S. 694 (1944); *Braswell* v. *United States* 487 U.S. 99 (1988).
[205] See text relating to n. 62.

and conviction (if they owned up)'.[206] There is also the concern raised by McCormack that high profile fraud cases may lead to victimisation of certain 'hate' figures who may be pilloried to divert attention away from regulatory failure.[207] Even if these arguments do not counterbalance the concessionary approach, there are considerable difficulties in determining an appropriate boundary. There are two aspects to setting the parameters: what *level* of involvement in the company might be caught, and how closely related to running the corporation must the alleged criminal acts be? The former might exclude all but directors, but would that include shadow directors?[208] What would be the situation of *de facto* directors?[209] Would the privilege be available to a dutiful wife as in *Re Red Label Fashions*,[210] where the respondent who had been in business with her director husband was held not to be a *de facto* director because she had acted as a 'dutiful wife' rather than a director?

The case of an executive director would perhaps be the easiest case – should the denial of privilege extend to non-executive directors, unpaid directors, the secretary, managers, all employees? There is certainly an argument that managers may occupy a position of equal or greater power in the running of the company than those adorning the board of directors.[211] There seems to be no obvious way of identifying the reach of the denial of privilege unless an approach similar to the organic theory set out by Lord Denning in *Bolton* v. *Graham*[212] were to be adopted. In determining when civil liability might be imposed on a company, Lord Denning reasoned:

A company may in many ways be likened to a human body. It has a brain and nerve centre which controls what it does. It also has hands which hold the tools and act in accordance with directions from the centre. Some of the people in the company are mere servants and agents who are nothing more than hands to do the work and cannot be said to represent the mind or will. Others are directors and managers who represent the directing mind and will of the company, and

---

[206] Per Goldberg J, *Murphy* v. *Waterfront Commission* 378 U.S. 52, 55 (1964), cited in Sedley, 'Wringing Out the Fault', p. 117 and raised by all other commentators cited in this chapter.

[207] G. McCormack, 'Self-Incrimination in the Corporate Context' (1992) JBL 442; Feldman, 'Corporate Rights', p. 393; A.T.H. Smith, 'The Right to Silence in Cases of Serious Fraud' in P. Birks (ed.), *Pressing Problems in the Law*, vol. 1, *Criminal Justice and Human Rights* (Oxford University Press, 1995).

[208] Companies Act 1985, s. 741, defines 'shadow director' as a person in accordance with whose directions or instructions the directors of the company are accustomed to act'.

[209] Companies Act 1985, s. 741, defines 'director' for the purposes of the statute as 'any person occupying the position of director by whatever name called'.

[210] [1999] BCC 308.   [211] Cheffins, *Company Law*, esp. p. 108 *et seq.*

[212] [1957] 1 QB 159.

control what it does. The state of mind of these managers is the state of mind of the company and is treated by the law as such.

This formula was subsequently adopted to determine that unless those representing the 'mind and will' of the company had made the decision leading to the commission of the crime, the company could not be convicted.[213] It would be feasible to adopt a view that the privilege should be denied to those who were the 'mind and will' of the company, but not others. Such an approach is widely discredited in the field of corporate criminal liability and should perhaps be approached with extreme caution.[214]

An alternative might be to rely on the nature of the charge. Would it be possible to identify 'charges relating to corporate behaviour'. It will be recalled that Saunders was charged with a wide variety of offences, some clearly relating to conduct within the corporation, such as contravention of s.151 of the Companies Act 1985, but also Theft Act offences. It would seem invidious to deny the privilege for 'Companies Act' offences and not for mainstream offences, particularly because there is considerable overlap.[215] Could a distinction be based on the seriousness of the offence? Quite apart from the complex discussions surrounding how to determine the seriousness of offences,[216] the policy arguments pull in opposite directions. The more serious the offence, the more protection ought to be afforded to the individual to ensure a fair outcome. On the other hand, the public policy arguments in favour of 'rooting out' corporate fraud become stronger as the seriousness of the offence increases.

If denial of the privilege cannot easily be tied to the nature of the offence, could there be a method of identifying behaviour in the 'conduct of the corporation' which would lead to denial of the privilege? This could be separate from or coupled to the status of the individual within the corporation. Such a test is not unknown to company law. In *Re A Company (No. 1761 of 1986)*[217] the court held that the acts of a shareholder in a personal capacity outside the conduct of the company's affairs were irrelevant to an action brought under Companies Act 1985, s. 459, alleging 'unfair prejudice in the conduct of company affairs'. The court

---

[213] *Tesco Supermarkets* v. *Nattrass* [1972] AC 153.

[214] J. Gobert, 'Corporate Killing at Home and Abroad – Reflections on the Government's Proposals' (2002) LQR 72; *Legislating the Criminal Code: Involuntary Manslaughter* (Law Com. No. 237, 1996); Home Office, *Reforming the Law on Involuntary Manslaughter* (2000).

[215] For a discussion of the relationship between offences see J. Dine, *Criminal Law in the Company Context* (Dartmouth, 1993).

[216] A. Ashworth, *Principles of Criminal Law* (3rd edn, Oxford University Press, 1999).

[217] [1987] BCLC 141.

was not interested in 'an attempt to blacken the respondent's name and to make the court look on her with disfavour as an immoral and attractive woman'.[218] The difficulties of applying such a test are clear from numerous cases. The court has faced difficult dilemmas in determining the extent to which a director is acting in her capacity as director. Just three examples will suffice. In *Regal Hastings Ltd* v. *Gulliver*,[219] the directors of the appellant company, which owned a cinema, were anxious to acquire two other cinemas. However, the appellant company could only afford to invest £2,000, not enough to secure the purchase. Accordingly, the directors and the company solicitor each contributed to the purchase price. The venture was a success but the House of Lords held that the directors were liable to account to the company for their profit: they had been acting as directors, not in a personal capacity, when they put up the funds for the purchase.

In *Industrial Developments* v. *Cooley*,[220] the defendant was managing director of the plaintiff company. While serving in that capacity he became aware of information that would have been valuable to the company, but instead of passing it on to the company he kept it to himself. He also obtained his release from the company by dishonest representations and for the purpose of obtaining a lucrative contract for himself. The plaintiff company could not have obtained the contract because the other party to the contract was opposed to the 'set-up' of the plaintiff company and the group of which it was a part. Despite this, and despite the fact that the defendant had made it clear to the other party to the contract that he was dealing with him on a personal basis and not in the capacity of managing director of the plaintiffs, the court held that the defendant must account to the plaintiff company for the profits that had been made from the contract.

A contrasting case is *Island Export Finance Ltd* v. *Umunna and another*.[221] In that case, the defendant was managing director of the plaintiff company. He secured for the company a contract for postal caller boxes in Cameroon. He subsequently resigned from the company solely due to dissatisfaction with it. At the time of his resignation the company was not seeking any further contracts for postal caller boxes. The defendant then procured two such contracts for his own company. The court held that there had been no breach of duty. It accepted that a duty could continue after resignation but the facts in this case pointed to there having been no breach. The facts singled out as particularly important in coming to this conclusion were:

---

[218] Are the two adjectives interchangeable?   [219] [1942] 1 All ER 378.
[220] [1972] 1 WLR 443.   [221] [1986] BCLC 460.

(i) the company had only a vague hope of further contracts rather than an expectation and were not actively seeking new contracts at the time of the defendant's resignation;

(ii) the resignation was not prompted or influenced by the desire to obtain the contracts for himself;

(iii) the information about the contracts was not confidential information, since it merely amounted to knowledge of the existence of a particular market. To prevent directors using such information would conflict with public policy on the restraint of trade.[222]

Adopting a boundary which relies on the defendant's involvement in corporate affairs is akin to determining whether a fiduciary duty owed by the defendant causes the privilege to be unavailable, an approach which was rejected in *Bishopgate Investment Management Ltd* v. *Maxwell*.[223] The Court of Appeal gave a clear answer to this question, holding that the existence of a fiduciary or agency duty did not prevent those subject to such duties from pleading the privilege against self-incrimination. While there is no reason why this finding should be determinative of the issue, the complexities involved in such an approach are clear.

This discussion of a tiny area of human rights law in relation to companies highlights how complex the issues are. Whatever the true position in relation to the self-incrimination debate, it serves to emphasise the care that must be taken to unravel complexity, particularly with regard to underlying purposes, from which rules have been developed.

---

[222] See also *Framlington Group Plc and another* v. *Anderson and others* [1995] 1 BCLC 475; *Thomas Marshall (Exports) Ltd* v. *Guinlie* [1979] Ch. 227.

[223] [1992] TLR 28. See also *Tate Access Floors Inc* v. *Boswell* [1991] Ch. 512; *Sociadade Nacional* v. *Lundqvist* [1991] 2 QB 310 and *Rank Flim Distributors Ltd* v. *Video Information Centre* [1992] AC 380. See also Dine, *Criminal Law in the Company Context*.

5   Corporate social responsibility

The move by companies to adopt a philosophy of 'corporate social responsibility'[1] (CSR) is partly driven by the extreme difficulty which has been experienced in imposing such a concept on corporations by legally binding regulations. This difficulty is particularly acute when the corporation in question is operating in different jurisdictions using branches, subsidiaries, franchising or exclusive delivery agreements. As we have seen, because companies are creatures of individual legal systems, controlling operations in different jurisdictions is an exceptionally complex legal problem,[2] compounded by the 'race to the bottom' which occurs when poor countries seek to attract foreign direct investment and are therefore unwilling to subject incoming companies to strict regulation. Korten quotes a Philippine government advertisement (1995): 'To attract companies like yours . . . we have felled mountains, razed jungles, filled swamps, moved rivers, relocated towns . . . all to make it easier for you and your business here.'[3]

Having moved the landscape, complete with its inhabitants, it seems unlikely that strict labour or environmental regulation will follow. Can companies become responsible, thus obviating the need for regulation? This chapter seeks to show that there needs to be a more fundamental approach to the problems of controlling companies than by asking for commitments to human rights or social responsibility. In effect, both of these cut across the structure of companies and their ethos as explained in chapters 1 and 2. There needs to be a complete rethink about corporate structures before social responsibility becomes an embedded reality within companies. Such an approach is explored in chapter 6.

---

[1] The reality of this move is accepted even by fierce opponents of CSR. See D. Henderson, *Misguided Virtue False Notions of Corporate Social Responsibility* (IEA, London, 2001).

[2] P. Muchlinski, *Multinational Enterprises and the Law* (Blackwell, Oxford, 1995); J. Dine, *The Governance of Corporate Groups* (Cambridge University Press, 2000); J. Woodroffe, 'Regulating Multinational Corporations in a World of Nation States' in M. Addo (ed.), *Human Rights Standards and the Responsibility of Transnational Corporations* (Kluwer, The Hague, 1999).

[3] D. Korten, *When Corporations Rule the World* (Kumarian Press, 1995), p. 159.

This means that, as well as jurisdictional complexities and the comparative economic power imbalance (some TNCs may be considerably more powerful than the regulating host state), philosophical and structural problems must be considered. Many of the TNCs based in the USA or United Kindom are driven by the concept of maximising shareholder value.[4] The introduction of ethical and social concerns is therefore hostile to the underlying philosophy and thus the way in which the rules regulating that company are structured. To take a simple example, in UK law, unless there is criminal fraud, only the shareholders may legally challenge the directors. The management is seen as responsible to the shareholders and much of the law concerned with directors' duties is concerned with aligning the interests of the directors with those of managers.

Attempts to conceptualise a company responsible to wider social concerns (usually designated as the 'stakeholder' debate) have met with significant problems. The theories are criticised as suffering from three significant and closely related problems. The first is the diffusion of goals, the second the absence of a yardstick to measure director performance and the third is the weight to be given to different interest groups.[5] Deakin and Hughes put the first issue well:

A major difficulty with stakeholder theory, at least as it has been applied in Britain, is that the term 'stakeholding' has been used to refer to a very wide range of interests which are loosely related at best . . . If the category of stakeholding interests is widened to include those of all potential consumers of the company's products, for example, or to refer to the *general* interest of society in the sustainability of the environment, there is a danger that the idea of stakeholding will cease to be relevant.[6]

The difficulties highlighted here are the problems of defining which groups or interests should validly be considered stakeholders, since few on this planet lead lives untouched by corporate activity, and the dangers of attempting to pursue diffuse (and possibly contradictory) goals. Does a road-building corporation have a responsibility to ensure a sustainable environment?

The second problem was the subject of a lively debate as long ago as the 1930s following the famous insight that the structure of modern corporations entails a separation of ownership and control.[7] Berle expressed the fear that any departure from the view that the board should use its

[4] Dine, *Governance of Corporate Groups*, esp. ch. 1.
[5] For a further discussion of this issue and a proposed way forward see chapter 6.
[6] S. Deakin and A. Hughes (eds), *Enterprise and Community: New Directions in Corporate Governance*, (Blackwell, Oxford, 1997), p. 4.
[7] A. Berle and G. Means, *Modern Corporation and Private Property* (Macmillan, New York, reprint 1962).

powers solely in the interests of shareholders was to abdicate responsibility over the board. The interest of the company must therefore remain co-extensive with the interests of shareholders or measurement of the directors' performance becomes impossible.[8]

The third difficulty is the weight to be allocated to each interest group's concerns. This, of course, is closely tied to the yardstick question. If no mechanism which creates a hierarchy of interests is created, how can we know that proper weight has been given to the interests of creditors, employees or the environment?[9] Will different interests gain prominence at different stages in a company's life?[10]

These are compelling criticisms and I have seen no theoretical solution which compellingly answers them.[11] However, as many commentators have pointed out, the German system of two-tier boards and employee participation has operated a stakeholder model, at least so far as employees are concerned, for some time. The *benefit of the company* means more than profit maximisation and includes some concept of community service.[12] The model works in practice without the requirement for lengthy debates about how to balance the competing interests involved or how to ensure management accountability. How is this possible? It appears to stem from the culture which has grown up over many years of the operation of the co-determinist system – the *procedures* of employee involvement and consultation have made it clear that their interests are internal to the interests of the company. Because of the difficulties identified above, it would be exceptionally difficult to move directly from a contractual, narrow understanding of the company to a stakeholder model: the current cultural understanding of companies would demand defined answers to the three (probably unanswerable) questions. It may be that the difficulty in addressing these questions lies in their relationship with a flawed understanding of the reality of corporate life.

---

[8] E. Dodd, 'For Whom are Corporate Managers Trustees' (1931) *Harvard Law Review* 1049; A. Berle, 'For Whom are Corporate Managers Trustees' (1932) *Harvard Law Review* 1365.

[9] C. Riley, 'Understanding and Regulating the Corporation' (1995) 58 *Modern Law Review* 595. See also Deakin and Hughes, *Enterprise and Community*.

[10] See discussion in Dine, *Governance of Corporate Groups*, pp. 33–4.

[11] Parkinson seeks to minimise the impact of these difficulties by calling for an 'ethical' fiduciary duty but this may be simply another way of attempting to change the culture from 'outside', it says nothing as to how to formulate and weight the ethical considerations: J. Parkinson, 'The Socially Responsible Company' in Addo, *Human Rights Standards*.

[12] J.-J. Du Plessis, 'Corporate Governance: Reflections on the German Two-Tier System' (1996) *Journal of South African Law* 315.

The inability of the law to achieve corporate social responsibility by 'command and control' regulation is accepted by Parkinson[13] who argues that the difficulties with 'stakeholder' theories identified above can be overcome by using:

self-regulation, involving filling the gaps in explicit regulation . . . It is not to replace profit seeking with an open-ended goal of maximising the welfare of affected groups. Profit accordingly retains its function of guiding management action, and of steering resources to their most valued uses. Indeed, the latter function will be enhanced where companies adopt constraints that reduce uncompensated costs ('negative externalities').[14]

It is hard to see why this is so. Payment (or benefits) provided to non-shareholder stakeholders beyond the minimum contracted for must decrease the pot available for shareholders if the profit maximisation theory holds and shareholders are entitled to the 'residue'. Parkinson further argues that 'it is no more appropriate to hold that honouring constraints of this kind renders a company's objectives indeterminate, however, than it is to describe as purposeless men and women who, in pursuing their individual goals, respect the ill-defined constraints of social morality'.[15] However, until the last judgment, no one will attempt to assess whether a person's life was purposeful or not but accountability of the directors of companies at present depends on whether they are pursuing a course which fulfils the objectives of the company. Parkinson accepts that the imposition of an obligation to have regard to ethical considerations could not be legally enforceable, thus, at least partially conceding the 'yardstick' point. Accountability rests, for Parkinson, on disclosure of information but this evades the distinction between judging the company and judging whether the directors have fulfilled their duty in pursuing the objectives of the company. Where those objectives are seen as maximum profit within the law, a more generous response to ethical considerations may still be *ultra vires* the directors' powers if not the company's objects.[16] However, that is not to dismiss the concept of some form of self-regulation as a way forward out of the difficulties. Nor should the concept of the provision of further information by companies be dismissed, particularly where it can be provided to the public in digestible forms and with some guarantees that it is not merely the product of the public relations department or a

---

[13] The discussion of John Parkinson's views in this chapter do not imply that I disagreed with many of his views. I was a friend and admirer of John and was deeply distressed by his untimely death in 2004.
[14] Parkinson, 'Socially Responsible Company'.   [15] *Ibid.*, p. 59.
[16] *Parke* v. *Daily News* [1962] 2 All ER 929.

cosy relationship with a friendly auditor. These aspects of CSR will be returned to later.

Corporate social responsibility: what is it?

According to the UN's 'Global Compact':

The Global Compact is not a regulatory instrument or code of conduct, but a value-based platform designed to promote institutional learning. It utilizes the power of transparency and dialogue to identify and disseminate good practices based on universal principles.

The Compact encompasses nine such principles, drawn from the Universal Declaration of Human Rights, the ILO's Fundamental Principles on Rights at Work and the Rio Principles on Environment and Development. And it asks companies to act on these principles in their own corporate domains. Thus, the Compact promotes good practices by corporations; it does not endorse companies.

The nine principles are:

Human rights

- Principle 1: support and respect the protection of international human rights within their sphere of influence; and
- Principle 2: make sure their own corporations are not complicit in human rights abuses.

Labour

The Secretary-General asked world business to uphold:

- Principle 3: freedom of association and the effective recognition of the right to collective bargaining;
- Principle 4: the elimination of all forms of forced and compulsory labour;
- Principle 5: the effective abolition of child labour; and
- Principle 6: the elimination of discrimination in respect of employment and occupation.

Environment

The Secretary-General asked world business to:

- Principle 7: support a precautionary approach to environmental challenges;

- Principle 8: undertake initiatives to promote greater environmental responsibility; and
- Principle 9: encourage the development and diffusion of environmentally friendly technologies.

Why should business participate in this initiative? Because as markets have gone global, so, too, must the principle and practice of corporate citizenship. In this new global economy, it makes good business sense for firms to internalize these principles as integral elements of corporate strategies and practice.[17]

For the EU Commission,[18] 'Corporate Social Responsibility is essentially a concept whereby companies decide voluntarily to contribute to a better society and a cleaner environment.'[19] The European Commission Green Paper, *Promoting a European Framework for Corporate Social Responsibility*,[20] considers as its first substantive issue, human resources management: 'Responsible recruitment practices, involving in particular non-discriminatory practices, could facilitate the recruitment of people from ethnic minorities, older workers, women and the long-term unemployed and people at a disadvantage.'

The UK government prefers to define the:

behaviour of a responsible organisation [which] does three things:

1. It recognises that its activities have a wider impact on the society in which it operates.
2. In response, it takes account of the economic, social, environmental and human rights impact of its activities across the world; and
3. It seeks to achieve benefits by working in partnership with other groups and organisations.[21]

Note that the 'benefit' accrues to 'it', the corporation since, 'CSR can help to build brand value, foster customer loyalty, motivate their staff, and contribute to a good reputation among a wide range of stakeholders.'[22] It has been claimed that CSR is 'outreach' which provides education for the disadvantaged.[23] For Hopkins, it means 'ethical behaviour of business towards its constituencies or stakeholders. I define stakeholders as consisting of seven azimuths or major groups' which are:

---

[17] www.un.org
[18] http://europa.eu.int/eur-lex/en/com/gpr/2001/com2001_0366en01.pdf
[19] Commission Green Paper, *Promoting a European Framework for Corporate Social Responsibility* (COM (2001) 366 final, Brussels, 18 July 2001).
[20] *Ibid.*
[21] *Business and Society: Corporate Social Responsibility Report* (Department of Trade and Industry, 2002).
[22] *Ibid.*, 'Foreword' by Douglas Alexander.
[23] *Corporate Citizenship* (The Smith Institute, 2000).

- owners/investors (share or stockholders);
- management;
- employees;
- customers;
- natural environment;
- the wider community;
- contractors/suppliers.[24]

The UK *Corporate and Social Responsibility Report*[25] states that '[t]he fundamentals of equal opportunities are a central plank of CSR'.[26] It should be noted, however, that the whole concept of CSR is not without its opponents. A comprehensive attack on 'global salvationism' and CSR in particular can be found in *Misguided Virtue*,[27] where it is argued that:

CSR embodies the notion that progress in relation to environmental and social issues lies in making norms and standards more stringent and more uniform, in part by corporations acting on their own initiative. This approach takes too little account of costs and benefits of extending regulation in ways that would reduce welfare. The effects of enforced uniformity are especially damaging in labour markets. The greatest potential for harm of this kind arises from attempts, whether by government or businesses in the name of CSR and 'Global Corporate Citizenship' to regulate the world as a whole. Imposing common international standards, despite the fact that circumstances may be widely different across countries, restricts the scope for mutually beneficial trade and investment flows. It is liable to hold back the development of poor countries through the suppression of employment opportunities within them.[28]

Others are lukewarm, acknowledging that many companies achieve admirable results under the CSR banner,[29] but raise other concerns:

Many of the arguments against CSR initiatives come down to the idea that they somehow distort or detract from the primary focus of the company, which is making money. Or that it will somehow require the imposition of a new regulatory layer on business.

I would agree that having too many rules, or creating institutions that have lives of their own, is as dangerous as not having any . . . The new democratic internationalism ought to be about standards and the rule of law, not controls. In other words, about ownership, property rights, rule of law, all the issues that are politely packaged in the politically correct slogan good governance.[30]

---

[24] M. Hopkins, *The Planetary Bargain* (Macmillan, Basingstoke, 1999).
[25] Department of Trade and Industry, 2002.
[26] *Ibid.*, p. 14.   [27] Henderson, *Misguided Virtue*.   [28] *Ibid.*, p. 17.
[29] N. Hertz, *The Silent Takeover* (Heinemann, London, 2001), esp. p. 143; M. Moore, *World Without Walls* (Cambridge University Press, 2002), p. 206 and see chapter 1.
[30] Moore, *World Without Walls*, p. 213.

Hertz points out that 'there is emerging a new dimension to corporate activity, one that puts corporations in the role of welfare providers and social engineers, environmentalists and mediators, in which corporations assume the traditional functions of the nation state. Business takes over the role of government'.[31] And, of course, they are not accountable to an electorate.

PR capture

The first and most obvious danger of the vagueness of these concepts and the focus on the benefit to the corporations is that the voluntary nature of codes and the imprecision of CSR provides an unparalleled opportunity for 'spin' for companies.

Corporations have . . . set out to persuade the public that the very *raison d'etre* of commerce has changed, and to co-opt the environmental debate. Companies are no longer insidious faceless corporations interested in profit at any cost, they were now caring corporations concerned about communities, consumers, children. They were committed to pollution prevention, to people, to the planet. There was only one problem with this strategy – on the whole, they were lying.[32]

Rowell alerts us to the huge effort put in by corporations and their 'white hat' networks and NGOs in order to present themselves as environmentally friendly from 'Paraquat and nature working in perfect harmony'[33] to 'The Japanese Power Reactor and Nuclear Development Corporation has created a green cartoon called "Mr Pluto" whose job it is to teach children that nuclear power is safe. "If everybody treats me with a peaceful and warm heart, I'll never be scary or dangerous" says the Smurf-like creature.'[34]

It is instructive that many CSR programmes are run by the public relations departments of companies. It was argued in chapter 2 that CSR can act as a moral deflection device. Those putting energy into such programmes can feel good about it while failing to address underlying issues. CSR as moral deflection also works by blaming companies for their actions while retaining the structure which pushes them to behave badly. The CSR movement thus adopts the 'blame the company' as a primary moral deflection device.

So far as monitoring CSR performance, many auditing firms have lucrative contracts to perform this function. However, as we have seen

---

[31] Hertz, *Silent Takeover*, p. 172.
[32] A. Rowell, *Green Backlash* (Routledge, London, 1996).
[33] Advert in *Malay Mail*, April 1993, depicting a scene of palm trees, birds and flowering plants in a rural idyll: Rowell, *Green Backlash*, p. 104.
[34] Rowell, *Green Backlash*, p. 105.

with the spectacular collapses at ENRON, WorldCom and Parmalat, external auditors cannot be relied on even to report on the correct state of the financial health of a corporation. Information issued on social responsibility is even less likely to be correct, even if apparently audited; many codes lie 'dormant' in company filing cabinets[35] and '[o]nly 18% of the environmental reports of the top 100 firms in Australia, Belgium, Denmark, Finland, France, Germany, the Netherlands, Norway, Sweden, the UK and the USA surveyed in 1999 by KPMG were found to have been independently verified',[36] (and the standard of verification was poor). That was some time ago and NGOs and the media have been diligent in pursuing cases of misreporting. Standards appear to be rising but the information asymmetry remains heavily tilted in favour of the company.

Vague principles and shaky foundations

The vagueness and breadth of the formulations at international, regional and national levels gives some credence to the claim that there is only a hollow 'presumption of agreement' and that CSR is a concept which has no real definition.[37] This reflects a number of problems, not the least of which is the power of corporations.[38] There are not only persistent squabbles as to what is meant by corporate social responsibility but also its basis and its relationship to that equally nebulous term 'corporate governance'. Addo writes:

There are practical and doctrinal uncertainties such as the precise scope of the various designations and the basis upon which social or moral responsibility can be imputed to an intangible entity such as a corporation which has no soul of its own to be damned, if necessary. There is a persistently unsatisfactory condition in which the various groups (NGOs, corporations, inter-governmental institutions etc.) attribute different meanings and explanations to designations of their choice. Good governance, good citizenship, or social responsibility can mean anything to anyone.[39]

As a way out of this wooliness, Addo starts by looking at the relationship between the shareholders and the managers, essentially leading us into the

---

[35] Hertz, *Silent Takeover*, p. 142.
[36] *Ibid.*, pp. 142–3, citing KMPG, *International Survey of Environmental Reporting* (1999).
[37] Henderson, *Misguided Virtue*, esp. ch. 3.
[38] George Monbiot, *Captive State* (Macmillan, London, 2000); Hertz, *Silent Takeover*; P. Drahos and J. Braithwaite, *Global Business Regulation* (Hart Publishing, 2000); Oxfam Report, *Rigged Rules and Double Standards* (2002), esp. ch. 7.
[39] M. Addo, 'Human Rights and Transnational Corporations: An Introduction' in M. Addo (ed.), *Human Rights and Transnational Corporations* (Kluwer, The Hague, 1999), pp. 13–14.

stakeholder debate which has been examined above, eventually arguing that:

It is not inconceivable . . . to suggest that managers must take a long-term view of the question of members' interests and to that extent to include, for example, the interests of future members of the company in today's policies and decisions. Taking into account the interests of future members of a company, who to all intents and purposes are yet unknown, the majority of whom could arguably be ethical investors . . . lends credibility to the suggestion that managers can take account of the interests of the wider community.[40]

But what if the directors look cynically at the young and decide that they will surely be a generation of profit maximisers, blind to their social and moral obligations? They will fall back on their duty to make profit so beloved of Friedman.[41] This form of the stakeholder debate fails to crack the difficulties in the definition of responsibility or in the 'stakeholder' debate at large.

Addo makes much more progress towards a solution to both these issues by examining the basis for attributing social or moral responsibility to corporations. As we shall see, it is a route which severely undermines the call for such responsibility to be 'voluntary' and gives us clues into the way in which such responsibility can be implemented within a company by redefining the 'corporate governance debate'.

Addo identifies two bases and three underlying 'principles' for attributing social responsibility/ethical requirements to companies. The bases are: an analogical extension of individual responsibility[42] and attribution of responsibility to the company as 'a responsible entity . . . capable of exercising control and able to make choices'.[43] In fact, the two approaches are very close since the extension of individual responsibility 'by analogy' usually accepts that 'organisations have and maintain different persona from the people who constitute it'[44] and that even if all the individuals involved in a corporation are persons of good conscience: 'having a conscience in the running of a large corporation does not translate automatically into running a conscientious corporation. The latter requires an "institutionalisation" of certain values, not simply the possession of

[40] Addo, *Human Rights and TNCs*.
[41] M. Friedman, 'The Social Responsibility of Business is to Make Profits' in G. Steiner and J. Steiner (eds), *Issues in Business and Society* (Random House, 1977).
[42] See James Coleman, 'Responsibility in Corporate Action: A Sociologist's View' in K. Hopt and G. Teubner (eds), *Corporate Governance and Directors' Liabilities* (de Gruyter, 1985).
[43] Addo, 'Human Rights and TNCs: Introduction', p. 16, citing H.L.A. Hart, *Punishment and Responsibility* (Oxford University Press, 1968). See also Celia Wells, *Corporations and Criminal Responsibility* (Clarendon, Oxford, 1993).
[44] Addo, 'Human Rights and TNCs: Introduction', p. 16.

those values in one part of the organisation (even if that part is at the top of the hierarchy)'.[45] Neither of these views are acceptable to the 'nexus of contracts' theorists who argue that the conception of a company as an institution is seriously misleading since 'companies, being merely a set of contractual relationships, are not different in kind from markets. It is held to follow that it is meaningless to suppose that companies can be under any obligation to operate in a socially or ethically responsible manner'.[46]

Addo and Wood identify a number of 'principles' underlying the imposition of responsibility,[47] whose first principle is essentially the concept of the corporation as existing by virtue of a concession by society: 'society grants legitimacy and power to business'.[48] As a consequence, companies must act responsibly. Again this is challenged by the 'nexus of contracts' theorists who argue that the risk undertaken by the shareholders means that they contract for an indefinite return. All other 'contractors' agree to a definite return on their contract. After these are paid, the shareholders are entitled to any surplus that remains.[49] This theory rests on several misconceptions, the first being that shareholders are entitled to a 'residue' when, in UK law at least, they have no entitlement to a dividend. The only residue that shareholders are entitled to is a division of a surplus in a solvent winding-up, not a proportion of profits. The second is equating a shareholder's right to return with 'maximisation' of that return. As Parkinson points out, even if the 'contracting shareholders' could be considered to be owners, that does not mean that they may insist that directors attempt to maximise profits in any way at all.[50]

Wood's second principle is an:

organisational principle which requires businesses to be responsible for the outcomes relating to the primary and secondary areas of their involvement with society. A car manufacturer for example, can be expected under this principle to share responsibility for environmental pollution, vehicle safety and initiatives addressing drivers' education . . . Corporate responsibility under this principle . . . demonstrates a credible relationship between the effects of corporate activities and the responsibilities sought to be imposed.[51]

[45] K. Goodpaster, 'The Concept of Corporate Responsibility' (1983), *Journal of Business Ethics* 1, at 10, cited in Addo, 'Human Rights and TNCs: Introduction', p. 16.

[46] Parkinson, 'Socially Responsible Company', p. 53 (citation of explanation does not imply agreement with the theory). See F. Easterbrook and D. Fischel, *The Economic Structure of Corporate Law* (Cambridge, Mass., 1991); Henderson, *Misguided Virtue*.

[47] D. Wood, 'Corporate Social Performance Revisited' (1991) 16 *Academy of Management Journal* 312.

[48] *Ibid.*, p. 314.

[49] Parkinson, 'Socially Responsible Company', p. 53. For an extensive analysis and critique of the economic theories underpinning these theories see Dine, *Governance of Corporate Groups*.

[50] Wood, 'Corporate Social Performance', p. 51. The concept of ownership in relation to companies is addressed in chapter 6.

[51] Addo, 'Human Rights and TNCs: Introduction', p. 18.

The third principle focuses on the individual moral choices made by managers in areas within their discretion.

Addo criticises the second principle on the basis that it 'can often lead to short term benefits only and overwhelm the need for long term planning such as research and development into environmentally friendly technology and the benefits of quitting smoking and drinking'. However, this principle seems to contain a much more fundamental flaw in that the company is essentially being asked to work against its own interests. It makes incoherent the concept of a decision made 'in the best interests of the company' as a commercial entity and must attract all the detriments pointed out by those who criticise the 'stakeholder' approach. The third principle may make for certain incremental changes within areas where discretion may be exercised but it is surely the first basis which is wholly convincing.

The concept of a delegation of power which requires reciprocal responsibility has been at the heart of the European conception of corporations[52] and, coupled with the realisation that the demands or requirements of society must be internalised in order for them to be effective, begins to give us a way of coupling corporate social responsibility with ideas of how the company actually works – corporate governance.

Concession on the international stage

Globalisation means that we are living in a world market. What does concession theory tell us about the behaviour of corporations in a world market? What international norms are available to guide us to select the correct parameters on corporate behaviour?

The first step is to identify the source of the 'concession' under which TNCs operate in a global market. It is then necessary to attempt to identify agreed norms which should be applied, and finally to identify an enforcement mechanism which might effectively deliver compliance. The original concession theories considered that the state, in the form of the monarch or Emperor, was the concession-granting source.[53] While this retains some resonance because the *mechanics* of the concession come via the exercise of state power (the grant of corporate personality and limited liability), the concession can be seen (at least from the perspective of democratic societies) in a wider context as a grant from society as a whole to carry on business provided the expectations of that society are met. Thus, the rules imposed on companies may spring from state apparatus but are a result of individual and collective expectations.

---

[52] This is argued (probably at tedious length) in Dine, *Governance of Corporate Groups*.
[53] See *ibid.*

'Corporations operate under the terms of two charters: a formal, written, legal charter; and an unwritten, but critically important, social charter ... it is the unwritten charter of societal expectations that determines the values to which the corporation must adhere and sets the terms under which the public grants legitimacy to the corporation.'[54] This may mean that the shaping and enforcement of the rules comes from state machinery but reflect the wider expectations of society. Where to find those expectations? They must be found by developing jurisprudence which refines and makes precise the vague aspirational goals which we see at present in the CSR debate. That this can be done is evident from the development over the past fifty years of precise jurisprudence on human rights; perhaps even more inspirational is the rapid development currently taking place in the field of economic, social and cultural rights. These need to be made concrete from just such vague aspirational statements as appear in the codes and much work remains to be done on this. Further, having identified society's concession boundaries, these need to be fed into the decision-making machinery of a company and extracted from the PR operation. That this can be done on a domestic front provides inspiration for the possibility of advances on an international stage.

Relationship between codes and corporate governance

Once it is possible to identify expectations with which companies can be expected to comply, a vital step in making them effective is to marry the concept of corporate governance with these expectations. At present, those concerning themselves with the *methods* of decision-making within companies and the enforcement mechanisms to ensure proper decision-making appear to be inhabiting a different planet from those drawing up guidelines and codes of conduct. Principally, the 'governance' debate accepts the primacy of shareholders whereas the codes formulation has extended far into stakeholder territory without concerning itself with how implementation may change the governance rules. The disparities between the OECD Guidelines and Principles can certainly be seen in this light. The Principles start from the premise that '[o]ne key element in improving economic efficiency is corporate governance'.[55] It commences with 'the rights of shareholders',[56] contains the principle that 'markets for corporate control should be allowed to function in an efficient and transparent manner'[57] and '[a]nti take-over devices should not be used to

[54] I. Wilson, *The New Rules of Corporate Conduct: Rewriting the Social Charter* (Quorum Books, Westport Connecticut, 2000), p. 3.
[55] OECD Code, Preamble.   [56] OECD Code, Principle I.
[57] OECD Code, Principle I E.

shield management from accountability',[58] but only nods to such 'stake-holders' as are 'established by law'.[59] There is no prescription as to which constituencies should be regarded as stakeholders. 'The degree to which stakeholders participate in corporate governance depends on national laws and practices, and may vary from company to company as well'.[60] This clearly adopts a number of principles taken from the UK-American neo-classical model of corporate governance.

This envisaged model of corporation law:

(1) relies heavily on the fiction of shareholder control over management;
(2) adopts the view that shareholder control over management will in some way be beneficial rather than simply increase the pressure for profit maximisation at all costs;
(3) adopts the 'market forces' alternative model of control – the market for corporate control, which if freely available, would prevent the adoption of corporate structures mentioned elsewhere in the code such as the representation of employees on boards.[61]

From the international perspective the most glaring omission is the absence of any recognition that a drive for economic efficiency on an international basis is at the root of many of the malpractices in which transnational corporations have been implicated.[62] Indeed, the excessive reliance on the existing models of corporate governance in member states could be seen as using the subsidiarity principle to shirk the responsibility to suggest best practice so far as the adoption of governance models. In that respect, it is extremely interesting that in the Principles of Corporate Governance a distinction is drawn between 'environmental and ethical concerns'[63] which 'are taken into account':[64] 'In addition to their commercial objectives, companies are encouraged to disclose policies relating to business ethics, the environment and other public policy commitments',[65] but both the international dimension and the 'ethical, environmental and other issues' are treated more explicitly in the OECD Guidelines for Multinational Enterprises.[66] The two documents read very differently. While neither document purports to be legally binding, the extreme difference of tone may perhaps be explained by the distinction between the suggested standards (Guidelines) and the methods of

---

[58] *Ibid.*   [59] OECD Code, Principle III A.   [60] OECD Code, Principle III D.
[61] Co-determination has long been accepted as a barrier to take-overs. See J. Dine and P. Hughes, *EC Company Law* (Jordans, looseleaf), ch. 12, esp. para. 12.19.
[62] Dine, *Governance of Corporate Groups*; Muchlinski, *Multinational Enterprises.*
[63] OECD Code, Preamble.   [64] *Ibid.*   [65] OECD Code, Principle IV A2.
[66] OECD Guidelines for Multinational Enterprises (DAFFE/IME/WPG(2000)9), available from OECD website (www.oecd.org).

achieving them (Principles of Corporate Governance). This paper argues
that, because of underlying philosophical difficulties in the structure of
the market place, there is an insufficient match between the exhortations
to achieve moral probity and the suggested governance methods. The
Guidelines arrived at in 2000 continue to adhere to the attitude that 'suggests that the Member Countries may have a moral duty to ensure that
the activities of their MNEs in host states do not contribute to the detriment of those states' economies, particularly if they are less developed'.[67]
Thus, '[t]he common aim of the governments adhering to the Guidelines
is to encourage the positive contributions that multinational enterprises
can make to the economic, environmental and social progress and to minimise the difficulties to which their various operations may give rise'.[68]
In particular, this process is to take place within the framework of 'sustainable development'. The puzzle is why there are two documents rather
than one and the answer may be of more fundamental importance than
would first appear. If the standards articulated in the Guidelines are to be
delivered, this can surely only be through corporate governance mechanisms. Yet there is an evident reluctance to see the sustainable development and environmental issues as a 'corporate governance' concern; for
example, the Principles of Corporate Governance state that the board
has responsibility 'to implement systems designed to ensure that the
corporation obeys applicable *laws*, including tax, competition, labour,
environmental, equal opportunity, health and safety *laws*'.[69] This is in
contrast to '[e]nterprises should, *within the framework of laws*, regulations
and administrative practices in the countries in which they operate, and
in consideration of relevant international agreements, principles, objectives and standards, take due account of the need to protect the environment, public health and safety, and generally to conduct their activities
in a manner contributing to the wider goal of sustainable development'
(Guidelines).[70] Despite the fact that both documents urge the setting up
of systems to monitor environmental performance, it remains clear that
the governance model requires adherence to environmental *laws*, whereas
the Guidelines exhort adherence to *the wider principle of 'sustainable
development'*. The only paragraphs in the Principles which have a wider
reach than proper compliance with law appear in the 'Disclosure and
Transparency' section.[71] On the basis that '[d]isclosure . . . helps improve
public understanding of the structure and activities of enterprises, corporate policies and performance with respect to environmental and ethical

[67] Muchlinski, *Multinational Enterprises*, p. 579.
[68] OECD Guidelines, Preface, para. 10.   [69] OECD Principle V.
[70] OECD Guideline V.   [71] OECD Code, Part IV.

standards, and companies' relationships with the communities in which they operate', companies are urged to 'disclose policies relating to business ethics, the environment and other public policy commitments' and 'risks relating to environmental activities'. However, '[d]isclosure requirements are not expected to place unreasonable administrative cost burdens on enterprises. Nor are companies expected to disclose information that may endanger their competitive position unless disclosure is necessary to fully inform the investment decision and to avoid misleading the investor.' So far as environmental damage is concerned, only problems that will affect the decisions of *investors* are material; informing the consumer is not necessary where a competitive disadvantage may be feared. This disclosure regime will only work to the benefit of the environment if we assume that all investors have an ethical approach. Thus, a statement that 'mahogany trees are being felled at a significant rate and turned into garden furniture netting a huge profit for investors' will be unlikely to deter non-ethical investors, whereas the other side of the story, 'we are chopping down ancient forests and creating a desert' could be withheld on the basis that it is not material for investors and it would put the company at a competitive disadvantage. The Guidelines are much more positive in the environmental field, requiring the maintenance of systems of environmental management, consultation with local communities, adoption of the precautionary principle and preparation of environmental impact reports.

There are several problems with the approaches in the Principles and the Guidelines. Apart from their non-binding nature and the controversy over the status of corporations in international law (addressed above), it is also problematic that the Guidelines represent a form of 'outside the company exhortation' and it will be unlikely to be effective unless mechanisms to achieve sustainable development can become part of the internal governance systems of companies rather than outside encouragement. A third and most fundamental problem is that it will not be possible to enlist company support for the wider meaning of 'sustainable development' until the underlying social understanding of the purpose companies serve changes fundamentally, particularly if 'sustainable development' retains its original ambience which included a significant redistributive agenda. The principal aim of MNEs is to maximise shareholder profit. It is for this reason that the mahogany statement may be regarded as acceptable disclosure to investors. Further, since the vast majority of the shareholders of MNEs live in the developed world, the repatriation of profits made in environmentally damaging ways represents a regressive redistribution of wealth which is the precise opposite of the aim of 'sustainable development'.

Loss of redistribution from 'sustainable development': the capacity for CSR to 'backfire'

In order to understand the way in which CSR could be misused, it is instructive to look at the way in which the concept of 'sustainable development' has evolved. This is a debate where the opposing values of responsibility and creating wealth collide, an exact mirror of the CSR/financial ambitions debate concerning companies. The aim of the Brundland Commission's sustainable development strategy was 'to promote harmony among human beings and between humanity and nature',[72] starting from the premise that it is 'futile to attempt to deal with environmental problems without a broader perspective that encompasses the factors underlying world poverty and international inequality'.[73] Adams identifies a 'subtle but extremely important transformation of the ecologically-based concept of sustainable development, by leading beyond concepts of physical sustainability to the socio-economic context of development . . . *Our Common Future* starts with people, and goes on to discuss what kinds of environmental policies are required to achieve certain socio-economic goals.'[74] This contrasts with the World Conservation Strategy which 'started from the premise of the need to conserve ecosystems and sought to demonstrate why this made good economic sense and – although the point was underplayed – could promote equity'.[75] Where this analysis fails is that the answers suggested by these two approaches are seen as 'remarkably similar'. Nothing could be further from the truth, as the world trading system is based on an economic vision which has caused and is causing extreme poverty. Thus, although there is an emphasis on 'growth' in the Brundtland Report it is 'growth, Jim, but not as we know it' and the attempt to keep familiar words such as 'growth' and 'development' in the formula have massively backfired. A huge 'capture' operation has undermined the radicalism which should have led to a complete rethink of world trading systems to create 'a new form of growth, sustainable, environmentally friendly, egalitarian, integrating economic and social development . . . and more equitable in its impact'.[76] How has it happened?

The single answer is, of course, the complexity of the issues which involve every field of human endeavour in a complex interrelationship. How much easier for 'experts' on corporate law not to talk to philosophers, chemists, sociologists and human rights proponents. The economic proponents of a free trade model of 'globalisation' see the world

---

[72] H. Brundtland, *Our Common Future* (Oxford University Press, 1987), p. 65.
[73] *Ibid.*, p. 3.   [74] W.M. Adams, *Green Development* (Routledge, London, 1990).
[75] *Ibid.*   [76] Brundtland, *Our Common Future*, p. 52.

as becoming a simpler place[77] – the exact opposite is true as a result of the construction of complex world trading systems.

Given the problems brought about by simplistic adherence to economic models, the contributions of 'green economists' to the debate about sustainability must be viewed cautiously. On the first page of *Blueprint for a Green Economy*[78] the following assumption is made:

Development is some set of desirable goals or objectives for society. Those goals undoubtedly include the basic aim to secure a rising level of real income per capita – what is traditionally regarded as the 'standard of living'. But most people would also now accept that there is more to development than rising incomes.

At first sight this appears to be a softening of the extreme neo-classical approach but it contains:

(a) the assumption that a rising standard of living is a basic and worthwhile goal (which it clearly is in poorer countries but may not be in wealthier ones);

(b) the sleight of hand which suggests that rising income is shared amongst the population, i.e. that growth will produce a rise of income 'per capita', which it will if the growth is divided by the population but not in reality where, as we have seen, unregulated growth leads to polarisation of incomes.

Distributional issues appear in the book, only to vanish again. Thus, 'sustainable development places emphasis on providing for the needs of the least advantaged in society',[79] a concept to be explained in chapter 2 of the book. Indeed, the position of the most disadvantaged is said to be an indicator of whether a society is developing but '[a] society which does not maintain or improve its real income per capita is unlikely to be "developing"' and '[a]chieving economic development without sacrificing an acceptable rate of economic growth may be said to define the problem of "sustainable development"'.[80] The 'wellbeing' of a defined population is the measure of whether or not there is sustainable development. However, the wellbeing indicators will be drawn from an aggregate of the whole population rather than its poorest sector. This 'optimal' way of conceiving the most benefit to society 'is in fact a utilitarian creation: it is concerned only with individual preferences, and it measures only totals for all individuals not distributions between them'.[81] Since the analysis is based on the presumption that satisfying consumer preferences is

---

[77] See, e.g., *Regulation Without the State* (Institute of Economic Affairs, London, 2000).

[78] D. Pearce, A. Markandya and E. Barbier, *Blueprint for a Green Economy* (Earthscan, 1989).

[79] *Ibid.*, p. 2.   [80] *Ibid.*, p. 30.

[81] M. Jacobs, 'The Limits to Neoclassicism' in M. Redclift and T. Benron (eds), *Social Theory and the Global Environment* (Routledge, London, 1994).

what matters, the results of wellbeing surveys will provide the answer to the 'correct' level of environmental protection. As Jacobs points out,[82] the neo-classical approach is founded on methodological individualism, based 'on the currently existing preferences of consumers'. At the same time, it is presented as morally neutral, seeking to discover an 'optimal' outcome which is nevertheless not presented as morally best.[83] Given a moral framework which derives from 'the greatest good of the greatest number', the 'optimal' elides with the normative 'morally best', absent some mystical dimension which can conveniently be derided by opponents (see below, discussion of 'green backlash'). Indeed, 'on the premise that satisfying consumer preferences is what matters, most neo-classicists would argue that [the optimal level of protection] is the level of protection which society therefore should choose'.[84]

The foundation of this economic approach is the desire to avoid the problem of externalities by turning 'the environment into a commodity which can be analysed just like other commodities'.[85] The motive may be to retain the economists' role as governmental advisers[86] or to seek genuine protection for the environment: because it has hitherto been free it has been significantly overused.

In valuing the environment it is argued that all aspects of the environment[87] can be valued with a money yardstick.[88] This is supported by the view that human life is valued by the amount of resources which a society will use to save life. This (unsupported) argument is unsound, confusing as it does the resources available to achieve a certain aim and the value of that which will be lost if the aim is not achieved. Jacobs[89] comments '[m]any environmentalists and Greens object to this treatment on

---

[82] Jacobs, 'Limits to Neoclassicism', p. 75.

[83] *Ibid.*, p. 70.   [84] *Ibid.*, p. 72.   [85] *Ibid.*   [86] *Ibid.*, p. 69.

[87] The apparently simplistic attribution of value to environmental commodities is mitigated by an attempt to factor into the equation not just 'use' value but 'option' value (the value of preserving something in case the consumer wishes to use it), 'Bequest' value, which is the value of options for future generations, and 'existence' value, which is the 'sentimental' value placed on the existence of whales etc. The poorer nations are mentioned as providing a rationale for natural capital conservation (which, to be fair, is the approach later adopted instead of a substitutability approach) and the process of exporting an unsustainable quantity of hardwood from poor nations is described as a policy choice on that basis: 'If we take the broader view [why broader?], based on total rather than natural capital only, the hardwood exporting countries may simply be converting their export revenue into investments which will sustain their future': *ibid.*, p. 70. The 'choice' exercised by these countries is then castigated: 'export proceeds are often turned into consumption'. The solution to this is *foreign aid for sustainable development*, a patronising solution which disguises the lack of choice that plagues these nations.

[88] Pearce, Markandya and Barbier, *Blueprint*, p. 53.

[89] Arguing along lines not dissimilar to R.M. Dworkin, 'Is Wealth a Value' (1980) 9 *Journal of Legal Studies* 191, discussed in chapter 2.

essentially moral grounds, namely that it devalues the cultural and spiritual meaning which the environment has for human society and ignores altogether the rights of other species'.[90] This confusion translates into an attempt to measure the *degree* of concern, i.e. the willingness of individuals to pay for the environment.[91] A further confusion arises in the assertion that 'preserving and improving the environment is never a free option; it costs money and uses up real resources'.[92] Again, the hidden assumption is that 'growth is good' since the cost of preservation may be 'in terms of some benefit foregone'. The inexpensive option of not developing is discounted. Jacobs,[93] in investigating the claim of this school of thought to moral neutrality, points out that in their analysis of the environment they depart completely from their analysis of 'public goods' the value of which cannot be derived from individual market preference. In departing from this tenet so far as environmental issues are concerned, they cease to analyse the real world: 'They are analysing what *might* happen *if* the environment were a set of commodities . . . Why should economists analyse a thing as if it were something else?' Two answers are given by Jacobs to this question: the first, that the creation of a pseudo-market creates protection from the overuse of 'free' environmental goods, the second, that individuals do in fact treat the environment as if it were a purchased commodity. Jacobs advances criticisms of both of these answers. On the issue of protecting the environment by use of market mechanisms, Jacobs argues that optimality may not be the sole criteria for allocating resources. We might, he argues 'tolerate some inefficiency in total allocation to ensure a more egalitarian sharing-out – for example, insisting that everyone should have access to the same quantity of drinking water.' The construction of hypothetical markets, especially on the basis of 'willingness to pay', 'cannot be divorced from ability to pay which leads inevitably to inegalitarian outcomes'.[94] The hypothetical market also leads to insufficient weight being placed on *rights* over the environment, particularly where destruction may lead to destruction of a culture. Further, it gives insufficient weight to the desires and wishes of future inhabitants, based as it is on the preferences of the present generation. These may 'express the interests of the present generation in [future] people'. They do not 'express the interests of future people'.[95] These alternative bases for social choice expose the hollowness of optimality as the foundation for action concerning the environment. Optimality is derived from individually expressed choices. Even supposing that this works with commodities where a market exists,

---

[90] Jacobs, 'Limits to Neoclassicism', p. 74.
[91] Pearce, Markandya and Barbier, *Blueprint*, p. 55.
[92] *Ibid.*, p. 56.   [93] Jacobs, 'Limits to Neoclassicism'.   [94] *Ibid.*, p. 76.
[95] And ignores the interests of other species: *ibid.* The extinction of species may be 'optimal'.

Jacobs points out that the individual preferences surrounding the hypothetical market are just that – hypothetical. Thus, 'in the case of the environment *there are no individually expressed preferences* . . . it is no use invoking the primacy of individual preferences to prove the primacy of individual preferences. The importance of optimality is simply a value judgment.'[96] The claim to ethical neutrality is a sham and the real issue is whether, because of the 'public goods' nature of the environment, a public forum should take account of moral criteria rather than individual self-interest. The second answer is met by evidence from contingent valuation exercises which tend to show that it is not the case that the environment is viewed as if it were merely another commodity, and explaining the significant failure to reach 'a priced environment' by the concept of 'category mistake': 'The environment belongs in the sphere not of monetary but of moral valuation: people choose what they believe to be *right* as "citizens", rather than what is in their *interests*, as "consumers".'[97] Jacobs suggests an alternative approach termed 'institutional environmental economics' which would research the way in which people actually value the environment, as consumers or citizens, or a complex mixture of them both, and would therefore address the ethical and moral effects of choices to be made and the political process through which choices must be processed, whether public or market-based.[98]

The sociologists

In order for sociologists to analyse environmental problems 'some deep-seated (and in important respects, *well-founded*) inhibitions need to be overcome'.[99] These include the recent experience of biological determinism, including the holocaust, racism and sexism, as well as the foundations of sociology which deliberately sought to create a human identity separate from nature. The 'dualist strategy of thinking about "nature" and "society" (or "culture") as qualitatively different realms offers one obvious and unambiguous way of resisting biological determinism'.[100] However, as Benton shows, dualist conceptions spawn a range of approaches from naturalistic reductionism, through technological determinism to sociological reductionism:

[96] *Ibid.*, p. 77.
[97] *Ibid.*, p. 81 and see M. Sagoff, *The Economy of the Earth* (Cambridge University Press, 1988).
[98] Jacobs, 'Limits to Neoclassicism', pp. 86–7.
[99] T. Benton and M. Redclift, 'Introduction' in *Social Theory and the Global Environment* (Routledge, 1994).
[100] T. Benton, 'Biology and Social Theory' in Benton and Redclift, *Social Theory*.

In each case 'nature' is counterpoised to 'society', but at the polar extremes one of these opposed terms tends to swallow up the other. In naturalistic reductionism human society is seen as part of the wider totality of nature, whereas in the more extreme forms of sociological (or discourse) reductionism, 'nature' becomes transmuted into its symbolic representations.[101]

That this tradition is alive and well appears from *Contested Natures*[102] in which Macnaughten and Urry argue against the claim that the environment is 'essentially a "real entity", which, in and of itself and substantially separate from social practices and human experience has the power to produce unambiguous, observable and rectifiable outcomes'.[103]

Benton and Redclift argue that a further difficulty arises from the parameters which have traditionally bounded sociological studies. The nation state has been seen as of considerable significance and the generalised, abstract nature of many theories ignores or minimises the impact of space and time.[104] The importance of breaking out of this way of thought is of vital importance given the power imbalance between nation states and TNCs. Sklair[105] introduces the concept of *transnational practices* to add to analyses which concern relations between states and state actors.[106] Taking the analysis of O'Riordan[107] that environmentalists can be classified as 'dry', 'shallow' and 'deep', Sklair postulates that the global environmental elite belonging to the two former categories are able to understand and work with the global capitalist elite who are active in the world's trading systems. This is because that cumulative elite believe in a 'technical fix' of problems (dry greens) or in neo-classical 'shallow green' economic analysis:

Clearly, the dominant forces in the global capitalist system have no option but to believe and act as if [the contradiction between capitalist development and global survival] can be resolved by a combination of economic-technological, political and culture ideology means. Part of this must involve the ways in which the capitalist system uses the Third World to resolve the contradiction.[108]

This powerful analysis would be a doomsday representation, particularly because of the scepticism shown of the 'deep green' alternative vision (see the analysis of social ecologists and the backlash below). However,

[101] *Ibid.*, p. 31.
[102] P. Macnaughten and J. Urry, *Contested Natures* (Sage, London, 1998).
[103] *Ibid.*, p. 1.   [104] Benton and Redclift, *Social Theory*, p. 5.
[105] L. Sklair, 'Global Sociology and Global Environmental Change' in Benton and Redclift, *Social Theory*.
[106] Sklair, 'Global Sociology', p. 205.
[107] T. O'Riordan, 'The New Environmentalism and Sustainable Development' (1991) 108 *Science of the Total Environment* 5.
[108] Sklair, 'Global Sociology', p. 221.

one significant factor is absent and that is a more detailed examination of 'capitalism' which, while it may be presented by neo-classical economists as inevitable, deregulated, impersonal and global, that is not a universal vision;[109] Hirst and Thompson argue that the globalisation of economic systems has been wildly exaggerated along with the impossibility of regulation at national and international level. This vision is therefore of a *controlled* capitalism. The lack of political will to control may well stem from the misrepresentation of free market globalisation as irresistable:[110] 'Markets do not regulate themselves and best outcomes do not happen spontaneously.'[111]

Formulating a course of action from sociological studies of man's interaction with the environment also entails choosing from different sociological traditions. 'The first and most pervasive of these contests is that between approaches which put human consciousness agency at the centre of analysis, and those which focus attention on the social-structural conditions for, and constraints on, action.'[112] The distribution of the power to choose is a crucial omission from the neo-classical economists' approach. The 'individualist' versus 'structuralist' debate has a further dimension in the assessment of risk; whether this can ever achieve a significant degree of objectivity is a difficult and contentious issue.[113]

The technocrats and risk assessment

Benton points out that the capitalist and communist versions of the 'cornucopian' vision of the technocrats differed little save for the communist understanding of competition and private property as a '*constraint* on the further development of human productive powers, and its emphasis on distributive justice rather than individual choice'.[114] The widespread perception that the capitalist mode of production has 'succeeded' in bringing material prosperity while the communist mode has 'failed' has left the field wide open to the capitalist elite and their environment elite brethren imbued with the optimism of the cornucopian vision that '[s]cience and technology promise an end to poverty, insecurity and disease, and a prospect of ever-growing material prosperity and cultural enrichment'.[115] The extent of this 'capture' of the environment elite can

---

[109] P. Hirst and G. Thompson, *Globalisation in Question* (2nd edn, Blackwell, Oxford, 1996).

[110] See *ibid.*, esp. chs 6 and 7.

[111] Will Hutton, 'Anthony Giddens and Will Hutton in Conversation' in W. Hutton and A. Giddens (eds), *On the Edge: Living with Global Capitalism* (Cape, London, 2000).

[112] Benton and Redclift, *Social Theory*, p. 7.   [113] *Ibid.*, p. 9.

[114] Benton, 'Biology and Social Theory', p. 32.   [115] *Ibid.*, p. 32.

perhaps be gleaned from *The Limits to Growth*,[116] which was a 'specific use' of scientific method.[117] Thus, the 'core assumptions . . . of a single-line cumulative growth of scientific knowledge . . . [and] that human well being, the "good life" consists in the ever-growing gratification of human desires by way of this technologically mediated mastery of nature'.[118] This 'directs attention away from gross global inequalities in power and resources which allow tens of millions, especially in Third World countries, to suffer and die as a result of ecological destruction'.[119] Further, the managerialist approach stems from the dominant vision of growth and development and therefore contemplates only 'the long-term sustainability of a *particular kind* of human culture and its dominant economic and political interests'.[120] The extent to which the 'technocratic' understanding of risk pervades is evident from examples such as the report to the European Commission Directorate-General for Science, Research and Development, reported in *Policies for Cleaner Technology*,[121] which concluded that developed economies had entrenched technologies that involved huge costs if radical change was desired.[122] An example is car use in developed nations. The conclusion is that research must be targeted at providing technically 'greener' technology and understanding the obstacles to implementation of these technical 'fixes' so that the most effective means of regulation can be devised. The use of sociology here is important because studies of the barriers to implementation are vital in this technological project. However, the study expressly rejects changing the 'linear growth' and development projection which supports only one particular type of culture.

A more radical approach may be based on Ulrich Beck's *Risk Society*,[123] which gives us two vital contributions to the present debate. One is the necessity of understanding the physical risks present in society and the way in which they cut across boundaries of nations, class and status. The second is the interdependence between disciplines in assessing these risks:

what becomes clear in risk discussions are the fissures and gaps between *scientific* and *social* rationality in dealing with the hazardous potential of civilization. The two sides talk past each other . . . The scientific concern with the risks of industrial development in fact relies on social expectations and value judgments, just as the social discussion and perception of risk depend on scientific arguments.

---

[116] D.H. Meadows, D.L. Meadows, J. Randers and W. Behrens, *The Limits to Growth* (Universe Books, New York, 1972).
[117] Benton, 'Biology and Social Theory', p. 33.   [118] *Ibid.*
[119] *Ibid.*, p. 37.   [120] *Ibid.*
[121] A. Clayton, G. Spinardi and R. Williams, *Policies for Cleaner Technology* (Earthscan, 1999).
[122] *Ibid.*, p. 6.   [123] U. Beck, *Risk Society* (translation published by Sage, London, 1992).

246 Companies, International Trade and Human Rights

Unfortunately, the subjective nature of risk is difficult to capture in international regulation. So, for example, the Cartagena Protocol on Biosafety[124] incorporated the precautionary approach contained in the Rio Declaration on Environment and Development but bases the risk assessment solely on the absence of 'scientific certainty', leaving more complex evaluations of risk to the parties. We live in a world where '[t]he environment, health, personal safety, and even the planet Earth itself appear to be under attack from enemies never before encountered. The goal of wresting society from the mercy of the laws of chance continues to elude us.'[125] It is likely that the decision-makers will take refuge in 'scientific' and 'mathematical' calculations of risk which are likely to disguise political consequences. As we have seen, the reduction of risk to mathematical symbols such as monetary value has precisely this consequence. Some methods of reversing the tendency to 'detached explication' and more concern with '*engagement* and *substantive* issues'[126] are needed. The mode of scientific explanation seeks to disguise the underlying fact that human perceptions reproduced in 'scientific discourses' define the 'modern environmental problem'.[127] To simply argue, therefore, that there is no environmental problem is 'self-defeatingly reductionist'[128] but reflects the postmodern view.

The introduction of redistributive justice into the Brundtland Report may have exacerbated the process, identified by Beck, whereby more and more processes have been made the objects of choice and responsibility and consequently become subject to individual risk assessment.[129] This process 'produces a condition where modern individuals are prone to states of heightened uncertainty and anxiety, as decisions proliferate and the cultural codes used to negotiate those decisions become more and more complex and varied'.[130] Szersynski, Lash and Wynne represent this tendency as 'one side of the problem of subjectivity in late modernity', with the 'other side' of the problem being 'objectification – the stripping away of human meanings on both inner and outer reality . . . through the ever-expanding reach of science and technology'.[131] However, the co-existence of these two problems may be more complex

---

[124] Agreed 29 January 2000 in Montreal, see A. Quereshi, 'The Cartagena Protocol on Biosafety and the WTO: Co-existence or Incoherence?' (2000) ICLQ 835.
[125] P. Bernstein, *Against the Gods: The Remarkable Story of Risk* (Wiley, London, 1996).
[126] B. Adams, 'Running Out of Time' in Benton and Redclift' Social Theory, pp. 92, 93.
[127] S. Lash, B. Szersynski and B. Wynne, *Risk, Environment and Modernity: Towards a New Ecology* (Sage, 1996), p. 2.
[128] *Ibid.*, p. 3.
[129] Beck, *Risk Society*, and 'Risk Society and the Provident State' in Lash, Szersynski and Wynne, *Risk, Environment*.
[130] Lash, Szersynski and Wynne, *Risk, Environment*, p. 13.   [131] *Ibid.*

since the 'management', 'technocratic' and 'positivist' responses have
the overwhelming attraction of permitting a simplification by partition of
the issues. Thus, not only is it possible to factor out cultural complexities but also each problem may be labelled and put in a technical box.
Thus, 'global warming', 'nuclear waste' and 'acid rain' become three
quite separate issues. Thus, the technocrats and economists are attractive because they reduce the fantastic complexity of our interrelatedness,
particularly as 'globalisation' shrinks the size of the world. Thus, the
two 'problems' are not just two faces of subjectivity – the technocratic
approach is an attempt, however misguided, to *solve* the first problem
of the tyranny of choice. Calls for the complexity to be re-recognised
thus become frightening, not just because recognition of political consequences of economic systems[132] may lead to rethinking of comfortable
and self-indulgent lifestyles, but because techniques for factoring in this
complexity are not well-developed. Habermas' concept of communica-
tive discourse, particularly as a method of rule-making[133] by rational
discourse amongst all who will feel the consequences of the imposition
of norms, is one method but without a structural map is likely to lead
to inaction.[134] However, elements of a number of alternative insights
may be harnessed to afford a plan for breaking the fear of risk and the
dependency cycle on technical fixes that has been the response. First,
we may look to the neo-classical economists for an understanding that
rational decision-making is based on 'complete information'; secondly,
to the work of Maarten Hajer, who argues that all understandings of the
environment are social constructions which simultaneously express and
disguise preferences about the kind of society we ought to have.[135] He
calls for a new discourse which would identify the hidden preferences of
the current lines of thought and use ecology as 'a keyword under which
society discusses the issues of "life politics" (Giddens) in a way which
allows for a rethinking of existing social arrangements'.[136] The third line
of approach might build on Beck's concept of risk in order to construct a
risk assessment framework which opened up the discourse to value rather
than price on the basis of an understanding of the multiple consequences
of differing actions and inactions, including the type of society which
is implicit in the choices made. This would re-open the debate about

[132] As suggested by R. Grove-White, 'Environmental Knowledge and Public Policy
Needs: On Humanising the Research Agenda' in Lash, Szersynski and Wynne, *Risk,
Environment*.
[133] J. Habermas, *Between Facts and Norms* (W. Rehg (trans.), Polity, Cambridge, 1996).
[134] Habermas is surely represented at most academic departmental meetings.
[135] M. Hajer, 'Ecological Modernisation as Cultural Politics' in Lash, Szersynski and
Wynne, *Risk, Environment*.
[136] *Ibid.*, pp. 265–6.

redistributive justice that has been buried by fear of the necessity for self-denial and the complexity of the interrelations between the world trading system and ecological concerns. It is this central importance of risk and its assessment that may give us a clue to formulating new methods of thought which can overcome the difficulties of the polarised and distant modes of thought considered above and begin to develop an approach to industrial processes which combines scientific and ethical thought. Some small steps have been taken in the field of corporate governance which may provide clues to a framework of thought.

Social ecologists argue that the ecological crisis is the outcome not of a generalised anthropocentrism but of distorted social relations at work in hierarchical systems where an elite subjugates others while 'pillaging the natural world for prestige, profit and control'.[137] The solution suggested is small societies 'which recognise that human wellbeing is inextricably bound up with the wellbeing of the natural world on which human life depends'.[138] Zimmerman's study of radical ecology shows how deeply diverse, even confused, its roots can be seen to be. Exposing the risk that tendencies to enthrone the 'natural' can lead to the rise of authoritarianism – '[i]n stressful times, people are all too willing to surrender to leaders promising to end humanity's alienation from nature'[139] – Zimmerman explores the roots of deep ecology through the 1960s counterculture, complete with psychotropic drugs, to religious and specifically christian roots of the ecological crisis in the 'domination of man' over nature.[140] The rejection of modernity's 'dark side: its control obsession, its logic of identity, its anthropocentric humanism' by the mainstream postmodernist theorists such as Derrida, Foucault, Lyotard and Deleuse have cross-fertilised with deep ecology despite some initial mutual suspicions.[141] Adding to this the feminist perspective that androcentrism is significantly to blame for the ecological crisis[142] (however justified), lays a fine foundation for a 'green backlash' which emphasises elitism, obscurity, anti-christianity, an out-of-touch attitude, anti-male attitudes and impossible and illogical solutions. 'Deep-green perspectives often rely on some version of an arcadian "golden age" in which humans lived in harmony with one another and with nature.'[143] The suggested solutions 'are remarkably consistent in their versions of the "cure": a return to a materially more simple, egalitarian and convivial, decentralized communal existence'.[144]

---

[137] M. Zimmerman, *Contesting Earth's Future* (University of California Press, Berkeley, 1994).
[138] *Ibid.*, p. 2.   [139] *Ibid.*, p. 7.   [140] See Genesis 2:48.
[141] Zimmerman, *Contesting Earth's Future*, p. 92.   [142] *Ibid.*, p. 277.
[143] Benton, 'Biology and Social Theory', p. 39.   [144] *Ibid.*

Conclusion

This study of one of the issues which lies at the heart of many of the codes of conduct, whether they are globally proposed or adopted by companies, shows how one small element of corporate social responsibility can become a matter of hot dispute and runs the risk of being subverted by market fundamentalists or become meaningless by an appeal to 'golden age' values. Much work remains to be done to identify a sound basis for responsibility, to identify the values that should be espoused by an international concession theory and to feed them into systems of corporate governance.[145] Some suggestions are made in chapter 6.

[145] See end of Bibliography for the list of Websites.

6   Understanding property rights: companies, states and the duty of international co-operation

Articles 1(2) of the International Covenant on Civil and Political Rights (ICCPR) and International Covenant on Economic, Social and Cultural Rights (ICESCR) read:

All peoples may, for their own ends, freely dispose of their natural wealth and resources without prejudice to any obligations arising out of international economic co-operation, based upon the principle of mutual benefit, and international law. In no case may a people be deprived of its own means of subsistence.

This paragraph sets out the right to own and dispose of property, but also sets limits to the use of that property. No property right is absolute, as Parkinson points out: 'Ownership rights are not absolute[1] (ownership of a knife does not entitle the owner to stab people with it). That shareholders might own companies does not mean that they may insist that directors attempt to maximise profits in any way at all.'[2]

This chapter analyses two different approaches to property rights, draws on the concept of human rights as providing a framework for building just institutions and uses the two together to argue that companies should be reconceptualised and that a responsible understanding of human rights, property rights and international co-operation should lead to a change in the relationship between nation states in the trading arena.

Different perspectives on property rights

Hutton has analysed very different attitudes which may be discerned in the USA and Europe.[3] His thesis is that the attitude to the ownership of property in the USA has been informed by a number of factors. One

---

[1] For a detailed analysis refuting the justifications for unlimited property rights see J. Harris, *Property and Justice* (Clarendon, Oxford, 1996).

[2] J. Parkinson, 'The Socially Responsible Company' in M. Addo (ed.), *Human Rights Standards and the Responsibility of Transnational Corporations* (Kluwer, The Hague, 1999).

[3] W. Hutton, *The World We're In* (Little Brown, London, 2002).

of these is the existence of the experience of the settlers who arrived at 'a wilderness pregnant with riches', had 'risked all crossing the Atlantic and who, as fervent Protestants, believed they had a direct relationship with God'. They believed that they were serving God's purpose by taking possession of the land and using it for their own individual purpose.[4] Hutton shows how the writings of John Locke encouraged the view that property both claimed by and created from the land belonged 'exclusively and completely' to the settler and, moreover, that the 'purpose of society and Government' was to 'further the enjoyment of property, and political power was only legitimate if it served this end'.[5] Two passages cited by Hutton seem particularly apt:

The only way whereby any one divests himself of his Natural Liberty and puts on the bonds of Civil Society is by agreeing with other Men to join and unite and into a Community, for their comfortable, safe and peaceable living one amongst another, in a secure Enjoyment of their Properties, and a greater Security against any that are not of it.[6]

An instructive viewpoint comes from competition law, which for many years has been struggling to identify the boundary between enjoyment of a right to property and an abusive use of the power that the right to property brings with it.

Every man has a property in his own person. There is no body has any right to it but himself. The labour of his body, and the work of his hands we may say are properly his. Whatsoever then he removes out of the state that nature has provided, and left it in, he hath mixed his labour with and joined to it something that is his own, and thereby makes his property.[7]

The war of independence and the writing of the Constitution did nothing to dispel this mind-set, the justification for revolution being the interference by King George III with the settler's rights to enjoy their property freely:[8] 'Any notion that property rights were a concession granted by the state in the name of the common interest – the European tradition . . . had been dispelled by the revolution.'[9]

The understanding of the nature of property rights, then, is founded in nature and religion, giving at once a mystical and religious significance to ownership. If a settler prospered it was evidence of a healthy relationship with God. The availability of vast stretches of land made any egalitarian notions realisable without the concept of redistribution becoming a problem, so that redistribution of property became contrary both to nature and

---

[4] *Ibid.*, pp. 52–3.   [5] *Ibid.*
[6] John Locke, *Two Treatises of Government* (P. Laslett (ed.), Cambridge University Press, 1988), p. 331.
[7] *Ibid.*, p. 288.   [8] Hutton, *The World We're In*, p. 56.   [9] *Ibid.*, pp. 58–9.

religion. The role of the central government was thus reduced to protection of individual property. The Constitution prevented states from doing anything that might impair obligations embodied in contracts. Once the right to own property and to contract had been granted to corporations as well as individuals,[10] and companies holding shares in other companies were equated with individual shareholders, the stage was set for the giant groups of companies that we see today. Further, the resistance to redistribution enshrined in the Fifth Amendment is a fertile ground for those seeking to resist regulation on the basis that it is a 'confiscation of property'. The Fifth Amendment prevents the government from depriving an individual of 'life, liberty and property without due process; nor shall property be taken for public use without just compensation'. Thus, although there was a long period between the 1930s and 1970 when property rights were regulated, the fundamental understanding of individual liberty as inextricably intertwined with ownership of property made it very much easier for the ultra-conservatives to build their anti-regulatory policies and have them widely accepted:

For the constitution remains explicit. Without powerful popular support and a clear sense of national crisis – as over slavery in the 1860s or unemployment in the 1930s – the American constitutional conception is that government at federal and state level is the custodian of private property rights; and the Supreme Court sees its task as policing that injunction.[11]

The old settler cast of mind provided fertile ground for Nozick's arguments that portray taxation to finance any minimum income for the poor as a form of forced labour and all forms of redistributive justice as co-ercive.[12] It also provided fertile soil for the concept that corporations are nothing but a 'nexus of contracts'[13] with the obvious result that government should not interfere in that 'contract'.

All these influences can be seen at work in the anti-environmentalist movements chronicled by Rowell[14] with the use of dominion theology (God gave man 'dominion' over the earth)[15] to justify exploitation of

---

[10] *Dartmouth College* v. *Woodward* 17 U.S. 518 (1819).

[11] Hutton, *The World We're In*, p. 60.

[12] R. Nozic, *Anarchy, State and Utopia* (Harvard University Press, 1973); Hutton, *The World We're In*, p. 68.

[13] R. Posner, *Economic Analysis of Law* (4th edn, Little Brown, Boston, 1992); F. Easterbrook and D. Fischel, *The Economic Structure of Corporate Law* (Harvard University Press, 1991); B. Cheffins, *Company Law: Theory, Structure and Operation* (Clarendon, Oxford, 1997); J. Dine, *The Governance of Corporate Groups* (Cambridge University Press, 2000).

[14] A. Rowell, *Green Backlash* (Routledge, London, 1996).

[15] Genesis 2:27–28: 'So God created man in his own image, in the image of God created he him; male and female created he them. And God blessed them, and God said to them, Be fruitful and multiply, and replenish the earth, and subdue it: and have dominion over the fish of the sea, and over the fowl of the air, and over every living thing that moveth on the earth.'

natural resources – 'you can't really hurt the planet because God wouldn't allow that. God wouldn't have given man chainsaws if he didn't think they were benign'[16] – coupled with allegations that environmental regulation destroys jobs and interferes with private property rights. One of the aims of Alliance for America is: 'To restore and protect constitutional private property rights'. Part of the 'Wise Use' movement, it assisted in constructing Gingrich's now notorious 'contract with America' which the National Resources Defence Council explained 'threatens to undermine virtually every federal environmental law on the books, meaning dirtier air, dirtier water and more species pushed to the brink'.[17] No wonder, then, that the government, in international trade negotiations, regards itself as acting to protect private property, in this case the interests of corporate America: 'One USTR [US Trade Representative] was remarkably frank in saying that the US has no intellectual plan about the long-term national interest, no consistent commitment to any principle. Rather the "client state" is the model of the USTR: "It's too socialist to plan . . . the businessman is the man who knows. So you respond to him."'[18] Given the underlying understanding of the moral value attached to property ownership coupled with the conceptualisation of corporations as individual property owners, there would seem no reason for the trade official not to be frank. He has every reason to be happy in his job of increasing the property ownership of American constituents.

What, then, of the 'European' conception of property ownership. Of course, it is not possible to reflect subtle and complex differences between the understanding of property across Europe. However, it may be possible to detect a general difference of view. Hutton cites Article 14 of the post-war German Constitution as capturing some of the flavour of the difference:

property is not seen in Europe as an absolute right, as it is by US conservatives. Rather, it is a privilege that confers reciprocal obligations – a notion captured by article 14 of the post-war German constitution, which specifies that 'property imposes duties. Its use should also serve the public weal.' Those who own and hold property are members of society, and society has a public dimension to which necessarily they must contribute as the quid pro quo for the privilege of exercising property rights.[19]

This conception of property ownership is coupled with a 'profound commitment to the notion that all citizens should have an equal right to

[16] Rowell, *Green Backlash*, p. 9, citing a speech by Chip Berlet.
[17] National Resources Defence Council, *Breach of Faith* (1995), cited in Rowell, *Green Backlash*, p. 32.
[18] P. Drahos and J. Braithwaite, *Global Business Regulation* (Cambridge University Press, 2000).
[19] Hutton, *The World We're In*, pp. 50–1.

participate in economic and social life, and that the state is more than a safety net of last resort: it is the fundamental vehicle for the delivery of this equality'.[20] To some extent, this attitude was driven by the different experiences vis-à-vis land ownership when notions of equality became important. In Europe, any attempt at equality meant redistribution, in the USA: 'When John Adams argued in 1776 that the acquisition of land should be made easy for every member of society in order to achieve equality and liberty, he could disregard European concerns with how the state had to intervene to construct a just society: a continent lay before him waiting to be claimed.'[21] The European state thus had a real and vital role to play in constructing a fair society, a far cry from a minimalist role in protecting individual property rights.

The rhetoric used in discussing property rights often ignores two aspects of property rights: one is the importance of always keeping in mind the insight that property rights are, in essence, rights against other people. This means that all property rights govern power relations between people. If property rights are seen as a person having rights over a thing, this ignores the fact that the rights actually lie against other persons, a right to exclude etc. This means that the role that property rights play in wealth distribution is ignored because the person to person relationship is clouded by the person to thing discussion. Thus:

A theorist who supposes that ownership interests in objects may be justified, say, by a natural-rights argument, but then ignores questions of wealth-distribution, tells only half the story. The same is true, in the opposite direction of one who advocates a certain distribution of 'resources' but who neglects the question whether person-thing ownership relations are to form part of a property-institutional design.[22]

It is because rights over things can never be absolute, but rather made up of a web of rights and responsibilities operating interpersonally, that the debate resonates with issues of wealth distribution and power relations. If property ownership meant that I have absolute dominion over three beans and the right to use them as I wished and you have similar rights over five beans, the property distribution debates would exist but they would be a mere matter of counting. Do I deserve more beans than you? Because the reality of property relations is that I may exclude some (but not others) from use of an item and I may use that item only in non-harmful ways, the discussion of rights and duties becomes infinitely more complex and balanced. It is important, then, to understand the nature of the bundle of rights called property rights and what it actually consists of.

[20] Ibid., p. 51.   [21] Ibid., p. 61.   [22] Harris, Property and Justice, p. 141.

Harris argues that the Hohfeldian 'bundle of rights' concept which emphasises rights against other persons, rather than rights over things, can best be expressed on an 'ownership' spectrum which enables an individual to have more or less exclusivity over the use of the property and more or less power to use it in designated ways. The concept of ownership is seen therefore as firmly rooted in social expectations which have come to be embedded in legal rules. These include '(1) trespassory rules, (2) property-limitation rules; (3) expropriation rules; (4) appropriation rules. (There may be as well property-duty rules and property-privilege rules)'.[23] This understanding means that attempts to infuse more weight into a particular side of the balance of interests by claiming it is a 'property' right is mere rhetoric designed to appeal to the conceptions underlying a particular society's view of the standing of 'property'. Of considerable interest in this context is the examination by Harris of 'expansive' definitions of property. In particular an expansive use of 'property rights' by economists can be discerned. This is property right as including 'any right – whether Hohfeldian claim-right, privilege, power or immunity – concerning the use of a resource, where "resource" means all bodily and mental capacities of the rightholder. In other words, all rights are property rights.'[24]

This expansion of the 'property rights' conception is, according to Harris, based on the conflation of owning and ownership. For Harris, 'it is one thing to say that a person is vested with ("owns") either a right or a bundle of rights; it is another to say that what he is vested with is that particular set of open ended privileges and powers over a resource which counts as an ownership interest'.[25] 'Conventional' property is 'cashable rights' such as bank accounts, shares etc. 'because expropriation and appropriation rules apply to them – they pass into a bankrupt's estate and they can be inherited . . . Cashable rights are the subject of real markets.'[26] Such an understanding would exclude 'social rights' such as the right to use public spaces, which some have claimed as property rights. While Harris is not in principle opposed to this extended use of property, he nevertheless does not see it as an aid to clarity: 'By all means let rights of all kinds be analysed in these terms. Calling all rights "property rights" is, however, anything but an aid to clarity for the enterprises at hand since both the analyst and the reader must constantly remind themselves that they are not talking about "property" as ordinarily understood.' More important, perhaps, is the insight that the use of 'property rights' is a rhetoric which will resonate with the reader according to the 'meaning' of property in a particular society:

[23] *Ibid.*   [24] *Ibid.*, p. 146.   [25] *Ibid.*, p. 147.   [26] *Ibid.*, p. 149.

The plausibility of rhetorical expedients of this sort is difficult to assess. They depend on the way you suppose 'property' will ring in the ears of an addressee and on his willingness to fall in line with the terminological shift. Imagine the following dialogue:

EGALITARIAN: 'For reasons of a, b and c, I maintain that everyone ought to have an enforceable right to work.'
CONSERVATIVE: 'For reasons of X, Y and Z, I disagree with you.'
EGALITARIAN: 'But you believe that property ought to be protected, don't you?'
CONSERVATIVE: 'I do.'
EGALITARIAN: 'Well the right to work is property.'
CONSERVATIVE RESPONSE 1: 'No it isn't.'
CONSERVATIVE RESPONSE 2: 'Why didn't you say that before? Of course, I now change my view to yours.'[27]

It can be seen that this discourse is intended to have the opposite effect from the attempts to understand companies by representing shareholder rights as property ownership rights. In the former case, the right to work is put forward as a 'property right' which can only be interfered with, with care and probably with compensation following. This is likely to have the effect of a redistribution of wealth to poorer communities. In the case of shareholders, since making a property claim about shareholder rights is an attempt to make them the focus for the company's efforts and those of the directors, giving us the structure which insists that directors should act in the service of shareholders and presumes this service to be profit maximisation,[28] the effect is likely to be reversed. In particular, strengthening the shareholders' rights excludes from consideration the interests of employees (and others on whom the company has an impact) and assumes that shareholders may profit at the expense of employees. This enhanced protection by representation of these rights as property rights is likely to have the effect of redistribution of wealth from employees to wealthy shareholders.

We need, therefore, to examine very closely the results which might be achieved by the use of any expanded property rhetoric. As Harris notes: 'The concept-expanding arguments . . . concede, at least arguendo, that property as conventionally understood really deserves prestige and that the rights contended for have an importance which is merely parallel to conventional proprietary interests . . . [the arguments] make too much of property.'[29]

[27] *Ibid.*, p. 160.
[28] Making a 'property claim' about intellectual property will have the same regressive effect.
[29] Harris, *Property and Justice*, p. 161.

In order to reach a proper understanding of what companies should be doing and of better governance it is extremely important to explode the 'shareholder-owner' myth, to see the company as a free-standing structure and to create mechanisms to reflect the responsibilities which the company has towards those over whom it has power by reason of the exercise of its property rights by its managers.[30]

The identification as a property right does not in any way, as Harris points out, identify its parameters – it merely appeals to the importance of 'property'. The 'property concept' tells us nothing about the limitations to be imposed. Any recognition of property rights involves (i) a bestowal of the right on one or more persons; (ii) a corresponding limitation of the rights of others and (iii) limitations on the use of the right by its owner. Where the balance should be struck cannot be deduced from the 'nature' of the rights but needs to be considered as a distributional issue of social justice. If I make and patent a crossbow, and that gives me 'natural' rights in it, this does not mean I may use those rights to injure or bully others.

Spectrum of responsibilities: more power, more responsibility

Focus on property rights tends to divert attention away from the duties and responsibilities that are associated with them. The exercise of ownership over any thing brings with it both moral and legal responsibilities. If I own a poisonous snake I have both a legal and a moral responsibility not to allow it to roam freely around a crowded shopping area. Just as rights over things give me rights against others – they may not steal my snake – they also give me responsibilities to others – I may not injure them by failing to confine my snake. Great attention has been paid to the 'spectrum' of rights which property ownership brings. How is the spectrum of responsibilities structured? Again, it is important to bear in mind that the responsibilities are to other persons, just as the rights are rights against other persons. The spectrum of ownership rights might be seen as a sliding scale, giving rights which vary from the nearly absolute – I am holding in my hand a bun which I am about to eat, thus exercising my absolute right to prevent you eating it – to a contingent right to inherit an incorporeal hereditament, which will take a gaggle of lawyers to unravel and gives me very limited power over others. The spectrum of responsibilities also may resemble a sliding scale, with the heaviest responsibilities being placed on owners whose property rights

---

[30] Although, as Paddy Ireland notes, this will be a difficult process: P. Ireland, 'Property and Contract in Contemporary Corporate Theory' (2004) *Legal Studies* 451.

give them the greatest power over other people. Thus, the ownership of the snake brings with it the possibility of exercising lethal power over others, and consequent heavy responsibility. When ownership of inanimate items is the issue there clearly is a similar responsibility not to use my knife to stab another. What about 'neutral' items which have no immediately obvious harm-potential. In those cases, the scarcity and necessity factors must come into play and, where items are both scarce and necessary for human dignified existence, ownership of the power to exclude others must bear a concomitant responsibility not to unfairly wield that power. The inequality of power has been a continuous theme throughout the book. The following section argues that wherever great power is being exercised over others by virtue of property rights, the consequent responsibilities are greater the greater the degree of inequality. Unfair use of such power may be regulated by well known concepts borrowed from competition law (see below).

Concepts of ownership: useful or a mirage?

Harris argues that the concept of 'ownership' retains value, as embedded within it are a bundle of expectations and understandings about the 'just' distribution of property. Ross has argued that ownership concepts are meaningless because they can be omitted from legal language with no loss.[31] This enables a moving on – a mere description of property rights as they stand cannot solve any controversial question. Ross argues that the concept of ownership is meaningless by describing an imaginary island community where people believe in an imaginary form of contamination which they call 'tu-tu'. If you eat the chief's food you become 'tu-tu'. If you become 'tu-tu', you have to undergo a purification ceremony. Ross argues that the rule could be rewritten: 'if you eat the chief's food, you must undergo a purification ceremony'.[32] In the same way, property rules could be rewritten, leaving out the concept of ownership: if X purchases goods he becomes owner; if he is owner he can sue to prevent interference with the item. In the same way as 'tu-tu', ownership could be taken out of this description: if X purchases the goods, he can sue to prevent interference with them. However, Harris argues that the concept of ownership has embedded in it the balance of interests that must be taken into account when judges decide a difficult and novel case lying on the borderline between different bundles of ownership rights. Discussing the *United Steel Workers* case,[33] where the court ruled that a corporation was, as owner of

---

[31] A. Ross, 'Tu-tu' (1957) 70 *Harvard Law Review* 625.
[32] *Ibid.*, cited in Harris, *Property and Justice*, p. 131.
[33] *United Steel Workers* v. *United States Steel Corporation* 631 F. 2d (1980).

the plant, free to demolish it and not obliged to sell it to the union even at a fair market price, Harris argues that:

An apologist for the court's ruling would argue as follows. There are sound reasons for conferring open-ended use-privileges and control powers over industrial plants on individuals and groups – for example, the inherent property-freedom argument and the market instrumental argument . . . Those property-specific justice reasons support liberty to act in a self-seeking way. When the judges invoked ownership they were keying into those reasons. They warrant the conclusion that the corporation could act for the benefit of the shareholders without regard to the effect of their decisions on others.[34]

In other words, the concept of ownership stands apart from the mere description of the bundle of rights and contains within it the notion of the arguments concerning the just allocation of those rights. This can be used to solve novel disputes about boundaries of rights.

On the other hand, it could equally be argued that the use of 'ownership or property rights' rhetoric may inhibit finding the solution to the distributional issues involved in a novel court decision, by concealing its distributional effect by the very use of 'property rights rhetoric', an argument that Harris himself espouses and illustrates with his dialogue between 'conservative' and 'egalitarian' (above).

The inherent distributional implications contained within any concept of property ownership causes Harris to wrestle with that intractable question of the 'just' distribution of property. This may be a red herring, as Harris himself points out that the major importance of unequal distributions of property is the domination potential. In a brief but compelling analysis, Richard Wilkinson shows how important inequality is. In *Mind the Gap*,[35] he demonstrates that 'inequality kills' and 'that income inequality affects health independently of average living standards, of the proportion of the population in absolute poverty, of expenditure on medical care, and of the prevalence of smoking'.[36] Further, inequality brings in its wake a significant increase in violence and social dislocation. It may well be that the extreme inequality of distribution causes unrest in society not only because of simple envy of material possessions but because of a system which perpetuates privilege and seeks to exclude the powerless from having a voice. Thus, an education system which continually perpetrates the rule of the monied classes may engender despair and exclusion in the remainder of the population.[37] Similarly, a world that refuses to

---

[34] Harris, *Property and Justice*, p. 137.
[35] R. Wilkinson, *Mind the Gap: Hierarchies, Health and Human Evolution* (Wiedenfield and Nicholson, London, 2000).
[36] Wilkinson, *Mind the Gap*, p. 11.   [37] *Ibid.*

permit the poorest to develop or have a say in the way the planet's affairs are run will have the same effect. This (Sen) is now accepted as one of the prime indicators of poverty. Thus, justice may not require a mathematical 'slicing of the cake' to ensure equality of resources beyond provision of basic needs but it may well require checks on the use of power brought by access to material things. This must be particularly so where the goods are scarce and essential to human existence.

Property and power

It can be seen, therefore, that problems are often caused not by the concept of property ownership itself but the potential which property ownership has to create unequal power relations. Thus, 'to concede a property relationship between one person and a thing, at any point along the property spectrum, is to negate the liberty of the rest of mankind to use the thing without the licence of the "owner"'.[38] The concept of property as power follows inexorably from the Hohfeldian/Honoré/ Harris understanding of property rights not as rights over things but as rights against persons. Inevitably, the property as power effect is exacerbated where there is huge inequality of property ownership:

Theorists who deplore great inequality, in wealth-holdings and recommend measures to alleviate it often have in mind, not the social-psychological argument against wealth disparities . . . but rather inequality's resultant domination-potential. It is not disparity in bank balances that matters. It is the influence over the lives of others which large property-holdings afford.[39]

So property ownership brings with it power, and the greater the inequality of property ownership the greater the domination-potential. This is particularly true where the supply of particular goods is in scarce supply:

If the supply of objects like clothing, furniture and books is drastically restricted, those few who own them could dominate their fellows by the egocentric exercise of their ownership power to control use. On the other hand, where such chattels are widely available, the use-channelling and use-policing functions of ownership interests . . . as compared with costly and intrusive regimes of communal use, clearly outweigh such dangers of domination.[40]

If property is understood as governing power relationships it is even more important in a company context to look at the management, who have the real power to deploy the assets of the company. Corporate governance becomes those restraints that control this power.

---

[38] Harris, *Property and Justice*, p. 264.   [39] *Ibid.*, p. 265.   [40] *Ibid.*, p. 265.

Companies as property

Paddy Ireland has made it clear that companies fit with difficulty into the property rights discourse.[41] This is because the traditional 'take' on companies is that they are 'the property of the shareholders' or 'in the "nexus of contracts" or "agency" theory of the company, in what amounts to the same thing, that the shareholders own not "the company" but "the capital", the company itself having been spirited out of existence'.[42] Ireland also shows that there is considerable convergence between the property rights of creditors and those of shareholders: each can be seen as essentially 'outsiders' having contractual rights against the company, rather than 'insiders' with membership rights. The remaining 'insider' rights of shareholders are relics of the time when joint-stock companies were run by members and of an even earlier time when lending for interest was banned but partnership for profit was not. An investment as a 'sleeping partner' was a convenient way to circumvent this rule. What are the relics? One is the rule that the residue of capital on a winding-up belongs to shareholders. The other is that they should have a significant role in the way the company is run. This latter rule has, of course, been significantly eroded by the managerial 'win' in the battle of Article 80 (see below) so that shareholders are left with the 'nuclear option' of dismissal of directors via Companies Act 1985, s.303 but no say in the day-to-day running of the company. For companies registered prior to 1 July 1985, the relationship between these two organs was usually governed by an article similar or identical to Article 80 of Table A annexed to the Companies Act 1948. This read:

> The business of the company shall be managed by the directors who may pay all expenses incurred in promoting and registering the company, and may exercise all such powers of the company as are not, by the Act, or by these regulations, required to be exercised by the company in general meeting, subject, nevertheless, to any of these regulations, to the provisions of the Act and to such regulations, being not inconsistent with the aforesaid regulations or provisions, as may be prescribed by the company in general meeting; but no regulations made by the company in general meeting shall invalidate any prior act of the directors which would have been valid if that regulation had not been made.

This appeared to reserve to the general meeting a power to make regulations to govern the conduct of directors. The scope of this power was most uncertain until the judges determined the balance of power

---

[41] P. Ireland, 'Company Law and the Myth of Shareholder Ownership' (1999) MLR 62. See also J. Hill, 'Visions and Revisions of the Shareholder' (2000) *Am. J Comparative Law* 39.

[42] Ireland, 'Myth of Shareholder Ownership'.

issue firmly in favour of the directors to the detriment of the powers of the general meeting. Thus, in *Automatic Self Cleansing Filter Syndicate Company Ltd v. Cunningham*,[43] the Court of Appeal held that a resolution passed by a simple majority of shareholders (an ordinary resolution) was not effective. The resolution purported to order the directors to go ahead with an agreement to sell the whole of the assets of the company. The directors believed that this was an unwise course. Warrington J said:

The effect of this resolution, if acted upon, would be to compel the directors to sell the whole of the assets of the company, not on such terms and conditions as they think fit, but upon such terms and conditions as a simple majority of the shareholders think fit. But it does not rest there. Article 96 [this was very similar to Article 80 of Table A to the 1948 Act above] provides that the management of the business and control of the company are to be vested in the directors. Now that article, which is for the protection of a minority of the shareholders, can only be altered by a special resolution, that is to say, by a resolution passed by a three-fourths majority, at a meeting called for the purpose, and confirmed at a subsequent meeting. If that provision could be revoked by a resolution of the shareholders passed by a simple majority, I can see no reason for the provision which is to be found in Article 81 that the directors can only be removed by a special resolution. It seems to me that if a majority of shareholders can, on a matter which is vested in the directors, overrule the discretion of the directors, there might just as well be no provision at all in the articles as to the removal of directors by special resolution. Moreover, pressed to its logical conclusion, the result would be that when a majority of the shareholders disagree with the policy of the directors, though they cannot remove the directors except by special resolution, they might carry on the whole of the business of the company as they pleased, and thus, though not able to remove the directors, overrule every act which the board might otherwise do. It seems to me on the true construction of these articles that the management of the business and control of the company are vested in the directors, and consequently that the control of the company as to any particular matter, or the management of any particular transaction or any particular part of the business of the company, can only be removed from the board by an alteration of the articles, such alteration, of course, requiring a special resolution.

This approach was subsequently adopted in *Breckland Group Holdings Ltd v. London and Suffolk Properties Ltd*,[44] where the court held that since the company's Articles of Association adopted Article 80 of Table A to the Companies Act 1948, the conduct of the business of the company was vested in the board of directors, and the shareholders in general meeting could not intervene to adopt unauthorised proceedings.

---

[43] [1906] 2 Ch. 34.   [44] [1989] BCLC 100.

It seems to have been the case that the general meeting could not interfere in management decisions by way of an ordinary resolution, even under the Companies Act 1948. The 1985 equivalent is Article 70 of Table A to the Companies Act 1985 (by virtue of SI 1985/805). This reads:

Subject to the provisions of the Act, the memorandum and the articles and to any directions given by special resolution, the business of the company shall be managed by the directors who may exercise all the powers of the company. No alteration of the memorandum or articles and no such direction shall invalidate any prior act of the directors which would have been valid if that alteration had not been made or that direction had not been given. The powers given by this regulation shall not be limited by any special power given to the directors by the articles and a meeting of directors at which a quorum is present may exercise all powers exercisable by the directors.

The justification for the insistence that there should be no interference in director control save by a special resolution was well expressed in *Gramophone and Typewriter Ltd* v. *Stanley*.[45] Buckley LJ said:

The directors are not servants to obey directions given by the shareholders as individuals; they are agents appointed by and bound to serve the shareholders as their principals. They are persons who may by the regulations be entrusted with the control of the business, and if so entrusted they can be dispossessed from that control only by the statutory majority which can alter the articles.

Now, it cannot be denied that a company may have significant assets. If shareholders do not have significant ownership rights, why is it that the 'myth' still persists? This is surely tied up with a particular use of the American expanded vision of property rights. As we have seen it is necessary, when expansionary property rhetoric is used, to examine the intended effect of that rhetoric. In this case the 'ownership' of the company leads to the understanding that the company must be run primarily in the interest of its 'owners' and that their interest in the company is in extracting maximum profit from 'their' capital. This has a direct result on the perception of directors' duties which become primarily a personal code of conduct to align their interests with those of the 'owners'. If we dismiss this exaggerated property rhetoric and look to those that are exercising property rights over the company we look to those who have the right to alienate the capital and the right to exclude others from participation. In other words, we look at the management. We should understand the company as truly owner of its assets with the managers exercising its ownership rights, at present uncontrolled since the claim to control by

---

[45] [1908] 2 KB 89.

shareholders is seen to be an unfounded use of property rhetoric.[46] If we then take the vision of the company not as a separation of ownership and control but of exercise of ownership residing in management, where can we seek for the domination-controlling rules which balance the power inherent in the exercise of ownership rights? As Harris points out:

The modern regulatory state has . . . enacted a raft of property-limitation and expropriation rules directed specifically at mitigating domination-potential. Use-privileges and control powers may be curtailed by safety and health regulations and transmissions and unfair dismissal rules. Expropriation rules may impose forced contributions to fund redundancy pay, pensions and insurance against sickness or disability.[47]

What are the consequences for company law, directors' duties and corporate social responsibility?

Uses for concession theory

Nowhere is there complete adherence to the theory that companies ought to be permitted to function free of all regulation: all states operate a 'mixed' system of market freedom and regulatory control.[48] However, traditional discussions of corporate governance give little weight to the web of regulation which surrounds every corporate operation and, in particular; the impact of regulations on corporate culture has not been examined in its legal context. Is the way in which companies actually work reflected in discussions of corporate governance and an adequate legal framework?

The imposition of regulations may easily be justified by traditional concessionary approaches: in its simplest form, this approach views the existence and operation of the company as a concession by the state, which grants the ability to trade using the corporate tool, particularly where it operates with limited liability. In return, this concession implies the right to impose limits on a company's freedom.[49] The imposition of regulations inevitably identifies those at most risk from particular corporate decisions and seeks to protect from or minimise that risk. Thus, environmental

---

[46] And in any case shareholder control of large companies is an unreal concept.

[47] Harris, *Property and Justice*, p. 268, although it should be noted that Harris is considering property limitation rules as if they were imposed on traditional 'owners', i.e. shareholders.

[48] Dine, *Governance of Corporate Groups*.

[49] *Ibid.* and S. Bottomley, 'Taking Corporations Seriously: Some Considerations for Corporate Regulation' (1990) 19 *Federal Law Review* 203; W. Briton Jnr, 'The New Economic Theory of the Firm: Critical Perspectives from History' (1989) *Stanford Law Review* 1471.

regulation identifies whole communities as at risk, financial regulation protects shareholders and health and safety regulation principally targets employees.

As Teubner rightly says: 'Putting it quite bluntly, a corporate enterprise does not exist simply as a self serving and self-realizing institution for the unique benefits of its shareholders and workers, but rather exists, above all, to fulfil a broader role in society.'[50]

Indeed, large companies have a huge influence on our social, economic and political lives. In the United Kingdom, the influence of companies is just as evident as in the USA. The food we eat is dependent on how it is grown, processed, packaged, advertised and sold to us. Every one of these stages is determined or influenced by companies. Increasingly, companies are involved in the provision of public services, with the government having created mechanisms such as private finance initiatives, and more recently the proposals for community interest companies. Such mechanisms are recognition of the influence of companies and their role in society. In such a context it seems that the two company law assumptions that share the structure of company law and corporate governance are not only anachronistic but in fact wholly inaccurate in their representation of the character of companies today. Teubner argues for a proceduralisation of fiduciary duties that enables non-shareholder interest groups to participate in the monitoring and decision-making functions. The role of the law, in Teubner's view, should be to control indirectly internal organisational structures, through external regulation. The role of the law is external mobilisation of internal control resources.[51] The organisational structures should allow for 'discursive unification processes as to allow the optimal balancing of company performance and company function by taking into account the requirements of the non-economic environment'. In short, Teubner advocates a constitutionalisation of the private corporation to make the corporate conscience work 'if that meant to force the organization to internalise outside conflicts in the decision structure itself in order to take into account the non-economic interests of workers, consumers, and the general public'.[52] Teubner highlights the role of disclosure, audit, justification, consultation and negotiation and the duty to organise. He emphasises the need to proceduralise. Ultimately, the point is to ensure that the decision-making processes allow

[50] Gunther Teubner, 'Corporate Fiduciary Duties and their Beneficiaries: A Functional Approach to the Legal Institutionalization of Corporate Responsibility' in K. Hopt and G. Teubner (eds), *Corporate Governance and Directors' Liabilities* (de Greuter, Berlin, 1987), p. 149, at p. 157.
[51] Teubner, 'Corporate Fiduciary Duties', at p. 160.   [52] *Ibid.*, p. 165.

participation by those affected by the decisions, whether in terms of profit, consumer choice, working conditions or environmental impact of corporate activities. If the decisions are made jointly with the directors, the monitoring role ought to reduce. Teubner's proceduralisation would mean a complete change in conceptualisation of the company and directors' duties. The following tries to put some 'flesh on the bones' in the context of a new look at UK company law.

As we have seen, Berle and Means identified the separation of ownership and control in the 1930s,[53] showing that, with dispersed ownership of shares, control of corporations lay less with shareholders and more with the professional managers of large companies. This led to corporate governance being discussed primarily as involving antidotes to such a separation, and, in particular with implementing mechanisms to align the managers' interests with those of shareholders. Today, there is a second shift in the governance of companies, this time strengthening the degree of separation between ownership and control and also shifting the focus and perhaps the power centre of decision-making to a lower level in the company. This second shift calls into question the reality of the vision of a company exclusively directed by the 'controlling minds' of managers but, by acknowledging that directors still have the ultimate decision-making power, is in line with the reconceptualisation of a company as owner; the directors are exercising their property rights' powers on behalf of the company. Limits on their decision-making, however, appear by way of providing them with information from throughout the organisation and insisting that the focus of their decision-making should be an assessment of risks to the organisation. This new understanding would reject the idea of the company being composed solely of its organs but, in some ways, embrace the 'organic' view of companies.[54] The organic analysis is borrowed from the analysis of states. Wolff[55] cites John Caspar Bluntschli who 'found something corresponding in the life of the State not only to every part of the human body but even to every human emotion, and designated e.g. the foreign relations of a State as its sexual impulses!'. In fact, the organic theory is remarkably wide in its vision; many current theories would omit the inclusion of the 'hands' at all, regarding employees as 'negative externalities' rather than as an integral part of the company's existence.

There are a multiplicity of regulations that companies must implement and, within companies, systems are set up to implement them. A simple

---

[53] A. Berle and G. Means, *Modern Corporation and Private Property* (Macmillan, New York, 1962).
[54] M. Wolff, 'On the Nature of Legal Persons' (1938) *Law Quarterly Review* 494.
[55] *Ibid.*, p. 499.

example (and the most obvious) is the systems which must be set up to ensure financial control. In the Barings collapse, one of the problems that was clearly identified was the lack of knowledge of the derivatives operation which was displayed by the directors. They were eventually disqualified as directors as being 'unfit' following their failure to put in place proper systems of financial control. However, in order to create effective systems they needed to familiarise themselves fully with the functioning of the derivatives operation. It is argued here that, because detailed knowledge of the operation of the systems which make up a functioning company are to be found elsewhere than at board level and that proper systems of control cannot be designed without this detailed knowledge, it is incumbent on the eventual decision-makers to take account of the knowledge and experience of those most intimately involved in the systems necessary to control the risks which are the subject matter of the regulations.

This is not to say that the power to take the eventual decision has moved, but that proper decisions cannot be made without wide consultation. This, in turn, gives the consultees standing to influence the decision-making process and, in particular, change the culture of the company from focusing on shareholder profit alone.

The example of financial controls is just a single example of the regulations which impinge on decision-making within companies. The company must remain within the criminal law and must have systems which ensure that this happens. This may extend to ensuring consistency between methods of working and achievable targets. For example, if time targets for repairs to electric signals on a railway cannot be achieved without electricians working excessively long hours, the inconsistency may in future be identified as a reason for holding the company (and its directors) criminally responsible for an ensuing disaster. Similarly, proper systems for implementation of health and safety and environmental regulations must rely on detailed knowledge of the 'way things actually work'.

In effect, the imposition of regulations which must be implemented, gives the company a greater degree of autonomy from the shareholders. As we have seen, the 'shareholder property rights' model led to a narrow definition of what is meant by 'corporate governance', with most commentators concerned only with the methods by which management action can be controlled in order to ensure management behaviour 'for the benefit of the company', meaning in the vast majority of situations, for the financial benefit of shareholders. This tendency has been reinforced by the 'legal boxes' which have been constructed, particularly in common law jurisdictions. 'Company law' is seen as a separate discipline from 'labour law', ignoring the fact of enormous proportions that the huge majority of employees work for companies and that companies cannot work without employees. Similarly, other regulatory structures impinge on corporate decision-making so that it is no longer open to the shareholders to insist on profit at the expense of compliance with health and safety standards, environmental regulations[56] or consultation with employees. Nor can systems to ensure compliance with criminal law be neglected.

In the recent American scandals, particularly those like Enron and Worldcom which involved manipulating accounts in order to maintain inflated share prices, we see a conflict between the old-fashioned view of 'corporate governance' which sought to create mechanisms for aligning the governance of the company with shareholders' interest in profit maximisation, and the vision described here which seeks, by regulation, to make sure that companies have proper systems in place to ensure their compliance with the requirements of society generally. Although it is true that directors of Enron and Worldcom stood to gain personally from inflated share prices, the primary motive for the 'creative accounting' was the pressure to do better than competitors so far as a continuously rising share price was concerned. The system of corporate governance which relies primarily on shareholder enforcement is shown not only to be inadequate but counterproductive, imposing pressures which are destructive of both the company and the wider interests of society, both in loss of faith in markets and destruction of, e.g., pension benefits.

The requirements of this web of regulation, imposed by society at large, means that the company gains a greater degree of autonomy from its 'owners' because it has discretion in responding to the imposition of control from a source other than the 'owner' shareholders. In this way, the separation of ownership and control is enhanced.[57]

At the same time, reliance on the knowledge of the employees at the 'coalface' to properly implement the systems creates a culture of inclusion which moves away from a simple conception of a company as a contract-based institution created by shareholders for their own benefit. This applies not only to financial and employee protection systems but to all systems designed to implement regulations relevant to a particular company's operation. For example, a company making chemicals will be

---

[56] See on this point M. Blecher, 'Environmental Officer: Management in an Ecological Quality Organisation' in G. Teubner (ed.), *Environmental Law and Ecological Responsibility: The Concept and Practice of Ecological Self-Organisation* (John Wiley, London, 1994).

[57] I am grateful to Bob Watt for this point.

unable to implement environmental control systems unless the designers
of the systems obtain detailed knowledge of the manufacturing process
so that risk (e.g. of spillage) may be minimised. This requires extensive
consultation if it is to be successful. In turn, the consultees have the
opportunity to influence decision-making. Similarly, implementation of
regulations designed to protect a 'wilderness area' may require extensive consultation with inhabitants and scientists if the aim of the regulations is to be properly achieved. The company becomes very much more
complex than a shareholder-driven profit maximisation machine. The
resultant company looks very different. What is clear is that, while this
understanding of companies is nearer the 'real picture' than the stylised
vision that we are given by theorists, company law and discussions of
corporate governance have not changed to embrace the new reality and
remain stuck in the 1930s, debating the consequences of the Berle and
Means understanding of separation and control by 'aligning' managers'
interests, with shareholder interests, rather than addressing the reality of
the complex web of systems of control which make up company decision-
making. This, coupled with the legal 'box' mentality, has inhibited the
understanding of directors' duties. They remain principally a code of
personal conduct designed to address the 'alignment of interests' issue
and no remedy is available in company law for failure to design proper
systems of control; no employee affected by the absence of health and
safety controls, damaged by poor environmental controls or disadvantaged by failure of consultation has a remedy against directors for failing
to implement regulations correctly.

The proper implementation of these regulations will and should entail
a change in the corporate culture, from a narrow contractual concept to
a more inclusive one, shifting decision-making powers in two separate
ways. First, the regulations may prevent the shareholders and directors
from taking certain decisions. More subtly, by requiring implementation
of control over operations where they involve complex detail known only
to those intimately involved, they require significant input from and give
significant influence on the eventual decision to those operating networks
at all levels of the organisation. The emphasis is on *proper* implementation of the regulations – if they are complied with in a 'box ticking'
or minimalist way it is unlikely that the regulations will function well,
leaving the company at risk of violation. Essentially, a process of internalisation will take place, with the decision-making processes absorb-
ing the underlying aims of the regulations as systems are designed to
achieve those aims. Parker explains the mechanisms relating to employees
well:

For exactly the same reasons that external command-and-control regulation will fail, a legalistic, top-down approach to compliance management within the company will also be a weak guarantee of compliance. At the simplest level, this is because a corporate compliance management system that fails to enter employees' 'zone of meanings' will not be effective at teaching them or convincing them of what it actually means to comply . . . At a deeper level, a self-regulation program that fails to connect with people's values and identities will fail to connect with anything that offers a robust motivation to commit to compliance – it will be dependent on extrinsic sanctions and rewards for success only, not intrinsic ones . . . Also, a compliance management approach that does not seriously engage with employee opinions, concerns and experiences about compliance will mean that employees distrust management's approach to compliance. There will be no bond that convinces them that it is worthwhile to comply to help the company. Finally, engaging with employee concerns and values about self-regulation builds up the integrity of the whole organisation by building up personal integrity, individual by individual. This is a bottom-up resource of connection with and permeability to the broader culture and its values.[58]

Two factors are at work here: one is the way in which company culture can be 'grown' as a result of implementation, the second is the nature of 'good' regulation.

The formation of a corporate culture can be significantly influenced not only by formal regulation but also by the 'issues of the day' which frequently surface in 'soft law' such as codes of conduct. Drahos and Braithwaite have noted the way in which codes and principles have influenced business conduct.[59] Issues such as sexual harassment or age discrimination become embedded in corporate culture as discussion of them is prompted by regulation or discussion which originated outside the organisation concerned.[60] Proper implementation of regulatory controls of all sorts will involve an internalisation process which needs to be individual to each organisation so that it works well within the existing culture and operations of a particular organisation. In order to facilitate this notion of internalisation it is necessary to adapt the core notions of corporate governance to give proper prominence to the complex web of risk control systems. The danger is that, if this is not done, compliance with regulatory control will continue to be seen as a marginal, moving concerns other than profitability to the status of 'negative externalities' rather than an essential part of the nature of corporate existence.[61]

---

[58] C. Parker, *The Open Corporation* (Cambridge University Press, 2002), p. 203.
[59] Drahos and Braithwaite, *Global Business Regulation*; see also J. Dine and B. Watt, 'Sexual Harassment: Hardening the Soft Law' (1994) ELR 104.
[60] C. Parker, *The Open Corporation* (Cambridge University Press, 2002), p. 16 and ch. 2.
[61] Cooter has analysed a reverse of this process: arguing that in a large organisation the self-interest of employees is imperfectly aligned with the interest of the organisation:

An institution absorbs and respects norms which are implemented within the organisation in response to outside regulation. The extent to which this occurs will depend to a large extent on the design of the regulations. Environmental awareness within companies has been enormously increased over recent years as a result both of the imposition of requirements of environmental audit and the general awareness of environmental issues in the general population.

Those who seek to regulate companies have been moving away from the simple 'command and control' model of prescribing the behaviour of companies by external regulation.[62] Instead, regulations increasingly follow the innovation in regulatory design suggested by Ayres and Braithwaite of enforced self-regulation,[63] although with a slight shift in emphasis. Ayres and Braithwaite envisaged individual firms proposing their own standards of regulation. The rules designed would have a public enforcement mechanism.[64] What seems to be emerging is a slight variant on this theme which perhaps we may call 'directed self-regulation'. Instead of each company setting its own standards of regulation, the standards or aim of the regulation is defined.[65] However, the two systems share in common the way in which the implementation is achieved. Parker uses the term 'new regulatory state' to describe the way in which 'the state is attempting to withdraw as the direct agent of command and control and public management, in favour of being an indirect regulator of internal control systems in both public (or formerly public) and private agencies'.[66] Detailed implementation is left to individual companies so that the mechanisms which suit that company may be established. While directed self-regulation lacks the flexibility of avoiding over-strict rules for small enterprises, it shares with enforced regulation the benefits of individual design of rules so that companies are likely to be more committed to them – both hostility to outside regulators and the confusion of two rulebooks is avoided.[67] In certain circumstances the full flexibility of enforced self-regulation may be established by regulators who are

---

'Internalising an occupational role involves accepting the norms of an occupation so intimately that they enter the individual's self-conception': R. Cooter, 'Law and Unified Social Theory' (1995) 22 *Journal of Law and Society* 50.

[62] Which a number of studies have shown to be ineffective and leading to deception and avoidance: see I. Ayres and J. Braithwaite, *Responsive Regulation* (Oxford University Press, 1992); R. Chambers, *Whose Reality Counts* (Intermediate Technology Publications, London, 1997); J. Dine, *Criminal Law in the Company Context* (Dartmouth, Aldershot, 1995); Dine, *Governance of Corporate Groups*.

[63] Ayres and Braithwaite, *Responsive Regulation*, p. 101.   [64] *Ibid.*, p. 102.

[65] A procedure not dissimilar to the original design for EEC Directives.

[66] Parker, *The Open Corporation*, p. 15.   [67] *Ibid.*, p. 116.

able to run a risk analysis over specific supervised sectors. The Financial Services Authority, for example, has established a sophisticated method of analysing financial risk which requires varying degrees of internal regulatory control, dependent on the assessment of the degree of risk posed by the operations of individual firms.[68]

Directors' responsibility to assess risk and establish systems

A key feature of such a legal framework is the imposition of a duty on directors to design and oversee systems which are capable of assessing and controlling the risks run by companies. Financial risks are the most obvious and the law already imposes duties to establish and maintain proper financial control systems. However, companies are at risk from a wide range of pressures imposed by society either directly (by regulation) or indirectly (by, for example, bad publicity). To fully understand the response of companies to regulatory and other pressures such as adverse publicity, we need to formulate a new concept of companies and their structural operation. If we move away from the idea of the company as separate 'organs' (shareholders in general meeting, directors with the duties of directors attempting to impose a code of personal conduct on directors) and consider the company as a series of interlocking systems, we can see that each system has a distinct role. One system will ensure that employees are paid correctly, another will establish the optimum method of ensuring a supply of raw materials, another will establish controls over financial affairs generally. Some of the systems will be established in response to external regulatory or publicity pressures. These systems established to control risks of regulatory or public condemnation and if properly designed and implemented, will change the culture of a company from one which has a narrow conception of its purpose as profit maximisation to an understanding of the purpose of companies which has internalised social values expressed by society as a whole. In turn, this means that directors' duties should be seen in a radically new light. No longer will it be sufficient to impose a code of conduct to ensure that the single stakeholders' interests are met, rather, they should be considered as responsible for establishing systems specifically designed for that company which adequately address the risks of regulatory condemnation and bad publicity, as well as systems which make the process of

[68] See detailed discussion of risk assessment, below.

production work. The importance of systems was analysed by Gladwell[69] in relation to the Enron failure, arguing that the collapse of the company was partially due to the culture of recruiting talented 'stars' and giving them unfettered discretion to operate, rather than establishing a settled network of operating systems.[70]

I have argued elsewhere that this new concept of risk management as a duty for directors is already becoming evident.[71] For the present, one example will suffice. *Re Barings plc and others (No. 5)*[72] resulted in the disqualification as directors of three directors of Barings on the grounds that their conduct as directors made them 'unfit to be concerned in the management of a company'.[73] The Secretary of State's case was that each respondent was guilty of serious failures of management in respect of the supervision of the conduct of Nick Leeson, thereby demonstrating incompetence of such a high degree as to justify a disqualification order. The three specific illustrations of management failure all relate to the failure to establish and maintain proper systems of control: first, over Leeson directly because he was both dealing and settling, i.e. dealing and auditing his own behaviour; secondly, by failing to maintain any procedure for enquiring into the massive requests for funding made by Leeson or attempting to reconcile the amounts requested with the underlying position; thirdly, the 'crass' and 'absolute' failure of any managerial controls over Leeson. The court held that each individual director owed duties to the company to inform himself about its affairs and to join with his co-directors in supervising and controlling them. Where functions had been delegated, the board retained a residual duty of supervision and control. In his evidence to the Board of Banking Supervision Inquiry, Peter Baring described the internal control failings as 'crass' and 'absolute',[74] a description with which the court agreed. However, the purpose of Mr Baring's description was to shift blame away from the board. His argument was that the board had properly delegated the establishment of supervision systems. Basing his decision on directors' duties of skill, care and judgment, Parker J refused to follow that line of argument, dismissing

[69] M. Gladwell, 'The Talent Myth', *The Times*, 20 August 2002.
[70] See also B. Mclean and P. Elkind, *The Smartest Guys in the Room* (Viking, London, 2003); B. Cruver, *Anatomy of Greed* (Arrow, 2003).
[71] J. Dine, 'Risks and Systems: A New Approach to Corporate Governance and the European Employee Consultation Stuctures?' (2001) 3(2) *International and Comparative Corporate Law Journal* 299.
[72] [1999] 1 BCLC 433.
[73] Under Company Directors Disqualification Act 1986, s. 6(1)(b).
[74] *Barings* (n. 73), judgment of Jonathan Parker, p. 481.

the idea that a 'flat' management structure, necessary for quick decision making involved:

any lesser degree of vigilance or diligence on the part of senior management in the performance of their managerial duties. Similarly, in my judgment, the mere fact that functions had been delegated to trusted colleagues whose capabilities are known and respected – in other words, the mere fact that the delegation was a proper one – does not relieve the delegator of the duty to supervise and monitor the discharge of those functions.[75]

This judgment emphasises that the ultimate responsibility for creating and supervising systems for the control of risk lie with the board. This does not imply that they have sole responsibility; the systems should also identify responsibilities throughout the company for design and participation in the systems.[76] Requiring and overseeing this aspect of systems design should be the responsibility of the board.

Of course, in the *Barings* case, the risk was of financial losses. However, financial loss may be caused by less direct failures and in particular by exposure to regulatory or public opinion condemnation. It seems evident that there is a direct responsibility on the board to assess these risks and respond to them by establishing adequate systems of control and that directors who do not do so are 'unfit' for that office. How may risks be assessed?

Risk assessment

Assessment of risk is a complex business even if it be accepted that it can be achieved with any degree of objectivity. The technical perception of risk as objective and measurable is losing ground:

the view that a separation can be maintained between 'objective' risk and 'subjective' and perceived risk has come under increasing attack, to the extent that it is no longer a mainstream position . . . Assessments of risk, whether they are based upon individual attitudes, the wider beliefs within a culture, or on the models of mathematical risk assessment, necessarily depend on human judgment.[77]

---

[75] *Ibid.*, p. 499.
[76] I am grateful for my colleagues at the Canberra Conference of Corporate Law Teachers Association of Australia and New Zealand 2004 for raising this issue. In the Australian HIH collapse a different division of responsibilities between managers and directors was suggested by the investigating Commission. See *Collapse* (CCH Australia, 2001).
[77] See Royal Society, *Risk: Analysis, Perception and Management* (Royal Society, 1992), p. 90. See also Julia Black, 'Perspectives on Derivatives Regulation' in A. Hudson (ed.), *Modern Financial Techniques, Derivatives and Law* (Kluwer, London, 2000); R. Baldwin, 'Introduction – Risk: The Legal Contribution' in R. Baldwin (ed.), *Law and Uncertainty: Risks and the Legal Processes* (Kluwer, Berlin, 1997).

This points to the necessity for directors to exercise their skill and judgment in assessing the exposure of their particular concerns. Some lessons may be learned from the work done by the Financial Services Authority, which is creating a 'risk assessment' approach to regulation.[78] The risk posed by a firm to the FSA's objectives[79] will be assessed by 'scoring' probability and impact factors. Probability factors take account of the likelihood of the risk happening and impact factors assess the 'scale and significance' of the harm should the risk occur. The FSA expresses it as:

$$\text{Priority} = \text{impact} \times \text{probability}^{80}$$

The FSA proposes a spectrum of supervision from maintaining a continuous relationship with firms which have a high impact risk rating to 'remote monitoring' of low impact firms. Firms in the latter category 'would not have a regular relationship with the FSA, but would be expected to submit periodic returns for automated analysis, and to inform the FSA of any major strategic developments'.[81]

This is a strategy which could clearly be adopted by the boards of companies towards their systems which implement regulation or seek to prevent market or financial risks from materialising. Indeed, such systems are required (although with unclear ambit) by the Combined Code which is the outcome of the Cadbury, Greenbury and Hampel Reports.[82] These exercises culminated in the Combined Code which requires amongst other things the maintenance of a 'sound system of internal control'.[83] The London Stock Exchange issued guidance on the implementation of this requirement,[84] which stresses management of significant risks since 'a company's system of internal control has a key role in the management of risks that are significant to the fulfilment of the company's business objectives'. In order to ensure a proper system of internal control the board must consider:

---

[78] Drawing (*inter alia*) on the work of the Basle Committee on Banking Supervision. See, e.g., Risk Management Guidelines for Derivatives, Bank for International Settlements (Basle, July 1994).

[79] Sections 2–6 of the Financial Services and Markets Act 2000 set out four objectives: to maintain confidence in the financial system, to promote public understanding of that system, to secure the appropriate degree of protection for consumers and to reduce the extent to which it is possible for a financial services business to be used for a purpose connected with financial crime.

[80] *Building the New Regulator* (Financial Services Authority, 2000).   [81] *Ibid.*, para. 25.

[82] See now the Combined Code, para. 12.43A, Listing Rules, in force 11 January 1999 (Stock Exchange, London).

[83] Code Principle D2.

[84] *Internal Control: Guidance for Directors on the Combined Code* (Stock Exchange, 27 September 1999).

- the nature of the risks facing the company;
- the likelihood of the risk materialising;
- the company's ability to reduce the impact of such risks if they do materialise;
- costs relative to benefits.

The DTI's suggested Operating and Financial Review[85] is moving in the same direction. It would include:

> where and to the extent material . . . An account of the company's and/or group's systems and structures for controlling and focussing the powers of management and securing an effective working relationship between members, directors and other senior management . . . Dynamics of the business – i.e. known events, trends, uncertainties and other factors which may substantially affect future performance, including investment programmes. For example risks, opportunities and related responses in connection with competition and changes in market conditions, customer/supplier dependencies, technological change, financial risks, health and safety, environmental costs and liabilities.[86]

This new culture of risk assessment and required response by setting up implementation systems is clearly an important element in company culture. Proper implementation systems will involve dialogue with those most closely involved in whatever it is that is posing a risk to the company's operation. Thus, if the risk is to the health and safety of employees, the only way in which that risk can be minimised is to understand the risk by undertaking consultations with those most at risk. Only in this way can the risk be properly understood and relevant systems devised to minimise it. In turn, this will involve a change of culture, from regarding health and safety systems as a negative externality to involve minimum compliance, to an integrated part of the corporate objective. In this way, 'stakeholders' become part of the company, not by formal identification, but by taking part in the decision-making process. This avoids the insuperable difficulties of the formal insertion of stakeholders – no longer must a formal 'weighting of interests' take place, each system operates to minimise the risks to the company and it is those risks that are to be weighed, not the moral or social claims of interest groups.

A corporate governance solution

However, one problem remains, and that is the difficulty of holding the directors to account. Clearly, all risks undertaken by the company will, if they materialise, have costs. Regulations will have their own enforcement

---

[85] *Modern Company Law: Developing the Framework* (DTI, 2001), para. 5.88.   [86] *Ibid.*

mechanisms, bad publicity will lead to drop in revenue etc. However, if the internalisation of the new understanding of companies as affecting a wide range of people is to be completed, enforcement mechanisms internal to the company are necessary. No longer should the risks run by employees be seen as imposing an external cost – 'red tape' for companies – their risks should be managed by internal systems with an integral enforcement mechanism. The dangers of not pursuing this route may be illustrated by the ineffective s. 309 of the Companies Act 1985 which infamously requires directors to take account of the interests of employees and provides that the enforcement mechanisms are to be the same as for any other duty of directors, i.e. exclusively in the hands of shareholders, with the result that it has been entirely ineffective.[87]

We have seen that directors' duties are being reformulated to cover devising and supervising systems of risk control, requiring them to assess the risk to the company of failing systems. Devising a proper internal enforcement mechanism, which widens the interest groups with *locus standi* to enforce those duties, requires an assessment of the risks run by the beneficiaries of those systems. Where the risk run by the protected beneficiary and the risk run to the company of a system failure are both significant and coincide, the protected beneficiary should have *locus* to enforce the duty of directors to put in place proper systems or to claim compensation for the failure to do so. This would be the enforcement of a duty owed to the company, brought by a person or group who has a 'direct and individual concern'[88] (or some similar formula) in the failure of such systems. The risk run by the individual would give them the standing to correct the failure to protect the company from risk. It must be emphasised that the creation of such a cause of action would be without prejudice to claims external to company law such as compensation claims. The point is to create a company law right to force companies, via their managers, to take on board the responsibilities inherent in the power that a company's property rights bestow on it. For an employee to be able to demand that proper systems of health and safety protection should be put in place might well be as valuable for her future as a compensation claim is for remedying past wrongs and they should not be mutually exclusive. Of course, so far as individual employees or others who are affected by companies are concerned, it is not difficult to grant *locus standi*. What should happen about a company's wider responsibilities for ethical

---

[87] Not only for lack of enforcement powers in the hands of employees qua employees but also because the wording of the section is vague and any enforcement action would probably have to show total disregard for employees' interests (the weight to be given to each interest group is introduced by this formal identification of stakeholders).

[88] EC Treaty, Article 230.

behaviour? Who should be the enforcers of human rights and corporate social responsibility, including environmental responsibilities? Here, I would draw on the Ayres and Braithwaite concept of 'tripartism'.[89] This involves the empowerment of public interest groups (PIGs). The strategy would be to identify a PIG which is directly concerned with the enforcement of the spirit behind a particular piece of legislation (environmental agencies for environmental law, employees for health and safety etc.). In order to prevent cosiness, competition between groups would be engendered. The role of these groups would then be to oversee the regulator/regulated relationship and step in where there was undue evidence of capture and corruption. The empowerment of PIGs is argued also from the standpoint of democratic involvement. 'An opportunity for participation by stakeholders in decisions over matters that affect their lives is a democratic good independent of any improved outcomes that follow from it.'[90] The authors' thesis is that a democracy limited simply to providing a vote for citizens will be undermined by the power accrued by the corporate sector. Selective empowerment of PIGs provides some element of counterbalance to that power. Further, empowerment of PIGs will of necessity cause the building of trusting relationships since there 'is no reason for us to trust those who have no influence over our lives; but once an actor is empowered in relation to us, we are well advised to build a relationship of trust with that actor'. The competition could be presided over in the United Kingdom by the DTI, FSA or the Stock Exchange and the NGOs (in place of PIGs) who were appointed would be charged with making sure that proper systems of CSR and rights compliance exist within the company. This would be done by comparison between claims made by the company and the reality as researched by the NGO. Disparities would require an explanation. Gross disparities would *prima facie* be a breach of directors' duties. Company responsibility for systems would extend to responsibility for supplies, subsidiaries and all over whom the property right gives significant dominion, whether at home or abroad. This system might well have the welcome side-effect of increased transparency for NGOs so that it would become easier to assess their independence.

So far as a standard of care is concerned, the courts already have a power to determine when company affairs are being conducted in a way unfairly prejudicial to the members.[91] And the jurisprudence relating to this concept could perhaps be adapted to embrace other interest groups.[92]

[89] I. Ayres and J. Braithwaite, *Responsive Regulation* (Oxford University Press, New York, 1992), ch. 3.
[90] *Ibid.*, p. 82.   [91] Companies Act 1985, s. 459.
[92] See *O'Neill* v. *Phillips* [1999] 2 BCLC 1.

However, a better approach might well be to use the standards being developed for the purposes of the disqualification of directors on the 'unfit' ground.[93] As noted above, the court in the *Barings* case made it plain that it remained the ultimate responsibility of the board to ensure that proper systems of financial control were in place, as the company was otherwise at extreme risk of collapse. Putting the company at risk from failure to create other systems protective of groups other than shareholders may equally be susceptible to a finding of 'unfitness' and such a finding could well be the basis for compensation or redress for groups other than shareholders.

In this way, it is suggested, the vision of companies can be changed and broadened. Of course, the assessment of risk carries with it difficulties and discretion and it is not suggested that such a remedy would arise frequently. However, the possibility of extending enforcement measures to groups other than shareholders would mean that the narrow objectives of service to shareholders would be changed and a more inclusive culture would understand that the objectives of society and the objectives of companies must be made to work in some degree of harmony.

Property rights in the international context

Here, the spectrum of responsibilities is particularly important. It will be remembered that the greater the power that property rights bestow, the greater the ensuing responsibilities. Further, the implication of restricted supply is that, although the 'owners' have the liberty to restrict the use of particular items, the liberty and freedom of others is thereby removed or restricted. Of course, where the relevant item is food or water, the freedom and liberty inherent in exercise of property rights becomes the death warrant of those whose access to the item is thereby restricted. This is the riposte to those who seek to elevate free use of property rights to a human rights status. Petersmann gives as examples of human rights 'property rights and freedom of contract', arguing that '[t]he neglect for economic liberty rights and property rights in the UN Covenant on economic and social human rights reflects an anti-market bias'.[94] Setting aside the fact (as noted earlier) that the ICCPR and the ICESCR share the same wording concerning the right to own and use property, the emphasis on the protection of property rights as an enhancement of liberty clearly depends on which side of the property right you are. If you

---

[93] Company Directors Disqualification Act 1986, s. 6.
[94] E. Petersmann, 'Time for a United Nations "Global Compact" for Integrating Human Rights into the Law of Worldwide Organisations: Lessons from European Integration' (2002) *European Journal of International Law* 621.

have the right to exclude then 'You're all right, Jack'. If you are excluded then the picture looks very different. Use of this expansionary vision of property rights clearly favours the 'haves' above the 'have nots'. A more balanced view of property rights would look carefully at the power that the rights will bestow and the consequent responsibilities that arise.

Here, we are concerned with the property rights of nation states and the way in which that property is used on the international stage, in particular the restraints to which that usage is subject because of 'obligations arising out of international economic co-operation, based on the principle of mutual benefit, and international law. In no case may a people be deprived of its own means of subsistence.' As with corporate property, the rules are created and followed by representatives of individuals.

Onora O'Neill points out that the allocation of obligations by human rights instruments, and, in particular, the Universal Declaration of Human Rights, is less than perfect. 'The Declaration approaches justice by proclaiming rights. It proclaims what is to be received, what entitlements everyone is to have; but it says very little about which agents and agencies must do what if these rights are to be secured.'[95] In the case of traditional liberty rights, O'Neill points out this is not a problem, they:

have to be matched and secured by universal obligations to respect those rights (if any agent or agency is exempt from that obligation, the right is compromised), other universal rights cannot be secured by assigning identical obligations to all agents and agencies. Universal rights to goods and services, to status and participation cannot be delivered by universal action. For these rights the allocation of obligations matters, and some means of designing and enforcing effective allocations is required, if any ascription of rights is to have practical import.[96]

The limitations on the property rights of nations are limited and defined by their other international obligations. The task is to define those limitations and identify which agencies are responsible for delivering the international economic co-operation which the Covenants define as the boundary to the right to enjoy natural property rights.

Whereas, as O'Neill has noted, the identification of obligation-holders in the Universal Declaration is rather 'scattergun' – 'Every individual and every organ of society, shall strive by teaching and education, to promote respect for these rights and freedoms and by progressive measures, national and international, to secure their universal and effective recognition and observance' – on the subject of international co-operation, the two Covenants diverge. The ICCPR clearly identifies

---

[95] Onora O'Neill, 'Agents of Justice' in T. Pogge (ed.), *Global Justice* (Blackwell, Oxford 2001).
[96] *Ibid.*, pp. 191–2.

the obligation-holders, which are the primary agents of justice,[97] and the recipients of the rights in that document: 'Each State Party to the present Covenant undertakes to respect and to ensure to all individuals within its territory the rights recognised in the present Covenant.'[98] However, the Preamble also places duties on individuals: 'Realising that the individual, having duties to other individuals and to the community to which he belongs, is under a responsibility to strive for the promotion and observance of the rights recognised in the present Covenant.' That Preamble is repeated in the ICESCR and the primary obligation-holder is similarly defined but the duty is very different:

Each State Party to the present Covenant undertakes to take steps, individually and through international assistance and co-operation, especially economic and technical, to the maximum of its available resources, with a view to achieving progressively the full realisation of the rights recognised in the present Covenant by all appropriate means, including the adoption of legislative measures.

The possible conflict between this duty and the right to utilise property is clear.[99] Further, Article 11(2) of the ICESCR reads:

The States Parties to the present Covenant, recognising the fundamental right of everyone to be free from hunger, shall take, individually and through international co-operation, the measures, including specific programmes which are needed: . . . (b) taking account of the problems of both food-exporting and food-importing countries, to ensure an equitable distribution of world food supplies in relation to need.

Does this impose a duty on resource-rich states to provide assistance?

The questions are: to what extent does the duty of international co-operation limit the right of states to enjoy their natural property? Is there a duty to provide aid or technical assistance or are the 'weasel-words' 'available resources' always there to provide a get-out?

To what extent must states, as primary obligation-holders, legislate to create or encourage secondary duty-holders, such as individuals, to carry forward this duty? Judith Bueno de Mesquita argues that, in accordance with Articles 1(b) and 29 of the Vienna Convention on the Law of Treaties, states that have ratified the Covenant are bound to give effect to its provisions at international level;[100] that while treaties traditionally have been considered to exert obligation in relation to the territory of

---

[97] *Ibid.*, p. 189.   [98] Article 2.
[99] See Skogly, *The Human Rights Obligations of the IMF and World Bank*, p. 128 (Cavendish, London, 2001).
[100] Judith Bueno de Mesquita, Senior Researcher, Human Rights Centre, Essex University, 'International Covenant on Economic, Social and Cultural Rights: International Co-operation and Assistance' (forthcoming).

a state party this is only the case unless 'a different intention appears from the treaty or is otherwise established'.[101] As Mesquita points out, the text of Article 2(1) clearly implies that extra-territorial obligations are required to realise the rights in the Vienna Convention. Alston and Quinn have argued that, although particular obligations have not yet been identified, 'it would be unjustified to go further and suggest that the relevant commitment is meaningless. It may, according to the circumstances, be possible to identify obligations to cooperate internationally that would appear to be mandatory on the basis of the undertaking contained in Article 2(1) of the Covenant.'[102] In particular, in relation to the rights to food and to development, the obligation of international co-operation is becoming clearer. Thus, the UN Committee on Economic, Social and Cultural Rights (CESCR) adopted a general comment on the right to food which invoked the international obligation 'to refrain at all times from food embargoes or similar measures which endanger conditions for food production and access to food in other countries'.[103] While the General Comments are not legally binding they have 'considerable legal weight' in providing 'jurisprudential insights'.[104] Similarly, by Article 3 of the Declaration of the Right to Development, 'States have the primary responsibility for the creation of national and international conditions favourable to the realization of the right to development' and:

States have the duty to co-operate with each other in ensuring development and eliminating obstacles to development. States should realize their rights and fulfil their obligations in such a manner as to promote a new international economic order based on sovereign equality, interdependence, mutual interest and co-operation among all States as well as to encourage the observation and realization of human rights.[105]

Although the analysis at the beginning of this chapter focused on American attitudes to property and it may seem strange to analyse American attitudes to property in the context of international co-operation, since

---

[101] Vienna Convention on the Law of Treaties (entry into force 27 January 1980) Article 29.
[102] P. Alston and G. Quinn, *The Nature and Scope of States Parties' Obligations under the International Covenant on Economic, Social and Cultural Rights* (1987) 9 HRQ 192, cited in Mesquita, 'ICESCR'.
[103] E/C. 12 1999/5, General Comment No. 12, 12 March 1999, para. 37.
[104] M. Craven, *The International Covenant on Economic, Social and Cultural Rights: A Perspective on its Development* (Oxford University Press, New York, 1995), p. 91; P. Alston, 'The Committee on Economic, Social and Cultural Rights' in P. Alston (ed.), *The United Nations and Human Rights: A Critical Appraisal* (Clarendon, Oxford, 1992), p. 494, both cited by Mesquita, 'ECESCR'.
[105] E/CN.4/ Sub.2/1999/12.

the USA has not even ratified the ICESCR, the purpose is to understand how obstacles to fulfilling that obligation may arise in any context.

Regulating trade and international co-operation

Now, of course, the contrast between 'American' and 'European' positions discussed above are unsubtle caricatures,[106] but they are also of real underlying significance and must be taken account of in determining the extent of the rights protected by Articles 1(2) of the two Covenants and whether, and to what extent, such rights might be limited by a duty of international co-operation. In particular, the more absolutist and expansionist view of property rights leads to an elevation of the notion of the sanctity of the rights of property owners and a disregard of those against whom those rights may be exercised. 'The naturalist ideology of the sanctity of property was especially appealing to the powerful class of landowners and to the legal functionaries they supported.'[107] How little changes! The focus on the protection of property rights will also distort the understanding of the state's obligations on the international stage and create an atmosphere which militates against the duty of co-operation. In particular, it reinforces a notion that a state should promote its own self-interest[108] and thus the interests of its citizens. Shue calls this the 'trustee/adversary theory of government'.[109] This is that 'the proper role of every national government is primarily or exclusively to represent and advance the interests of its own nation'.[110] Clearly, this notion is wholly accepted by the US Trade Representatives' alignment of the interests of 'corporate America' with the interests of the state and their wholehearted commitment to deliver whatever property owners desire. Indeed, as Shue acknowledges, '[t]his view is so widely assumed that it is ordinarily taken to be obviously correct'.[111] This notion may be based on a taxation argument: 'the government is spending our money so the

---

[106] They do not, e.g., include consideration of Rawls' views on the American side of the equation. See J. Rawls, *A Theory of Justice* (Oxford University Press, 1973); Rawls, 'The Law of Peoples' in S. Shute and S. Hurley (eds), *On Human Rights* (Basic Books, New York, 1993) extensively considered in Pogge, *Global Justice*, and for a discussion of these ideas in relation to neo-classical economics see M. Salter, 'Hegel and the Social Dynamics of Property Law' in J. Harris (ed.), *Property Problems: From Genes to Pension Funds* (Kluwer, 1997).

[107] J. Getzler, 'Theories of Property and Economic Development' in Harris, *Property Problems*.

[108] K. Arambulo, *Strengthening the Supervision of the International Covenant on Economic, Social and Cultural Rights: Theoretical and Procedural Aspects* (Intersentia, Antwerpen, 1999), p. 66.

[109] H. Shue, *Basic Rights* (2nd edn, Princetown University Press, 1996), p. 139 *et seq.*

[110] Shue, *Basic Rights*, p. 139.   [111] *Ibid.*, p. 140.

government ought to be serving our interests. This appeals to a principle that he who pays the piper is morally entitled to call the tune.'[112] Alternatively, the argument might be that the government is representative of those who elect it so that failure to secure the best deal for them is a breach of trust.[113] Faithful representation of these interests at an international level, where there is conflict with the interests of others, will require an adversarial role. Shue identifies two significant failures of this simplistic view of a government's role: one is that in representing their population, one 'interest that . . . citizens [might] wish to have served may be their interest in seeing their transnational duties to aid fulfilled'.[114] Thus, the pursuit of the protection of property rights is limited by an individual's duty under the Universal Declaration of Human Rights and the obligations placed on states by the ICESCR. The second 'weakness' in the theory identified by Shue is the disparity between the difference in the structure of national and international bargaining:

> Within individual nations a great deal is determined simply by the competition of adversaries representing conflicting interests, but not everything is. Institutions also exist to care for those unable to compete or unsuccessful in the competition, to provide for goods that cannot derive from competition, to regulate competition within generally beneficial rules . . . So far comparable restraining institutions at international level are virtually non-existent.[115]

This insight is supported by the rhetoric of the enthusiasts for an open, global market. Since restraining institutions have not appeared, the duties on states must be developed in order to fill this vacuum. Once Pogge's concept of institution-building to deliver human rights is seen in the context of the duty of international co-operation, the duty to build a fair trading system becomes very clear indeed. In chapter 5, the devotion of trade negotiators to gaining the best advantage for their country was noted. This attitude is informed by the various concepts of nationalism. In seeking to address the boundaries which should apply to naked self-interest in international trade bargaining, Pogge starts from the requirements imposed on a public official to set aside family considerations when, for example, employing an aide. Pogge points out the inconsistency between the condemnation of corruption which favours family or friends in national debates and the acceptance that such partiality is acceptable or even required at international level. Such a 'limit on the scope of common nationalism is not widely accepted today. But its rejection smacks of inconsistency. How can we despise those who seek to slant the national playing field in favour of themselves and their relatives and yet applaud

---

[112] *Ibid.*   [113] *Ibid.*   [114] *Ibid.*, p. 141.   [115] *Ibid.*

those who seek to slant the international playing field in favour of themselves and their compatriots?'[116] The avoidance of moral constraints by the appointment of an 'agency', be it government or companies, makes no moral sense.

Further, the practice of human rights conditionalities in trade agreement becomes even more suspect. The duty-holders under the duty of international co-operation will be the most powerful as it is their very power that can ensure the establishment of equitable institutions. Why, then, would they be entitled to use conditionalities imposed by contract in order to supplement their primary failure to build systems which deliver human rights? An opponent of this view would need to adopt one of the principles described by Pogge as 'explanatory nationalism'.

The right to own and use property may be limited in two, quite different and important ways. It might be limited by an egalitarian desire to even out inequality in ownership, based on social or theological notions of morality.[117] Peter Singer famously argued that assisting those without enough food is morally required. Failure to contribute at least 10 per cent of our incomes to the hungry is morally wrong.[118] This argument is supported by Shue's perspective on human rights. He argues that subsistence rights, including the right to food, are basic rights, that is, rights on which the exercise of all other rights and freedoms depend.[119] Shue suggests that all basic rights give rise to three types of duty:

- 'I Duties to avoid depriving';
- 'II Duties to protect from deprivation';
- 'III Duties to aid the deprived'.[120]

Translated on to an international stage, Shue argues that the duty of international co-operation requires the transfer of assets, at least so far as food aid is concerned.[121]

However, the duty to transfer assets may be seen as one end of a spectrum of what is meant by the duty of international co-operation. At this early stage of conceptualising the duty of international co-operation, much more work is needed to flesh it out, not least by understanding what might be meant by the 'maximum available resources' which are to

---

[116] T. Pogge, *World Poverty and Human Rights* (Polity Press, Oxford, 2002), p. 124.
[117] See G. Cohen, *If You're an Egalitarian, How Come You're so Rich?* (Harvard University Press, 2000).
[118] P. Singer, 'Reconsidering the Famine Relief Argument' in P. Brown and H. Shue (eds), *Food Policy: The Responsibility of the United States in the Life and Death Choices* (Free Press, New York, 1977). See also the contributions of P. Brown, S. Gorovitz and H. Shue in the same volume.
[119] This view is supported by Pogge: see Pogge, *World Poverty*.
[120] Shue, *Basic Rights*.   [121] *Ibid.*, ch. 7.

be applied in the fulfilment of this duty. This is not to say that such a clarification is unimportant but to propose a less radical starting point.

The duty of international co-operation contains the well-known spectrum of obligations: to respect, protect and fulfil.[122] In ascending In order this requires refraining from violating rights, preventing others from violating rights and taking steps to fulfil those rights.[123] Shue's arguments require the imposition of an international duty to fulfil rights but it is possible to achieve much by arguing for the less radical duty to respect rights. As we saw in chapter 4, Skolgky has argued that the international co-operation duty of states requires them to use their votes within the International Monetary Fund (IMF) and World Bank in a way that ensures the rights of people in other nations are not infringed.[124] The CESCR asks all nations about the way in which states use their voting rights in these two institutions. There is no reason why this argument does not apply equally to the way in which international trade agreements are arrived at and to domestic policies which affect international trade. Indeed, the CESCR requires that 'States Parties should, in international agreements whenever relevant, ensure that the right to adequate food is given due attention and consider the development of further international legal instruments to that end.'[125]

However, in international trade negotiations presided over by the World Trade Organisation, as in the operation of policies of the IMF and World Bank, there is a great deal of evidence that a narrowly defined trustee/adversary position has been adopted by powerful states in simple pursuit of the property interests of their nationals, using not their right to own and 'freely dispose of property' as such but the naked power that the ability to do so brings.[126] Drahos and Braithwaite show that in numerous cases the rules of the international trading system have been arrived at by 'economic coercion', often by the powerful 'Quad' combination of trading blocks, Canada, Japan, the USA and EU.[127] In particular, in a system supposedly dedicated to international freedom of markets, agricultural subsidies paid by industrialised countries to their farmers 'amount to more than $1 billion a day', preventing developing countries from any possibility of competing.[128] Failure to address this issue and provision of apparently favourable terms of trade (Generalised System of

---

[122] P. Hunt, *Reclaiming Social Rights* (Dartmouth, Aldershot, 1996), p. 31.

[123] *Ibid*. See also K. Arambulo, *Economic, Social and Cultural Rights: Strengthening the Supervision of the International Covenant* (Intersentia, Antwerpen, 1999), p. 73.

[124] Skolgky, *Human Rights Obligations*.   [125] General Comment 12, paras 36–37.

[126] Drahos and Braithwaite, *Global Business Regulation*; Hutton, *The World We're In*; Oxfam Report, *Rigged Rules and Double Standards* (Oxfam, 2002); D. Korten, *When Corporations Rule the World* (Kumarian Press, 1998).

[127] Drahos and Braithwaite, *Global Business Regulation*.   [128] Oxfam, *Rigged Rules*, p. 11.

Preferences) hedged round with conditions which make the possibility of take-up very low[129] are estimated to cost developing countries in the region of US$100 billion per annum. In the light of the jurisprudence on the right to food and the right to development, use of power to achieve this result cannot be justified as a use of property *simpliciter* and must surely be a breach of the duty of international co-operation. It is suggested here that reconciliation between the right to own property and the duty of international co-operation requires, at a minimal level, the regulation of the use of this power – together with the regulation of the power of TNCs.[130] I make no suggestions here as to an institutional framework for providing these restraints, but hope to provide a conceptual framework drawn from twin disciplines which have at their heart the regulation of power – human rights law and competition law. It is axiomatic that human rights law was intended to regulate power. Central to the Universal Declaration is the acknowledgement that 'disregard for human rights have resulted in barbarous acts which have outraged the conscience of mankind'. That disregard manifested itself as much on the international as the national stage. However, trade concerns have been considered to be in the realm of economic, social and cultural rights which, as we have seen, have been indisputably the 'junior branch' of human rights law.[131]

The well documented neglect of economic, social and cultural rights requires the development of conceptual tools to enhance the understanding of the parameters of rights and duties which principally concern economic relations.

It is suggested here that the content of the duties may take some elements from a body of law which also seeks to limit and regulate power, with the added advantage that one of its particular concerns is the limitation of power which occurs as a result of the accumulation of great wealth.

In order to see a way to answer this dilemma, it is useful once again to 'de-bundle' property rights.

---

[129] UN Conference on Trade and Development, *The Least Developed Countries Report 2002* (United Nations, 2002).

[130] Note that this could be supplemented by Paul Hunt's idea that developing countries could use their human rights responsibilities as a 'shield' to prevent the non-fulfilment of human rights because of IFI imposed plans. The duty of international co-operation should prevent states voting for such plans and from exercising muscle in the WTO where it would have the same effect. See P. Hunt, 'Relations between the UN Committee on Economic, Social and Cultural Rights and International Financial Institutions' in W. Genugten, P. Hunt and S. Mathews (eds), *World Bank, IMF and Human Rights* (Wolf Legal Publishers, Nijmegan, 2003).

[131] See A. Eide, C. Krause and A. Rosas (eds), *Economic Social and Cultural Rights* (2nd edn, Martinus Nijhoff, 2001), p. 15; Hunt *Reclaiming Social Rights*; Arambulo, *Strengthening the Supervision*; Dine, *Corporate Governance of Groups*.

Property is more than merely a right of exclusive possession against all the world. It is a bundle of nested rights, that is, rights building upon each other, which include (1) possession of the physical thing owned; (2) rights to exploit, change, re-order, and manage; (3) rights to the flow of income from rights 1 and 2; (4) rights to transfer, exchange and destroy rights 1, 2 and 3; and (5) rights to transfer right 4.[132]

A distinction is thus made between the 'dephysicalised expectation of income'[133] attached to the possession of the 'thing' and the 'thing' itself. Each of these different aspects of property rights may require a distinct legal approach to their regulation, both at national and international level. Crucially, these regulations will concern the impact of property owners on each other:

the 'right' of property is diminished primarily by the prospect of competitive injury to physical control and income flow caused by the actions of rival property holders in exploiting their holdings . . . It can be difficult for the law to discriminate between legitimate price competition and co-ercive interference with assets . . . there is a complex relationship between the 'right' to private property and the legitimacy of injurious competition.[134]

It is precisely this difficulty which competition law and policy seeks to address. Peritz writes 'On the one hand, competition policy has prohibited corporate mergers that result in firms whose market power might allow them to dominate their rivals. On the other, enjoining owners from selling their business impinges upon a fundamental right to sell or exchange property.'[135]

Drahos and Braithwaite argue for an extension of competition policy to the world stage in order to prevent the accumulation of vast power by multinational corporations.[136] The following argument takes a particular aspect of competition law and explores its implications in the light of states' obligations of international co-operation, and in particular how that can be seen as limiting the dephysicalised components of their property rights, the rights to exploit their possessions. Competition policy in the EU has developed 'fairness' tests in order to limit unfair exploitation of the power that property ownership brings, thus providing a conceptual structure that can be used to give content to the duty of international co-operation. One way in which EU competition law limits exploitation

[132] J. Getzler, 'Theories of Property and Economic Development' in Harris, *Property Problems*, p. 203.
[133] *Ibid.*   [134] *Ibid.*, p. 204.
[135] R. Peritz, *Competition Policy in American History, Rhetoric, Law* (Oxford University Press, 2000).
[136] Drahos and Braithwaite, *Global Business Regulation*.

of property rights is by the concept of 'abuse of a dominant position'.[137] Article 82 reads:

Any abuse by one or more undertakings of a dominant position within the common market or in a substantial part of it shall be prohibited as incompatible with the common market.

Examples given of when such abuse may be detected at first sight 'suggest a concern to place limits on the capacity of a dominant firm to exploit its customers or consumers by extracting monopoly rents from them by such practices as excessive pricing, limiting markets, tie-ins etc'.[138] However, as Anderman points out, 'Article 86 [now 82] has been interpreted to apply more widely than merely prohibiting exploitative abuses; it is also aimed at "structural" or "anti-competitive" abuses directed against competitors.'[139] The concept of 'abuse' thus relates to unfair behaviour which is possible because of the power accumulated by dominance in a particular market. The WTO administers a global market and rules are made for specific markets within that umbrella. Thus, the geographic market administered is global, the specific markets will be defined by identifying the relevant 'product' although 'the Commission's choice of relevant product market has on occasion been heavily influenced by the type of abuse that is alleged to have occurred'.[140] The definition of the 'relevant market' may be heavily influenced by the way in which the 'abuse' is being perpetrated. In the 'Soda Ash' case the Commission stated that in determining 'the area of business in which conditions of competition and market power of the allegedly dominant undertaking fall to be assessed . . . account has to be taken of the nature of the abuse being alleged and of the particular manner in which competition is impaired in the case in question'.[141]

In other words, the precise definition of the product market in question can be adjusted to reach a finding of dominance and subsequently an abuse of that dominance where the nature of the behaviour is seen as unfair. It is not a scientific determination but depends on the underlying understanding of what level of exploitation of property rights is to be tolerated. As Peritz has shown, this may change radically over the years according to the dominant economic philosophy, to the extent that he sees competition policy in the recent years as an 'inverted' version of

---

[137] Article 82 EC.
[138] S. Anderman, *EC Competition Law and Intellectual Property Rights* (Clarendon, Oxford, 1998), p. 181.
[139] *Ibid.*   [140] Anderman, *EC Competition Law*, p. 161.
[141] *ICI* v. *Solvay*, [1991] OJ L=152/21, para. 42, cited in Anderman, *EC Competition Law*, p. 161.

its previous role: 'There is little concern about market power and none about corporate size . . . the Regan-Bush years produced an antitrust inversion. Consistent with the conservative Republicans' deregulatory ideology of freeing commercial enterprise from government restraints, antitrust doctrine emerged as a weapon for privately owned businesses to attack the power of political subdivisions.'[142]

Care must therefore be taken to select an underlying understanding of 'fairness' and its opposing concept 'abuse' in balancing the unconstrained use of power and enjoyment of property rights. However, at the level of international markets, there is a growing realisation that the system that has been created by using the trustee/adversary justification for self-interested negotiation, backed by economic coercion, has created an unfair and unsustainable position in which powerful nations have abused their dominant position in the international markets at the expense of the poorest:

Over one quarter of the children are undernourished in 33 out of 43 Least Developed Countries (LDCs) for which data are available. Nineteen out of 33 African LDCs have maternal mortality rates above 1 per hundred live births. The chance of a child dying under the age of five is more than 1 in 10 in 38 out of 49 LDCs. On average, under 50 per cent of the adult female population is literate in LDCs.[143]

If this can even partially be caused by 'rigged rules and double standards'[144] operating on a grand scale then the concept of abuse may be helpful in limiting the unconstrained use of property power by states in constructing and operating a trading system that delivers such appalling outcomes.

A research agenda

In writing this book I have sought to show that any easy solutions or quick fixes are unlikely to help and may often be counterproductive. In looking for solutions I have concentrated on the restructuring of our view of corporations. It follows that many ideas which are seen as routes to ameliorate the grave inequalities in the world deserve far more attention than I have been able to give them in the time span available and in the light of my limited understanding. So for the future may I hope that the following ideas receive further attention.

The first is the concept of the free movement of workers. It seems strange that while this concept forms one of the central pillars of the European market, it has been widely neglected in the creation of the global

---

[142] Peritz, *Competition Policy*, p. 273.   [143] UNCTAD, *Least Developed Countries*, p. 21.
[144] Oxfam, *Rigged Rules*.

market. Nigel Harris points out that '[d]iscussions on immigration do not start from the interests of the world, the universal, but from those of the minority, the country'.[145] This is beginning to change with a number of authors making the case for free movement, in particular mooting the possibility that freedom of movement would benefit rich countries as well as poorer ones.[146] But much more research is needed.

A second possibility is to revise the position of nation states and soften the absoluteness of sovereignty. Concepts of multilevel governance are being developed:[147]

> just as it is nonsense to suppose that, in a juridical condition, sovereignty *must* rest with one of the branches of government, it is similarly nonsensical to think that in a multilayered order, sovereignty *must* be concentrated on one level exclusively. As the history of federalist regimes clearly shows, a vertical division of sovereignty can work quite well in practice, even while it leaves some conflicts over the constitutional allocation of powers without a reliable legal path of authoritative resolution.[148]

Quite a challenge for international law but one which would also entail different representation mechanisms and decision mechanisms in the IFIs and WTO.[149]

A third focus could be reforms to the international financial architecture. There is an enormous literature on this but one burning issue is that of taxation. Mulitnationals seem able to minimise the tax take because of a lack of international agreement about fair tax rates. Again, the absolute concept of sovereignty means that less powerful countries 'agree' low tax rates. Maybe the duty of international co-operation should decree that there be international agreement on base rates of tax. Such measures might also go hand in hand with creating an international fund by imposing a Tobin tax on financial speculation[150] or by denying the rich countries' claim to have absolute sovereignty over their assets and creating a 'global resources dividend'.[151] As Pogge points out, sovereignty also

---

[145] N. Harris, *The New Untouchables: Immigration and the New World Worker* (Tauris & Co. Ltd, New York, 1995), p. 219.

[146] See T. Hayter, *Open Borders: The Case Against Immigration Controls* (Pluto, London, 2000); N. Harris, *Thinking the Unthinkable: The Immigration Myth Exposed* (Tauris & Co. Ltd, London and New York, 2002).

[147] N. Bernard, *Multilevel Governance in the European Union* (Kluwer International, The Hague, 2002).

[148] Pogge, *World Poverty*, p. 179.

[149] See on this D. Jacobs, 'Reforming Economic Governance in the Interests of the Poor' (djacobs@oxfamamerica.org) paper presented at Conference on 'Alternatives to Neo-liberalism', Washington 23–24 May 2002.

[150] *Debating the Tobin Tax*, New Rules for the Global Finance Coalition, Washington DC, November 2003.

[151] Pogge, *World Poverty*, ch. 8.

means that there is an incentive for non-democratic coups in the immediate recognition that the winners of the coup will have the ability to
dispose of the whole wealth of that country and have access to the 'international borrowing privilege'. Pogge suggests that this could be lessened
by democratic states making constitutional amendments to deny future
authoritarian governments access to this privilege; subsequent loans to
these governments in breach of the constitution might be discouraged
by public pressure in the rich democracies.[152] And, of course the debt
cancellation schemes should be incrementally speeded up. Eichengreen
and Ruhl suggest 'collective action clauses' should be included in loans
made by private sector banks to developing countries. These would provide for orderly restructuring in the event of a default and permit the IMF
to stand aside.[153] There would be less likelihood of herd withdrawal of
funds. More radically, the IMF has considered some form of bankruptcy
procedures for states.[154] And, at the micro level, further extension of
micro loans should be part of the PRSP procedure.[155] So much to do, so
little time . . .

[152] *Ibid.*, ch. 6.
[153] B. Eichengreen and C. Ruhl, 'The Bail-in Problem: Systematic Goals, Ad Hoc Means'
(http://emlab.berkeley.edu/users/eichengr/).
[154] www.imf.org.
[155] M. Yunus, *Banker to the Poor: The Story of the Grameen Bank* (Aurum Press, London,
1998, 2003).

Bibliography

Adams, B., 'Running Out of Time' in T. Benton and M. Redclift (eds), *Social Theory and the Global Environment* (Routledge, 1994)

Adams, W.M., *Green Development* (Routledge, London, 1990)

Addo, M., 'Justiciability Re-examined' in R. Beddard and D. Hill (eds), *Economic Social and Cultural Rights: Progress and Achievements* (Macmillan, 1992)

'Human Rights and Transnational Corporations: An Introduction' in M. Addo (ed.), *Human Rights and Transnational Corporations* (Kluwer, The Hague, 1999), pp. 3–14

Alston, P., 'US Ratification of the Covenant on Economic Social and Cultural Rights: The Need for an Entirely New Strategy' (1990) 84 *Am. J International Law* 365

'The Committee on Economic, Social and Cultural Rights' in P. Alston (ed.), *The United Nations and Human Rights: A Critical Appraisal* (Clarendon, Oxford, 1992)

'Resisting the Merger and Acquisition of Human Rights by Trade Law: A Reply to Petersmann' (2002) 13 EJIL 815

Alston, P. and Quinn, G., 'The Nature and Scope of States Parties' Obligations under the International Covenant on Economic, Social and Cultural Rights' (1987) HRQ 9

Anderman, S., *EC Competition Law and Intellectual Property Rights* (Clarendon, Oxford, 1998)

Management Decisions and Workers' Rights (4th edn, Butterworths, London, 2000)

Anderson, S. and Cavanaugh, J., *The Rise of Global Corporate Power* (Institute for Policy Studies, Washington DC, 1996)

Arambulo, K., *Strengthening the Supervision of the International Covenant on Economic, Social and Cultural Rights: Theoretical and Procedural Aspects* (Intersentia, Antwerpen, 1999)

Arup, C., *The New World Trade Organisation Agreements: Globalising Law through Services and Intellectual Property* (CUP, 2000)

Ashworth, A., *Principles of Criminal Law* (3rd edn, OUP, 1999)

Athukorala, P., *Crisis and Recovery in Asia: The Role of Capital Controls* (E. Elgar, Cheltenham, 2003)

Ayres, I. and Braithwaite, J., *Responsive Regulation* (OUP, 1992)

Bal, S., 'International Free Trade Agreements and Human Rights: Reinterpreting Article XX of the Gatt' (2001) 10 *Minn. J Global Trade* 62

Baldwin, R., 'Introduction – Risk: The Legal Contribution' in R. Baldwin (ed.), *Law and Uncertainty: Risks and the Legal Processes* (Kluwer, Berlin, 1997)

Beetham, D., 'What Future for Economic and Social Rights?' (1995) *Political Studies Association* 43

Belcher, A., 'The Boundaries of the Firm: The Theories of Coase, Knight and Weitzman' (1997) 17(1) *Legal Studies* 22

Benton, T. and Redclift, M., *Social Theory and the Global Environment* (Routledge, 1994)

Berle, A., 'For Whom are Corporate Managers Trustees' (1932) *Harvard Law Review* 1365

Berle, A. and Means, G., *Modern Corporation and Private Property* (Macmillan, New York, reprint, 1962)

Bernard, N., *Multilevel Governance in the European Union* (Kluwer International, The Hague, 2002)

Bernstein, A., *Against the Gods: The Remarkable Story of Risk* (Wiley, London, 1996)

Betten, L. and Grief, N., *EU Law and Human Rights* (Longman, 1998)

Bingham, T., 'The Law Favours Liberty: Slavery and the English Common Law', Essex Law Lecture, 2003

Black, J., 'Perspectives on Derivatives Regulation' in A. Hudson (ed.), *Modern Financial Techniques, Derivatives and Law* (Kluwer, London, 2000)

Blecher, M., 'Environmental Officer: Management in an Ecological Quality Organisation' in G. Teubner (ed.), *Environmental Law and Ecological Responsibility: The Concept and Practice of Ecological Self-Organisation* (Wiley, London, 1994)

Blumberg, P., 'The American Law of Corporate Groups' in J. McCaherty, S. Picciotto and C. Scott (eds), *Corporate Control and Accountability* (Clarendon, Oxford, 1993)

Borensztein, E., de Gregorio, J. and Lee, J., 'How Does Foreign Direct Investment Affect Economic Growth?' (2002) *Journal of International Economics* 45

Bottomley, S., 'Taking Corporations Seriously: Some Considerations for Corporate Regulation' (1990) 19 *Federal Law Review* 203

Bottomley, S. and Kinley, D., *Commercial Law and Human Rights* (Ashgate, Dartmouth, Aldershot, 2002)

Brenton, P., *Integrating the Least Developed Countries into the World Trading System: The Current Impact of EU Preferences under Everything But Arms* (World Bank, Washington, 27 February 2003)

Briton, W. Jnr, 'The New Economic Theory of the Firm: Critical Perspectives from History' (1989) *Stanford Law Review* 1471

Brown, P., 'Food as National Property' in H. Shue (ed.), *Food Policy: The Responsibility of the United States in Life and Death Choices* (Free Press, Macmillan, London 1977)

Brundtland, H., *Our Common Future* (OUP, 1987)

Bueno de Mesquita, J., 'International Covenant on Economic, Social and Cultural Rights: International Co-operation and Assistance' (forthcoming)

Butler, A., '*Funke v France* and the Right Against Self-incrimination: A Critical Analysis' (2001) *Criminal Law Forum* 461

Cahn, J., 'Challenging the New Imperial Authority: The World Bank and the Democratization of Development' (1993) 6 *Harvard Human Rights Journal* 160

Campbell, D., 'Why Regulate the Modern Corporation? The Failure of Market Failure' in J. McCahery, S. Picciotto and C. Scott (eds), *Corporate Control and Accountability* (Clarendon, Oxford, 1993)

    'Reflexivity and Welfarism in the Modern Law of Contract' (2000) *Oxford Journal of Legal Studies* 477

Cateau, H. and Carrington, S. (eds), *Capitalism and Slavery Fifty Years Later* (Peter Lang Publishing, New York, 2000)

Chambers, R., *Whose Reality Counts* (Intermediate Technology, 1997)

Chatterjee, C., 'The OECD Guidelines for Multinational Enterprises: An Analysis' (2002) *Amicus Curiae* 18

Cheffins, B., *Company Law: Theory, Structure and Operation* (Clarendon, Oxford, 1997)

Chomsky, N., *Profit Over People* (Seven Stories Press, New York, 1999)

Chossudovsky, M., *The Globalisation of Poverty* (Pluto, Halifax, Nova Scotia, 1998)

Cockburn, A., '21st Century Slaves', *National Geographic*, September 2003

Cohen, G., *If You're an Egalitarian How Come You're so Rich?* (Harvard University Press, Cambridge, Mass, 2000)

Coleman, J., 'Responsibility in Corporate Action: A Sociologist's View' in K. Hopt and G. Teubner (eds), *Corporate Governance and Directors' Liabilities* (de Gruyter, 1985)

Collapse (CCH Australia, 2001)

Colling, T., *Employee Relations in the Public Services* (Routledge, 1999)

Cooter, R., 'Law and Unified Social Theory' (1995) 22 *Journal of Law and Society* 50

Craven, M., *The International Covenant on Economic, Social and Cultural Rights: A Perspective on its Development* (OUP, New York, 1995)

Cruver, B., *Anatomy of Greed* (Arrow, 2003)

Cullett, P., 'Patents and Medicines: The Relationship between TRIPS and the Human Right to Health' (2003) *International Affairs* 79

Czinkota, M., I. Ronksinen and M. Moffett, *International Business* (4th edn, Dryden, 1996)

Darity, W., 'British Industry and the West Indies Plantations' in J. Inikori, S. Engerman (eds), *The Atlantic Slave Trade* (Duke University Press, 1992)

Deakin, S. and Hughes, A. (eds), *Enterprise and Community: New Directions in Corporate Governance* (Blackwell, Oxford, 1997)

Deakin, S. and Morris, G., *Labour Law* (3rd edn, Butterworths, London, 2001)

Dennis, I., 'Instrumental Protection, Human Right or Functional Necessity? Reassessing the Privilege Against Self-Incrimination' (1995) *Cambridge Law Journal* 342

Department of Trade and Industry, *Business and Society: Corporate Social Responsibility Report* (DTI, 2001)

White Paper on Competitiveness (1998)

Dine, J., *Criminal Law in the Company Context* (Dartmouth, 1995)

The Governance of Corporate Groups (CUP, 2000)

'Risks and Systems: A New Approach to Corporate Governance and the European Employee Consultation Stuctures?' (2001) 3(2) *International and Comparative Corporate Law Journal* 299

Dine, J. and Watt, B., 'Sexual Harassment: Hardening the Soft Law' (1994) ELR 104

Dine, J. and Hughes, P., *EC Company Law* (Jordans, looseleaf)

Dodd, E., 'For Whom are Corporate Managers Trustees' (1931) *Harvard Law Review* 1049

Dommen, C., 'Raising Human Rights Concerns in the World Trade Organisation: Actors, Processes and Possible Strategies' (2001) *Human Rights Quarterly* 30

Drahos, P., 'Bilateralism in Intellectual Property', paper prepared for Oxfam, 2003

Drahos, P. and Braithwaite, J., *Global Business Regulation* (CUP, 2000)

Drzewicki, K. 'The Right to Work and Rights at Work' in A. Eide, C. Krause and A. Rosas (eds), *Economic Social and Cultural Rights* (2nd edn, Martinus Nijhoff, 2001)

Du Plessis, J.-J., 'Corporate Governance: Reflections on the German Two-Tier System' (1996) *Journal of South African Law* 315

Dunn, R., *Sugar and Slaves: The Rise of the Planter Class in the English West Indies, 1624–1713* (University of North Carolina Press, 1972, 2000)

Dunning, J. (ed.), *Making Globalisation Work* (OUP, 2003)

Dworkin, R., 'Is Wealth a Value?' (1980) *Journal of Legal Studies* 191

Easterbrook, F. and Fischel, D., *The Economic Structure of Corporate Law* (Harvard University Press, Cambridge, Mass, 1991)

Economic Analysis of Law (2nd edn, Little Brown, Boston, 1977)

Eatwell, J., 'International Capital Liberalisation: The Impact on World Development', Working Paper Series III, Center for Economic Policy Analysis (New York, 1996)

Eatwell, J. and Taylor, L., *Global Finance at Risk* (New Press, New York, 2000)

Ehrenreich, B., *Nickel and Dimed* (Granta, London, 2002)

Eichengreen, B. and Ruhl, C., 'The Bail-in Problem: Systematic Goals, Ad Hoc Means' (http:::/emlab.berkeley.edu/users/eichengr/)

Eide, A. Krause, C. and Rosas, A. (eds), *Economic Social and Cultural Rights* (2nd edn, Martinus Nijhoff, 2001)

Erikson, E. and Fritzell, K., 'The Effects of the Social Welfare System on the Well-being of Children and the Elderly' in A. Palmer, T. Smeeding and E. Torrey (eds), *The Vulnerable* (University of Chicago Press, 1988)

European Commission Green Paper, *Promoting a European Framework for Corporate Social Responsibility* (COM (2001) 366 final, Brussels, 18 July 2001)

European Commission Staff Working Paper, 'Reforming the European Union's Sugar Policy' (Brussels, SEC (2003))

Ewing, K., 'Britain and the ILO' in K. Ewing, C. Gearty and B. Hepple (eds), *Human Rights and Labour Law: Essays for Paul O'Higgins* (Mansell, London, 1994)

Fairclough, N., *New Labour, New Language* (Routledge, London, 2000)

J. Farrah and B. Hannigan, *Farrar's Company Law* (Butterworths, London, 1998)

Findlay, R., 'Trade and Growth in the Industrial Revolution' in C. Kindleberger and G. di Tella (eds), *Essays in Honour of W.W. Rostow*, vol. I, *Models and Methodology* (New York University Press, 1982)

Finger, J., 'The GATT as International Discipline over Trade Restrictions: A Public Interest Approach' in R. Vaubel and T. Willett (eds), *The Political Economy of International Organisations: A Public Choice Approach* (Westview Press, Boulder, Colorado, 1991)

Flickling, D., 'Misery of Rag-Trade Slaves in America's Pacific Outpost', *Guardian*, 1 March 2003

Forrester, D., *Christian Justice and Public Policy* (CUP, 1997)

Francioni, F. (ed), *Environment, Human Rights and International Trade* (Hart, Oxford, 2001)

Frankel, J. and Roubini, N., 'The Role of Industrial Policies in Emerging Market Crises', US National Bureau of Economic Research Working Paper 8634 (2000)

French, D., 'Reappraising Sovereignty in Light of Global Environmental Concerns' (2001) *Legal Studies* 1

Friedman, M., 'Greed is Good', *New York Times Magazine*, 13 September 1970 'The Social Responsibility of Business is to Make Profits' in G. Steiner and J. Steiner (eds), *Issues in Business and Society* (Random House, 1977)

Friedmann, W., *Law in a Changing Society* (2nd edn, Penguin Books, London, 1971)

Gaja, G., 'How Flexible is Flexibility under the Amsterdam Treaty' (1998) *Common Market Law Review* 975

Getzler, J., 'Theories of Property and Economic Development' in J. Harris (ed.), *Property Problems: From Genes to Pension Funds* (Kluwer, 1997)

Gladwell, M., 'The Talent Myth', *The Times*, 20 August 2002

Gless, S. and Zeitler, H., 'Fair Trial Rights and the European Community's Fight Against Fraud' (2001) *European Law Journal* 219

'Global 500: The World's Largest Corporations', *Fortune*, 7 August 1995

Global Witness, 'Time for Transparency: Coming Clean on Oil, Mining and Gas Revenues' (www.globalwitness.org) 24 March 2004

Gobert, J., 'Corporate Killing at Home and Abroad – Reflections on the Government's Proposals' (2002) LQR 72

Goodpaster, K., 'The Concept of Corporate Responsibility' (1983) 2 *Journal of Business Ethics* 1

Gower, *Principles of Modern Company Law* (6th edn, P. Davies, (ed.), Sweet and Maxwell, London, 1997)

Greenfield, K., 'From Rights to Regulation' in F. Patfield (ed.), *Perspectives on Company Law* I (Kluwer, 1997)

Habermas, J., *Between Facts and Norms* (W. Rehg (trans.), Polity Press, Cambridge, 1996)

Hadden, T., 'An International Perspective on Groups' in J. McCahery, S. Picciotto, and C. Scott (eds), *Corporate Control and Accountability* (Clarendon, Oxford, 1993)

Hale, B., 'Power Giant Buys Town to Avoid Pollution Lawsuits', *The Times*, 14 May 2002

Hanson, G., 'Should Countries Promote Foreign Direct Investment?', UNCTAD G-24 Discussion Paper Series 9 (Geneva, 2001)

Harris, J., *Property and Justice* (Clarendon, Oxford, 1996)

Harris, N., *The New Untouchables: Immigration and the New World Worker* (Tauris & Co. Ltd, New York, 1995)

    Thinking the Unthinkable: The Immigration Myth Exposed (Tauris & Co. Ltd, London and New York, 2002)

Harrison, P., *Inside the Third World* (3rd edn, Penguin, Harmondsworth, 1993)

Hayden, P., *John Rawls: Towards a Just World Order* (University of Wales Press, Cardiff, 2002)

Hayek, F., *Law, Legislation and Liberty*, vol. II, *The Mirage of Social Justice* (2nd edn, Routledge, London, 1982)

    Law, Legislation and Liberty, vol. III, *The Political Order of a Free People* (2nd edn, Routledge, London, 1982)

Hayter, T., *Open Borders: The Case Against Immigration Controls* (Pluto, London, 2000)

Hazeltine, H., Lapsley, G. and Winfield, P. (eds), *Maitland Selected Essays* (CUP, 1936)

Heerings, H. and Zeldenrust, I., *Elusive Saviours* (International Books, Utrecht, 1995)

Henderson, D., *Misguided Virtue* (IEA, London, 2001)

Henkin, L., *International Law: Policies and Values* (Martinus Nijhoff, Dordrecht, 1995)

Hertsgaard, M., *Earth Odyssey* (Abacus, London, 1999)

Hertz, N., *The Silent Takeover* (Heinemann, 2001)

Higgins, R., *Problems and Process: International Law and How We Use It* (Clarendon, Oxford, 1994)

Higgins, R., *The Development of International Law through the Political Organs of the United Nations* (OUP, London, 1963)

Hill, J., 'Visions and Revisions of the Shareholder' (2000) *Am. J Comparative Law* 39

Hindley, B., 'What Subjects are Suitable for WTO Agreement?' in D. Kennedy and J. Southwick, *The Political Economy of World Trade* (CUP, 2002)

Hirst, P. and Thompson, G., *Globalisation in Question* (2nd edn, Blackwell, Oxford, 1996)

Hoekman, B. and Kostecki, M., *The Political Economy of the World Trading System* (2nd edn, OUP, 2001)

Home Office, *Reforming the Law on Involuntary Manslaughter* (2000)

Hopkins, M., *The Planetary Bargain* (Macmillan, Basingstoke, 1999)

Horowitz, S., 'Marxian Economics and Modern Economic Theory' in S. Horowitz (ed.), *Marx and Modern Economics* (Macgibbon & Key, London, 1968)

Howse, R., 'The Early Years of WTO Jurisprudence' in J. Weiler (ed.), *The EU, the WTO and NAFTA* (Oxford, 2000)

'Human Rights in the WTO: Whose Rights, What Humanity? Comment on Petersmann' (2002 13 EJIL) 651

Hunt, P., *Reclaiming Social Rights* (Ashgate, Aldershot, 1996)

'Relations between the UN Committee on Economic, Social and Cultural Rights and International Financial Institutions' in W. Genugten, P. Hunt and S. Mathews, *World Bank, IMF and Human Rights* (Wolf Legal Publishers, Nijmegan, 2003)

Hutton, W., 'Anthony Giddens and Will Hutton in Conversation' in W. Hutton and A. Giddens (eds), *On the Edge: Living with Global Capitalism* (Cape, London, 2000)

The World We're In (Little Brown, London, 2002)

ILO, *A Fair Globalisation: The Final Report of the World Commission on the Social Dimension of Globalisation* (ILO, Geneva, 2004)

IMF, *World Economic Outlook* (IMF, Washington DC, 1998)

(IMF, Washington DC, 1998)

'Conditionality: Fostering Sustained Policy Implementation' in L. McQuillan and P. Montgomery (eds), *The International Monetary Fund* (Hoover Institution Press, Stanford, 1999)

Inikori, J., 'Slavery and the Revolution in Cotton Textile Production in England' in J. Inikori and S. Engerman (ed.), *The Atlantic Slave Trade* (Duke University Press, 1992)

'Capitalism and Slavery, Fifty Years After: Eric Williams and the Changing Explanations of the Industrial Revolution' in H. Cateau and S. Carrington (eds), *Capitalism and Slavery Fifty Years Later* (Peter Lang Publishing, New York, 2000)

Inikori, J., Bailey, R., Darity, W. and Richardson, D., 'Slavery, Trade and Economic Growth in Eighteenth Century New England' in B. Solow (ed.), *Slavery and the Rise of the Atlantic System* (CUP, 1991)

International Council on Human Rights, *Beyond Voluntarism* (2002), (www.international-council.org)

Ireland, P., 'Company Law and the Myth of Shareholder Ownership' (1999) MLR 62

'Property and Contract in Contemporary Corporate Theory' (2004) *Legal Studies* 451

Irwin, D., *Free Trade Under Fire* (Princeton University Press, New Jersey, 2002)

Jackson, J., *The Jurisprudence of GATT and the WTO: Insights on Treaty Law and Economic Relations* (CUP, 2000)

Jacobs, D., 'Reforming Economic, Governance in the Interests of the Poor' (djacobs@oxfamamerica.org), paper presented at Conference on 'Alternatives to Neo-liberalism', 23–24 May 2002, Washington

Jacobs, M., 'The Limits to Neoclassicism' in T. Benton and M. Redclift (eds), *Social Theory and the Global Environment* (Routledge, 1994)

Jagers, N., 'The Legal Status of Multinational Corporations under International Law' in M. Addo (ed.), *Human Rights Standards and the Responsibility of Transnational Corporations* (Kluwer, 1999)

James, M., *Social Problems and Policy during the Puritan Revolution, 1640–1660* (London, 1930)

Johnson, B. and Schaefer, B., 'Why the IMF is Ineffective' in L. McQuillan and P. Montgomery (eds), *The International Monetary Fund* (Hoover Institution Press, Stanford, 1999)

Kahn-Freund, O., 'Some Reflections on Company Law Reform' (1944) 7 MLR 54

Karl, J., 'The OECD Guidelines for Multinational Enterprises' in M. Addo (ed.), *Human Rights Standards and the Responsibility of Transnational Corporations'*, (Kluwer, 1999)

Karl, K., 'Economic Partnership Agreements: Hopes, Fears and Challenges' (2002) 195 *Courier ACP-EU* (November–December)

Karliner, J., *The Corporate Planet* (Sierra Club, San Fransisco, 1997)

Kenen, P., *The International Economy* (4th edn, CUP, 2000)

Kennedy, D. and Southwick, J. (eds), *The Political Economy of the World Trading System* (CUP, 2002)

Kerse, C., *EC Antitrust Procedure* (4th edn, Sweet and Maxwell, London, 1998)

Khan, M., 'The Macroeconomic Effects of Fund-Supported Adjustment Programs' in L. McQuillan and P. Montgomery (eds), *The International Monetary Fund* (Hoover Institution Press, Stanford, 1999)

Klein, M. and Olivei, G., 'Capital Account Liberalisation: Financial Depth and Economic Growth', National Bureau of Economic Research Working Paper 7384 (Cambridge, Mass, 1999)

Klein, N., *No Logo* (Picador, 1999)
Fences and Windows (Picador, 2002)

Korten, D., *When Corporations Rule the World* (Kumarian Press, 1995)

Kristol, I., 'Human Rights: the Hidden Agenda' (1986/7) 3 *National Interest* (winter)

Krugman, P., 'Currency Crises' in M. Feldstein (ed.), *International Capital Flows* (University of Chicago Press, 1999)

Kwa, A., 'Power Politics in the WTO', *Focus on the Global South*, January 2003 (www.focusweb.org)

Kwesi Johnson, L., 'Jamacia Uncovered', *Guardian*, 28 February 2003, reviewing 'Life and Debt', a film by Stephanie Black

Larsson, T., *The Race to the Top: The Real Story of Globalisation* (Cato Institute, Washington, 1999)

Lash, S., Szersynski, B. and Wynne, B., *Risk, Environment and Modernity: Towards a New Ecology* (Sage, 1996)

Law Commission, *Legislating the Criminal Code: Involuntary Manslaughter* (Report No. 237, 1996)

Leader, S., *Freedom of Association* (Yale University Press, 1992)

Locke, J., *Two Treatises of Government* (P. Laslett (ed.), CUP, 1988)

Lukes, S., *Individualism* (Blackwells, Oxford, 1979)

MacIntyre, A., *Marxism and Christianity* (Duckworth, London, 1969)

Macmillan, F., *WTO and the Environment* (Sweet and Maxwell, London, 2001)

Marceau, G., 'A Call for Coherence in International Law: Praises for the Prohibition against "Clinical Isolation" in WTO Disputes' (1999) *Journal of World Trade* 87

Marx, K., *Capital Punishment, New York Daily Tribune*, 18 February 1853

McCormack, G., 'Self-Incrimination in the Corporate Context' (1992) JBL 442

Mclean, B. and Elkind, P., *The Smartest Guys in the Room* (Viking, London, 2003)

McQuillan, L. and Montgomery, P. (eds), *The International Monetary Fund: Financial Medic to the World?* (Hoover Institution Press, Stanford, 1999)

Meadows, D. H., Meadows, D. L., Randers, J. and Behrens, W., *The Limits to Growth* (Universe Books, New York, 1972)

Mill, J.S., *On Liberty* (Penguin, Harmondsworth, 1974)

Monbiot, G., *Captive State: The Corporate Takeover of Britain* (Macmillan, 2000)

Monsod, S., 'Human Rights and Human Development' in *Human Development and Human Rights* (Human Development Report Office, 1998)

Moore, M., *World Without Walls* (CUP, 2002)

Moxham, R., *The Great Hedge of India* (Constable and Robinson, London, 2001)

Muchlinski, P., *Multinational Enterprises and the Law* (Blackwell, Oxford, 1995)
'Corporations in International Litigation: Problems of Jurisdiction and the United Kingdom Asbestos Case' (2001) ICLQ 1

Munk, D., 'Lula's Dreams for Brazil are Delayed as the Realities of Power Hit Home', *Guardian*, 31 December 2003

Murphy, J., 'Marxism and Retribution' in *Marx, Justice and History* (Princetown University Press, 1980)

Naismith, S., 'Self-incrimination: Fairness or Freedom?' (1997) *European Human Rights Law Review* 229

Narayan, D., Petesch, P., Shah, M. and Chambers, R., *World Bank Development Report 2000–2001: Voices of the Poor – Can Anyone Hear Us?* (OUP, New York, 2000)

Nash, G., 'Foreward' in R. Dunn, *Sugar and Slaves: The Rise of the Planter Class in the English West Indies, 1624–1713* (University of North Carolina Press, 1972, 2000)

New Rules for Global Finance Coalition, *Debating the Tobin Tax* (Washington DC, November 2003)

Novak, M., *UN Covenant on Civil and Political Rights: CCPR Commentary* (Engel, Kehl, 1993)

Nozic, R., *Anarchy, State and Utopia* (Harvard University Press, 1973)

O'Neill, O., 'Agents of Justice' in T. Pogge (ed.), *Global Justice* (Blackwell, Oxford, 2001)

Ogus, A., *Regulation: Legal Form and Economic Theory* (Clarendon, Oxford, 1994)

Oppenheim, L., *International Law: A Treatise* (2nd edn, David McKay & Co, New York, 1912)

Ostrey, S., 'The Uruguay Round North-South Grand Bargain' in D. Kennedy and J. Southwick, *The Political Economy of The World Trading System* (CUP, 2002)

Oxfam, 'Tax Havens: Releasing the Hidden Billions for Poverty Eradication' (Oxfam Policy Papers, Oxford, 2000)
America Oil, Gas and Mining: Poor Communities Pay the Price (Oxfam, Boston, 2001)
Global Finance Hurts the Poor (Oxfam America, 2002)

Page, S. and Hewitt, A., 'The New European Trade Preferences: Does "Everything But Arms" (EBA) Help the Poor' (2002) 20(1) *Development Policy Review* 91

Palast, G., *The Best Democracy Money Can buy* (Pluto, 2002)

Parker, C., *The Open Corporation* (CUP, 2002)

Parkinson, J., *Corporate Power and Responsibility* (Clarendon, Oxford, 1995)
  'The Socially Responsible Company' in M. Addo (ed.), *Human Rights Standards and the Responsibility of Transnational Corporations* (Kluwer, The Hague, 1999)

Paust, J., 'Human Rights Responsibilities of Private Corporations' (2002) *Vanderbilt Journal of Transnational Law* 801

Peers, S., 'Fundamental Right or Political Whim? WTO Law and the European Court of Justice' in G. de Burca and J. Scott (eds), *WTO and the European Court of Justice* (Hart, Oxford, 2001)

Peritz, R., *Competition Policy in American History, Rhetoric, Law* (OUP, 2000)

Petersmann, E., 'The EEC as a GATT Member: Legal Conflicts between GATT Law and European Community Law' in M. Hilf, F.G. Jacobs and E. Petersmann (eds), *The European Community and GATT* (Kluwer, Deventer, 1986)
  'Constitutional Principles Governing the EEC's Commercial Policy' in M. Maresceau (ed.), *The European Community's Commercial Policy After 1992: The Legal Dimension* (Martinus Nijhoff, Dordrecht, 1993)
  'International Trade Law and International Environmental Law: Environmental Taxes and Border Tax Adjustment in WTO and EC Law' in Revesz, Sands and Stewart (eds), *Environmental Law, the Economy, and Sustainable Development* (CUP, 2000)
  'Time for a United Nations "Global Compact" for Integrating Human Rights into the Law of Worldwide Organisations: Lessons from European Integration' (2002) 13 EJIL 621

Pettet, B., *Company Law* (Pearson Education, Edinburgh, 2001)

Pilger, J., *The New Rulers of the World* (Verso, London, 2002)

Pogge, T., *Realising Rawls* (Cornell University Press, Ithaca, NY, 1989)
  'Rawls on International Justice' (2001) 51 *Philosophical Quarterly* 246
  World Poverty and Human Rights (Polity Press, Oxford, 2002)
  'The First Millennium Development Goal' (www.etikk.ne/globaljustice/)

Pogge, T. (ed.), *Global Justice* (Blackwell, Oxford, 2001)

Posner, R., *Economic Analysis of Law* (4th edn, Little Brown, Boston, 1992)

Prentice, D., 'Some Comments on the Law of Groups' in (J. McCahery, S. Picciotto and C. Scott (eds), *Corporate Control and Accountability* (Clarendon, Oxford, 1993)
  'Corporate Personality, Limited Liability, and the Protection of Creditors' in R. Grantham and C. Rickett (eds), *Corporate Personality in the 20th Century* (Hart, Oxford, 1998)

Quereshi, A., *International Economic Law* (Sweet and Maxwell, London, 1999)
  'The Cartagena Protocal on Biosafety and the WTO: Co-existence or Incoherence?' (2000) ICLQ 835

Quinn, D., 'The Correlates of Change in International Financial Regulation' (1997) 91(3) *American Political Science Reviewe* 531

Rampersad, F., *Critical Issues in Caribbean Development, No. 2* (Ian Randle Publishers, 1997)

Rawls, J., *A Theory of Justice* (Harvard University Press, Cambridge, Mass, 1971, revised edn 1999)
Political Liberalism (Columbia University Press, New York, 1993)
The Law of Peoples (Harvard University Press, Cambridge, Mass, 1999)
'The Law of Peoples' in S. Shute and S. Hurley (eds), *On Human Rights* (Basic Books, New York, 1993)
Reddy, S. and Pogge, T., 'How Not to Count the Poor' (www.socialanalysis.org)
Renucci, J., *Droit européen des droits de l'homme* (2nd edn, 2001)
Riley, A., 'The ECHR Implications of the Investigative Provisions of the Draft Competition Regulation' (2002) ICLQ 55
Riley, C., 'Understanding and Regulating the Corporation' (1995) 58 *Modern Law Review* 595
Rixon, F., 'Lifting the Veil between Holding and Subsidiary Companies' (1986) 102 LQR 415
Rodrik, D., *Has Globalisation Gone too Far?* (Institute for International Economics, Washington, DC, 1997)
'Who Needs Capital Account Convertibility?' (1998) *Princeton Essays in International Finance* 55
Rolston, B., '"A Lying Old Scoundrel": Waddell Cunningham and Belfast's Role in the Slave Trade' (www.historyireland.com/magazine/features/11.1Feat.html, 8 October 2003)
Ross, A., 'Tu-tu' (1957) 70 *Harvard Law Review* 625
Rowell, A., *Green Backlash: Global Subversion of the Environment Movement* (Routledge, 1996)
Royal Society, *Risk: Analysis, Perception and Management* (Royal Society, 1992)
Sachdev, S., *Contracting Culture: From CCT to PPPs* (UNISON, 2001)
Sacks, D. and Thiel, P., 'The IMF's Big Wealth Transfer' in L. McQuillan and P. Montgomery (eds), *The International Monetary Fund* (Hoover Institution Press, Stanford, 1999)
Sagoff, M., *The Economy of the Earth* (CUP, 1988)
Salter, M., 'Hegel and the Social Dynamics of Property Law' in J. Harris (ed.), *Property Problems* (Kluwer, 1997)
Schlosser, E., *Fast Food Nation* (Penguin, London, 2002)
Scott, J., 'Corporate Groups and Network Structure' in J. McCaherty, S. Picciotto and C. Scott (eds), *Corporate Control and Accountability* (Clarendon, Oxford, 1993)
'Trade and Environment in the EU and WTO' in J. Weiler (ed.), *The EU, the WTO and the NAFTA: Towards a Common Law of International Trade* (OUP, 2000)
Sedley, 'Wringing out the Fault: Self-Incrimination in the 21st Century' (2001) *Northern Ireland Legal Quarterly* 115
Sen, A., *Development as Freedom* (OUP, 1999)
Sharma, S., *The Asian Financial Crisis* (Manchester University Press, 2003)
Shue, H., *Basic Rights* (2nd edn, Princeton University Press, New Jersey, 1996)
Singer, P., 'Reconsidering the Famine Relief Argument' in P. Brown and H. Shue (eds), *Food Policy: The Responsibility of the United States in the Life and Death Choices* (Free Press, New York, 1977)

Sklair, L., *Global Sociology and Global Environmental Change* in T. Benton and M. Redclift, *Social Theory and the Global Environment* (Routledge, 1994)

Skogly, S., *The Human Rights Obligations of the World Bank and IMF* (Cavendish Publishing, London, 2001)

Skogly, S. and Gibney, M., 'Transnational Human Rights Obligations' (2002) *Human Rights Quarterly* 781

Smith, A., *The Wealth of Nations* (J.M. Dent & Sons, London, 1910)

Smith, A., 'The Right to Silence in Cases of Serious Fraud' in P. Birks (ed.), *Pressing Problems in the Law*, vol. 1, *Criminal Justice and Human Rights* (OUP, 1995)

Soros, G., *The Crisis of Global Capitalism: Open Society Endangered* (Public Affairs, New York, 1998)

Spielman, D., 'Human Rights Case Law in the Strasbourg and Luxembourg Courts: Conflicts, Inconsistencies and Complementarities' in P. Alston, M. Bustelo and J. Heenan (eds), *The EU and Human Rights* (OUP, 1999)

Stiglitz, J., 'Capital Market Liberalisation, Economic Growth and Instability' (2000) 28(6) *World Development* 1075
Globalisation and its Discontents (Allen Lane, London, 2002)
The Roaring Nineties (Allen Lane, London, 2003)

Stokes, M., 'Company Law and Legal Theory' in W. Twining (ed.), *Legal Theory and Common Law* (Blackwell, Oxford, 1986)

Stoljar, S.J., *Groups and Entities: An Enquiry into Corporate Theory* (ANU Press, Canberra, 1973)

Story, J., 'Reform: What has been Written?' in G. Underhill and X. Zhang (eds), *International Financial Governance Under Stress* (CUP, 2003)

Sugarman, D. and Rubin, G., *Law, Economy and Society* (Professional Books, Abingdon, 1984)

Sullivan, D. and Conlon, D., 'Crisis and Transition in Corporate Governance Paradigms: The Role of the Chancery Court of Delaware' (1997) *Law and Society Review* 713

Taylor, I. and Eatwell, J., *Global Finance at Risk* (New Press, New York, 2000)

Teubner, G., 'Corporate Fiduciary Duties and their Beneficiaries: A Functional Approach to the Legal Institutionalization of Corporate Responsibility' in G. Hopt and H. Teubner (eds), *Corporate Governance and Directors' Liabilities* (de Greuter, Berlin, 1987)
'Enterprise Corporatism: New Industrial Policy and the "Essence of the Legal Person"' (1988) 36 *Am. J Comparative Law* 130

Third World Network, 'A World in Social Crisis: Basic Facts on Poverty, Unemployment and Social Disintegration' (1994) 52 *Third World Resurgence*

Thomas, H., *The Slave Trade* (Papermac, London, 1997)

Toynbee, P., *Hard Work* (Bloomsbury, London, 2003)
'A Cringing Appeasement of the Rich and Powerful', *Guardian*, 24 March 2004

Uchitelle, L., 'A Bad Side of Bailouts: Some Go Unpenalized' in L. McQuillan and P. Montgomery (eds), *The International Monetary Fund* (Hoover Institution Press, Stanford, 1999)

UNCTAD, *Trade and Investment Report 1997* (UNCTAD, Geneva, 1997)

UNCTAD, *Transnational Corporations and Competitiveness* (New York, 1999)

UNCTAD, *Trade and Development Report 2000: Global Economic Growth and Imbalances* (UN, Geneva, 2000)

UNCTAD, *Least Developed Countries Report 2002* (UN, Geneva, 2002)

UN Development Programme, *Human Development Report 1992* (OUP, 1992)
Human Development Report 1996 (OUP, New York, 1996)

UN Economic and Social Council, *Work on the Formulation of the United Nations Code of Conduct on Transnational Corporations: Outstanding Issues in the Draft Code of Conduct on Transnational Corporations* (E/C10/1985/5/2, 22 May 1985)

UN Executive Committee on Economic and Social Affairs, *Towards a New International Financial Architecture* (Economic Commission for Latin America and the Caribbean, Santiago, 1999)

Underhill, G. and Zhang, X., *International Financial Governance Under Stress: Global Structures versus National Imperatives* (CUP, 2003)
'Global Structures and Political Imperatives: in Search of Normative Underpinnings for International Financial Order' in G. Underhill and X. Zhang (eds), *International Financial Governance Under Stress* (CUP, 2003)

United Population Fund, *The State of World Population 1992* (New York, 1992)

van Houtte, H., *The Law of International Trade* (2nd edn, Sweet and Maxwell, London, 2002)

van Leeuwen, A., *Critique of Heaven* (Lutterworth, London, 1972)

Vidal, J., 'Hewit Joins Angels on Farm Visit, Agriculture Minister Blames IMF for Problems in Honduras', *Guardian*, 13 September 2003

Walsh, K. and Davis, H., *Competition and Service: The Impact of the Local Government Act 1988* (HMSO, 1993)

Warren, L., 'Inhuman Profit', *National Geographic*, September 2003

Wateraid, *The Education Drain* (www.wateraid.org.uk)

Watson, A., *Slave Law in the Americas* (University of Georgia Press, 1989)

Weber, M., 'The Meaning of "Ethical Neutrality" in Sociology and Economics' (1917) in E. Shils and H. Finch (eds), *Max Weber on the Methodology of the Social Sciences* (Glencoe, 1949)

Weiler, J. (ed.), *The EU, the WTO and the NAFTA: Towards a Common Law of International Trade* (OUP, 2000)

Wells, C., *Corporations and Criminal Responsibility* (Clarendon, Oxford, 1993)

Wilder, L., 'Local Futures: From Denunciation to Revalorisation of the Indigenous Other' in G. Teubner (ed.), *Global Law Without a State* (Dartmouth, Aldershot, 1996)

Wilkinson, R., *Mind the Gap: Hierarchies, Health and Human Evolution* (Wiedenfield and Nicholson, London, 2000)

Williams E., *Capitalism and Slavery* (1944) (University of North Carolina Press, 1994)

Williams, F., 'WTO Minnows Cry Foul on Mediation', *Financial Times*, 24 October 2002

Williamson, J., 'Costs and Benefits of Financial Globalisation' in G. Underhill and X. Zhang, *International Financial Governance Under Stress* (CUP, 2003)

Williamson, O., 'Contract Analysis: The Transaction Cost Approach' in P. Burrows and C.G. Velanovski (eds), *The Economic Approach to Law* (Butterworths, London, 1981)

'Transaction-Cost Economics: The Governance of Contractual Relations' (1994) 21 *Journal of Law and Society* 168

Wilson, I., *The New Rules of Corporate Conduct: Rewriting the Social Charter* (Quorum Books, Westport Connecticut, 2000)

Wolff, M., 'On the Nature of Legal Persons' (1938) *Law Quarterly Review* 494

Wood, D., 'Corporate Social Performance Revisited' (1991) 16 *Academy of Management Journal* 312

Woodroffe, S., 'Regulating Multinational Corporations in a World of Nation States' in M. Addo (ed.), *Human Rights Standards and the Responsibility of Transnational Corporations* (Kluwer, The Hague, 1999)

Woodward, D., *The Next Crisis? Direct and Equity Investment in Developing Countries* (Zed, London, 2001)

World Bank, *Global Economic Prospects* (World Bank, Washington DC, 1999)

Curbing the Epidemic: Governments and the Economics of Tobacco Control (World Bank, Washington DC, 1999)

Global Development Finance 2001 (World Bank, Washington DC, 2001)

World Health Organisation, *The World Health Report 2001* (WHO Publications, Geneva, 2001)

Yunus, M., *Banker to the Poor: The Story of the Grameen Bank* (Aurum Press, London, 1998, 2003)

Zarrilli, S., 'International Trade in Genetically Modified Organisms and Multilateral Negotiations: A New Dilemma for Developing Countries' in F. Francioni (ed.), *Environment, Human Rights and International Trade* (Hart, Oxford, 2001)

Zimmerman, M., *Contesting Earth's Future* (University of California Press, 1994)

Websites

http://www.europa.eu.int/comm/enterprise/csr/index.htm EU

http://www.europa.eu.int/comm/enterprise/csr/official_doc.htm EU PAPERS AND CONSULTATIONS

http://www.europa.eu.int/comm/enterprise/csr/forum.htm A FORUM ON CORPORATE SOCIAL RESPONSIBILITY/MINUTES/IDEAS/ OPINION OF NGOs

http://www.europa.eu.int/comm/employment_social/soc-dial/csr/csr_index.htm EMPLOYMENT AND SOCIAL AFFAIRS DG/DOCUMENTS – PAPERS

http://www.europa.eu.int/comm/trade/issues/global/csr/index_en.htm DG TRADE/LINKS

http://www.europa.eu.int/comm/environment/eussd/index.htm DG ENVIRONMENT/SUSTAINABLE DEVELOPMENT

http://www2.marksandspencer.com/thecompany/ ourcommitmenttosociety/index.

shtml spencer
http://www.mallenbaker.net/csr/
http://www.mallenbaker.net/csr/CSRfiles/page.php?Story_ID=890
http://www.bsdglobal.com/issues/sr_csrm.asp monitor – interesting
http://www.chibus.com/news/2001/11/05/Perspectives/A.Companys.
    Social.Responsibility-139790.shtml article
http://www.btplc.com/Thegroup/Companyprofile/
    Corporatesocialresponsibility/british telecom
http://www.btplc.com/Societyandenvironment/Betterworldreport/
    index.htmmore british telecom
http://www.hp.com/hpinfo/globalcitizenship/csr/
http://grants.hp.com/
http://www.societyandbusiness.gov.uk/ the opinion of dti
http://www.standardlife.com/page.php?sctn=76 standard life group
http://www.fordmotorcompany.co.za/corporatesocial/   ford motor company
http://society.guardian.co.uk/voluntary/story/0,7890,1128788,00.html . . . and
    the opinion of guardian
http://www.edf.fr/index.php4?coe_i_id=24058 edf group
http://www.bayer.com/about_bayer/social_responsibility/philosophy/
    objectives/page1179.htm bayer gropu
http://www.shell.com/home/Framework?siteId=nigeria shell
http://www.worldbank.org/privatesector/csr/   the world bank group and reports
http://www.levistrauss.com/responsibility/   levi strauss
http://www.economist.com/business/displayStory.cfm?story_id= 2369912 the
    opinion of the Economist
http://www.unido.org/en/doc/5162 a view from the UN
http://66.102.9.104/search?q=cache:nWGyP769pyYJ:www.oecd.org/
    dataoecd/54/13/2407958.pdf+company+social+responsibility&hl=
    en&ie=UTF-8   and the respective from the OECD
http://www.oecd.org/document/37/0,2340,en_2649_201185_2429925
    _1_1_1_1,00.html   OECD again
http://www.state.gov/e/eb/rls/othr/25246.htm   the department of State
http://matsushita.co.jp/csr/en/panasonic
http://www.daimlerchrysler.com/dccom/0,,0-5-7167-1-57099-1-0-0-0-
    0-0-114-7167-0-0-0-0-0-0,00.html   DaimlerChrysler
and
http://66.102.9.104/search?q=cache:E68PvzFODFQJ:www.imfmetal.
    org/main/files/DC%2520code%2520in%2520English.pdf+company+
    social+responsibility&hl=en&ie=UTF-8
www.cmsproject.com/resources/PDF/CMS_CSR.pdf+company+social+
    responsibility&hl=en&ie=UTF-8 an article
http://www.volvo.com/group/global/en-gb/Volvo+Group/ourvalues/
    socialresponsibility/   VOLVO
http://www.rocheusa.com/about/responsibility.html   Hofmann-La Roche
http://www.dhl.co.jp/eng/dhl/contribution.html   DHL
http://www.usa.canon.com/templatedata/AboutCanon/ciwenprmsg.html
    Canon

http://www.vodafone.co.uk/cgi-bin/COUK/portal/ep/browse.do?
    channelPath=%2FVodafone+Portal%2FAbout+Vodafone%2FSocial+
    responsibility&BV_SessionID=@@@@1577734507.1079107485
    @@@@&BV_EngineID=cccjadcklmlfdihcflgcegjdgnfdff   n.0 Vodafone
http://www.vodafone.com/section_article/0,7765,CATEGORY_ID%
    253D304%2526LANGUAGE_ID%253D0%2526CONTENT_ID%
    253D203794,00.html Vodafone Reports on Corporate Social
    Responsibility
http://www.adidas-salomon.com/en/sustainability/values/default.asp
Adidas
http://www.bp.com/genericsection.do?categoryId=39&contentId= 2008106 BP

Index

Lightning Source UK Ltd.
Milton Keynes UK
UKOW05f1836031213

222334UK00001B/126/P